The History and Annals of Northallerton

J. L. Saywell

Alpha Editions

This edition published in 2019

ISBN : 9789353601287

Design and Setting By
Alpha Editions
email - alphaedis@gmail.com

This book is a reproduction of an important historical work. Alpha Editions uses the best technology to reproduce historical work in the same manner it was first published to preserve its original nature. Any marks or number seen are left intentionally to preserve its true form.

THE HISTORY

AND

ANNALS OF NORTHALLERTON.

THE HISTORY

AND

ANNALS OF NORTHALLERTON,

YORKSHIRE,

WITH NOTES AND VOLUMINOUS APPENDIX,

COMPILED FROM AUTHENTIC AND RELIABLE SOURCES

BY THE

REV. J. L. SAYWELL, F.S.Sc.,

EXAMINER IN HISTORY TO THE SOCIETY OF SCIENCE, LONDON;
FELLOW OF THE ROYAL HISTORICAL SOCIETY; MEMBER OF THE
YORKSHIRE ARCHÆOLOGICAL AND TOPOGRAPHICAL ASSOCIATION;
AND FORMERLY CURATE OF NORTHALLERTON.

"Quis nescit, primam esse historiæ legem, ne quid falsi dicere audeat; deinde, ne quid veri non audeat; ne quid suspicio gratiæ sit in scribendo; ne quid simultatis."
"Hæc scilicet fundamenta nota sunt omnibus."
Cicero Orat. ii, 15.

"Forsan et hæc olim meminisse juvabit."
Virgil, Æn. i, 203.

NORTHALLERTON:
PRINTED AT THE OFFICE OF J. VASEY.
1885.

LONDON: SIMPKIN, MARSHALL, & CO.

TO

THE RIGHT HONOURABLE AND MOST REVEREND

WILLIAM THOMSON, D.D., F.R.S.,

LORD ARCHBISHOP OF YORK, PRIMATE OF ENGLAND
AND METROPOLITAN;

AND TO

GEORGE WILLIAM ELLIOT, ESQ.,

FOR ELEVEN YEARS MEMBER OF PARLIAMENT FOR THE
PARLIAMENTARY BOROUGH OF NORTHALLERTON,
AND DEPUTY-LIEUTENANT FOR THE COUNTY OF MONMOUTH;

THIS WORK IS

BY SPECIAL PERMISSION, DEDICATED BY THE COMPILER.

PREFACE.

The necessity for a new edition of the History of Northallerton is the compiler's apology for issuing the present work. An historical work is necessarily one which must from time to time be enlarged and improved. The histories by Gale, Langdale, and Ingledew have come and gone, having served their day and generation ; and the compiler trusts that the same kind consideration and patronage will be extended to him and his work as were enjoyed by his predecessors. It is hoped that the "*History and Annals of Northallerton*" will be found more complete, reliable, and interesting than any previous history of the town : much new and important matter has been added, and the whole brought down to the present date. With a view to a continuation of the work by other hands at some future time, and to preclude the necessity of an index, the compiler has arranged his information under successive years, care being taken to eliminate everything of an unimportant and uninteresting nature. If the work tends in any degree to maintain the prestige and reputation of the " capital of the North-Riding," to which title Northallerton has an undoubted claim, the compiler will be amply rewarded. To all those who have encouraged and assisted him in the work he begs to return his most sincere thanks.

J. L. S.

ACKWORTH,
September, 1885.

☞ The Plates in this work are from negatives kindly supplied by MR. JAMES COOPER, Photographer, Ivy House, Bondgate, Darlington.

The History and Annals
OF
NORTHALLERTON,
YORKSHIRE.

THE ancient and historic town of Northallerton occupies a **Situation.**
central but somewhat secluded position in the vale of
York, between the Hambleton Hills and the river Swale.
Its origin, says Gale, dates back to a very early period, **Origin.**
so early indeed as to be almost involved in obscurity. It
appears clearly to have been a Saxon borough, and, like
many others, to have risen out of the ashes of some old
Roman station, the name of which is considered very
doubtful. That this is no improbable conjecture may be
gathered from the fact that the old Roman road* from York

---

* Whilst engaged in constructing a new road on the estate of Mr. Hirst, at Crosby, some labourers discovered the old Roman strata. Its course is as follows: York to Aldby (Derventia) by Easingwold, Thirsk, Thornton-le-Street, Romanby to Catterick, where it joins the great Erming Street, thence to Crosby, crossing the Tees at Sockburne, it continued to Durham, Chester-le-Street, and Gateshead to Tynemouth. These roads, or military ways, were a national trust and pride. The noblest office in the state was their superintendence. A Roman inspectorship of roads corresponded with our rangership of parks. Augustus himself watched over those in the neighbourhood of Rome. It is singular that the plan adopted in their construction should have been proved to be the best, and that the experiments of centuries have only re-discovered the practice of the ancients. They laid the foundation with stones and cement; and broken granite, used in a similar way, has been recently introduced as the first layer in the great streets of our sumptuous metropolis. Still the Roman road defies the rivalry of modern skill. Fourteen hundred years have not obliterated them. They have withstood all storms, and all weathers; the plough has not torn them up; the trample of armies has not beaten them down; the more insidious ravages of antiquarian researches have not entirely spoiled them.

to Tynemouth, known as Watling Street, which joined the great Erming Street at Scotch Corner, passed through the village of Romanby *(Romundebi)*. This is confirmed by the high and ancient mounds or intrenchments in the vicinity of the town, now thought to have been Roman works, from which Romanby *(Romanorum habitatio)* probably takes its name; and also by the discovery of Roman coins, pottery, and other relics. Sir Thomas Saville, in a letter* to Camden, the celebrated antiquary, conjectures the Roman city of Camulodunum† to be identical with Northallerton, and adds, that the bishop of Durham had a charter in which "*Parti de Camuloduno, continens iii lencas in latitudine, atque xv in longitudine, ab Edivino Northanhumbrorum rege episcopis Dunelmensis conceditur;*" and that the see of Durham, under this very charter, enjoyed the territory of Northallerton at that day and to that extent. Supposing the above claim to be established, we learn from Tacitus that the Roman general, Publius Ostorius, whilst subduing the Silures, a naturally fierce tribe of Britons, commanded by Caractacus, established a colony of strong bodied veterans at Camulodunum, on the conquered lands, as a defence against the rebels, and as a means of imbuing the allies with respect for our laws.‡ Here also, a temple dedicated to Claudius had been raised, the priests of which committed infamous exactions, under the pretence of honouring religion. These new settlers in the colony of Camulodunum drove people out of their houses, ejected them from their farms, called them captives and slaves, and the lawlessness of the veterans was encouraged by the soldiers, who lived a similar life and hoped for similar license.§ Meanwhile, without any evident cause, the statue of victory at Camulodunum fell prostrate, and turned its back to the enemy, as though it fled before them; whereupon the alarmed veterans took refuge in the temple, which was shortly afterwards burnt down, the colony dispersed, and the soldiers slaughtered by the exasperated and blood-thirsty Britons.‖

Name.

In Domesday Book the town is called Alvertune, Aluertun, and Allerton. Simeon of Durham, who flourished about 1100, calls it Alvertona; and Peter de Longtoft, Alverton, as it is generally designated in all other ancient records. Gale thinks it is derived from the great King Alfred, and was originally called Alveredtune, which was

---

* Illustrium vivorum epistolæ, 1691, p. 9.
† This place is frequently mentioned by Pliny, Ptolemy, and Tacitus. Northallerton, Malton, Maldon, and Colchester all claim to be identified with the ancient Camulodunum.
‡ Cornelii Taciti. Lib. xii, cap. 32. § Ib. Lib. xiv, cap. 31.
‖ Cornelii Taciti. Lib. xiv, cap. 32.

afterwards softened into Alvertun and Allerton. But as there are several other Allertons in the county of York, it seems more reasonable to suppose with Thoresby, that the name is a mere incident to the situation of the place; indeed it was common in former times for towns and territories to receive their names from the sort of wood with which they abounded.*
It is very likely, therefore, that the name is derived from the Alder-tree which flourishes in watery and boggy places, and which may have formerly abounded in and around the vicinity. The town is called *North*-Allerton to distinguish it from Allerton Mauleverer † which lies to the south.

<small>Derivation.</small>

The Shire contains the following parishes and townships, those marked with an asterisk not being included in the Magisterial division:—Birkby, Borrowby, Brompton, Brawith, Cotcliffe, Crosby, Deighton, Ellerbeck, Foxton,* Girsby,* High Worsall,* Holme,* Hornby, Hutton Bonville, Hutton Sessay, Hutton Conyers,* North Kilvington, North Otterington, Northallerton, Knayton, Landmoth-with-Catto, Lazenby, Leake, Little Smeaton, Norton Conyers,* Osmotherley, Over Dinsdale,* Romanby, Kirby Sigston, Sowerby-under-Cotcliffe, Thimbleby, Thornton-le-Beans, Thornton-le-Street, West Harlsey, West Rounton, and Winton with Stank and Hallikeld.

<small>Allertonshire.</small>

The Parish of Northallerton includes the Parliamentary Borough and Market-town of Northallerton, with Lazenby, the Chapelries of Brompton, Deighton, and High Worsall, with the township of Romanby.

<small>The Parish.</small>

The township of Lazenby only contains six houses. It was formerly within the ecclesiastical parish of Northallerton, but it is now attached to Danby Wiske. It is still within the County Court district, Magisterial division, Union, and Parliamentary Borough of Northallerton.

<small>Lazenby.</small>

The Chapelry of Brompton is now a vicarage,‡ in the gift of the dean and chapter of Durham. The living, according to Crockford, derives £30 from glebe lands, and £352 from the Tithe-rent Commissioners. There is a good vicarage house and garden. The church, dedicated to St. Thomas, is built entirely of stone, and newly restored. It is small but pretty, and possesses a ring of three bells, several elegant stained glass windows, and a chaste reredos. The village is a large one, of considerable antiquity, being mentioned in Domesday Book by the names of Bromptuna and Brunton. The parish registers date from 1700.

<small>Brompton.</small>

---

* Ackworth, near Pontefract, derives its name *(Aken-worth)* from the oaks with which it formerly abounded.
† The seat of a family now extinct. Vide page 75.
‡ Vide Terrier, in Appendix II.

Deighton. The village of Deighton, seven miles distant, is a chapelry in the ecclesiastical parish of Northallerton. The church, which is a small stone Gothic building, bearing date 1715, is a chapel-of-ease to the parish church of Northallerton. There is only one glebe farm.*

High Worsall The Chapelry of High Worsall was in the ecclesiastical parish of Northallerton until 1720. The living which is valued at £77 per annum, is in the gift of the vicar of Northallerton. There is no residence for the incumbent, who is generally the curate of Yarm. The church, which was built in 1719, from the ruins and on the site of a more ancient chapel, is small but well preserved. The population is about 150. The terrier says there was a chapel-of-ease to the parish church of Northallerton, until the chapelry was augmented by the bounty of Queen Anne, which was about the year 1720.

Romanby. The picturesque village of Romanby is also in the ecclesiastical parish of Northallerton, and quite as ancient. A very small but substantial church, dedicated to St. James, has recently been erected as a chapel-of-ease.†

Agricola. In the year 85, Julius Agricola, the Roman general, subdued Scotland and perhaps encamped at Northallerton both going and returning. In a descriptive poem of the ancient town and borough of Northallerton, written by Miss Crosfield, and published by Langdale, of Northallerton, in 1789, the following words occur:—

> "The brave *Agricola* whose wisdom beam'd
> A double lustre on triumphant Rome,
> Perhaps encamp'd his hardy veterans here,
> When in the daring march they northward bent,
> And conquering all before him, drove thy sons,
> Fierce Caledonia! to their inmost mountains.‡

The Parish Church. The earliest date which can be accepted with any degree of certainty connected with the town is A.D. 630, in which year a church, for the most part of wood, is supposed by many eminent archæologists to have been built, around which a more substantial Saxon edifice of stone was subsequently erected by St. Paulinus, the first bishop of York, and domestic chaplain to Ethelburga, wife of Edwin, king of Northumbria.

Dr. Stukely,§ the learned antiquarian, in a paper read before the Antiquarian Society, Oct. 30th, 1755, says,

---

* Vide Terrier, in Appendix.   † Vide p. 203.   ‡ Vide Appendix.
§ Rev. William Stukely, M.D., F.S.A., was born at Holbeach, in Lincolnshire, in 1687; mar. Elizabeth, eldest dau. of the Rev. Thomas Gale, D.D., and sister to Roger Gale, esq., M.P. for Northallerton. In 1747 the duke of Montague gave him the rectory of St. George the Martyr, Queen-square, where he died, 1765. His principal works are "Itinerarium Curiosum"; "Descriptions of Stonehenge and Aubury"; "History of Carausius"; "An account of Richard of Cirencester"; &c.

"Paulinus built many parish churches in Yorkshire. Some I have seen and taken drawings of them; particularly that of Godmundham, where is the original font in which he baptized the heathen high-priest Coifi. He built Northallerton Church, now remaining. His effigy is placed on the outside of it."* There is no doubt that Paulinus was baptized in the Swale not far from Northallerton, in or about the year 630, for Gregory the Great, in an epistle to St. Eulogius, Patriarch of Alexandria, on the Conversion of the Britons, thus writes respecting the progress of missionary labour in the neighbourhood of Northallerton:—" On the day of Christ's nativitie, he (Paulinus) did regenerate by lively baptisme above ten thousand men, besides an innumerable multitude of women and children. Having hallowed and blessed the river, called in English, Swale, the archbishop commanded by the voice of criers and maisters that the people should enter the river confidently, two by two, and in the name of the Trinitie baptise one another in turnes. Thus were they all born againe with no lesse a miracle than in times past, the people of Israel passed over the sea divided, and likewise Jordan when it turned backe; for even so, they were transported to the banke on the other side; and notwithstanding so deepe a current and channel, so great and so divers differences of sex and age, not one person took harme. A greate miracle no doubt, but this miracle as it was, a greater pre-eminence doth surmount: in that all feebleness and infirmitie was laid off in that river; whosoever was sick and deformed returned out of it whole and reformed."

Another argument in favour of the Saxon origin of Northallerton church is the discovery, during the restoration of 1883-4, of a large quantity of Saxon crosses, and other stone work; and this is backed up by its dedication to All Saints, which is usually regarded as indicative of a Saxon origin.†

The church as it now stands is a fine and interesting old pile. The effigy of St. Paulinus, mentioned by Dr. Stukely, has disappeared, but the niche remains. The building consists of nave, aisles, transepts, chancel, vestry, and organ chamber, the whole externally presenting a cathedral-like aspect, in the cruciform style. Its total length from east to west is 138 feet, and its breadth across the transepts 84 feet. The northern arcade is Norman, the southern, early English. The tower is a handsome structure 80 feet high, erected by bishop Hatfield, of Durham, in the fifteenth century.‡ The fine perpendicular chancel, just erected, corresponds with

---

* Archæologia, i, 44.
† Vide Arch. and Top. Journal, part xxxiii.
‡ A description of the bells will be found in the Appendix.

the tower, and the great five-light window of bishop Nevill, in the south transept, and is the fifth chancel erected on the site. 1. Saxon. 2. Norman. 3. Early English. 4. Rude Gothic. 5. Perpendicular. The history of the church may be easily read on the surface of its stones, both inside and out. The remains of a pre-reformation altar,* with its adjacent piscina, discovered in 1883, may be seen in the south transept, and a mutilated benetura in the south porch. All the Saxon, Norman, and Early English remains of any interest have been carefully preserved inside the church. On the west buttress of the south transept outside, about 18 feet from the ground, there is a square sun-dial in good condition, bearing the motto "*Ora et labora*," but no date appears upon it. Several minor features are noticed in the body of this work. The various changes of spoliation and renovation, through which the church has passed, will be found recorded under their respective dates.

A.D. 769. The first historical event connected with Northallerton is
The town destroyed. its destruction by fire in 769, by Beornredus, or Earnredus, a tyrant king of Northumbria, who at the same time burnt down Catterick, the Roman Cataractonium. The Saxon church at Northallerton would most likely be destroyed at the same time.†

865. Ninety-six peaceful years intervene, and then a sharp
Battles at conflict is said to have taken place at Northallerton, between
Alvertoun. king Alfred and five Danish kings, who had invaded the kingdom with a great host. The latter were not defeated until a second sanguinary battle had been fought, although they were victorious elsewhere, and ultimately succeeded in subduing the country. Peter de Langtoft (an Austin friar, born in this county, who wrote a chronicle of the Danish invasion in French verse, in the time of Edward II.,) thus speaks of the struggle:—

> "Tille Alfred our kyng com tythings starke,
> That fyve kyngs and fyve earles ver comen of Denmarke,
> That wild on him renne, and reve him the coroune,
> With alle ther grete folk, thei lay in Alvertoune."

883. About this time king Alfred the Great caused all the
King Alfred. country between the Humber and Tweed, which had been laid waste in 769, to be re-inhabited.

1069. In 1069, William the Conqueror provoked‡ by the murder
A singular of Robert Cumin, whom he had appointed to the earldom of
phenomenon. Northumberland, sent an army against the Northumbrians to

---
* The altar-slab is unfortunately missing. † Gale's MSS.
‡ William was heard to swear by his usual oath, "By God's splendour," he would not leave a soul alive.

avenge his death, but when the army reached Northallerton, A.D. 1069. so great a darkness arose that one man could scarcely perceive his comrade, nor were they able by any means to discover which way to go. While thus they remained in a state of astonishment and suspense, they were told that the people of the city of Durham, whither they were going, had a certain Saint* who was always their protector in adversity, and to this they ascribed the sudden darkness which had overtaken them. Having either too much piety or prudence to think of waging war with heaven, the army returned to York, where William joined them, and leading them back again, ravaged and destroyed the country on all sides. Upon this occasion the town of Northallerton was again depopulated and destroyed.†

Ordericus Vitalis, a Norman monk, who wrote in the reign of Henry I., after giving an account of the horrible desolation of Yorkshire, in which statement he says, there perished above one hundred thousand human beings, adds the following reflections: " I have no doubt in asserting, that so horrid a butchery is a crime that cannot pass unpunished; for an Omnipotent judge and most rigorous avenger will strictly scrutinize the actions, and punish the guilt of the highest, as well as the lowest delinquent."‡

A further account of this great devastation in old English verse may not be unacceptable to the reader.§

> Now William has sojourned and slayne alle his Enmy's,
> And to the southe is turned, als King that won the Pris.
> Tidings cam him fulle stout, that a grete Oste and Stark,
> With Harold and with Knoute, the King's sonnes of Denmark,
> Were aryved in Humbere, and an Earl Turkylle,
> With Foulke withouten numbere the Norreis sell tham tille,

* St. Cuthbert, the patron Saint of Durham.

† "It was shocking," says Simeon of Durham, "to see in the houses, the streets, and highways, human carcases swarming with worms, dissolving in putridity, and emitting a most horrible stench; nor were any left alive to cover them with earth, all having perished by sword or by famine, or stimulated by hunger, had abandoned their native land. During the space of nine years the country lay totally uncultivated. Between York and Durham not a house was inhabited, all was a lonely wilderness, the retreat of wild beasts and robbers, and the terror of travellers. The admirers of William the Conqueror must confess that in cruelty no pagan tyrant ever surpassed, and few ever have equalled, this christian (?) destroyer." It is supposed that above 100,000 human beings perished at this time. The recollection of the cruelties William had committed made him exclaim on his death-bed, "Multis, gravibusque peccatis onustus contremisco, et mox ad tremendum dei judicium rapiendus, quid faciam ignoro." In a general survey made a few years afterwards, Northallerton is described as "modo wastum est."

‡ Indubitanter assero quod impune non remittitur tam fatalis occisio; summos emin et imos intuetur Omnipotens Judex ac æque omnium facta discutiet ac puniet districtissimus vindex. Order. Vital, lib. 4, p. 514.

§ Langtoft's Chronicle.

8 ANNALS OF

A.D. 1069.

Comen to the Earl Edgar, with all thos of his kinde,
Sir Walthof he is thar, tho with that he met finde
Marlfwain Turkille Son, ond Swayne o doughty Knyght;
Of Scotlande Gospatrick, with them at all his myght.
The Normans in the Southe were in so grete affaray,
Of Kastelles and of Tonnes, they com oute alle Day.
To York ran ilk a man, to rescit in that Tonne,
That no Danes Man the Walles to breke doune.
Sir William Mellet was Warden of the Cuntres,
Sibrigh the Gaunt was set with to keep the Pees.
Thise two brought tydying, thei were comen by that Coste.
Therefore William the King did turne agayn his Hoste,
And swore a grete Othe, that he suld never spare,
Neither Lithe nor Lose, Northeren whut so thei were.
William turned agayn, and held what he had sworn,
All mad he wasteyn, Pasture, Medow, and Korne.
And slough both Fader and Sonne, Women lete thei gon,
Hors and Houndes thei ete, uncithis skaped non.
Now dwellis William efte, full bare was money wone,
Of gode men er none lefte, but slayn er ilk one.
Grete Sin did William, that swilk Wo did work,
So grete Vengeance he nam, of men of holy Kirk,
That did no wem to him, ne no Trespass,
Fro York unto Durham no wonyng Stede was,
Nien yere, says my Buke, lasted so grete Sorrow,
The Bishop Clerkes tuke their Lives for two borrows.*

1087.
The Manor.

William Rufus gave the Manor of Alverton to William Carilepho, Bishop of Durham, but it was afterwards confiscated.

1130.
The Castle.

The castle of Northallerton was erected near the town on the west side, by Geoffrey, surnamed Rufus, Bishop of Durham, in the time of King Henry I, but much nearer to it than the old Roman castrum. A short distance W.N.W. from the Bishop of Durham's Palace,† says Leland, "bee the ditches and the dungeon hille wher the castelle of Alverton some tyme stood."‡ These castles were built for the protection of the town and neighbourhood in those times of feudal tyranny, when the inferior inhabitants of the country from the depressed state of their minds, and the severity of unequal laws, were not able to protect themselves.§

1135.
Stephen's feud with the Scots

Stephen's accession to the throne raised the indignation of David, king of Scotland, who had taken an oath to support the claims of the empress Matilda, his niece. Levying an army with all possible speed, he marched against Stephen, possessing himself of all the castles, fortresses, and towns upon the route. The two monarchs met and concluded a peace at Durham, but subsequent claims made by David, to

* *i.e.* two sureties.
† Northallerton Cemetery occupies the site of the Palace.
‡ Now known as the "Castle Hills."
§ All this was rectified by the celebrated "Magna Charta," 1215.

which Stephen would not submit, served only to irritate the king of Scotland, and hostilities recommenced. Stephen being absent on continental affairs, a truce was effected until his return, but on his arrival in England the country was again exposed to the miseries of intestine war. In March, 1138, king David crossed the Tweed at the head of an army which he had collected from every part of his kingdom, to defend the title of his niece Matilda.* Chroniclers describe the Scotch army as a wild and barbarous multitude, many of whom gathered from the recesses of the Highlands, were men fierce and untutored, half clad, and with only the rudest weapons of war. This undisciplined host passed through Northumberland, devastating the country, reducing towns to ashes, dismantling fortresses, and committing unheard of barbarities upon the miserable inhabitants. It is related of them that they behaved after the manner of wild beasts, slaying all who came in their way, sparing neither old age in its helplessness, nor beauty in its spring, nor infant in the womb.

The fury of these massacres exasperated the northern nobility, who might otherwise have been disposed to join the king of Scotland. Thurstan, archbishop of York, an aged man, seemed to derive new youth from the crisis which demanded the exertion of his energies. He shook off the weight of years, and, organising an army, he earnestly exhorted the barons and soldiers to defend their country from the ravages of the invaders. William, earl of Albemarle, Roger Mowbray, Robert de Ferrers, William Piercy, Walter L'Espec, and others of their compeers, assembled their troops, and encamped at Elfer-tun, now called Northallerton, and there awaited the enemy. The advance of the Scots had been so rapid, that Stephen, who was occupied with repressing the rebellion in the south,† had not time to reach the scene of action.

The hostile armies were brought face to face, and the standard raised by the English on Cowton Moor, three miles north of Northallerton, on Monday, October 22, 1138.

The Scottish army, the first division of which was led by prince Henry, son of David, crossed the Tees in several divisions, bearing as a standard a lance, to which was fixed a bunch of the "blooming heather." They did not form, as was the case, with more disciplined armies, distinct bodies of horse and foot, but each man brought to the field of battle

---

* It is a true saying that women and wine are, directly or indirectly, the cause of all evil and misery. (Ecclus. xix, 2.)
† The confederacy organised by Robert, Earl of Gloucester.

A.D. 1138.

such arms as he could obtain. With the exception of the French or Norman knights whom the king of Scotland brought with him, and who were armed *cap-a-pie*, with complete suits of mail, the great mass of his soldiers displayed a disorderly equipment. The men of Galloway and other parts of the west wore no defensive armour, and bore long and sharp pikes or javelins as their only weapon. The inhabitants of the Lowlands, who formed the chief part of the infantry, were armed with spears and breastplates; while the Highlanders, who wore a bonnet adorned with plumes, and a plaid cloak fastened at the waist by a leathern belt, appeared in the fight with a small wooden shield on the left arm, while in the right hand they bore the claymore or broadsword. The chiefs wore the same armour as their soldiers, from whom they were only distinguished by the length of their plumes.

The army being drawn up for battle, Robert de Brus (Bruce) eloquently addressed the soldiers, representing to them :—

Speech of Robert de Brus.

"That though he was rightfully a subject to the king of England, nevertheless, from his youth, he had been a friend and familiar to the king of Scots; and, therefore, being an old soldier, and sufficiently skilled in military affairs; as also not ignorant of the danger impending, considering likewise the ancient friendship between himself and that king; and that he stood obliged to him, not only by the band of friendship, but by a kind of necessary fidelity, desired leave of his fellow soldiers to go to him, with purpose either to dissuade him from fighting or friendly to leave him. And, accordingly coming into his presence told him, that what he had to advise, should be honourable to himself and profitable to his realm; adding that the English had been his best friends, and that they had so approved themselves to Duncan and Edgar, his brothers, in their greatest exigence, instancing sundry particulars wherein they had obliged him when he stood most in need of their aid; demonstrating likewise to him the unavoidable consequences of war, viz., rapine, spoil, and destruction. And that though his army was more numerous, yet the English were more valiant and strong, and resolved to conquer or lose their lives.

"Which expressions so wrought upon the Scotch king, that he forthwith brake out into tears, and had condescended to a peaceable accord, but that William Mac Duncan, his nephew (a person of extraordinary courage, and the chief instigator of this invasion) came in, and in great fury charging Brus with treachery, dissuaded the king from hearkening unto him."

"Whereupon, returning with sorrow to the English host, (we) prepared for battle."*

A.D. 1138.

Walter Espec then ascended a platform which was made about the standard, and did, by the following oration, encourage the English army to fight :—

"Putting them in mind of the famous exploits which had been done of old by the valor of their ancesters in foreign parts, and in particular against the Scottish nation, assuring them that to vindicate the vile profanations which that barbarous people had made in all holy places where they came, St. Michael and his angels, and St. Peter, with the Apostles (whose churches were by them made stables) would fight, yea, the martyrs with their glorious company, whose altars they had defiled, would lead them on : likewise, that the sacred virgin would intercede for them, by her devout prayers, and that Christ Himself would take up His shield, and rise up to their aid." And having ended his speech, turned himself to the Earl of Albermarl, and gave him his hand, saying, '*I faithfully promise you that I will conquer the Scotts this day, or lose my life by them.*'

Speech of Walter Espec

"Which courageous expression did put such spirit into all the noblemen there, that each of them made the like vow to the other, and to take away all opportunity of flight, sent their horses to a distance, resolving to fight on foot, and conquer or lose their lives."†

Thurstan, archbishop of York, was prevented by illness from accompanying the army further than Thirsk ; he therefore commissioned Ralph, bishop of Orkney,‡ to fill his place, who, standing on an eminence in the centre of the English army, roused their courage with words to this effect :—

"Brave nobles of England, Normans by birth, for it is well that on the eve of battle you should call to mind who you are, and from whom you are sprung : no one ever withstood you with success. Gallant France fell beneath your arms ; fertile England you subdued ; rich Apulia flourished again under your auspices ; Jerusalem, renowned in story, and the noble Antioch, both submitted to you. Now, however, Scotland, which was your own rightly, has taken you at a disadvantage, her rashness more fitting a skirmish than a battle. Her people have neither military skill nor order in fighting, nor self-commaud, there is therefore no reason for fear, whatever there may be for indignation, at finding those whom we have hitherto sought and conquered in their own country, madly reversing the order, making an irruption into

Speech of Bishop Ralph

* Vide Ord's Cleveland.
† Vide Haile's Annals of Scotland, vol. 1, p. 90.
‡ Some say Ranulph, bishop of Durham, but this is doubtful, for that prelate would most likely be in league with David of Scotland.

A.D. 1138. ours. But that which I, a bishop, and by Divine permission, standing here as the representative of our archbishop, tell you, is this: that those who in this land have violated the temples of the Lord, polluted His altars, slain His priests, and spared neither children nor women with child, shall on this same soil receive condign punishment for their crime. This most just fulfilment of His will, God shall this day accomplish by your hands. Rouse yourselves then, gallant soldiers, and bear down on an accursed enemy, with the courage of your race, and in the presence of God. Let not their impetuosity shake you, since the many tokens of our valour do not deter them. They do not cover themselves with armour* in war; you are in the constant practice of arms in the time of peace, that you may be at no loss in the chances of the day of battle. Your head is covered with the helmet, your breast with a coat of mail, your legs with greaves, and your whole body with the shield. Where can the enemy strike you when it finds you sheathed in steel? What have we to fear in attacking the naked bodies of men, who know not the use of armour? Is it their numbers? It is not so much the multitude of a host, as the valour of a few, that is decisive. Numbers without discipline are a hindrance to success in the attack, and to retreat in the defeat.† Your ancestors were often victorious when they were but a few against many. What then does the renown of your fathers, your practice of arms, your military discipline avail, unless they make you, few though you are in numbers, invincible against the enemies' hosts? But I close my discourse, as I perceive them rushing on, and I am delighted to see that they are advancing in disorder.‡

Absolution granted to all those who should fall in battle.

"Now, then, if any of you who this day are called to avenge the atrocities committed in the houses of God, against the priests of the Lord, and His little flock, should fall in the battle, I, in the name of your archbishop, absolve them from all spot of sin, in the name of the Father, whose creatures the foe hath foully and horribly slain, and of the Son, whose altars they have defiled, and of the Holy Ghost, from whose grace they have desperately fallen."

---

* The rank and file of the Scots used no defensive armour, and perhaps like their posterity, only wore the kilt.

† The *pauci contra multos* principle is not always a safe one. The early Britons, although naked and savage, the Germans in the Franco-German war, and more recently the Zulus, often secured victory by their number against well-armed and disciplined troops.

‡ The Scots, in their council of war, disagreed in their sentiments, about the manner of beginning the engagement. The Galloway men descended from the ancient Picts, claimed it as their right to be in the van, and make the first attack. Though David did not care to gratify them, yet to avoid the ill consequences of a quarrel, hastily gave orders for them to form the first battalion, and begin the battle.

Then all the English replied with a shout, and the mountains and hills re-echoed, "Amen! Amen!"

At the same moment the Scots raised their country's war-cry, "*Albanigh! Albanigh!*" till it reached the clouds.* These sounds were drowned amid the crash of arms.

The Galloway corps began the charge with such fury that the English archers at first gave ground; but being sustained by the firmness of the rest of their body, and deriving great advantage from their armour in close engagement, they quickly rallied; whilst the ranks of the Galloway men, galled by the bowmen of Yorkshire and Lincolnshire, who poured in flights of arrows upon the enemy, and having lost their two leaders, were broken up, and the Scots fled in great confusion. {*The commencement of the attack.*}

Prince Henry, forcing himself through the advancing English, passed beyond the Standard, fell upon a party of cavalry posted behind the main body, and drove them before him, followed by the rest of his forces. The English, terrified by the impetuosity of the attack, were on the point of quitting the field, when they were stopped by the stratagem of an artful and experienced warrior; who, cutting off the head of one who was slain, held it up on his lance, crying out, "*this is the head of king David!*" On hearing this the English renewed the battle with greater vigour than before. The Scots, discouraged by the flight of the Galloway men, and the rumour of the death of their king, fled on all sides;† leaving David, who had hitherto fought on foot, to retreat on horseback, guarded by his knights. Those who fled, seeing the royal banner, on which a dragon was painted, waving in the air, concluded immediately that the king was not dead; and, rallying, joined his corps in such numbers, as to render it dangerous to the pursuers. Some of these latter were taken prisoners, but the rest, with David, retired unmolested to Carlisle, where the king remained for two days in great trouble about his son, of whom he could hear no tidings. {*An artful stratagem. Total defeat of the Scots. Escape of the King.*}

Prince Henry finding himself with a few followers in the midst of the English army, made them throw off their marks of distinction, and mixing with the enemy, found means at last to get from them. After being severely wounded, and encountering many difficulties, the prince arrived at Carlisle three days after his father. {*Prince Henry wounded.*}

* By this they meant to announce themselves as descended from the ancient inhabitants of Scotland, called of old Albyn and Albania. When they were repulsed, the English called in scorn "*Eyrych! Eyrych!*" (Irish! Irish!) which was true of the wild Scots of Galloway, who are undoubtedly Scotch-Irish.

† Galwegians, light as ocean's gale,
And London's knights all sheathed in mail,
And the bold men of Teviotdale,
   Before the standard fled.   (vide Appendix.)

A.D. 1138.
Losses of the Scots.
English loss.

The loss of the Scots on the field of battle was not great; but thousands who fled were slain in the different counties, through which they endeavoured to escape. The total was computed at 10,000 men. The English loss was very small; Gilbert de Lacy being the only knight slain. This battle has ever since been called the "*Battle of the Standard*," from a long pole which Thurstan brought from the convent of Beverley:—

> "Standard, from stand, this fight we aptly call,
> Our men here stood to conquer, or to fall." *

Description of the Standard.

The Standard was fixed upon a four-wheeled carriage, and had on the top of it a silver crucifix, beneath which were suspended the banners of St. Peter of York, St. John of Beverley, and St. Wilfrid of Ripon, and at the top of the mast, in a silver pix, the consecrated host or sacramental wafers. The object of this was to rouse the sacred feelings of the English soldiers, and to its presence they ascribe their victory.

The scene of action is still known by the name of "*Standard Hill*," and the holes into which the dead Scots were thrown by that of the "*Scot-pits*."

> In Stephen's troubled reign, in as tumultuous days,
> As England ever knew, the Archbishop of York
> Stout Thurstan, and with him joined in that war-like work,
> Ralph (both for wit and arms) of Durham, Bishop then †
> Renown'd, that called were the valiant clergymen,
> With th' Earl of Albemarle, Espec, and Peverell, Knights,
> And of the Lacies two, oft try'd in bloody fights,
> 'Twixt Allerton and York, the doubtful battle got,
> On David and his son, whilst of th' invading Scot.
> Ten thousand strew'd the earth, and whilst they lay to bleed,
> Ours follow'd them that fled, beyond our sister Tweed.‡

Three days after this defeat, the king of Scotland arrived at Carlisle, where he rallied his scattered forces, and subsequently laid siege to Wark castle which fell into his hands. Notwithstanding the result of the *Battle of the Standard*, the counties of Cumberland, Westmoreland, and Northumberland remained for many years free from Norman dominion, and attached to the kingdom of Scotland.

1139.
Robert de Ferrars.

Robert de Ferrars commanded the Derbyshire men in the Battle of the Standard, for which service Stephen advanced him to the Earldom of Derby; he died soon afterwards.

Walter de Gant.

Walter de Gant, eldest son of Gilbert de Gant, was a person of great humanity and piety, and when advanced in years and near his death, commanded a brave regiment of Flemings and Normans in the Battle of the Standard.

---

* Hugh de Sotevagina. † Vide third footnote, page 11.
‡ Drayton's Polly Olbion.

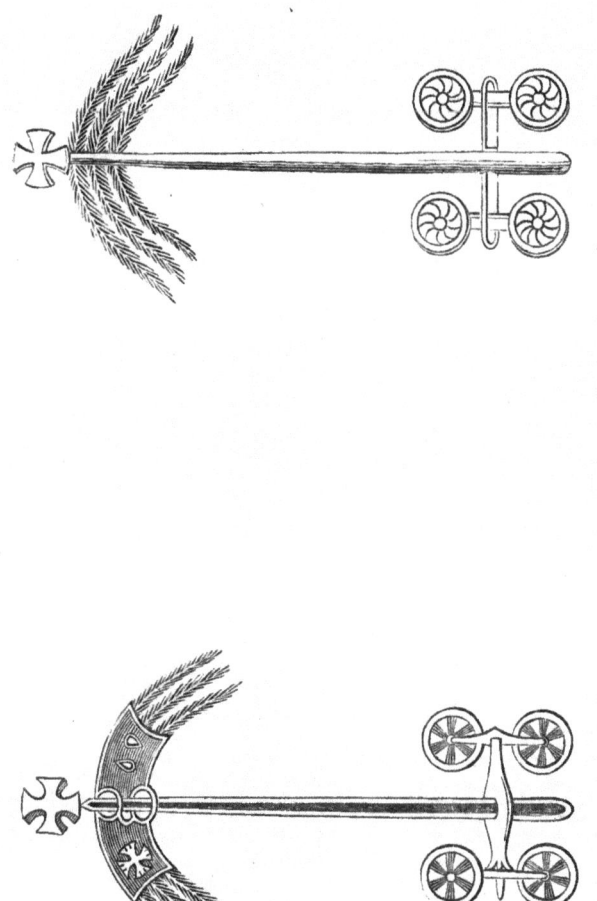

Figures of the Standard.

FROM A PRINTED COPY OF THE MS. OF ÆLREDUS, PUBLISHED IN *DECEM SCRIPTORES* IN 1652.

"*Signum quod vulgo Standard dicetur.*"

The Gants held Hundmanby, in Yorkshire, and their name is still kept up by the inhabitants. A.D. 1139.

"Gilbert Gant
Left Hundmanby moor
To Hundmanby poor,
That they might never want."

and—

"Gilbert de Gant—
And in those days good women were scant;
Some said they were few and some said they were many;
But in the days of Robert Couitas
One was sold at the market cross for a penny."

Such are the rhymes formerly sung round the market cross there every Shrove Tuesday, in remembrance of the good donor.

William Peverell led the forces of Nottinghamshire in the Battle of the Standard, and was taken prisoner with Stephen at the Battle of Lincoln, and his castle of Nottingham, given by the empress Maud to William Painell, but in the following year Peverell's retainers recovered it by stratagem in the night. He founded and endowed several religious houses for the health of the souls of himself, of Aveline his wife, William his son, and all his other children. William Peverell.

William Cumin, chaplain to bishop Rufus at the time of the bishop's last sickness, perceiving the bishop's dissolution approaching, gained the confidence of those about his person, and particularly such as had the custody of the castle of Durham, who entered into a confederacy to deliver up the palace and town to him immediately on the bishop's death. He concealed his project with the greatest assiduity from the prior and archdeacon, and made a journey to the court of Scotland, to consult his sovereign's pleasure, and obtain his assistance in gaining the bishopric. During his absence the bishop departed this life; and, in the night following his death (it not being possible to keep the corpse otherwise), the bowels were drawn, and the body embalmed. In order that the prelate's death might not be suspected abroad, when the prior and archdeacon came to the castle, in their usual manner, to pay their visit, they were refused admittance. His death was kept secret until the Friday following, at the end of which time the clamour of the people being great, and the rumour of the prelate's death having gone abroad, they prepared for his funeral as if he were just dead, and he was interred on Sunday. 1140. The Castle taken.

On the Sunday following Cumin returned to the castle, armed with powers from the king of Scotland, who favoured his project; and, by every influence he could exert, he induced the people to submit to his authority; Fordun

A.D. 1140. expressly says, "he took possession of the castle by the command of the empress." He experienced no great difficulty in gaining over several of the most powerful of the barons; notwithstanding that before the battle of North Allerton, on David refusing to retire on the terms they had proposed in order to save the horrid carnage, Robert Brus and Bernard Baliol had deserted the Scottish standard, and fought under Stephen's banner; yet these two, to protect the palatine, were the first who appeared on behalf of the empress Matilda, whose nominee they esteemed Cumin. They were joined by Eustace de Baliol and Hugh de Moreville. With every persuasion, argument, and threat they could use, they endeavoured to influence the prior and archdeacon to elect Cumin to the bishopric; which they steadily refused, as being inconsistent and irregular. All efforts proving vain, it was proposed to consult the legate; and persons were appointed by Cumin's party who were sworn to act impartially in this business. But the legate gave judgment against such intrusion, and pronounced an interdict against Cumin, if he should assume the episcopal function without a due election. Notwithstanding these oppositions, Cumin prepared to receive the pastoral staff and ring from the empress on the day of St. John the Baptist; and he would have assumed the same accordingly, had not the trouble of the state obliged the empress, with the king of Scotland and their partisans, previously to leave London.

Robert, an archdeacon of Cumin's creation, with the barons of the bishopric, returned to Durham, bearing the empress's letter, directed to the chapter, requiring them to nominate Cumin. He was with the empress at Winchester, and a party in the miseries of her flight; so that it was near Michaelmas before he returned to Durham, where he found the king of Scotland, who had arrived a short time before him, entertained by the convent. He therefore immediately entered the castle, and found the prior and convent, together with the old archdeacon, still remaining inexorable to every argument. The king of Scotland, therefore, left Cumin in possession of the castle, as *custos* of the temporalities of the see for the empress; the king pledging himself to the convent, that they should suffer no injury under the authority of Cumin. But Cumin after the king's departure, not regarding himself as *custos*, but as possessing the authority of bishop, received the homage of all the barons, except Roger de Coniers, and made the burgesses of Durham swear fealty to him.

At length, a monk of the Cistercian order arrived at Durham, and straightway was admitted into secret confidence by Cumin. He was soon sent abroad to accomplish a project they had concerted between them, and which afterwards came fully to light. A proper time having elapsed, the monk returned, bringing forged letters from the pope, with a counterfeit seal, resembling the apostolical seal, by which the holy see expressed satisfaction at Cumin's election, and commanding Henry, bishop of Winchester, the legate, no further to molest him in his episcopal function. Cumin then sent him to David king of Scotland, with other forged letters, wherein the pope expressed his approbation of the oath the king had taken to the empress Matilda, and that Cumin should hold the bishopric of Durham by her appointment, The fraud was soon afterwards discovered, the monk confessing he was instigated by Cumin. Innumerable injuries were devised against the convent by the usurper. He had the custody of the city gates, so that he prevented all messages being sent to the monks. He had possession of the chapter seal, and used it as his pleasure dictated; and he is said to have built the castle at North Allerton, which he gave to William his nephew, who espoused the niece of the earl of Albermarle. His part, however, in the construction of the castle was probably little more than repairing the structure already raised by Galfrid, with perhaps some extension of the fortifications.

A.D. 1140.

This prelate was commissioned by Thurstan, archbishop of York, to represent him at the Battle of the Standard. Bishop Ralph's speech to the British army on that occasion, will be handed down to posterity as his memorial.

Ralph, Bishop of Orkney.

Torffœus, the Danish historian, doubts the accounts given of the early bishops of the Orkney isles. The archbishops of York had used to consecrate bishops with the title of Orkney, but Torffœus is of opinion that they were merely titulars, to give a greater show of authority to the see of York; and he is positive that this bishop never did reside in the Isles of Orkney, and that Ralph, designed bishop of Orkney, had been a presbyter at York.

Thurstan, the twenty-eighth archbishop of York, was elected in 1114, but was not consecrated till 1119. He was lord-lieutenant of the north, and organized the troops that fought in the battle of the Standard, though he was left at Thirsk sick. He protected the thirteen monks who fled from St. Mary's abbey, York, in 1132, and gave them the ground near Ripon, on which was afterwards founded the beautiful abbey of Fountains. Thurstan is remarkable for having never acknowledged the precedence of the see of Canterbury over that of York. In 1137, while he was archbishop, the minster was partly destroyed by fire. He resigned 21st Jan., 1139.

Thurstan, Archbishop of York.

"Thus within two years after the battle, the aged Thurstan felt his vital vigour to decay, and prepared for

A.D. 1140.
a more solemn hour of conflict. He set his house in order; and assembling the priests of the cathedral of York in his own chapel, made his last confession before them; and laid with bared body on the ground before the altar of St. Andrew, received from some of their hands the discipline of the scourge, with tears bursting from his contrite heart. And remembering a vow made in his youth at Clugny, the famous monastery in Burgundy, he went to Pontefract, to a newly founded house of Cluniac monks, followed by an honorable procession of the priests of the Church of York, and a great number of laymen. There, on the festival of the conversion of St. Paul, he took the habit of a monk in the regular way, received the abbot's blessing, and for the remainder of his life gave himself entirely to the care of the salvation of his soul. On the 6th of February, 1140, twenty-six years and six months after his accession to the archbishopric, the canons of the church of York and other religious persons standing round, the hour of his departure being at hand, he celebrated the vigils in commemoration of the dead in Christ, read the lesson himself, and with a clear voice, pausing and sometimes groaning in spirit, chanted the solemn verses of the hymn, *Dies iræ*. At the end of this solemn service of humiliation he sank to the earth, and while the monks gathered round and prayed for him, breathed his last."*

1141.
Robert de Brus.

Robert de Brus took an active part in the Battle of the Standard, and was no less distinguished for piety than valour. He founded Guisborough priory, gave the church of Middlesbrough to Whitby, and died at a good old age, and was buried within the venerable pile at Guisborough which he had reared.

1143.
Transfer of the Castle.

On the 14th March, 1143, the convent having escaped from Durham to York, elected William de St. Barbara,† dean of York, to the see of Durham. After long resistance and bloodshed, the legal bishop, accompanied by the archbishop of York and the bishop of Carlisle, entered the city of Durham on the festival of St. Luke; Cumin in deep contrition for his offences, prostrated himself at the bishop's feet, and voluntarily delivered up the castle, together with the whole territories of the palatinate. Some authors allege, that on

* Churton's early English Church.

† Consecrated 20th June, 1143, at Winchester, from whence he returned to York; privately enthroned 18th Aug., 1143, enthroned duly 18th Oct., 1144; died 14th Nov., 1152. He is described as a person of good stature, with venerable grey locks, remarkable for his hospitality and liberality to the poor, of exemplary manners, true piety, much wisdom, and great perspicuity of judgment. He was endowed with profound knowledge in the several branches of the literature of that age, and graced it with persuasive eloquence. Ever intent on works of charity and the service of God, his memory went down to posterity, distinguished by uniform virtue and propriety.

Cumin's surrender, the bishop granted the honor and castle of North Allerton, with their appendages, to Richard, another nephew of Cumin.* A.D. 1143.

It appears that Cumin soon began the war again, but whether from not meeting with his usual success, either from his being now broken with age and infirmities, or from the death of his nephew William,† which happened about this time, or from other causes, he soon afterwards made submission to the bishop, took an oath to make good the damages the see had suffered, and left the bishop to enjoy the see in 1144.

Roger de Mowbray, one of the commanders in the Battle of the Standard, was, with king Stephen, at the Battle of Lincoln, and there taken prisoner. He afterwards accompanied Lewis, king of France, in his crusade to the Holy Land, where he was again taken prisoner by Saladin, and redeemed by the Knights Templars. Being concerned in the rebellion, he had to forfeit his castle of Thirsk, which the king (Henry II) caused to be pulled down. He was buried in the abbey of Byland. 1148. Roger de Mowbray.

Walter Espec was one of the principal commanders in the Battle of the Standard, and although this is the only engagement in which we find him, his address to the soldiers shows him to have been a man of valour in the defence of his country. He founded and amply endowed the abbeys of Kirkham and Rievaulx. He had only one son, who was killed by the fall of his horse, to the great grief of his father, who, being thus bereft of his issue, resolved to "*make Christ heir of part of his lands.*" He was buried in the abbey of Rievaulx, where two years before he became a monk. 1153. Walter Espec.

The foundation of the hospital,‡ situated about a mile on the road to York, and dedicated to St. James, has usually been ascribed to Hugh Pudsey, bishop of Durham, in the reign of Henry II. Tanner says, in the reprises upon the valuation, the chaplains here are said to be appointed to pray for the soul of Philip de Poicteu,§ bishop of Durham, who was successor to bishop Pudsey. The churches of Thornton-le-Street and North Otterington were given to this hospital; it was also endowed with the town of Ellerbeck and the mill, half a plough-land at Romanby, and eight oxgangs at Otterington. 1155. St. James' Hospital, Romanby.

* Jo. Hagulst. Sim. Dun. Gale's Historical account.
† He died at Merrington, as he was endeavouring to convert into a fortress the church of St. John. It was not unusual to make church towers serve as fortresses: Bedale tower has a fire-place, portcullis groove, and even a forica of stone throughout.
‡ A farm-house now stands on the site, which still retains the name of *Spital*.
§ Elected at Northallerton, 1195, consecrated May 12th, 1197. Excommunicated for contumacy, and buried like a dog in 1208.

20   ANNALS OF

A.D. 1162.
Ecclesiastical dispute.

Prior Thomas, the first, engaged with bishop Pudsey in a dispute about the church of Allerton, and a violent contention arose, in which the monks not supporting their prior, as they ought to have done, in protection of the rights of the church, the prior was deposed by the bishop in the year 1163, and retired to the island of Farne, in which St. Cuthbert formerly had his residence, and restoring some of the buildings, lived the life of a recluse.* He was succeeded by Germanus.

1166.
The judgment by water

In the twelfth year of Henry II., the soke of North Alverton was amerced ten marks † for putting a man to the judgment of water, without the knowledge or presence of the king's servant. The judgment alluded to was this:—the culprit, bound hand and foot, was thrown into a pond; if he sank he was considered guilty, and if he floated innocent. The process, however, was supposed to be watched by a government official, who in this instance did not happen to be present, hence the penalty.

1167.
Adam de Brus

Adam de Brus fought side by side with his father (Robert de Brus) in the Battle of the Standard. Having adhered faithfully to king Stephen throughout his stormy and disastrous career, he incurred the displeasure of Henry II., who deprived him of his noble castle at Danby in Cleveland. He emulated his father in deeds of piety, and gave to the Knights Templars, lands at Ingleby and Yarm; he also founded the nunnery at Hutton Lowcross. He was buried at Guisborough.

1173.
Fortification of the Castle.

Hugh de Pudsey,‡ the sixth of the Norman bishops, nephew of king Stephen, greatly enlarged the castle at North Allerton about 1173, for the security of the town and his estates in Allertonshire; and at many other places he repaired or rebuilt the residences of his predecessors, "raising stately buildings," says the Durham historian, "thinking it the most honorable course to leave his successors no ground of complaint against his memory."§ He strongly fortified the castle of Norham, and repaired at great cost the castle at Durham, and the city walls.

* Ang. Sac. 721. Geoff. de Cold.
† £6 13s. 4d.
‡ Treasurer of York, and archdeacon of Winchester. Elected 13th Feb., 1152, consecrated 20th Dec., 1153. He was bishop nearly forty-two years, and did many good and memorable deeds, though, Godfridus de Coldingham says "his magnificent works were monuments which pride raised to his memory, inscribed with the perpetuation of those sins he committed on his distressed province." He died at Howden, 3rd Mar., 1194, æt. 70; leaving many valuable presents to the church. His bible in four large volumes, in the dean and chapter's library, is one of the finest MSS. there, though the illuminations have suffered from Dr. Dobson's lady or nurse, who on rainy days amused his child in the library and cut out the "bonny shows" for it to play with.
§ Hist. Dun. c. vii.

NORTHALLERTON. 21

After the defeat and capture of William, king of Scotland, the king (Henry II.) lost not a moment in pursuing the correction of his diffident barons; and in less than a month, compelled them to surrender their castles and persons. A.D. 1174. Defence of the Castle.

Bishop Pudsey appeared before the king at Northampton to make his submission. He was the only prelate in the realm who had given cause to suspect his loyalty. He had, in the previous year, permitted the Scottish army to march through his territories without opposition; and lately had sent for a body of Flemings, consisting of 40 knights and 500 foot soldiers, to come over into England, under the command of his nephew Hugh, count de Bar. They landed at Hartlepool on the very day the king of Scotland was made prisoner; the news of which event induced the bishop immediately to send back the foot, but he retained the knights, and committed the care of his castle at North Allerton to his nephew, with that force for its defence.*

The bishop, under the present situation of State affairs, was glad to acommodate his offences with the king upon any terms he could obtain; to which end he paid a large sum of money into the royal coffers, and surrendered his castles of Durham, North Allerton, and Norham. The manor was obtained, but he could not rescue his castle of North Allerton, which the king ordered to be razed to its foundation.†

Bishop Pudsey gave the church of Durham many rich ornaments, and greatly enlarged the power of the monastery; the Yorkshire churches, until the time of this prelate, appertained to the bishops, as appears from a deed of composition made with the archbishop of York; but Pudsey granted them to the convent. Episcopal bounty.

After the Battle of the Standard, Bernard de Baliol adhered to king Stephen in his greatest troubles, and was taken prisoner with his royal master at the Battle of Lincoln. He is supposed to be the founder of the castle, thence called Bernard Castle. When the Scots besieged Alnwick Castle, Bernard joined the British barons, and on their march to the relief, it was advised they should halt on account of a dense fog, but Bernard said "*Let them stay that will, I am resolved to go on, though none follow me, rather than dishonour myself by staying here.*" Following his example, they went forward, surprised the enemy, and in a short but fierce skirmish, took the king prisoner, and conveyed him to Richmond Castle. Bernard de Baliol

Northallerton again became prominent in the rebellion between Henry II and his son. In the early part of 1175, the king sent an army to put down the rebellion, and Roger 1175. Another battle.

* Hovenden. Lel. Col.
† Gale's Historical Account.

A.D. 1175.   de Mowbray who headed the insurgents was totally defeated by the royal troops, near Northallerton, on the 11th of March.

Northallerton burnt by Wallace(?)   There is an apocryphal account that Wallace * the knight of Elrisle, fought a sanguinary battle on the outskirts of the town with "Shyr Rawff Rymut, captaine of Maltoun," and after lying some time in expectation of a visit from Edward I, burnt the town, but this account is considered by eminent antiquarians to be both unfounded and romantic.†

Defeat of Roger de Mowbray at Northallerton.   On the 13th of March Roger de Mowbray was again defeated by the troops of King Henry II. at Northallerton, whilst hastening to relieve his nephew, John de Mowbray, who was valiantly defending their ancestral castle at Thirsk.

1177. The Castle destroyed.   "Eodem anno Ds. rex fecit demoliri castellum & mœnia Leicestriæ, & castellum de Grosby, & castellum de Tresk, & castellum de Malseart, & castellum novum de Allerton, & castellum de Fremingham, & de Bungey, & fere omnia castella Angl. & Norman, quæ fuerint contra eum tempore guerræ."‡

Several historians say, that bishop Pudsey actually gave the king 1,000 marks, "*pro amore suo habendo et ut castello sua starent.*"§ Lambarde says, that this bishop "among many things that he compassed at Richard I.'s hands, what tyme he made his expedition towards Jerusalem, obtained that this castle might stand, notwithstanding that, order was taken for the pullinge down of al other which had bene lately buylt in tyme of cyville warre." "But for al that," he adds, "the king caused it to be rased sone after." This, however, must be a mistake, since Geoffrey de Collingham, an ancient Durham historian, ‖ speaking of the acts of Bishop Hugh, in the time of Henry II., says, "that he fortified the town (or castle) of Alverton, having obtained that when all other castles were destroyed, this alone should remain entire. Yet the king afterwards commanded it to be overthrown and laid level with the ground." Hoveden says, "that this and other castles were demolished by Henry in 1177, and calls it *castellum novum de Alverton*."

* "Wallace tranountyt on the secund day,
   Fra York thai passit rycht in gud aray;
   North-west thai past in battaill buskyt boun,
   Thar lugeyng tuk besyd Northallyrtoun."

" Then *Wallace* maid full mony byggyng hayt;
   Thai rassyt fyr, brynt np Northallyrtoun,
   Agayne throuch York-schyre bauldly maid thaim boun,
   Destroyed the land, as fer as evir thai ryde,
   Sewyn myle about thai brynt on athir syde."
                    Regist. Honor de Richmond, p. 156.

† Jefferson of Thirsk, a local historian, is the authority for the above apocryphal account.
‡ Lel. Col. I. 133.   § Benedict. Abbas. Brompton, ap. x Script.
‖ Ang. Sac. I. 723.

"The winding labyrinths, the hostile tower,
  Where danger threaten'd, and tyrannic power,
  The jealous draw-bridge, and the moat profound,
  The lonely dungeon, in the cavern'd ground,
  The sullen dome above those central caves,
  Where liv'd one tyrant and a host of slaves!"

A.D. 1177

The materials of the castle were undoubtedly used in erecting the Episcopal Palace or Manor house, which stood on the same site, about 200 yards west of the church. Leland says, "at the west side of Northalverton, a little from the chirch, is the bishop of Dyrham's palace, strong of building and well motid."* By whom built uncertain; it was for several generations the occasional residence of succeeding bishops of Durham, many important transactions occurring during their sojourn.

This gallant baron fought in the Battle of the Standard, and was advanced to the earldom of Yorkshire as a reward for his prowess. He was also distinguished for his liberality towards the religious orders. He founded the abbeys of Vandey, in Lincolnshire; Ment, in Yorkshire; and the ancient and stupendous castle, once the glory and still the ornament of Scarborough.†

1180. William de Gross.

King William (Rufus) II., out of gratitude for the friendship and fidelity which William, bishop of Durham, had shewn both to him and his father, gave to the said bishop and his successors, the town of Northallerton, with all its rights and appendages.‡

1187. Royal gift.

The following extracts from the Exchequer rolls serve to throw some little light on the history of the manor during the period corresponding with the dates:—

1197. Extract from Exchequer rolls.

A.D. 1197. 8 Richard I. Roll 20. memb. 1.
  The account of Gilbert Fitz-Reinfrid and Richard Briewerre, of the Bishopric of Durham, for three parts of a year, whilst it was in the hand of the king.

Gilbert Fitz-Reinfrid and Richard Briewerre, Richard de Marisco and Master Anketil for them, render account of £100 54s. 4½d. of stock of the same bishoprick sold. In the treasury, £80 104s. 8d. And to Stephen de Hendon 40s., which he had for service which he rendered to Hugh bishop of Durham for three parts of a year by the aforesaid writ. And they owe £15 9s. 8½d., of which the town of Aluerton owes £8 11s. 0½d. And Roger de Gloccr', 40s. 8d. And Serlo, son of Walsi de Eborac, £4 8s. And Stephen de Hendon, 10s., as the aforesaid keepers say.

Of the debt which Hugh, bishop of Durham, owed the king by the roll of the king.

* In the bishop's accounts in the auditor's office, at Durham, are several entries for the payment of keeping swans in this moat.
† Roll of Battle Abbey.   ‡ Simeon Dunelmensis, cap. 67.

A.D. 1197.   Of those who rendered nothing of the aforesaid debt.
Roger, son of Jukel de Aluerton, owes 40s. for a certain house for the same. Nicholas, the parson of Leck, owes 2 marks of amercement for the same.
The tallage of the manors of the bishoprick by the aforesaid.
Of those who have rendered the whole.
The same render account of £200 55s. 10d. of the tallage of the manors of the bishoprick, the names of which, and the particulars of the debts, are noted down in the roll which the aforesaid have rendered in the treasury. They have paid in the treasury. And they are quit. The town of Aluerton renders account of £30 for the same. In the treasury, £10 16s. 2d. And it owes £19 3s. 10d.
The scutage of the same bishoprick made by the same.
Of those who have rendered the whole.
John de Romundeb (Romanby) renders account of one marc for the same. In the treasury half a marc. And he owes half a marc.

1200.
The Vicarage

The Vicarage, which is in charge, was formerly appropriated to the prior and convent of Durham, and is still in the gift of the dean and chapter of that church. The present vicarage-house is of comparatively recent date, being built on the site of a much older edifice. The following inscription appears on a stone slab above the front door:—

DOMUM HANC,
Vetustate collabentem instauratam ampliatam commodiore *loco positam*, sibi et successoribus suis Dei Opt Max numine invocato dicat,
GEORGIUS TOWNSEND, A.M.,
Vicarius de Northallerton,
A.D. MDCCCXXVIII.
Pios tecta hæc tutentur et Fideles.*

---

* *Translation.*—George Townsend, A.M., Vicar of Northallerton, devotes this house, decaying through old age, having been restored, enlarged, and placed in a more convenient situation, to himself and his successors, when he had invoked the blessing of the Greatest and Best GOD, A.D. 1828.
May these walls overshadow the pious and the faithful.

The proprietor of the rectorial tithes is Sir Henry Beresford Pierse, whose ancestor Henry Pierse, Esq., then M.P. for the Borough, purchased the rectory from Edmund Prissick, Esq., of Carlton, in Cleveland, to whom it had been sold by the Earl of Ailesbury, in whose family it had been long vested. A list of Vicars from a very remote period, and a further description of the Vicarage, will be found in the appendix. A.D. 1200.

Permission to hold fairs in Northallerton was granted by king John in 1200; there were formerly only two during the year; at the present time there are four. (1) *Candlemas Fair*, for horses and cattle, held on the 14th February. (2) *St. George's Fair*, granted by Queen Mary, is held on the 5th and 6th of May, for horses, cattle, and sheep; it is also a fancy fair, and is a great resort of the fair sex. One of the half-yearly hirings takes place at this fair. (3) *September Fair* (S. Bartholomew), is held on the 5th of that month, but is not very well attended. (4) *St. Matthew's Fair*, granted by James I., is held on the 3rd of October, for cattle and sheep, and for the hiring of farm labourers. The Market is held on Wednesdays, and is supplied with various descriptions of produce. The Cheese Fair, formerly held on the second Wednesday in October, has been discontinued for many years. The following Latin stanzas (to which a translation is affixed) are extracted from Barnaby's Journal, (part iii). Fairs and Markets.

> Veni *Alerton*, ubi oves,
> Tauri, vaccæ, vituli boves,
> Aliaque campi pecora,
> Oppidana erant decora:
> Forum fuit jumentorum,
> Mihi autem cella forum.
> Veni *Alerton*, lætam, latam,
> Mercatori perquam gratam,
> In utiliorem actum,
> Eligo locum pecori aptum.
>
> *(Translation.)*
>
> Thence to Alerton, rank'd in battle,
> Sheep, kine, oxen, other cattle;
> As I fortun'd to pass by there,
> Were the town's best beautifier:
> Fair for beasts at that time fell there,
> But I made my fare the cellar.
> Thence to Alerton, cheerful, fruitful,
> To the seller very grateful;
> There to choose a place, I'm chariest,
> Where my beasts may shew the fairest.

The centre of activity at these fairs and markets was the cross which stood in the midst of the market-place, as a signal for upright intention and fair dealing, and designed as a check on a worldly spirit. On the north of the cross stood two double rows of shabby shambles, and on the south side an unsightly toll booth ; both are now removed. The migratory habits of rats are well known, and it is said that large numbers have frequently been seen to proceed from the toll booth and shambles to drink at the Sun-beck when swollen. On the south side of the toll booth stood the stocks, "though lost to sight, to memory dear," and in which many ardent worshippers of Bacchus had time and opportunity given to them wherein to study the delightful science of astronomy.

A.D. 1211.
Extract from Exchequer rolls.

13 John A.D. 1211. Roll 4. memb. 1.

The account of the bishopric of Durham from the feast of saint John the Baptist, in the tenth year, to the feast of saint Martin next following. And from thence for the three years next following.

Eimeric, archdeacon of Durham, and Philip de Ulecote render account of £198 12s. 8½d. of the balance of the account of the bishopric of Durham, as it is contained in the roll of the eighth year of king Richard. And of 100s. of Reginald clerk of Aluerton for disseisin. And of 2 marcs of John de Rodmundbi. And of 30 marcs of the town of Aluerton. And of 2 marcs of Jukell de Smitheton. And of 20s. of Nicholas, the parson of Leke.

1213.

14 John, 1213. Roll. 5. memb. 2.

The account of the bishopric of Durham, by Eimeric, archdeacon of Durham, and Philip de Ulecote, from the feast of saint Martin, in the 13th year, to the feast of saint Martin the year of this roll.

The aforesaid Eimeric and Philip render account of £7 4s. 10d., in work done at the houses of Aluerton, by the same writ, and on sight of the aforesaid.

1218.
The Pope's legate at Northallerton

This year Gualo, the pope's legate, summoned the clergy of the neighbourhood to appear before him in Northallerton Church at Easter, where he gave absolution to some who satisfied his demands, obliged some to repair to the court at Rome, and passed on others sentences of suspension or deposition on the different degrees of obstinacy in the persons accused, as his own views of gain directed.*

1230.

A charter was granted by bishop Richard Poor,† reciting divers liberties to the burgesses of Hartlepool. Given by the hand of Valens, at Alverton, 3 kal. Oct., in the third year of our episcopacy.‡

* Vide Ridpath's Border History.
† Translated from Salisbury, 22nd July, 1228. He made himself honorable by clearing his predecessor's (De Marisco) debts. He died 15th April, 1237, and was buried in the nunnery at Tarent, built by himself.
‡ Sharpe's Hartlepool, 59.

From the calendar of charters in the Bodleian Library, it is ascertained that Philip de Collevill granted to the hospital of St. James, near Alverton, two acres of land in Dritdale. A.D. 1230. Grant of land.

Gilbertus, Vicar of Northallerton about 1240. He was presented to the living by the prior and convent of Durham, and died in 1267. 1240. Gilbertus.

John de Derlington, formerly vicar of S. Oswald, Durham, became vicar of Northallerton in the same year. 1267. John de Derlington.

In 1274, prior Richard of Durham conveyed Robert de Insula, prior of Finchale, to London. The latter had just been elected bishop of Durham, and the train in attendance, upon so important an occasion as journeying to seek confirmation of the appointment by the king, must have been very considerable. Their rate of motion cannot be taken as a fair criterion of the ordinary speed of travelling, as every convenience and aid would be specially supplied. They reached London on the 15th day after leaving Durham. Two kinds of carriages are mentioned, *carectæ* and *bigæ*. The former were four-wheeled carriages, the latter two-wheeled. The road pursued was by North Allerton, Boroughbridge, and Pontefract, to Doncaster; the first night was passed at Ketton, where the monastery possessed a grange. The party appears not to have paid by the meal, but by what they actually consumed, for they had prepared a stock of provisions to be carried in their carts, and a stock of herrings was despatched from North Allerton to Doncaster against their arrival at that town. At Ketton they paid for kitchen stuff, drink and bread, all other accommodation being ready and gratis. Further on, charges occur for forerunners, oats, hay, and litter for their horses, beer and wine. There must have been an inn at Ketton where the beer and wine were purchased, the expression being "In taberna ibidem." The whole journey up cost £75 15s. 5d. The return was more rapid, the party reached Ketton by a ten days travel.* 1274. A Bishop of Durham's journey to London.

Bishop Robert de Insula† by deed, dated at Alverton, 6 id. Sep., 1279, granted to Henry de Horncastre, prior of Coldingham, and to the monks of that cell, for ever, a place for an habitation in the village of Holy Island.‡ 1279. Deed of grant

* Longstaffe's Darlington.

† Prior of Finchley, elected 24 Sep., 1274. The bishop was of humble origin. To his mother he gave an honorable establishment, and once when he went to see her, he asked "And how fares my sweet mother?" "Never worse," quoth she. "And what ails thee, or troubles thee? hast thou not men, and women, and attendants sufficient?" "Yea," quoth she, "and more than enough; I say to one 'Go,' and he runs; to another, 'Come hither, fellow,' and the varlet falls down on his knees; and in short all things go on so abominably smooth, that my heart is bursting for something to spite me, and pick a qurrel withal." He died at Middleham, 7th June, 1283, and was buried in the chapter house at Durham, before the bishop's seat, under a beautiful stone, curiously engraven, and adorned with images.

‡ Raine's North Durham.

A.D. 1282.
Warinus de Alverton. Warinus de Alverton was presented by the master and brethren of the hospital of St. James, juxta Northalverton, to the vicarage of North Otterington.

1291. Royal visit. King Edward I. visited Northallerton, on his way to the north, April 13th.

1292. The Episcopal Palace. There is no documentary or other evidence which conclusively points to the date of the erection of the episcopal palace of the prince bishops of Durham, in Northallerton. In or about the year 1292 is the most probable date.

Ecclesiastical disputes. The Metropolitan see of York having commenced a claim of jurisdiction over the see of Durham, sent their notary-public and his clerk to Durham, by the pope's authority, with official letters of citation and canonical mandates. On their arrival at the castle of Durham, the bishop's officers imprisoned the messengers in the castle, and kept them in "durance vile" until compelled to release them by a sentence of interdict thundered out by the archbishop of York against his brother prelate the bishop of Durham, confirmed by a process issued from the king's secular courts. After this, the archbishop issued his precept to the prior of Bolton to excommunicate the bishop of Durham in his own churches of Alverton, Darlington, and other places. The prior obeyed, and the case came before parliament. The archbishop then found himself in a more awkward predicament than his predecessor, who fled from Durham on a one-eared palfrey in an attempt at visitation. Parliament adjudged the archbishop to be committed to the Tower, notwithstanding his pall; and enforced to enter into a recognizance, with sureties, to pay a fine of 4,000 marks* to the king.†

Royal visit. King Edward I. visited Northallerton on the 15th and 16th August in this year.

1293. Episcopal grant. At the instance of Anthony Beke,‡ bishop of Durham, John de Lythege, and Alice his wife, granted to John Hansard their manor of Werkersale, and in consideration for the same, Hansard granted his manor of Evenwood and Fuley to bishop

---

* £2,666 13s. 4d.
† This dispute as to jurisdiction between the sees of York and Durham has continued down to the present time, but it has recently been decided that Northallerton is not a peculiar jurisdiction in the diocese of York in matters ecclesiastical, although in the gift of the Dean and Chapter of Durham.
‡ Archdeacon of Durham, patriarch of Jerusalem. He had also from the king the principality of Man. Elected to the see of Durham, 9th July, 1283; died 3rd March, 1310. In his time the court of Durham exhibited all the appendages of royalty; nobles addressed the palatine sovereign kneeling, and instead of menial servants, knights waited in his presence chamber, and at his table, bareheaded and standing. At one time he had present with him at the king's wars in Scotland, twenty ancient bearers of his own family. He was the first bishop that was buried in the cathedral; reverence for St. Cuthbert prevented his predecessors from being buried there.

Beke, and the bishop made compensation to Lythege and his wife, by granting to them £40 per annum for their lives out of the manor of Allerton.* *A.D. 1293.*

Bishop Lewis Beaumont demised to certain foreign merchants, called in the records *Alienigenis*, (but of what country not easily determined, though supposed to be Italians, the Forum Alieni being thought to be Ferrara; or perhaps they were of Alias in France), his manors of Allerton, Howden, and Richall, for a term of ten years.

King Edward I. visited Northallerton January 20th, 1293. *Royal visit.*

Stephen de North Alverton was in 1295 vicar of Marske, near Redcar. This gentleman derived his name either from his birth or residence at Northallerton. *1295. Stephen de Northallerton.*

King Edward I. visited Northallerton on the 9th and 10th October, 1296. *1296. Royal visit.*

Certain Scotch nobility who, being summoned had refused to attend a parliament held at York, Edward I. assembled an army at Alverton, and marched from thence against his contumacious lords. The dispute was settled by the battle of Falkirk, which was fought on July 22nd, 1298, the king gaining a complete and decisive victory. *1298. Northallerton a military rendezvous.*

The borough of Northallerton first sent members to parliament in the 26th year of Edward I. John le Clerk and Stephen Maunsell were the names of the worthies on whom the choice of the electors fell. How they conducted themselves, how they voted, and how their wages were paid, we have no information. No members were afterwards returned for 342 years, probably on account of the expense of their wages, which must have been a heavy burden on the inhabitants.† *First Members of Parliament.*

Peter de Killawe became vicar of Northallerton. *1302. Peter de Killawe.*

King Edward I. visited Northallerton on the 7th March, 1302. *Royal visit.*

King Edward I. visited Northallerton on the 27th and 28th April, 1303. *1303. Royal visit.*

It is somewhat remarkable that no event worth recording took place at Northallerton between the two royal visits of king Edward, during this otherwise eventful period.

In 1304, £4,000 sterling passed through Northallerton on its way from York to Scotland. The money was packed in eight barrels, made out of three empty casks, which were placed in a cart, guarded by five carters, twelve archers, and six men-at-arms. *1304. Transit of specie.*

King Edward I. visited Northallerton on the 1st October, 1304. *Royal visit.*

* Randall's MSS.
† For list of Members of Parliament, see appendix.

A.D. 1309.
Fortification of the Bishop's Palace.

Davyd Eosselyn, a partisan of Thomas, Earl of Lancaster, and who was ultimately executed for robbery, fortified the manor of Allerton in the time of Edward II. At this time it is described by Leland as being "stronge of building and welle moted."*

1311.

Peter de Fishburn succeeded Peter de Killawe as vicar of Northallerton, in 1311.

Roger de Northallerton.

In Burton's MS. we find that Dr. Ro(d)ger de Northalverton was vicar of Skipwith, in Howdenshire, at this time.

1312.
Royal visit.

King Edward II. visited Northallerton on the 6th and 8th April, 1312.

1317.
The illiterate Bishop of Durham.

Lewis Beaumont, the illiterate bishop of Durham (who had been consecrated because he was a descendant of the royal family of France and a near relative of the Queen of England), accompanied by two cardinals and a splendid retinue, met the prior of Durham at Northallerton, and such was the bishop's ignorance, that his deed of consecration had to be read by the prior, because the bishop was unable to read it himself! It is a source of gratification to know that in this respect at least *tempora mutantur, nos et mutamur in illis.*

The Bishop's Palace rifled.

Towards the close of this year, a noted robber, Sir Goselene Denville, descended from honourable parents at Northallerton, and whose family came over with William the Conqueror, attacked the bishop's palace at Northallerton, and completely rifled it. He was associated with a numerous band, who did not, without a desperate conflict, yield to the sheriff and five hundred men; after which the desperadoes, who had been the terror of the county, were led to the scaffold at York.

1318.
Battle of Bannockburn.

Not long after the lamentable battle of Bannockburn, in which the English were totally defeated by Robert Bruce†, the victorious Scots, headed by Sir James Douglas, made a dash at York with the hope of carrying off Edward's Queen, Isabella; but a prisoner, whom the English had taken, betrayed their scheme just in time to prevent its success. On their route they laid waste the country with fire and sword. At Northallerton, they received 1,000 marks ‡ to spare the town, but whether enraged at the opposition of the castles of Skipton and Knaresborough, or from some other motives, it is certain they burnt both Ripon and Northallerton, and continuing their depredations, advanced to the walls of York. The few inhabitants that remained in Northallerton after its partial destruction, were exempted by the king from the payment of taxes, in consideration that they had been ruined by his enemies and rebels.

A scheme frustrated.

Northallerton partially burnt.

1319.
Its inhabitants exempted from taxation.

---

* I am told that about a hundred and twenty years ago, a good piece of the gatehouse was standing; but through the injuries of time and the violence of illiterate hands, not the smallest vestige of it now remains.—J.L.S.

† The anecdote of Bruce and the spider is well known to every schoolboy.

‡ £666 13s. 4d.

The town, or what remained of it, was totally destroyed by fire by the Scots on their return from the expedition of 1322, after which they appear to have made themselves masters of the whole of the north of England. *[A.D. 1322. Totally destroyed by the Scots.]*

In several succeeding reigns, Yorkshire was the seat of intestine wars with all their attendant horrors. The Scots, urged by ambition and aggression, took every opportunity of invading the northern frontiers, frequently penetrating as far as York.

In order to check these inroads, Edward II. issued a commission to raise as speedily as possible, in every town and place in the wapentake of Alverton, all the defensible men between the ages of sixteen and sixty of all classes, each man being duly arrayed according to his estate. *[1323. Another military levy.]*

Alan de Chiredon, S.T.P., appointed vicar of Northallerton, in 1323.

Edward III., although only fourteen years of age, marched against the Scots, who under Robert Bruce, were ravaging the northern parts of England, and another levy was made under a writ, dated at Northallerton, in order to raise troops* for the occasion. These being duly appointed and arrayed, were led by night and by day, by hasty marches, to join the king at Carlisle; but before an encounter could take place peace was concluded, and David the heir of Scotland was married to Edward's sister Jane, called *Joan of the Tower*, and by the Scots *Joan make peace*. This, however, did not finally cement the friendship of the two nations, for in less than five years we find Edward marching north, entering Scotland in aid of Edward Baliol, and closing the campaign by the glorious victory of Halidown Hill. *[1327. Military levy. British victory of Halidown Hill.]*

King Edward III., visited Northallerton, in July, 1327. *[1327. Royal visit.]*

When this school was founded it is impossible to say, but the earliest document relating to it is dated 1327. It is free and open to the reception of four free scholars, being children of poor parents belonging to the parish of Northallerton. It is poorly endowed. The property belonging to it includes the house and garden, and some land at Catto, subject to the payment of 20s. yearly. It, however, possesses several university advantages: five scholarships at Peterhouse, Cambridge, of £10 a year each, failing of applicants from the school of Durham, and also contingent interests in twelve exhibitions of £20 per annum at Lincoln College, Oxford. The master is appointed by the vicar of Northallerton, and licensed by the dean and chapter of Durham. *[The Grammar School.]*

---

* " The men of Thirsk, Northallerton beside,
    With Topcliffe heroes, show a comely pride."
                                    Madox's Exch.

A.D. 1327. The free scholars are admitted into the school on application to the master, with the concurrence of the vicar. Formerly the school enjoyed great reputation, and was well attended by the children from the town and neighbourhood, but during the time the Rev. James Wilkinson was master, in consequence of the decline in the demand for classical education, the school was conducted for some years as an English reading and writing school. This change did not give universal satisfaction, and on the appointment of the Rev. John Bowness, it was determined to replace the school on the former footing of a grammar school.

Brief notices of the eminent men who were educated at this school, and who have been an honour to the town, will be found under their respective dates.

1328. An episcopal dispute. Bishop Beaumont had a dispute with William de Melton, archbishop of York, concerning the right of visitation in the jurisdiction of Allerton; and whenever the metropolitan came thither to visit, the bishop of Durham opposed him with an armed force. After much litigation, a compromise and agreement* took place in the year 1330, and the archbishop appropriated the church of Leak† for the maintenance of the bishop's table; with the reserve of an annual pension to himself, and another to the chapter of York.‡

1331. Gift of land. William de Alverton gave land to the Austin Friars in this town, 14 Edw. III. He was the 14th Abbot of Fountains.

1332. Richard Askeby, vicar of Northallerton, resigned the living in 1332, for the rectory of Sigston.

1334. Another levy. The Scots still continued to be a thorn in the side of the English, and in 1334 another levy was made similar to that of 1323, Northallerton being chosen as the rendezvous.

An interesting inquisition. By an inquisition taken at Northalverton, in the seventh year of the reign of king Edward III., before Ralph de Neville, *custos* of the bishopric of Durham, then vacant and in the king's hands, it was found that the men of this town were free and of free condition *(liberi et liberæ conditionis§)*, and had and held the same town with the tofts and crofts ||

---

* See 1 Reg. Eccl. Dun. 121.

† In the church of Leak, in the north aisle, is a screen of rich parclose of the 14th century, it retains its original paintings of birds and flowers, and in the south aisle are two beautifully carved stall ends bearing date, 1519. On one of the bells, said to have been brought from Rievaux, is the following inscription,

✠ O: PATER: AELREDE: GRENDALE: MISERI: MISERERE.

"O Father, commisserate the miserable Aelred Grendale."

‡ Rob. de Graystanes. Ang. Sac. 760.

§ The *Liberi Homines* were such as held in military service, and were not knighted or *nulites*.

|| A *toft* is the enclosure in which the house stands, and the *croft*, a little garth or close adjoining to the toft.

therein; and also the market and fair thereof, with all the profits thence arising, of the bishop of Durham in fee, at the rent of 40 marks* of silver without other customs and services. It was also found that in all the pleas of lands or tenements within the same town, the men thereof were to compose the jury; and that if any one of the town were impleaded in the free court of the lord bishop at Northalverton, the two *præpositi* or *reves* of the same town, or one of them, with his bailiff there, should come to court, and assign to the parties the third day of plea in the Toll-booth *(theslonio)*. It was likewise found that Anthony, bishop of Durham, deceased, and the late and present king had taken £20 from the townsmen by extortion† or against their will. It further appears from the inquisition, that the bishop had plea of *hymsoken, blodewite, and replevin*, with the amends of the assize of bread and ale broken, of butchers and forestallers ‡; liberties which he still preserves in the name of Court-Leet and Court-Baron, held twice a year, after Easter and Michaelmas, the latter of these courts having a great number of copyholders upon it, who pay a moderate fine on alienation. But neither the above rent of 40 marks, nor any other, is now paid to him by the town.

A.D. 1334.

A writ was issued to Richard Dousyng, Adam de Cupendale, and Adam Tyrwhit, jointly and severally, to array and train to arms all men within the liberties of Beverley; to send within three days, under the command of Adam de Cupendale and Adam Tyrwhit, fifty hobelars and fifty foot soldiers, whether expert archers or not; and to train all other men, between sixteen and sixty years of age. It appears the expected detachment from Beverley did not join the king, in obedience to his writ, for Adam de Cupendale abandoned the command, and Thomas de Holm was appointed in his place, and he was commanded without further delay to send them to Richmond and Northallerton, to act against the Scots.§

Writs issued to raise troops

The people of Beverley appear to have been averse to meeting the king's wishes on this subject, for the men were not yet sent. Another writ was issued (19th June,) in which the arrayers were not only accused of negligence and disobe-

---

* £169 10s.
† The burgesses and tradesmen in large towns had, in the reign of Edward the Confessor, their patrons, under whose protection they traded and paid acknowledgment therefore, or else were in a more servile condition, as being *in Dominio Regis vel aliorum, i.e.* altogether under the power of the king or other lords.
‡ Plea of *hymsoken* and *blodewite*, is judicial cognizance of *forcible entry* and *bloodshed*. *Wite* is a mulct or penalty. *Replevin*, an action for recovering goods wrongfully detained.
§ Rot. Scot. (6 June,) 7 Edw. III.

A.D. 1334. dience, but their omission was imputed to peculation, and other causes of a still baser nature; and they were threatened with summary and signal punishment, if they did not send them without further notice. This threat was decisive, the men were forthwith sent.

1335. Edmund Cruer, vicar of Northallerton, resigned the living in 1335 for the vicarage of Haltwhistle, and was succeeded by Robert Dighton.

1336. Fresh levies. Edward was obliged again to assemble an army to attack the Scots, and four writs successively followed each other, for arming and arraying men in Holderness; the first is addressed to Simon de Grimsby and John de Sutton; the second, in French, "de tris centy homes a sue en la fraunchise de Holdernesse"; the third, to Thomas de Monceaux, John Sourdeville, Roger de Sprotele, and John de Wyneton, signed by the king himself, at Carlisle; the fourth appoints John de Sourdeval, Roger Gilt de Sprotele, Walter de Twywell, William Rust de Dringhoe, Thomas Hogg de Wynestede, Thomas Porter, William Godebour, Roger Donell, Robert de Bellerby, and Thomas de Stanley; these troops were to be marched to Northallerton.*

1338. Talbot de Northalverton During the episcopacy of bishop Bury, Talbot de Northalverton, by his deed granted to John de Menevyll and Agnes his wife, and their heirs, a rent charge out of lands in Great Haswell.

1340. A monastery of Austin friars. In 1340, William de Alverton gave the Austin friars eight acres of ground in this town to build them a church and habitation thereon. The site of this house was on the east side of the town, now occupied by the Fleece Inn, and two houses adjoining on the south side.†

Church rebuilt 1345-81. The church was rebuilt about this time, after its destruction by the Scots.

1346. Northallerton desolated. David Bruce, king of Scotland, taking advantage of the absence of Edward III. in France, entered England with an army of 50,000 men, and devastated the country up to the very gates of York, "foure tounes only" according to Hollinshed, being exempt from burning, to witte, Hexham, Corbridge, Durham, and Darlington, to the ende he might in them lay up such stores of vitayls, as he shall provide abrode in the country, wherewith to susteyne his army during the

---

* Rot. Scot. 9th Edw. III. 320, 369, 393. Poulson's Holderness.

† The habit of the monks of this order was a white garment and scapulary; when outside, over the former a caul and hood, both black, girt with a black leathern thong. The order was one of the mendicants. They had all things in common; they employed the first part of the day in labour, and the remainder in reading and devotion. Saturday was allowed to provide necessaries, and on Sunday they were allowed to drink wine. The strictest chastity was enjoined.

time of his abyding in those partes." This is, at least, A.D. 1346.
negative evidence that if Northallerton had recovered from
its destruction in 1318, it was again desolated in this year.

Queen Philippa, being then in York, collected all her
forces, and marching against the Scots, overtook them at
Neville's Cross, near Durham, and after an obstinate resistance they were wholly routed, leaving 15,000 dead upon the
field, and their king a prisoner in the hand of a squire named
John Copeland, who had ridden off with him, no one knew
whither. The queen ordered him to be sought out and told
"that he had done what was not agreeable to her, in carrying
off her prisoner without leave." Next day Philippa wrote
with her own hand to John Copeland, commanding him to
surrender the king of Scots to her. He replied to Philippa,
that, " He would not give up his royal prisoner to woman or
child, but only to his own lord king Edward, for to him he
had sworn allegiance, and not to any woman." Philippa
wrote to the king her husband, who ordered Copeland to go
to him at Calais. John, when he came into the presence of
the king, fell on one knee and said, " Sire, do not take amiss
if I did not surrender king David to the orders of my lady
queen, for I hold my lands of you, and not of her, and my
oath is to you and not to her, unless, indeed, through choice."
King Edward answered, " John, the loyal service you have
done us, and our esteem for your valour is so great, that it
may well serve you as an excuse, and shame fall on all those
who bear you any ill-will. You will now return home, and
take your prisoner, the king of Scotland, and convey him to
my wife; and by way of remuneration, I assign lands, as near
your house as you can choose them, to the amount of £500 a
year, for you and your heirs." He was likewise made a
knight-banneret. Upon his return, he assembled his friends
and neighbours, and, in company with them, took the king of
Scots to York, where he presented him, in the name of king
Edward, to queen Philippa, and made such excuses that she
was satisfied.*

About the year 1354 Thomas Hatfield, bishop of Durham, A monastery
granted to the monks of the order of Mount Carmel† a croft of Carmelite
and pasture together containing 3a. 1r., upon which to build friars.
them a religious house. Bequests and gifts of various kinds
too numerous to mention were subsequently made at different
times to this monastery. Walter Kellaw, superior of the

---

* Strickland's Queens of England.

† The Carmelite friars were a mendicant order of great austerity, founded
by Albert, Patriarch of Jerusalem, in 1122, on Mount Carmel, from which
they were expelled by the Saracens. They rose early, slept in their coffins,
observed strict silence, and never tasted flesh meat.

36   ANNALS OF

A.D. 1354. convent and provincial of Carmelites in England, died and was buried here, being probably the first prior.* Leland had heard that one of the earls of Westmoreland was buried here. The site is situated on the east side of the town near the church, and still retains the name of the Friarage; no vestige remains, save the modern wall which was built of the stone from the old fabric.†

1378. Liber Vitæ. This beautiful book, richly covered with gold and silver, was laid on the high altar of the cathedral church at Durham, and contained the names of all the benefactors towards St. Cuthbert's church. The names were generally written with gold and silver ink, and it was the hope and the prayer that the same names might at last find a place in the "*Book of Life*," in which those are enrolled who shall be found faithful unto death. Amongst the names recorded in the " Liber Vitæ" are those of Hugo diaconus de Alvertona, Robertus de Alvertona, Johannes de Alvertona, and Rogerus de Alvertona; also John de Alverton, feretrar or shrine-keeper of St. Cuthbert.

1382. John de Haytor, vicar of Northallerton, resigned the living in 1382, for that of Lynton.

1390. Bequests. Sir John Clervaux,‡ of Croft, infirm in body—to be buried in the parish church of St. Peter, of Croft—to the patron of the church of Croft 10s. [the convent of St. Mary's, York, were patrons at the time]—the friars minor of Richmond 6s. 8d.—the friars of Yarum 6s. 8d.—the friars of Allerton 6s. 8d.—son John 8 oxen for one plough, silver cup with a cover after the death of my wife Beatrix, and one whole best bed but one—friar John de Yougelby 6s. 8d. to celebrate for my soul—Robert de Rokeby, chaplain, 6s. 8d.—son John 12 silver spoons after the decease of my wife Beatrix. [Daughter of Sir John Mauleverer.]

1393. John de Gilling, vicar of Northallerton, died in 1393.

1396. William Kamel, vicar of Northallerton, removed in 1396 to St. Ann's, London.

1402. Richard de Allerton. Richard de Allerton was an executor to the will of Matilda, wife of John de Smeton, proved March 13th, 1402.

1403. Robert Ridmereshill, vicar of Northallerton, resigned the living in 1403, for the Rectory of Barningham, near Richmond, and was succeeded by John Staynfield.

1412. John Corbridge, Vicar of Northallerton, somewhere about 1412.

* Cole's MSS.

† The site is now being used as a gravel pit, and human bones and skulls have from time to time been unearthed by the workmen.

‡ For an account of the house of Clervaux, I refer my readers to Mr. Longstaffe's elaborate pedigree in his History of Darlington.

William Barker, S.T.P., vicar of Northallerton, resigned the living in 1421, and was succeeded by William Middleton, who also resigned in the following year. *(A.D. 1421.)*

Robert Wyclyf, master of Kepyer hospital, and rector of Hutton Rudby, by his will dated Octavo die mensis Septembris, Anno Domini Millesimo cccc. vicesimo tercio, left the following: "Item lego cuilibet ordini Fratrum mendicancium, videlicet Allerton, Richemond, et Hartilpole xx." This affords a striking example of the difference in religious opinion which frequently prevails in the same family. The illustrious John Wycliffe, the reformer, probably the uncle, but certainly the very near relative of this Robert, had directed the whole of his learning and abilities towards exposing the vices and corrupt habits of this particular order. "I shall not die, but live, and still further declare the evil deeds of the friars," said he, to a party of sycophants, who, when he was once severely indisposed, forced themselves into his bedroom, and demanded to hear his recantation. *(1423. Bequests.)*

The village of Deighton, about seven miles N.E. of Northallerton, is at present a chapelry in the parish of Northallerton. The church, which is small, is a comparatively modern one, dating from about the middle of the seventeenth century, but it evidently stands upon the site of a more ancient one; indeed it would seem that in the thirteenth century Deighton (or Dighton) was a rectory, and the village was a much larger one than it is now. In an old list of burials at the priory church of Mount Grace, the following entry appears:—"William Ainthorp, rector of Deighton, by will, proved in 1432, desired to be buried in St. Mary's church, Mount Grace, and gave thereto a chalice of silver and twelve silver spoons." An old moat proving the existence of a castle at some early period is still to be seen. *(1432. Deighton.)*

John Thorneton was appointed vicar of Northallerton in 1437, and died in 1447. He was succeeded by John Levesham, who resigned the living in 1455 for that of Eslington. *(1437.)*

On the 9th June, 1441, Cardinal Kemp, archbishop of York, granted an indulgence of a hundred days relaxation of penance to all such as liberally contributed to the honour and conservation of the *Gild* or *Fraternity*, instituted in the church at Northallerton, or to those who resorted thereunto, on account of the devotion of those saints in whose honour and memory it was celebrated.* *(1441. An indulgence granted.)*

---

* Burton's MSS. The Rev. J. L. Saywell, curate, has succeeded in resuscitating this ancient Guild, which, we trust, will go on prospering and infusing spiritual life into the church, like the leaven in the barrel of meal.

A.D. 1443.
Bequests.

Sir John Clervaux,* by his will dated 13 July, 1443, to be buried in the church of St. Peter the Apostle, at Croft—to every parson and beneficed vicar being at my exequies and burial 20d., and to every chaplain at the same 12d., and every clerk 6d.—friars of Yarum 6s. 8d.—of Northallerton 6s. 8d. —of Richmond 13s. 4d.—the friars Carmelite of York 20s.— residue to Margaret my wife, and she shall find for me and her good estate one chaplain to perform divine offices in her presence for her whole life, and that such chaplain have 100s. for one year's celebrating for me in the church of Croft—said Margaret my capital messuage in Saint Savorgate, York; also 4 of my better mares—son Richard 3 covered cups and two without covers with twelve spoons and half of my vessels of brass and pewdyr and a hanging with a tostor of arrase for the hall and one bed with curtyns and tostors in the new chamber, and 5 other beds without curtyns and tostors; all my draught animals, &c.; 24 oxen and cows with a bull, 8 calves at Croft and half of my mares not bequeathed; and one silver salt without cover—Wm. Gybson chaplain 20s. beyond his salary due to him—Margaret Clerionet 10 marks of silver, 3 cows, 4 bullocks, and 3 styrk—Henry Taylboys [his brother-in-law] one covered cup—Wm. Vincent † [the same] one covered cup—Rich. Mason a draught fily, a cow, an acre of wheat, and part of my vestments, viz., a hayk of skarlatt and a hood—Wm. Cabery a draught fily—every servant of mine a vestment—Wm. Leds a draught fily or a stage and a dublet—Tho. Blakman a cow and a mark of silver.

1452.
Wars of the Roses.

It is somewhat singular that either the town did not play any conspicuous part during the famous wars of the Roses, or if it did, historians have omitted all mention of it. This is the more remarkable when we remember that the conflict was between the rival houses of York and Lancaster. It is, however, very probable, that the town was directly or indirectly the scene of various battles, skirmishes, military gatherings, and levies; indeed it is almost impossible to conjecture how it could have been otherwise, seeing that it occupied so accessible and central a position to both armies.

* Sir John married Margaret, daughter of sir Ralph Lumley, knt., by Eleanor, daughter of John lord Neville, by Maud, daughter of Henry Percy.

† William Vincent, esq., of Great Smeaton, m. Margaret Clervaux; on whom and his intended wife her father settled in free marriage his property in Great Smetheton, in 1416. William Vincent, in 1450 enfeoffed trustees of property in Atelaucouton and Southekylvyngton, for his son William; Berningham, Shetesby, Whitewell, Great Cowton, for son Roger; manor of Great Smetheton for said Roger and heirs, rem. Ric. Clarevaux and the heirs of his body; residue of Smeton for said Roger; Brompton juxta Alverton, for said Roger and heirs, rem. right heirs of John Syneflete; Carleton juxta Forset, and Richemond, for Wm. Vynsent, jun.

Sir William Plumpton, knight of Plumpton, co. York, rode through Northallerton northward with the forces mustered by Henry Percy, earl of Northumberland,* warden of the east marches, for the purpose of making an incursion upon the Scottish borders.

A.D. 1456. Incursion upon the Scotch Borders.

It was on this march that Sir William Plumpton first notified his secret marriage with Joan, daughter and co-heir of Thomas Wintringham, of Wintringham Hall, to Sir Robert Littester, chaplain, in these words:—"Robert, do you now return home; and I beg of you to listen well to all I am going to say, and, above all, to what concerns my weal and honour in my household. And because the event of war is dubious, and the solemnization of marriage between me and Joan Wintringham, my wife, has not yet been openly and publicly notified, I hereby make known to you that the said Joan is my true married wife and I her true married husband. And this I wish and desire you, as you love me, if I happen to die in battle, to testify for the future wherever it may be necessary."†

John Treyndon, vicar of Northallerton, died in 1465, and was succeeded by Robert Walker who resigned the living in the same year.

1465.

Bartholomew Radcliff appointed vicar of Northallerton in 1471, and died in 1474. He was succeeded by Richard Rolleston, A.B., who resigned the living shortly afterwards.

1471.

William Halyman appointed vicar of Northallerton in 1475, and died in 1491.

1475.

The original deed constituting this foundation is in the possession of the earl of Carlisle, and is dated October 1st, 1476.

1476. The Maison Dieu Hospital

By the will and appointment of Richard Moore (who established the chantry) thirteen poor persons were appointed to reside and perform hospitality in the tenements in Northallerton called "*Massendew,*" and that such poor persons out of the rents of certain land, messuages, and tenements, enfeoffed for that purpose, should receive annually 20s. to buy sea coals, and find two beds for poor wandering travellers for one night, and no longer, and to buy other necessaries for the said poor at certain times. From the want of documentary evidence, the subsequent history of this charity cannot be traced, but it appears to have long subsisted as an hospital or alms-house for poor widows, whose numbers have of late years been decreased to four.

The hospital premises are situate on the east side of the

---

* Slain at the battle of Towton in 1461, and being attainted, his honours became forfeited.
† Plumpton Correspondence, Camd. Soc.

40 ANNALS OF

A.D. 1476. high street of Northallerton, near the church, and consist of two buildings, separated from each other by a small garden; one of the buildings was rebuilt on the site of the ancient alms-house, and the other was erected since 1796, and contains four separate apartments on the ground floor. The alms-women are appointed at meetings of the select vestry, as vacancies occur, and are chosen from poor widows belonging to Northallerton. Each of them at present receives out of the rents an annual stipend of £8 by quarterly payments, and a ton of coals.

A chantry in Northallerton Church. By indenture dated October 1st, 1476, Richard Moore left certain lands, messuages, and tenements therein mentioned, in Northallerton and elsewhere, to establish a chantry in the church at Northallerton, and appoint a chantry priest, with a salary of £4 13s. 4d. per annum.

1487. Grant of privilege. From the calendar of charters preserved in the Bodleian Library, we find that James, prior of the house of Carmelite friars in Northalverton, granted to Thomas Gayneng and Agnes his wife, privilege of participation in spiritual benefits of the convent.

1490. Ralph Rokeby. Somewhere about this time there was bred in the woods of Rokeby, a wild sow of so ferocious a nature that

"She was mare than other three,
The grisliest beast that ere might be,"

and

"Her force it was so ful,"

that

"Ralph* of Rokeby, with good will,
The friars of Richmond gave her till,"
Full well to gane them fare;

but

"Fryer Middleton by his name,
He was sent to fetch her hame,
That rued him sare full sare."†

1491. Rev. John Fisher. John Fisher, M.A., 1491, resigned in 1494; elected bishop of Rochester in 1504. He assisted Henry VIII. in his book against Martin Luther, which procured the king, from the pope, the title of "Defender of the Faith." Henry being determined to shake off the papal yoke, and Fisher refusing to acknowledge the king's supremacy in ecclesiastical affairs, the latter was imprisoned in the tower, 21st April, 1534, and beheaded on Tower Hill, 22nd June, 1535. The unmerited

* Ralph Rokeby married Margery, eldest daughter and co-heir of Robert Danby, Esq., of Yafforth, near Northallerton.
† Ingledew's "Ballads and Songs of Yorkshire," p 94.

fate of this prelate affords an instance of firmness and devotion to the dictates of his conscience; attesting the one by a steady defence of the persecuted Katherine of Arragon when abandoned by the rest of the world, and proving the other by refusing, at the expense of his life, to acknowledge his sovereign's pretensions.

A.D. 1491.

He wrote " A Treatise concernynge the fruytful saynges of David the king and prophete in the seven penytencyal psalmes, devyded in ten sermons, was made and compyled by the ryght reverente fader in God, Johan Fyssher, doctour of dyvinyte and bysshop of Rochester, at the exortacion and sterynge of the most excellent pryncesse Margarete, countesse of Richmount and Derby, and moder to our souverayne lord kynge Henry the VII." At the beginning of the book, " sur une garde en velin," there is written in a very neat hand the following verses; the profession of faith of Thomas More and his friend bishop Fisher:—

> "The surest meanes for to attaine
> The perfect waye to endlesse blisse
> Are happier lief and to remaine
> Within ye church where virtue is:
> And if thy conscience be sae sounde
> To thinke thy faith is truth indeede
> Beware in thee noe schisme be founde
> That unitie may have her meede;
> If unitie thow doe embrace
> In heaven joy possesse thy place."

Beneath—

> "Qui non recte vivit in unitate ecclesiæ
> Catholicæ, salvus esse non potest."

> "Thomas Morus dus cancellarius Angliæ
> Joh. Fisher Epus Roffensis."*

Robert Clay appointed vicar of Northallerton 1494, died 1522.

1494.

In 1502 Margaret, eldest daughter of king Henry VII., with her train of nobles stayed at the episcopal palace at Northallerton, from whence she took her journey to Scotland, on her marriage with James IV, king of Scotland. This alliance had been negociated during three years, though interrupted by several broils; and Henry hoped, from the completion of it, to remove all source of discord with that kingdom, by whose animosity England had so long been infested.

1502. A royal sojourn at Northallerton

The ceremonial of attending the princess is recorded in an account styled " The Fyancelles of Margaret, eldest daughter

* Techener's Bulleton du Bibliophile. This treatise is in the library at Douay.

A.D. 1502.

of king Henry VII., to James, king of Scotland: together with her departure from England, journey into Scotland, her reception and marriage there, and the great feasts held on that account. Written by John Younge, *Somerset Herald*, who attended the said Princess on her journey." This worthy says,

" The XVIIth Day of the sayd Monneth (July) the sayd Quene departed fro the sayd Cite of York in varey fair companye and ordre, rychly appoynted, the archbyschop of York and byschops of Morrey, and of Norwyche, and Durham (Richard Fox) the Lords Willeby, Lord Scroup and his son the Lord Latimer, the Lord Hastynge, Therle of Kent, and his son Lord Straunge, Therle of Northumberlande, Therle of Surrey, the Lord Chamberlain, the officers of armes, and the Serjents, with the Ladyes in waiting, including the Countess of Surrey bareing her Trane, the Countess of Northumberlande, well accompanyed of many Knights and Gentylmen, and Ladyes and Gentylwomen. Also the Lord Mair, Scheryffs and the Aldermen, the streytts and the wyndows so full of people that it was a fair thynge for to see.

" And after this doon, she took hyr way to Newbrough the Priorie, to the which place she was receyved by the said Prior and Religyous, honnestly revested with the Crosse, at the Gatt of the Church.

" The XVIIth day of the said Monneth the Quene departed fro the said Newbrough to Allerton, and at the Intrynge of the said Place, sche was receyved by the Vicayr and Folks of the Church with the Freres Carmelites in Processyon, and the Byschop Morrey did as before. From that Place she was conveyed, as Custome was, to the Manayr of the said Bischop of Durham.

" The XIXth day of the said Monneth, the Queene departed fro Allerton, in sayr Aray and noble Companyd; and Sir James Straungwysch, Knyght, Sheryff of the said Lordschyp for the said Byschop, mett hyr welle accompanyed."

It is related of Margaret's affianced, that, having taken arms against his father, he imposed on himself the penance of continually wearing an iron chain about his waist. Some amusing stanzas on the marriage occur in Evan's ballads :—

"O fair, fairest of every fair,
Princess most pleasant and preclare,
The lustiest alive that be,
Welcome to Scotland to be queen.

Young tender plant of pulchritude,
Descended of imperial blood,
Fresh fragrant flower of fairhood sheen,
Welcome to Scotland to be queen.

> Sweet lusty imp of beauty clear,
> Most mighty king's daughter dear,
> Born of a princess most serene,
> Welcome of Scotland to be queen.
>
> Welcome the rose both red and white,
> Welcome the flower of our delight,
> Our spirit rejoicing from the spleen,
> Welcome of Scotland to be queen."

A.D. 1502.

The princess rode on a " fair palfrey, but after her was conveyed by two footmen, one varey riche litere, borne by two faire coursers, varey nobly drest, in which litere the sayd queene was borne in the intryng of the good townes, or otherways to her good playsur."

> "When Queene Elizabethe came to the crowne,
> A coach in England then was scarcely knowne;
> Then.'twas as rare to see one, as to spye
> A tradesman that had never told a lye."*

The will of Joan Hastings, widow of Sir Richard Hastings, dated March 19th, 1504, directs—
"My body to be buried in the church of the Friars Minors, within Newgate in London, in the vault there purposely made for my said husband and me. I will that six priests shall pray for me, whereof one priest shall sing for ever in the monastery of Mount Grace, another in the chantry founded by my father† in the parish church of North Allerton; to the four orders of friars iv pounds to pray for my soul; and also to sing *placebo* and *dirige*, and mass of *requeim*, with a trentall of masses for my soul and the soul of my lord my husband."

1504.
A pious direction.

Among the names of the pilgrims from England to Rome in April, 1507, in the records of the English college at Rome, is that of Thomas de Northallerton, dioc Eborac.

1507.
Pilgrimage to Rome.

Matthew de Allerton gave land in Northallerton to the abbey of Byland.

Gift of land.

In the sanctuary register of St. John's, Beverley, is inserted an entry concerning John Henisle, of Northallerton, a delinquent, who claimed and obtained the privilege of sanctuary. Certain privileges of sanctuary have been recognised from the earliest ages. Moses was directed to appoint three cities of refuge " *that the slayer might flee thither, which should kill his neighbour unawares, and hated him not in times past; and that fleeing into one of these cities he might live.*"‡ In heathen countries, the temples and sacred inclosures offered an asylum to those who fled to them. There is ample proof that the custom of taking sanctuary in christian churches

1509.
Privilege of Sanctuary.

---

* Taylor, the Water Poet.
† Richard, Lord Welles.
‡ Deut. iv., 41-43.

A.D. 1509. existed in the fourth century, but the privilege does not appear to have received the papal sanction in Britain until the year 620. It was formally noticed and established by William the Conqueror in 1070. The privileges of sanctuary were greatly curtailed at different periods, and finally abolished in 1624. A method of claiming sanctuary and the ceremonies observed seem to have varied according to the custom of different churches. At Durham persons who took refuge fled to the north door, and knocked for admission; the knocker remains. Men slept in two chambers over the door, for the purpose of admitting such fugitives at any hour of the night. As soon as any one was so admitted, the "Galilee bell" was tolled to give notice that some one had taken sanctuary. The offender was required to declare before certain credible witnesses the nature of his offence, and to toll a bell in token of his demanding privileges of sanctuary. Every one who had the privileges of sanctuary was provided with a gown of black cloth, with a yellow cross, called St. Cuthbert's Cross, upon the left shoulder; a grate was expressly provided near the south door of the Galilee for such offenders to sleep upon, and they had a sufficient quantity of provision and bedding at the expense of the house for thirty-seven days, when they were required to quit the country.

At Beverley, offenders were treated with still greater kindness. An oath of allegiance to the archbishop and king was imposed upon each person on admission to the sanctuary at Beverley. The general privilege of sanctuary was intended to be only temporary. Within forty days after a felon or murderer had taken refuge, he was to appear before the coroner, clothed in sack-cloth, and there confess his crime, and abandon the realm. This abjuration lasted only during the lifetime of the reigning sovereign, after whose death, they might, if not previously pardoned, return unquestioned to their homes. The privilege of sanctuary was greatly abused, yet it was a custom not unfitted to the age in which it existed.

1513. Remarkable instance of longevity. Death of Jenkins.

Bishop Lyttleton, in a paper communicated to the Society of Antiquaries in 1766, speaks of a certain Henry Jenkins, who, when about 150 years of age, went to live at Bolton-upon-Swale. He died at Ellerton-upon-Swale, aged 169, and was buried in Bolton church-yard, December 6th, 1670, where a monument was erected to his memory. What a multitude of events must have taken place during this man's long and wonderful life, which is exceeded only in duration by that of "Old Parr," who died at the age of 175.

Mrs. Anne Saville says, "When I came first to live at Bolton, I was told several particulars of the great age of Henry Jenkins, but I believed little of the story, till one day he coming to beg alms, I desired him to tell me truly how old

he was. He paused a little and then said, that to the best of A.D. 1513.
his remembrance, he was about 163. And I asked, 'What
kings he remembered?' He said, 'Henry the Eight.'
I asked, 'What public things he could longest remember?'
He said 'Flowden Field.'* I asked, 'Whether the king was
there?' He said, 'No, he was in France, and the earl of
Surrey was general.' I asked him, 'How old he might be
then?' He said, 'I believe I might be between 10 and 12;'
for says he 'I was sent to Northallerton with a horse load of
arrows, but they sent a bigger boy from thence to the army
with them.' All this agreed with the history of that time, for
bows and arrows were then used; the earl he named was
general, and king Henry the Eight was then at Tournay.
And yet it is observable that this Jenkins could neither write
nor read. There were also four or five in the same parish
that were reputed, all of them, to be 100 years old, or within
two or three years of it, and they all said he was an elderly
man ever since they knew him, for he was born in another
parish, and before any registers were in churches, as it is said:
he told me then, too, that he was butler to the lord Conyers,
and remembered the abbot of Fountains Abbey very well,
before the dissolution of the monasteries. Henry Jenkins,
departed this life December, 1670, at Ellerton-upon-Swale, in
Yorkshire; the battle of Flodden Field was fought September,
9, 1516, and he was about 12 years old when that battle Battle of
was fought. So that this Henry Jenkins lived 169 years, and, Flodden Field
with the exception of "Old Parr," was the oldest man born
upon the ruins of this post diluvian world. In the last
century of his life he was a fisherman, and used to trade in
the streams; his diet was coarse and sour, but towards the
latter end of his days he begged up and down. He had
sworn in chancery and other courts to above 140 years
memory, and was often at the assizes at York, where he
generally went on foot; and I have heard some of the country
gentlemen affirm that he frequently swam in the rivers after
he was past the age of 100 years. In the king's Remem-
brancer's office in the Exchequer, is a record of a deposition
in a cause by English bill, between Anthony Clark and
Smithson, taken 1665, at Kettering, in Yorkshire, where
Henry Jenkins, of Ellerton-upon-Swale, labourer, aged 157
years, was produced, and deposed as a witness."

In the parish church of Bolton-on-Swale, on a mural Jenkins'
tablet of black marble is inscribed the following epitaph, Monument.
composed by Dr. Thomas Chapman, Master of Magdalen
College, Cambridge:—

* Flodden. The Scotch king, four prelates, twenty-five nobles, and four
hundred knights and gentlemen were slain in this disastrous encounter.

A.D. 1513.   Blush not, marble, to rescue from oblivion the memory of Henry Jenkins: A person obscure in birth, but of a life truly memorable; for he was enriched with the goods of nature, If not of fortune, and happy In the duration, If not variety, Of his enjoyments: and, tho' the partial world Despised and Disregarded His low and Humble State, the Equal Eye of Providence Beheld, and blessed it with a Patriarch's Health and Length of Days: to teach mistaken man, these blessings were entailed on Temperance, or, a life of labour, and a mind at ease. He lived to the amazing age of 169; was interred here Dec. 6th (lege 9), 1670, and had this justice done to his memory, 1743.

In the same churchyard is erected a monument to the memory of "Henry Jenkins, the oldest Yorkshireman,"—the subject of the preceding inscription. It consists of a base, 4 feet 4 inches square by 4 feet 6 inches high, surmounted by a pyramid 11 feet high. On the west side is inscribed—

This Monument was
Erected by contribution
In ye year 1743, to ye Memory
of Henry Jenkins.

On the west side—

Henry Jenkins,
Aged 169.

1514. Bishop Gheast   Edmund Gheast was born at Northallerton in 1514, received his education at York School, and eventually became Fellow of King's College, Cambridge. Nominated to the archdeaconry of Canterbury in 1559, he became the first protestant bishop of Rochester in 1560. He was also Lord Almoner to Queen Elizabeth; and Fuller says "he must be both a wise and good man whom she would trust with her purse." On the death of bishop Jewell, bishop Gheast was translated to the see of Salisbury. He died in 1577, and was interred in the choir of his cathedral. He was the principal compiler of the Liturgy of the Church of England now in use.

1522.   Leonard Hutchinson, M.A., of Baliol College, Oxon, senior proctor, and afterwards master of University College, appointed vicar of Northallerton in 1522. He resigned the living for that of Crowlton.

1523. Wolsey's doings at Romanby.   The memory of this ambitious, arrogant, overbearing, haughty, pompous, yet withal shrewd, talented, and learned prelate, will not be revered by the people of Romanby. A short time after his elevation to the prince-bishopric of the county palatine of Durham, he held an episcopal visitation throughout his new diocese, and, when holding at Northallerton, he gave orders for the pulling down and destruction of the parochial chapel* at Romanby, in consequence of the then incumbent of Northallerton, having questioned his

---

* The remains of a small monastery for Carmelites, built here in 1356, by Thomas Hatfield, Secretary of State to Edward III, after he was promoted to the see of Durham were also totally destroyed by Cardinal Wolsey. (vide Mann-Dowson Todd's MSS.)

authority; which destruction subsequently took place, and the materials of the fabric were sold, as also the glebe land, with the site upon which the chapel stood.* Whether Wolsey or his royal master, the " Eighth Harry," pocketed the money, historians of that date do not mention. But Hodgson in his history of Allertonshire and Birdforth, says that "the king and the cardinal went *snacks*, and divided the money betwixt themselves, the cardinal having first deducted his expenses.†

A.D. 1523.

Although it is uncertain when the idea of dissolving the monasteries was first talked of, it is certain that the axe was first laid to the tree by Cardinal Wolsey, who obtained grants for suppressing a number of the smaller monasteries in order to found a college at Oxford (now Christ Church) and another at Ipswich. Wolsey himself (in his letter to the king, printed in Ellis, orig. lett. second series, ii. p. 18) calls them "certain exile‡ and small monasteries, wherein neither God is served ne religion kept." The zealous catholics were alarmed by this measure, and justly regarded it as an example which would not fail to lead to a more general demolition of the religious houses. Some of the abbots attempted to avert the danger by offering sums of money for his scholastic foundation instead of the abbey lands, as in the case of Edmund Walley, abbot of St. Mary's, at York, who in a letter to the cardinal, says,—" I am right interely contented, for your tenderinge of the premisses, to gyve unto your grace ccc. markes sterlinge, which shall be delivered unto your grace immediately." There were even some tumultuous outbreaks of popular dissatisfaction. Grafton§ says,—" You have heard before how the cardinall suppressed many monasteries, of the which one was called Beggam, in Sussex, the which was verie commodious to the countrey: but so befell the cause, that a riotus company, disguised and unknown, with painted faces and visers, came to the same monasteries, and brought with them the chanons, and put them in their place againe, and promised them that whensoever they rang the bell, that they would come with a great power and defend them. Thys doyng came to the eare of the king's counsayle, which caused the chanons to be taken, and they confessed the capitaynes, which were

1530.
Dissolution of Carmelite Friary at Northallerton.

---

* Vide Rymer, Crossfield.
† A portion of the glebe called the Hall Garth Fields, which was sold by Cardinal Wolsey after the destruction of the chapel, has been, by a lineal descendant of the purchaser, vested in trustees for the support of widows and deserving clergymen resident in Allertonshire and the North-Riding of Yorkshire.
‡ Poor, lean, endowed with small revenues, Lat. *exilis*, (not *alien priories*.) It is a word of no uncommon occurrence in the writings of that age.
§ Chron. p. 382, new edition.

A.D. 1530. imprisoned and sore punished." When Wolsey was beginning to decline in the royal favour, the suppression of these religious houses was one of the first charges brought against him.

The question of breaking up the monasteries was formally proposed by secretary Cromwell* in the year 1535. When the king consulted with his council on this subject, one was of opinion that "There is a due place left for monasteries; yet, when they grow up to that multitude, that either the just proportion they bear in a state is exceeded, or they become a receptacle only for lazy persons, it is fit to apply some convenient remedy, therefore be pleased, sir, not to think so much of their overthrow as their reformation." Another of the council remarked that, "The clergy had one-fourth part of all the revenues of the kingdom; that this was an undue proportion; and that two or three monasteries left in every shire would be sufficient."

After much consultation, a general visitation of the monasteries by commissioners was ordered, who carried on everywhere a rigorous inquiry with regard to the conduct and deportment of all the friars. Great irregularities were discovered to exist, especially in the lesser monasteries; the result was the passing of a bill, entitled "An Acte whereby Relygious Houses of Monkes, Chanons, and Nonnes, whiche may dyspend Manors, Landes, Tenementes, and Heredytaments, above the clere yerly value of ij.c.li. are given to the Kinges Highnes, his heires and successours, for ever." (27 Hen. VIII. c. 28.) By this act all the monasteries possessing revenues below two hundred pounds a year, to the number of three hundred and seventy-six, were suppressed, their revenues, amounting to thirty-two thousand pounds a year, were granted to the king; besides their goods, chattels and plate, computed at a hundred thousand pounds more. Hollingshed says, "Ten thousand monks were turned out on the dissolution of the lesser monasteries." In this category was the Carmelite friary of North Allerton, as appears from the original deed of surrender, deposited in the Augmentation office.

By the suppression of the monasteries, literature suffered an irremediable loss, by the neglect to provide a receptacle for the libraries. The monasteries at that time had a prodigious number of valuable manuscripts. Indeed, it was said, England contained more than any country of equal size in the world. Many an old MS. bible was cut to pieces, to cover pamphlets. The following is a complaint of Bale to Edward VI., A.D. 1549.

* Created baron Cromwell of Okeham, 9 July, 1536, and earl of Essex, 10 April, 1539, K.G. Attainted and beheaded, 1540, when his honors became forfeited.

"A number of those persons, who bought the monasteries, reserved of the library books thereof, some to serve their jakes; some to scour their candlesticks, and some to rub their boots; some they sold to the grocers and soap-sellers, and some they sent over-sea to the bookbinders, not in small numbers, but at times whole ships full. Even the universities of this realm were not all clear in this detestable fact. I know a merchant-man that bought the contents of two noble libraries for forty shillings price! The stuff thereof he hath occupied, instead of grey paper, by the space of more than these ten years; and yet he hath store enough for as many years to come. Our posterity may well curse this wicked fall of our age, this unreasonable spoil of England's most noble antiquities."

A.D. 1530. Wholesale vandalism.

"On the pretence," says Dodd, "of rooting out superstition, visitors were sent about. Upon this occasion was destroyed the famous Angervilian library, first composed by Angerville,* bishop of Durham. The two libraries of Cobham, bishop of Winchester, and duke Humphrey, of Gloucester, underwent the same fate."†

Innumerable works of art were destroyed, and magnificent specimens of architecture were defaced and left roofless. The friaries were adorned with curiously painted glass, and the names of the benefactors were recorded on the windows or walls of their cells, hence in "Pierce and Ploughman's Crede" a minor friar speaks thus to one who wanted to be taught his creed:—

"We haven forsaken the world, and in wo libbeth,
In penaunce and pourerte, and prechethe the puple,
By ensample of oure lif, souls to helpen
And in pouerte preien, for al owr parteneres,
That gyueth us any good, God to honouren
Other bel other book, or bred to owr foode,
Other catel other cloth, to coueren with our bones.
Moneye, other moneye worth, here mede is in heuen,
For we buildeth a burwgh, a brod and a large,
A chirch and a chapitle, with chambers alofte.
With wide wyndowes yurought, and walles wel heyne
That mote ben portreid, and paint and pulched ful clene,
With gay glitering glas, glowyng as the sunne,

* Richard Angerville, alias De Bury, was tutor to prince Edward, afterwards Edw. III., at whose instance he was elected bishop of Durham, 7th Dec., 1333. He was much esteemed for his learning; and though his great knowledge in state affairs gained him frequent employment at court, and in embassies, he omitted no opportunity to apply to his studies. So violent was his love of books, that, as he says himself, it put him in a kind of rapture, and made him neglect all other business. He wrote several books; his principal work was "Philobiblos," a treatise for the management of his splendid library, which he founded for the students at Oxford. He held the several offices of lord privy seal, lord treasurer, and lord chancellor. He died 14 April, 1345, and was buried before Mary Magdalene's altar, in his cathedral.

† Vide Fuller's Church History.

A.D. 1530.

  And mighteston amenden us with moneye of thyn owen,
  Thou chouldest kneyl bifore Christ in compas of gold,
  In the wyde window westward wel neigh in the myddel,
  And Sainte Frauncis hym self, shal folden the in his cope,
  And present the to the Trinite, and pray for thy synnes.
  Thy name shall noblich ben wryten and wrought for the nones,
  And in remembrance of the, yrad there for euere."

Alas! little did the writer of the above dream of the events which have produced such mighty changes. The names written and painted on the walls, to be " yrad there for euere," have long since perished and are forgotten, and their existence is among the things that are past.

1533. Robert Askew, vicar of Northallerton in 1533, died in 1547.

1534. Northallerton and the Bishopric of Durham. The following account of the valuation of the bishopric of Durham in 1534 is copied from an old book in the possession of a gentleman at Lintz Colliery:—

	£	s.	d.
The scite of the Castle of Durham, with the coinage of money	8	6	3
Rents, farms, and office of Coroner in Chester Ward	486	6	5
Rents in Darlington Ward, and office of Coroner	212	15	1
Rents, &c., in Easington	396	2	4
Ditto in Stockton	214	14	5
Ditto in Sadberg	290	12	8
Ditto, &c., in Auckland, Gateshead, Whickam, &c.	630	0	0
Spirituals	87	13	4
In Norhamshire, the scite of the Castle, &c., of Norham	120	0	0
In Allerton and Allertonshire, the scite of the mansion	241	11	3
Spirituals in Allerton and Allertonshire	18	0	0
In the liberty of Crayke the scite of the castle, &c.	46	2	0
In Hoveden and Hovedenshire	284	10	3
The Mansion of the Bishop of London	18	1	4
	3056	5	9
Deduct reprises	307	6	3
Clear value	£2748	19	6

The Bishop of Durham retained the privilege of coining money in his Mint from the year 1196, in the reign of Richard I., to the year 1540.

1536. The Pilgrimage of Grace. The suppression of the abbeys and monasteries caused such discontent, that a rebellion broke out in the northern counties under Robert Aske.

  Forthe shall come a worme, an Aske with one eye,
  He shall be the chiefe of the mainye;
  He shall gather of chivalrie a fulle faire flocke
  Half capon and half cocke,
  The chicken shall the capon slay
  And after thatte shall be no May.*

---

* These rhymes, alleged to be taken from the ancient prophecies of Merlin, it is said, were recited in the host as an ambiguous prediction of their expedition and its chief.

This rebellion, known by the name of the *Pilgrimage of Grace*, was joined by about 40,000 men. York, Hull, and Pontefract were soon captured by them, but listening to offers, they appointed deputies to treat with Henry; this ended in a general pardon, and a promise that their grievances should be discussed. But the king, neglecting to redeem his promise, the "pilgrims" were induced again to rise in arms in 1537, when they were speedily defeated by the duke of Norfolk, and their leader, with the abbots of Fountains, Jorevalle, and Rievaulx, the prior of Bridlington, and other chiefs, comprising some of the best blood in the north, were taken and executed. It is difficult to ascertain what part Northallerton took in the transaction, as a mystery hangs over the affair.* The more effectually to suppress this insurrection, Henry, in August re-appointed the famous council of the north, Cuthbert Tunstall, bishop of Durham, being its president. It continued to sit until the time of Charles I., having exercised a tyrannical and hateful jurisdiction for more than a century.

[marginal note: 1536.]

About the year 1538, Leland, the famous antiquary began his peregrinations, under a commission from Henry VIII. In his report the following account is given: "From Kirkeby Wisk to Northallerton a VI miles by pasture and corne ground. I markid by much of the way as I roode from Tollerton onto Wisk Bridge most communely caullid Smithon Bridge, that I passid yn a meately fertile valley bytwixt Blackemore Hills by east, and Richmontshire Hills by weste, a good distance being bytwixt them. There is very little wood in Northalvertonshire, and but one park at Hutton now without deere. There is good corne in Northalverton, yet a great peace of the grounde that I saw at hand bytwixt Northalverton and Smithon Bridge is low pasture and mores, whereof part beere sum fyrres. From Alverton to Smithon Bridge a VI miles wher Wisk renneth cumming a VI miles of by est from Smithon."

[marginal note: 1538. Leland, the Antiquary. His Report.]

The endowment made by king Henry VIII. of the cathedral church of Durham, bears date the 16th May, 1541, wherein ecclesiastical jurisdiction in the manors of Northallerton, Howden, and Hemyngburg, are granted to the dean and chapter, in as full a form as they possessed the same before the dissolution. The statute of king Edward VI. reversed part of the grant, and the two collegiate churches were reduced.†

[marginal note: 1541. Royal Endowment.]

During the war with James V. king of Scotland which ended in the glorious victory of Solway, a long letter was

[marginal note: 1542. Battle of Solway.]

---

* Doubtless the names of many Northallerton men would appear upon the roll of Pilgrims.
† Hutchinson.

A.D. 1542.

Letter from Norfolk to Wriothesley.

1547.

1553.

1555.
The family of Metcalfe.

written to Henry VIII. dated from Northallerton, November 5th, 1542, at 8 at night, concerning several political and constitutional matters, and signed by three noblemen and two others.

The following letter was also written the same night.

With most herty recommendacions. This shall be to advertise you, that sith the wryting of my last letters to you, I have be so extremely handled with my disease of the lax, that, and gode help of medicynes had not stoped it, I think I shuld never have sene you. It is skant credeble that any man shuld have avoyed that I dyd on Fryday, fro six at night unto 10 o'clok in the mornyng. But now, thanked be Almyghty God, I am stopped, and feale myselff right well.

And where I wrote you consernying the howse of Bath-place, I requyre you by the next post to advertise what answer ye have had therein, and also how the Kynges Majeste is content with me; assewrying you that for asmoche as of a longe tyme I have had no letter fro you, nor none other of my frendes of the counsell, I am not a little afferd that His Majeste shuld not be content with my procedynges; wich if it be trew, I am sewer it shall apere by the report of all men that I have wrong: for though all things wer not accomplished, as I wold they had be, yet I dout not it shall appere no man coude have done more than I have done to have broght it well to pas; as God knowith, who have you in His tuicion.

Fro Allerton, the 5th of November, [1542] at nyght.

Your assewred frend,
(Signed) T. NORFOLK.*

(Superscribed)
To my right worshipfull frende, Sir
  Thomas Wriothesley, Knight, one of
  the Kinge's Majesties twoo Principal
  Secretaries.

Lancelot Thornton, vicar of Northallerton in 1547. He resigned the living in the same year.

William Todd, D.D., was presented to the vicarage of Northallerton in 1553, but he resigned it 1561, and became prebendary of the fifth stall in Durham cathedral, and subsequently archdeacon of Bedford.

The family of Metcalfe is of great antiquity in Yorkshire, and so numerous that there is scarcely a town or village in the North-Riding which does not possess an inhabitant of that name, and in 1607 it was counted the most numerous family in England; indeed there are several families of

* Attainted in 1546, when his honors became forfeited; he would have been executed had not Henry VIII. died the day before the warrant was to have been put in force. His honors were restored in 1553; died 1554.

Metcalfe in Northallerton at the present time. Dr. Whittaker resolves the name, which is locally pronounced *Mecca*, into Mechalgh from *Mec*, a Saxon personal name, and *halgh*, a low and watery flat. Ingledew relates a tradition, which says, that two men being in the woods together at evening, seeing a four-footed animal coming towards them, one said "have you not heard of lions being in these woods?" the other replied that he had, but had never seen such a thing. The animal coming nearer, one ran away, whilst the other resolved to meet it; which proving to be a *red calf*, he that met it got the name of *Metcalfe*, and he that ran away *Lightfoot*.

A.D. 1555.

A tradition.

The above conjectures as to the origin of the name, however, are absurd; the following is probably the true one. In 7 Edward I. (1278) we find that Richard de Steynbrigge de Deneke (Dent) slew in single combat "Adam de Medecalf de eâdem et statim fugit." A fell or mountain called "The Calf," is in the near neighbourhood of Dent, and another mountain called "Calf Top," is two miles to the west of Dent. A portion of the fell is said to be called by the shepherds "Midcalf." The prefix *Mede*, *Mete*, or *Met*, signifies middle, limit, landmark, or boundary; hence the name "*Metcalfe*."

True origin of the name.

Camden, the historian, who wrote in the time of Elizabeth and James I, relates of Sir Christopher Metcalfe, of Nappa, that when high sheriff of Yorkshire in 1555, he rode out of York with a retinue of 300 men of his name and family, clad in his cloth or livery, and all well mounted on white horses, to meet the judges of assize, and conduct them to York.

A regiment of Metcalfes.

* **Metcalfe of Nappa.**

* *Arms.*—Quarterly of six.—1. Argent, three calves passant sable (*Metcalfe*). 2. Argent, a lion rampant gules (*De Hertlyngton*). 3. Sable, three pickaxes argent (*Pigott*). 4. Argent, a chevron gules between three eagles displayed sable (*Leedes*). 5. Argent, on a fess cottised gules three fleurs-de-lys of the field (*Normanville*). 6. As the first.

54 ANNALS OF

A.D. 1558.
The Quarter
Sessions.

The Quarter Sessions were held from this time at the Guild Hall, afterwards the workhouse, and now the site of the present Savings' Bank, until the year 1720.

1559.
Royal confiscation.

By an act, made in the first year of the reign of queen Elizabeth, (cap. 19,) "giving authority to the queen's majesty upon the avoidance of any bishopric, to take into her hands certain of the temporal possessions thereof," the see of Durham suffered a great diminution in revenue; for by bishop Pilkington's * address to secretary sir William Cecil, it appears the queen seized upon Allerton and the shire, of the yearly value of £218 9s. 1¼d.; Norham and the shire £120; Creik £39 7s. 4½d., &c.

Letters patent recite, that queen Elizabeth had taken from the bishopric of Durham, in the year 1559 and 1560, the manors of Allerton, Allertonshire, Norham, Norhamshire, &c., and so had exempted them out of the restitution of the temporalities to bishop Pilkington, dated 25th March, 1561. Other patents specify, that by a new restitution of the temporalities, dated 13th June, 1566, all were restored, except Norham and Norhamshire; so that hitherto the see lost little, except paying its pension of £1,000 per annum † till bishop Barnes.‡

1561.

Mark Metcalfe, vicar of Northallerton in 1561, died in 1593.§

1564.
Knight service.

In aº 6 Eliz. the co-heirs of sir Ralph Bulmer held twenty messuages of the manors of Allerton, Long Cowton, Ottering-

* Pilkington was the first protestant bishop of Durham. During the persecution under Mary, he was obliged to leave the kingdom, but on the accession of Elizabeth he was preferred to this see, 20th Feb., 1560-1. He died 23rd Jan., 1575, and was buried at Auckland, but was afterwards removed to the choir of Durham cathedral. He wrote some valuable commentaries on the scriptures.

† The queen having heard that he (bishop Pilkington) had given his daughter a £10,000 portion, as much as Henry VIII. had bequeathed to herself, scotched the see of £1,000 a year, and settled it on her garrison at Berwick.—*Strype*.

‡ Vide Rymer's Fœdera.

§ On a slab commemorating him in the south transept of the church is the following inscription :—" Hic jacet in hoc tumulo Marcus Metcalfe, filius Lucæ Metcalfe de Bedale, frater quoque et hæres Nicholai Metcalfe, armigeri, unius sex clericorum eximiæ curiæ cancellariæ defuncti. Qui quidem Marcus vicarius fuit matricis ecclesiæ Omnium Sanctorum de Northallerton, incumbens ibidem XXXII annos. Vixit LIV. ann. tandem sepultus XXIV die mensis maii, anno Domini 1593." At the head of the stone is a shield: quarterly one and four three calves for *Metcalfe;* two and three a chevron between three quatrefoils pierced for *Roughton*, impaling *Tomlinson* or *Thomlinson*, of Gateshead, co. Durham. Glover, in his visitation says, Mark Metcalfe, of Bellerby, vicar of Northallerton, was 4th son of Lucus Metcalfe, of Bedale, by his wife Katherine, 2nd daughter of Robert Jackson, of Bedale, mar. Elizabeth, daughter of Antony Tomlinson, of Galeside, co. Durham, gent., by whom he had issue, Maria, aged 8 years in 1585; Martha 7; and Magdalen. The registers of baptisms, marriages, and burials preserved in the parish church date from the incumbency of Mark Metcalfe, in 1593.

ton, Newby and Wiske, Ainderby in the Mire,* &c., of our lady the queen, as of her honor of Richmond, by knight service.† {A.D. 1564.}

During this memorable period the town of Northallerton figures so conspicuously that we are obliged to trouble the reader with particulars which at first sight may seem dry and uninteresting, but a patient perusal will convince him to the contrary. {1569. The rising of the north.}

The zealous adherents of the Romish religion being dissatisfied at the change, formed the design of re-establishing that faith, restoring Mary of Scotland to her liberty, and placing her on the throne of England. Thomas Percy, earl of Northumberland, and Charles Neville, earl of Westmoreland, who possessed great power in the north, having held together several conferences, orders were despatched by Elizabeth to these two noblemen to appear at court, and answer for their conduct.‡ On the night of the day on which the earl of Northumberland received the queen's letters in his manor-house at Topcliffe, certain conspirators perceiving him to be wavering, caused a servant to bustle in and knock at his chamber door, willing him in haste to shift for himself, for his enemies had beset him, whereupon he arose, and conveyed himself to his keeper's house: in the same instant they caused the bells of the town to be rung backward, and so raised as many as they could.§ Northumberland hastened to his associate Westmoreland, whom he found surrounded with his friends and vassals, and deliberating with regard to the measures which he should follow in the present emergency. They determined to begin the insurrection without delay; and committed themselves irrevocably by entering Durham in arms, on the 14th November, 1569. {A conspiracy. Commencement of the insurrection.}

> "Now was the north in arms:—they shine
> In warlike trim from Tweed to Tyne
> At Percy's voice; and Neville sees
> His followers gathering in from Tees,
> From Were, and all the little rills,
> Conceal'd among the forked hills.
> Seven hundred knights, retainers all
> Of Nevile, at their master's call
> Had sate together in Raby Hall!
> Such strength that earldom held of yore,
> Nor wanted at this time rich store
> Of well-appointed chivalry,
> —Not loth the sleepy lance to wield,

---

* Morton-upon-Swale. MS. Vinc. A. 8, 547., in Coll. Arms.

† Knight service *(Servitium Militare,)* was a tenure, whereby several lands in this kingdom were held of the king; which drew after it homage and service in war.

‡ Haynes, 552.   § Hollinshed.

A.D. 1569.

> And greet the old paternal shield,
> They heard the summons; and furthermore
> Came foot and horsemen of each degree
> Unbound by pledge of fealty;
> Appear'd with free and open hate
> Of Novelties in church and state,
> Knight, burgher, yeoman, and esquire,
> And th' holy priest, in priest's attire."*

Diary of Sir George Bowes The earliest document relating to this rebellion, is the following diary of Sir George Bowes—apparently the copy of a letter giving an account of his time:—

"I met the Earl of Westmerland of Saturday next after St. Matthew's day [21st September] or thereabout, as our ways crossed, his to Branspeth, and mine to the Isle: and appointed then to meet the said Earl of Westmerland of Wednesday next, after our hawking; which appointment I kept, but he came not, nor sent, though he were not far thence.

"I received a letter, directed from the Lord President to the Earl of Westmerland, Lord Eurye, and me, to be at York the next Sunday after Michaelmas day, which, after I had read, I returned to the said Earl again.

"Thursday I stayed at the Isle. Friday being the thirtieth of September, I rode to Streytlam, where I received a commandment from the Sheriff of Yorkshire, to be at York, with the Lord President, in the [Sunday] morning next after, by eight of the clock.

"I rode of Saturday to Aske; of Sunday to York, where I found the Lord President and the Lord of Hunsdon.

"I rode of Monday after to Cawood, and rested there that night; Tuesday to York; and Wednesday after, to Cawood again, where I met Francis Slingesbye, and tarried there that night, and rode of Thursday to York.

"Friday to Allerton; where I met by the way, at Borowebrige, with Francis Tankerde, which brought me word from Francis Slingesbye, that I should be laid for, to be taken, which caused me that night, after I had supped, to remove my lodgings to Danbye, a servant's house of mine.

"Saturday, the courts at Allerton,† whereunto I returned, and that night, riding by Sockburne, I went to the Ile."‡

Letter from Earl of Sussex to Sir George Bowes. Sir George,—I receyved this daye one letter from you, dated the Xth, at midnight, and one other letter, dated this daye, at three in the mornyng: and perceyving, as well

* Wordsworth.
† He was the Bishop's Seneschal by letters patent, 10th March, 1567. Appointed Steward, 1560.
‡ See Sharp's Memorials of the Rebellion. Bowes' MS. vol. 2.

thereby as by divers other advertisements, that th' Erles, and all that depend upon them, ride openly armed and weaponed, and assemble daily forces unlawfully, whereof th' end muste be open rebellion if they be hable: We have resolved to levy force presently, and to sett forwards so soon as it shall be levyed; and to that ende you shall receyve comyssion by the berer to levye what force you maye in the Byshoprick, Richmondshire, and Allertonshire, and to repaire therewith to such place as shall be best for the Queen's service, and most for your suertie.

Military levy.

I heartely praye you, fynd the meanes to cause the letters herewith sent, to be conveyed to Sir John Foster and Mr. Gower; and if you cannot safely convey Mr. Gower's letter, then send it to Sir John Foster to convey it. In haste, this XIIth of November, 1569.*

Yr. assured frend,
T. SUSSEX.

My bounded dewtye premysed: pleaseth yt your good Lordshippe, I have yesterdaye receyved frome your L. by my servant, Thomas Dande, three commyssyons dyrected to me, and others, of the contrees of Rychmondshyre, Allertonshyre, and the countye of Durham; with also your L. letter to Thomas Gower, and a commyssion to Sir Henyre Pearcye† and others, which latter letter and commyssion I have sent awaye, as I truste in greate savetye, to be delyvered accordinge to the derection. And for the better executyon of the other commyssyons, I have dyspatched my letters, together with the said, or copyes of the same, to everye commyssyoner in Allertonshire and Richmondshyre; requesting them, that immedyatelye upon syghte thereof, they shall repayre to me, and in theire waye execute suche parte of the commyssyon as was to be doyne presentlye, soo as I looke for them, or the more part of them, thys mornynge. And hayth, upon great respect, required them to come to Barnard Castell, somethinge myslykinge the inhabytants of the town of Rychmond, being the onlye people to be dowted of in these parts; for which purpose I have thought yt more to the Quene's and savetye of the people, to make oure assemble elsewhere; and,

Sir George Bowes to Earl of Sussex.

Disloyalty of Richmond.

---

* Bowes' MS. vol. I.
† Younger brother of the Earl of Northumberland, and his successor in his honours. He stood firm to the Queen, took an active part against his brother, and held the appointment of Captain of Tynemouth Castle for a considerable time. But afterwards being suspected of participating in the conspiracies in favour of Mary Queen of Scots, he was thrown into the Tower, where after a long imprisonment, he shot himself on the 21st of June, 1585, being the seventh Earl, and the thirteenth member of the Percy family, who died an untimely death. He was succeeded by his son Henry, 9th Earl, K.G., by his wife Katherine, eldest dau. and co-heir of John Neville, Baron Latimer.

beynge assemblyd, we maye resorte thether, or elsewhere, as shall stand with your Lordship's pleasure. But in respecte of this Castelle, I thought yt good to begin th' assemblye here, where ys alredye comed unto me, with greate haste, and well appoynted, to serve as light horsemen, the whole gentlemen dwellinge upon the ryver of Teyse of both syds, whose names I thoughte good to advertyse your Lordship of. And as I judge, they brought with them ny abowt a hundred lighte horsemen, well mounted, and armed with playte coyts and speares, and I have of my owne very nye an hundred light horsemen. And there ys also assembled hether of the countrethes next adjoynyng, two hundred able men, armed and weapened with playte coyt, jack, bowes and arrows, and bylles, and twenty corslets of my owne, and thirtie harquebusses; the effect of which nomber ys a choyse of my owne tenants and others under my rewle, of the Quene's Majestie's tennants of Barnard Castell Lordship. And most dewtyfullye and obedyentlye the people nye these parts assemblythe styll, whereof the best lyke, in person and furnyture I staye, and the reste with thanks, and good words, I returne home: thus much for Richmondshyre. And thys parte of the byshoprige is redye, and I howrlye looke for the commyssyoners, that we maye proceede to the execution of oure commyssyons, in every behalfe. And I have also sent the commyssyon for the Countye Palentyne of Durham to the commyssyoners, with my letter, appoyntinge fytt places for the assembles of theys, by north the ryver of Weare, to come together, without perill of anye attempte to be agaynste them, or suche lyke inconvenyence; sodenlye to growe by unapte places of assemble, trustinge that the same shall take good effecte. And havinge here with me, my brother, Robert Bowes, whoo, beinge the Sheryffe of thys Countye of Durham, laytlye returned into theys parts, and redye with hys whole power and delygence to serve the Quene's Majestie; I have, therefore, for my better helpe, in so manye trobles, imployed him in thys present servyce, and also thought good to sygnifye unto your L. hys returne and redynes, that here upon your L. may, from hencefurth, dyrecte and bestowe hym in all servyces, as beste lyketh your good L. The other parts of the byshoprige, towards Stockton and to Durham, I have onlye sent for the justyces, to make their repayre to me with spede, meanynge by them to doye as shall be thoughte most convenyent; but wyll not there muche styrre the people, lest when they shulde be together, there assemble for favor to some persons myghte rather turne to harm then good. I have also in the afternone yeasterday receyved the twoo commyssyons, together with your L. letter, by which commyssions your L. hath sygnyfyed what number of footmen yowe will have in Rychmond and

Allertonshyre; which, indede, was not appoynted before. A.D. 1569.
For the affayres heare; most of th' Erle of Westmerland's
tennants, and some fewe of his reteyners, be returned to there
howses, and theyre numbers muche abayted, as by outwarde
appearance; yet dothe theyr dalye, people armed and well
mownted, come northwards over Teyse, as of Sundaye laste,
in the afternone, came over at Crofte and Newsam (where I
have contynuall watche) within eight persons of an hundreth,
well horsed, and lyke to have privye coyts, but wer nott
warrelyke weaponed, except some daggers.

There came yesterdaye, in cloaks, lyke the Sheryff's
leverage, twenty-two, northwards, also verye well horsed, but
had noo weapon, but as before; and sewer the numbers,
where they lye, by anye advertysement I can gett, dothe
rather demynyshe than increase, soo that I gather, they ryde
of the nyghte southwards, and cometh agayne of the daye
northwards, to make shewes, for what intent I knowe not;
but yt ys thought there cometh ever some small numbers of
unknown faces and horses. And sewer, I dare avoche, that
after the departure of theys forsid tennants to th'Erle of
Westmerland, there remayned not above five hundrethe men.

Th'Erles kepe together, and Rychard Norton;* all the
reste hathe elsewhere bestowed themselfes, and kepeth close.
And sewer, of Sundaye laste there sprange a generall reporte,
that they shulde that nyght meet together, and make some
attempte agaynst me or my things; and I was at many hands
certyfyed thys, but in the ende it turned to nothinge. And Defections
nowe the beste intelligence I have, advertyseth that Marken- amongst the
fielde, Reed, Tempeste, and Swynburne are fledd; and my insurgents.

* The family of Norton appears to have been deeply concerned in this
enterprise, Richard Norton, of Norton Conyers, Esq., being Standard Bearer.
  Lord Westmorland his ancyent raisde,
   The Dum Bull he rays'd on hye;
  Three Dogs with golden collars brave,
   Where there sett out most royallye.
  Earl Percy there his ancyent spred,
   The Halfe Moon shining all so faire;
  The Nortons' ancyent had the crosse,
   And the five wounds our Lord did beare.

On the suppression of the insurrection he and his sons were especially
marked out for vengeance.
  Thee, Norton, wi' thine eight good sonnes,
   They doomed to dye, alas! for ruth!
  Thy reverend lockes could thee not save,
   Nor them their faire and blooming youthe.

However, his seventh son Christopher was the only member of the family
that was put to death; of the others one or two were pardoned, and the rest,
together with their aged father, escaped abroad and died in exile. Their estate
of Norton Conyers was granted to a Musgrave, who sold it to an ancestor of
Sir B. R. Graham, Bt., the present owner.

A.D. 1569. Ladye (the Countess of Westmoreland) braste owte agaynste them with great curses, as well for their unhappye counselling, as nowe there cowerd flyghte. But all the evyll counsellors be not yett gone, for in trewth, Mr. Christopher Nevill* hath doyne more harme to that noble young Erle, hys nephewe, than can be thoughte, and doeth yet remayne aboute hym. I wyshe he were further off.

For any rate, at a pennye the meal, or a pennye leverage, Darneton, I have sent to knowe; but there was, nor ys noo suche, neither any lyenge there, save th'Erle of Northumberland's fawkener, with hys hawks. And for the watche at Durham, I have sent to knowe the truth, but it ys not certyfyed; and, for suche causes of service as I suppose maye be doyne, I have sent unto your Lordship this bearer, my kynsman Robert Bowes, Under-Sheryff of the Bishoprige, unto whome I humblye praye your Lordship to gyve credytt. And, so restinge, redye to serve the Queen's Majestie, as I shall receyve dyrections from your Lordship, I take my leave.

From Barnarde Castelle, the XVth of Nov., 1569.†

Sir George Bowes to Earl of Sussex.

My bownden dewty premised, pleaseth yt your Lo. to be advertysed; the two Earles yesterday passed to Richmond, and ther made proclamation, which, by cause of the difference of reports in some parts, I omitte to advertise; and the rest was, that where as ther was certaine counsellors cropen in abocte the Prince, which had excluded the nobility from the Prince, and had set furthe laws contrary to the honor of God, and the welth of the Realme, which they ment to reforme; whereupon they had assembled themselves, trustinge that the people would taike their parte, which they requyred. And then they dowted not but they should restore the ancient laws, as masse and other things now laide awaye. And at Darnton was made the like proclamation, where they offer great wages to suche as will serve them; and hath not only stayed the people in many parts of Richmondshire for assembling to me, and the commissioners hither, but hath in the bishoprick called all the people of Darnton together, and this daye they make their musters there, and appoint Captaines to such number of fotemen as they have levied. They have constreined, by force, sundrie to followe them; as the people of Bishopton, tenants of John Conyers‡

Proclamation by the insurgent Earls.

---

* Of Kirbymoorside. Upon the dispersion of this rebellion, he escaped abroad, and died in exile a pensioner of the King of Spain.
† Cotton. MS. B. IX, 342.
‡ John Conyers, of Sockburn, Esq., the lineal representative of the "Faulchion Knight," of Sockburn, and of the Lords of Bishopton, Barons of the Bishopric. He was Knighted by James I. on his first entrance into England, in 1603; died at Sockburn, where he was buried, 2nd Feb., 1609-10.

my sonne in law, being readie to come forwards to serve the Quene's Majestie under him heare, they not only forced them to go with them, but compelled the rest of the towne, armed and unarmed, to go to Darnton; and owrly advertisement cometh, of their constreining men to serve them. And the feare is so increased, that in a manner no man dare travell; yet for anything·I can learne, the whole people of Richmondshire meaneth to be dutifull, but dare not assemble towards us here, for feare of interceptinge, as one towards me is intercepted, and yet not hurt; but knowing he was a servant to a gentleman, my servant, now sycke, they have commanded him to warn his master, upon paine of spoile, that to-morrow he be with them at Allerton. And so nowe they occupye much of the bottome of the countrye; and for all that, they exceeded not yesterday four hundred horsemen, and five hundred fotemen, the more part of which fotemen are clearly unarmed. Christopher Nevill is gone into Kirbymoreside to raise people, and comethe thorowe Cleveland. The matter groweth very hot, and sure in my opinion requireth to be expedited; as what with feare, of fair speche, or moneye, they drawe awaye the harts of people; and sure besydes my owne, and those apperteyning such of my friends, as will with me adventure all, their eis not heare as yet above seventy men, and manye of them not the best furnished.

Yesterday, Francis Norton,* with the nomber of one hundred horsemen, hath entred John Sayers' house, at Worsall, and therein taken his sone, and some portion of armour, which is not great; but much discomforteth him for his sone. The armour is six corslets, two or three harquebushes, and six muryons, which he weith not.

This day, young Nicholas Fairfax, with a great companye, hath entred the house of Anthony Kattrick, and taken therein his two sons in law, Lambert and Mennell†; which Mennell was but gone thither, meaninge of the morowe to come hither; and his servant to the Earl of Leicester.

They soght for my children, where they were at scole,

A.D. 1569.

Progress of the rebellion.

Insurgent raids.

---

* Eldest of the "eight good sonnes" of Richard Norton, who, after the failure of this enterprise, escaped to Flanders, where, after several attempts in vain to secure a pardon, he died in exile, a pensioner of the King of Spain.

† Roger Mennell, of North Kilvington, co. York, called a servant, or retainer, of the Earl of Leicester, mar. Margaret, dau. of Anthony Cattrick, of Stanwick. He was not attainted; yet he appears to have suffered severely, as Lord Scroop writes to Cecil, 6th Nov., 1570, to solicit his pardon, stating, that he was forcibly taken away from Stanwick, "and from thence conveyed to the Rebelles, and with whom he remaynned a whyle, against his will; and, fearing the extremity of the laws against them, fled into Scotland." He adds, that both Sir George Bowes, and Robert Bowes, his brother, have made reports of the truth of this statement, and, at the desire of Sir George Bowes and others, he now signifies the same.—*State Papers.*

A.D. 1569. but yesterdaye I brought them hyther; but in the towns, in a manner, everywhere, they take away the whole people; and we come too late with our commandments, which yet we proceed with, and shall do the best I may, havinge manye things to dele in, bothe for feare of the worst, and comfortinge the fearfull, faynt, or false. I doubt to get any more advertisements, but wisheth spede be made, and promiseth dutifull obedience and diligence, to the full of my wytts and power; and will and shall ende with a dutifull and obedient hart, yielding my breath in truthe to everie authority; and thus commending my service to your Lordship's directions, promising to preserve the people comed under my charge, withoute any attempte, but in defence. I humbly take my leave, in haste, at Barnard Castle, the 17th Nov., 1569, at nine of the clocke.

Protestations of loyalty.

Movements of insurgents.

They, this daye, at Richmonde, made a great muster; but what is further done I am nott yet advertised.

They use the Quene's Majesties name in their calls, with threatening to burne suche as absent themselves. The Erle of Northumberland beareth a guydon before his troope.

Masse was yesterday at Darnton; and John Swinburn, with a staffe, drove before him the poor folks, to hasten them to hear the same.

Threats and coercion by the insurgents

After the wryting hereof, two of the most substantialest men of the town of Richmond did come unto us, and declared the commandments that the Erle of Northumberland had given them; and how he had required, firste by faire speche, and after by offers of money, and lastlye by threats of burning and spoilinge, that they should give him ayde of an hundreth men; but they wold not confesse to grant any. Lastly, they had day given, to make answer to of the morrowe, at which time they were newly provoked, and practises made to bring them to it, but they still refused; then it was told them, that the most parte of the gentlemen with me was escaped hence, and was come to them; but, finallye, after manye speeches, it was required that they would conduct him, being not above sixty persons, to the other Erle, to Allerton, whereunto they were content to bring him to the bounds of their town, but not further. Whereupon he would have them armed, and desyred but one hundrethe; but they saide they wold all go, but unarmed; whereupon they went indede, to the nomber of three hundred men, of all sorts; and at the out lymits of their bounds they would have departed, but there they were newly set on againe, but it could not prevaile, and so they departed. And, in goinge awaye, sundry of the Erle's servants offered to take some stele caps and bylls from them, but they wylled them to staye, or they shoulde wyn them with strypes; whereupon they all

Northallerton, the headquarters of Earl of Westmoreland.

returned home: yet the Erle, at their parting, saide, that if they sent him not one hundrethe men to-morrow, to Leaming, or at the furthest, that night, to Ryppon, he, in his return, would burne and spoile the towne. They have nowe, by thes men, promised dutyful obedience, and promised to notyfye the effecte of the comyssion delivered me this daye, dated yesterdaye, which satisfiethe much people, which I earnestly seke, therefore, to get known everie where, and order is nowe geven for the same. *A.D. 1569. Threat to burn Northallerton.*

The Erles seme they will lie this night at Allerton, and to morrow at night to Rippon; but my intelligence sayeth that they will this night to Rippon, where they are in great hope much to be incresed; and sayeth further, that they will either attempte you at York, yf they like their force, or else drawe towards Lankashire. But good, my Lord, looke to your owne safetye, for therein lyethe all the hope of the good speade of the whole affayres; and for advertisements I must now cease, for that they are drawn farr from me. Sir John Nevell hathe promised to meate them at Ryppon, and they want much of others also, but they will staye much of small occasion. Sure their threats be great towards me, promising, upon their return, to assalte me; but I trust, by Godde's helpe, the old adage, in them, shall be verified, "*God sendeth an evyll wylled cow with short hornes.*" Fynally, for trewthe, this day, at noone, they no way altogether, could make five hundred horsemen and five hundred fotemen, as before, which fotemen, for the most part, be without armour or weapon; but no doubt they will nowe growe great of these simple people, rather shapes than matter. But now to complain: our lacks, which is armour, and weapon, and money, for the contreth of Yorkshire never goeth to war but for wages; the people already complaineth, and yet have I bestowed the little I had amongst them, and hath prepared such store of victall that they shall not lack, which hathe and dothe both pleasure and content them well. But, would to God I had your Lordship's warrant to the Quene's Majestie's armour at Newcastle, for I wold make a convey in their absence to get some, for that, indeed, is our greatest lack. And thus again, I end: wishing again that your Lordship take good heed to yourselfe. From Barnard Castle, the XVIIth Nov., at twelve of the clock at night, 1569.* *Insurgent camp at Northallerton. A true saying.*

The two Earles, accompanied with Richard Norton, Thomas Markenfeld,† with many other gentlemen of the *Sir G. Bowes to Captain Drury.*

---

* Orig. Calig. IX, 353. Copy, Bowes' MS. Vol. II. No. 6.
† Sir Thomas Markenfeld, on the failure of this rebellion, took refuge in a foreign country. His estate of Markenfield, near Ripon, was forfeited, and

A.D. 1569.
Sacrilege.

Bishopricke, and none of reputation, else, wente on Monday last to Durham, and have burned the service bookes, and broken the communion table. They made, by the mowthe of another, an oration, commending themselves, desiringe the aid of the people. On Tuesdaie, to Darlington, there they sente for the sundrie precepts : proclamations most wicked. Wednesdaie, to Richmond, where they altered the manner of their proclamation, whiche is suche, if they be suche as the copies delivered, purporte, that it would grieve any honest hearte to heare it. I have some other of their doings, whereat there owne hands are, which be bad enough; the which I have one, of the copy whereof I send you, and for the other, because it toucheth so muche, and I have it not under their hands, I spare to certify the copy of. Thurs-

The people of Northallerton coerced.

daye they went to Allerton, and in their waye forced the whole people to followe them, muche againste most of their wills ; and in the morning, by three of the clock, knowinge there was a muster appointed at Ryppon, they went thither, and put Sir William Ingleby, appointed for the purpose, from the said muster, in some danger ; but he escaped well. It is thought they are now fourteen or fifteen hundred lighte horsemen, well appointed, and footmen a great number ; the most part whereof is unarmed, and broughte forwards by coercion. I wish much to know what is become of Reade ; and I advise you to look about you, for Jeffurth and two other disguised, is gone northwards, by Bransbethe. By Mr. Gower I may heare, for I divers times send thither. Thus scribbled, in haste, at the Quene's Majestie's castle at Barnard Castle, the XXth of November, 1569.*

Lord Hunsdon to Secretary Cecil, Nov. xxxth.

Yesterday came hither Nicholas Errington, who came from Berwyk to my Lord Lt. and me, who was taken by the way, by the rebells at North Allerton : and so caryed too Rychmond, too the Erle of Northumberland, where he was detayned three days before he cowld get away. He sayethe, that they are 1,000 horsemen, and better, well appointed ; but for theyre footmen, they are symple creatures, nothynge so well as they have byn accowntyd : so as yf we had heare 500 or 1,000 horsemen, and 300 shott, we wold nothing dowght the overthrow of them, for all theyr strenkth ys yn ther horsemen.†

---

subsequently granted to the lord chancellor Egerton, by whose descendant, the celebrated duke of Bridgwater, it was sold to Sir Fletcher Norton, ancestor to lord Grantley, the present owner.

* Bowes' MS. Vol. II.
† State Papers.

NORTHALLERTON.   65

My good Lord,—Understanding, this day, that Sir George Bowes is so besieged by the rebelles, as neither I can send to him, nor he to me; and doubting how he is furnished of victuells, I think it convenient to sett forwards with all the possible sped I may; and, therefore, have sent this bearer to waite upon your Lo. to bring me certen worde when the 300 shott, 300 armed pikes, and the horse, that shall come from your Lo. may be at Wetherby, to th ende that they from thence, and I from hence may set forwards to meete at North Allerton. It were great pitie such a gentleman sholde be lost.† *[margin: A.D. 1569. Earl of Sussex to the Lord Admiral* Dec. vith. Conveyance of arms to Northallerton]*

On the XIth Dec., the earl of Sussex writes to Cecil from York:—"This day the footmen be set forwards out of this cittye; and to morrow I overtake them with the horsemen, and wyll lye at Allerton on Tuesday."† *[margin: Earl of Sussex lies in wait at Northallerton]*

Sir George Bowes,—We authorize you, by these presents, forthwith to levye, and take upp, within Richmondshire, the Bishoprike of Duresme, and Allertonshire, so many horsemen as ye can gett, that be sufficiently furnished with horse and armor, for the warres, and have not been in the confederacie or ayde of the rebells; and to take, within the same places, armor and speares for the supplieing of your lacks, of all persons that be not appointed to be in the Q. Majestie's paye, for her service at this tyme. And, further, to levy one hundreth fotemen where you shall think fetest and them to furnish with such armor and weapen as you can gett, and shall be fetest for her Majestie's service. For the doinge whereof, these shal be your sufficient dischardge. Dated xiij Decemb., 1569.
[margin: Lord Lieutenant to Sir George Bowes. Levy of troops.]

T. SUSSEX.

The earl of Sussex writes to sir William Cecil, from North Allerton, on the XIVth Dec. "Symond Musgrave (Sheriff co. Cumb. 11th Eliz.) is arived with 400 horsemen."—"If the rebells offer the fyght, I wyll not refuse it, considering my L. of Warwyk and my L. Admirall be at my backe."† *[margin: Preparation for war.]*

On the same day the earl of Rutland writes to Cecil.—"I am sure you are not ignorant of sir G. Bowes' deliverance out of Barney Castle.‡ We are now at Allerton, marching towards the rebells.§ *[margin: Action imminent.]*

* Edward, lord Clinton, K.G., who, with the earl of Warwick, commanded the Southern army; created earl of Lincoln, 4th May, 1572, ob. 1585.
† State Papers.
‡ Sir G. Bowes was compelled to retire from Barnard Castle, through the desertion of many of his men 12th Dec.
§ State Papers.

E

A.D. 1569.
Loyalty of Yorkshire.

On the XVth, sir Ralph Sadler writes to Cecil, informing him, "the rebells do now gather all the forces they can make. And I lerne all Clevelande, Allertonshire, Rychmondshire, and the Bishopricke, ar all hollie gon unto them, such is their affection to the cause of religion; by meanes whereof they are grown to the force of greate nombers, but yet confused, without order, armor, or weapon."*

Barnard Castle besieged.

Whilst sir George Bowes was closely besieged in Barnard Castle,† the rebels took possession of his castle at Streatlam, and destroyed, or carried away, the whole of his goods, after having committed every possible excess. To repair his great losses, the earl of Sussex gave him the household goods of the earl of Northumberland, remaining at Brakenborough and Topcliff; which grant was confirmed by the commander of the southern army, on the XXVIIth (Dec.)

Confiscation of insurgent property.

Where we have authorised Sir George Bowes, Knighte, Marshall of the Q. Majestie's armie levied in the northe, to take and receive all such stuffe and other things as did belonge and appertaine to the Earl of Northumberland, now remayning in Brackenbourg or Topcliff, and the lodge. These be to will and commande all other persons, not to meddell or take anie parte thereof; but to suffer the sayed Sir George Bowes quietly to take and carrie away the same. Dated at North Allerton, the XVIth of Decemb. 1569.

T. Sussex.‡

Dispersion of the rebels.

The Queen's troops being increased to 7,000 men, under the command of the earl of Sussex; 12,000 under lord Clinton; the earl of Cumberland and lord Scroop, being near Carlisle, with a numerous army, so intimidated the rebels, that they dispersed without striking a blow. The leaders fled into Scotland, and left their deluded followers in the hands of the provost marshal, who is said to have executed on a gallows sixty-six petty constables, and some hundreds of others,§ the rest being pardoned.

> Full many a gallant wight,
> They cruellye bereav'd of life;
> And many a childe made fatherlesse,
> And widowed many a tender wife. ||

* Sadler's State Papers, vol. 2, p. 66.
† "Coward, a coward, of Barney Castell,
Dare not come out to fight a battell."
Popular Rhyme.
‡ Bowes' MS. Vol. 1.
§ Tradition ascribes to Bowes the expression on hanging one Harrison in his own orchard, "that the best fruit a tree could bear, was a dead traitor."
|| Popular Song entitled "The rising of the north."

On the IVth Jan. 1570, sir George Bowes received orders where the executions should take place.

A.D. 1570. Northallerton appointed a place of execution.

At Allerton.—All the constables of Allertonshire and Langbarth, the townsmen of Allerton and the servinge men.*

Sir George Bowes,—For that Sir Henrie Gates is directed by the Q. Ma. to go in to Scotland, I will wryte to my L. Evers and Mr. Layton to mete you at Allerton, at suche daye as you shall appointe to assist you in th examening of the constables and others appointed thether who also shall take paines with you at Thruske. And, therefore, I pray you appoint your dayes certen, and give them notice thereof in tyme, and take order in the meane tyme for th apprehending of constables. Sir Thomas Gargrave hathe I think alredie examined all the West Ryding; so as you may send to him for a note of his doings, and thereby you may appointe your daye at Rippon accordinglye, and appointe under ministers to the other townes to make the more expedicon. Fare you hartely well. From Duresme, the VIIIth of Januarie, 1569 (70). Yr. assured frend,

T. Sussex.†

Examination of Constables.

My humble dewtie remembred, pleaseth your good L. I send you herewith all the books of Alvertonshire and Cleveland, to have your L. directions for the numbers to be appointed furth of them to be executed. I fynd very fewe, or none, (savinge the market townes) eyther in Alvertonshire or Cleveland, that did goe with the rebells in the first jorney, and sure in Cleveland there are none; and it is very fewe that went in ther returne, and as it seemyth to me rather went coarsed then otherwyse of good will, wherefore I would be glad to know your L. pleasure in thes cawses. I do this day intend to wryte unto Mr. Gargrave and to make appointment for my beinge at Rypon, and so to followe on my course accordinge to your L. former direction, yf I be not countermanded by your L. and intending to be there of Wednesday, in the morninge att furthest. I wold be glad to know your L. pleasure yf there be any prisoners of these parts in my command your L. will have to be brought to be executed ther, that I may doo it with convenyent spede. Humblie desieringe your L. that I may have comandment to the justices of peace, and gentlemen in thes parts of the west riddinge, that I may have there assystance as well in the apprehension of prisoners, as also unto my mynysters for th doinge of execution. I also send your L. herewith, a note of suche prysoners as I of late received from the L. Scrope,

Sir G. Bowes to Earl of Sussex.

Directions concerning executions.

---

* Bowes' MS. vol. 12. † Bowes' MS. vol. 1, p. 21.

which in effect be but meane serving men, yet very proper men. Desirous to knowe your L. pleasure what shall be done with them. Thus restinge readie att your L. comandement, I humblie take my leave. From Alverton, this XIIIth January.*

Sir George Bowes was now on his "circut," in compliance with the orders of the earl of Sussex. He held courts for the trial of the parties implicated; but the minutes of these courts are not preserved, and the proceedings must have been brief and expeditious, as the queen was impatient to be relieved from further expense. Sir George, in a letter to the earl of Huntingdon, lord president of the north, says, "that none were executed by him, who did not confess that they were in actual rebellion two days at least after the first pardon, and stirrers of the rest of their neighbours."†

He appears to have been at Northallerton, or in the immediate neighbourhood, from the 13th January to the 23rd.

Judgments were given at Allerton, on the 16th, for execution :—

Allerton. — Xpor Hancock, Richard Wynde, Randall Horner, Robert Heckley, Henrye Thompson, Allan Lynsley, William Taylor. *Xpor Lambe, hangman.*

Evill men beyng fled which are necessarye to be executed, yf they may be had :—*Norton Conyers*, Thomas Tatam ; *West Rougton*, Thomas Mabson ; *Romaldbye*, William Markenfield ; *Birtbye*, George Lupton ; *Borowbye*, John Prest.‡

In the list of judgments given 18th Jan., at Northallerton, for executions in Cleveland, appears Robert Peters, of Gisburgh; who was stayed at the earnest suit of Anthony Wycliff.§

The speedy defeat of Leonard Dacres, on the 20th February, and the inroad of the earl of Sussex on the Scottish borders, finally relieved the north from all apprehension; and tranquility was gradually restored. The principal rebels fled to the continent, as Scotland was unable to afford them a safe refuge; but the earl of Northumberland was brought to York and beheaded on the pavement, near St. Crux church, August, 1572.

---

* Bowes' MS. vol. 18, p. 7.
† The earl of Sussex implores the queen to spare the life of John Gower, son of Ralph Gower of Richmond, who had been attainted for his share in this ill-fated enterprise, and that he may also be allowed to compound for his estates.—" 1. Because of the simplicity of the yonge manne, who symply was ledde to this his firste faulte. 2. Because the queen shall be no loser. 3. His lordship wolde gratifye Sergent Wraye, (afterwards Lord Chief Justice) uncle to the partie. 4. Cottrell, his servant, would marry his mother." The request was granted.
‡ Bowes' MS. vol. 14, p. 19. § Idem, p. 20.

A common custom in the sixteenth century was the insertion of stones, bearing the date of any alterations made at this period, and for about a century after the reformation. Northallerton church seems to afford an example of this custom; for outside under the great window of the south transept, near the ground, may be seen two stone tablet insertions; the one to the west had doubtless an inscription, but it is now entirely obliterated; on the stone to the east is the following inscription, much mutilated:—

>   COR MVNDV̄ CREA IN
>   ME DEVS: ET SPIRI
>   TVM RECTVM INNO
>   VA IN VISCERIBVS
>   MEIS ✣ CREDO
>   VIDERE BONA DN̄I
>   .... Aº 1576.

The last line is quite indistinct, with the exception of the date; the whole inscription, as deciphered by the late Dr. Green, of Lewisham, in Kent, was "*Cor mundum crea in me Deus: et spiritum rectum innova in visceribus meis.*" "*Credo videre bona Domini: in terra viventium.*"† The date certainly seems to synchronise with the time when the aisles received their last alterations, as far as the walls are concerned; yet it is but right to say that it may be a monumental tablet, though the former verse seems inconsistent with this supposition, even if we were to consider the belief in the doctrine of purgatory to have had an influence, which, however, was not an article of the faith of the church of England in the year 1576.

In 1577, the comfort to be prepared for travellers had become a science. Harrison speaks in ecstacy of the linen used at table being washed daily, and each new comer having clean sheets. The constables appear to have received fees, I suppose for taking care of the strangers' luggage, as appears

---

* "*Create a clean heart in me, O God; and renew a right spirit within my bowels.*"—Psalm li. 10 (l. 10 vulgate.)
† "*I believe to see the goodness of the Lord in the land of the living.*"—Psalm xxvii. 15 (xxvi. 19 vulgate.)

A.D. 1577. from the following posting charges of William Davison, esq., who was sent by Elizabeth on a special message to James of Scotland, in December, 1582. "For ten post horses from Allerton to Derlington (16 miles), 20s.; to two guides, 12d.; to the constables at Allerton, 12d."*

1584. Porch House.

This historical building, which, though much modernised, bears evident marks of antiquity, was built in the year 1584, by Richard Metcalfe, the great-great grandson of Thomas Metcalfe, of Nappa, in Wensleydale, Chancellor of the Duchy and County Palatine of Lancaster, and a Privy Councillor in the reign of Richard III; which Thomas was son of James Metcalfe, of Beare Park and Nappa, who was a captain in the battle of Agincourt, in the retinue of Richard, Lord Scrope, of Bolton. That the house was built by Richard Metcalfe is confirmed by the initials and date — R.M., 1584, M.M., carved on an oak beam exposed to view during some alterations at the Porch House in the year 1844. The initials stand for Richard Metcalfe, and Margaret Metcalfe, his wife (daughter of Roger Wilson, of Danby Wiske). In the gable of the porch are carved the initials and date — W.M., 1674, A.M., for William Metcalfe, and Anna Metcalfe, his wife, daughter of Sir George Marwood, Bart., of Little Busby.

† Metcalfe of Northallerton.

A tradition. Langdale in his "History of Northallerton" relates the tradition that King Charles I. once stayed at the Porch

---

* Longstaffe's Darlington.

† *Arms.*—Argent, three calves passant sable, a canton gules for difference. *Crest.*—A satyr affronté proper, with a girdle of oak leaves round his loins, vert; holding in the dexter hand, over the right shoulder, a spiked club, or morning star, or. In Dugdale's visitation of Yorkshire, 1665, there are pedigrees of three houses of this family, Metcalfe of Nappa, Metcalfe of Northallerton, and Metcalfe of Thornborough. The arms of the latter were at that time differenced by a canton, red and blue respectively, by Sir William Dugdale, then Norroy King of Arms. The elder line seated at Nappa Hall, bore the ancient undifferenced coat, viz., three black calves on a silver field.

House as a guest of the Metcalfes on one of his progresses A.D. 1584. or marches to the north. This was probably on the 29th of August, 1640, when the king rode from York to Northallerton on his way to join his army in the north, opposed to the Scottish Covenanters. While at Northallerton, news came of the defeat of his troops at Newburn Ford, on the Tyne, and of the taking of Newcastle by the Scots, upon which he returned to York.

King Charles's visit at the Porch House may, however, have been on some other occasion, as he was much in the north between the year 1640 and the setting up of his standard at Nottingham, on the 22nd of August, 1642.

In February, 1647, Charles I. again rested at the Porch House, but he was then a prisoner in the hands of the Commissioners of the Parliament, who had been sent down to Newcastle-upon-Tyne to receive him from the Scots, and who were conducting him, under a strong guard, but with every mark of respect, to his new prison at Holmby.

Tradition says that the king made an attempt to escape Another tradi- out of a window at the south end of the house, in which tion. attempt he probably had such assistance as the Metcalfes, then young children (the eldest, Elizabeth, could only have been a girl of about twenty) and their serving men and women could render him. George Metcalfe, their father, was dead, and, it would appear, their mother also. Dugdale, in his visitation, gives 1642 as the date of the father's death, but his will was not proved till 1647. He left five young children; William, his heir (born 1635), Richard, Elizabeth, Catherine, and Mary, all of whom are named in his will, dated 28th May, 1642.* Elizabeth, the eldest daughter, married Timothy Mauleverer, of Arncliffe Hall, Esq., J.P.; Catherine married Henry Crosland, of Helmsley, younger brother of Sir Jordan Crosland, of Newby, near Ripon, Governor of Scarborough Castle; and Mary married Lancelot Pinkney, of Silton Paynell, and of Ingleby-under-Arncliffe. There being no mention in George Metcalfe's will of his wife Elizabeth (Talbot) to whom he was married 29th July, 1624, at St. Helen's, York, it is probable that she died before 1642. As she belonged to a family remarkable for devotion to the royal cause—the ancient and knightly family of Talbot of Thorneton and Bashall—no doubt her little children were staunch royalists. John Talbot, of Wood End, Thornton- le-Street, her cousin, was a colonel in the royal army, his son Roger was a Cavalier captain, and passed through many dangers in the king's service, and John Talbot, a younger brother of Roger, was also a captain in the army of Charles I.

* Vide page 85.

A.D. 1584.

George Metcalfe's kinsman, Scrope Metcalfe, a son of Sir Thomas Metcalfe of Nappa, was a major in a Cavalier regiment of horse, and died at Oxford 13th Sept., 1645, of wounds received in a cavalry skirmish at Thame, when the Cavaliers beat up the quarters of the Parliamentarians there on the 7th of September.

The Porch House seems to have been rarely occupied by the Metcalfes during the early part of the 18th century, the immediate successors of William Metcalfe living much at York or at Sand Hutton, another seat of the family, near York.

From the initials and date 16 $_{W.\ A.}^{M.}$ 79 over the entrance to an ancient house at Landmoth, sometimes called Marygold Hall, probably from the large marygold or rose, carved in stone above the door, it would appear that William Metcalfe at that time made some alterations and additions with the intention of residing there. The estate of Landmoth had been bought by his father of a family of some note named Green, a short pedigree of which family may be found in the visitation of 1612, made by Sir Richard St. George, Norroy King of Arms. The initials $_{W.\ A.}^{M.}$ evidently stand for William and Anna Metcalfe. Anna Metcalfe was a legatee in the will of her father, Sir George Marwood, who died in the year 1679. William Metcalfe's daughter, Henrietta Katherine, married first John Batte, of Okewell Hall, and secondly John Smyth, of Heath Hall, near Wakefield. His daughter, Margaret Metcalfe, married in 1672, Daniel Lascelles, Esq., of Stank Hall and Northallerton, M.P. for Northallerton in 1702, and High Sheriff of Yorkshire in 1719. Her grandson, Edwin Lascelles, of Harewood Castle, Stank Hall, and Northallerton, born 1713, was M.P. for Scarborough; for Northallerton in 1754, again from 1780-90, and created Baron Harewood, of Harewood Castle, in 1790. In 1759 he laid the foundation of the princely building named Harewood House, which has since been the residence of the successive Earls of Harewood.

Alterations in the Porch House.

In the year 1784 the Porch House appears to have suffered the transformation, from a picturesque and interesting building, with mullioned windows, of the time of Queen Elizabeth, to its present modernized and comparatively uninteresting appearance. A manuscript sketch of the life of Anne Metcalfe, widow of the Rev. Thomas Metcalfe, M.A., Trinity Coll., Camb., of Northallerton and Sand Hutton, vicar of Tilton and rector of Narborough, in Leicestershire, and subsequently rector of Kirkby Overblows, Yorkshire, written by her niece, Ann Jesse Cholmley, wife of Nathaniel Cholmley, of Howsham and Whitby Abbey, states that Mrs. Metcalfe

MARKET PLACE FROM THE SOUTH.

THE PORCH HOUSE.

went to live in a house at St. Saviour's Gate, York, in 1780, "where she stayed four years until the old family house of the Metcalfes at Northallerton was repaired, where she remained until the day of her death." She died at the Porch House, 13th Feb., 1804, aged 87 years, and is buried at Stokesley with her husband, who died 16th Feb., 1774. Their monument is in the chancel of Stokesley Church. The Rev. Thomas Metcalfe sold Sand Hutton.

A.D. 1584.

Anne Metcalfe's father, William Smelt, of Kirkby Fleetham Hall, and Leases Hall, by Bedale, Esquire, was Member of Parliament for Northallerton, from 1740 to 1745, in which year he was appointed Receiver-General of Revenues in the island of Barbadoes. Her mother was Dorothy Cayley, daughter of Cornelius Cayley, counsellor-at-law, son of Sir William Cayley, of Brompton, baronet, by Dorothy, eldest daughter of Sir William St. Quintin, of Harpham, baronet.

Captain Leonard Smelt, of Langton Hall, Anne Metcalfe's brother, was Sub-Governor to the Prince of Wales and the Bishop of Osnaburg (the Duke of York) from 1771 to 1776, under their nominal Governor, the Earl of Holderness.

The Rev. Thomas Metcalfe is thus named in the will of his kinsman, Thomas Metcalfe, of Nappa, the last of the elder line seated at Nappa Hall, in Wensleydale, who died at Nappa, in 1756. " To my godson, son of the Rev. Mr. Metcalfe, of Tilton, in Leicestershire, my seal with my coat of arms and crest set in gold, and two pair of stone buttons set in gold, as a mark of my wishes for his success in the world." The Rev. Thomas Metcalfe's sister, Anne Metcalfe, married Waring Ashby, Esq., of Quenby Hall, Leicestershire, near Tilton, High Sheriff of Leicestershire in 1733.

The sons and daughters of the Rev. Thomas Metcalfe and Anne his wife, who were the last of the family to reside at the Porch House, were—

1. William Metcalfe, eldest son and heir, who became possessed of the estates of Little Busby in Cleveland, under the will of his cousin Jane Marwood, widow of Cholmley Turner, Esq., of Kirkleatham, and in compliance therewith took the surname and arms of Marwood in lieu of Metcalfe, by Act of Parliament, 5 Geo. III. (1765). He died without issue in 1809.
2. Rev. George Metcalfe, M.A., Trinity College, Cambridge, Canon of Chichester, who succeeded his brother William in the Metcalfe and Marwood estates in 1809, and assumed the name and arms of Marwood.
3. Cornelius Metcalfe had issue Thomas, (who married Christiana Brisbane Cranstoun, only daughter and heiress of Henry Kerr Cranstoun, eldest son of

A.D. 1584.

George, fourth son of William, fifth Lord Cranstoun, of Creeling, co. Roxburgh, by his wife Jean, daughter of William Kerr, second Marquess of Lothian), and four daughters.

4. Thomas Metcalfe, died aged 13.
5. John Metcalfe, died aged 19 (unmarried).
6. Leonard Metcalfe, died an infant.
7. Rev. Francis Metcalfe, M.A., Trinity College, Cambridge, vicar of Rudston, near Bridlington, and rector of Kirkbride, in Cumberland, the advowson of which rectory belonged to him. He married Harriet, daughter of John Clough, of York, and Newbald Hall, Beverley, by his wife Rebecca, daughter of Jacob Costobadie (or de Costobadie), of York, a proctor in the Ecclesiastical Court, and sister to Jacob Costobadie, who was for 52 years rector of Wensley, in Wensleydale.

The de Costobadies were a French Huguenot refugee family, from Auvergne, in France. Jean de Costobadie, de Tonneins, fled to England on the revocation of the Edict of Nantes, and settled in York in the year 1686.

1. Henrietta-Anne-Katherine Metcalfe died unmarried 29th June, 1781, aged 36, and was buried at Stokesley. She appears to have been the family genealogist, for a pedigree written by her in 1775, is now remaining at the College of Arms in the Collections of John Charles Brooke, Somerset Herald, who died in 1794.
2. Dorothy Metcalfe was living at the Porch House (unmarried) in the year 1810. She sometime afterwards purchased a house on the banks of Lake Windermere, and removed thither, taking with her the old family portraits long preserved at the Porch House. These portraits, dating from the time of King Charles I. to the end of the last century, were subsequently taken to Busby Hall, in Cleveland, where they now remain.

Dorothy, the last of the family who lived at the Porch House, survived all her brothers and sisters, and died (unmarried) at Bowness, on the 10th Feb., 1842, aged 88. Her monument is in Bowness Church. Windermere.

---

* I am indebted to John Henry Metcalfe, Esq., of Leyburn, in Wensleydale for the above and other information relating to the Metcalfe and Marwood families. Mr. Metcalfe is the now sole representative in Yorkshire both of the Nappa Hall, Wensleydale; and the Porch House, Northallerton, families of Metcalfe, being the grandson and representative of the Rev. Francis Metcalfe, M.A., Rector of Kirkbride, and only son of the late Captain John Metcalfe, H.E.I.C.S.—*J.L.S.*

The Porch House is now the property of George Frederick Marwood, of Little Busby Hall, near Stokesley, the great grandson of the Rev. George Metcalfe, M.A., Canon of Chichester, who succeeded his brother, William Metcalfe (called Marwood) both in the Metcalfe and Marwood estates, and assumed the surname and arms of Marwood in lieu of Metcalfe, in 1809. No family of importance has been more identified with the history of Northallerton than that of the Metcalfes.

A.D. 1584. The Porch House now Marwood property.

Respecting this ancient family, Longstaff, in his "Richmondshire" remarks, "The Metcalfes were to Wensleydale what the Featherstons and Waltons were to Weardale. Their clanship was wonderful."

*Marwood of Busby.

Leland, our first antiquary, who wrote in the time of Henry VIII., in his "Itinerary" says, that Nappa and other places "there aboute be able to make a 300 men yn very knowen consanguinitie of the Metcalfes."

Sir Christopher Metcalfe, of Nappa, who died in the 16th of Elizabeth (1574) put this assertion to the proof, as related at page 53.

In one of the windows of the Church, in painted glass, were two armorial shields, bearing on the dexter side, sable, three greyhounds courant in pale argent, being the arms of Mauleverer. These were impaled in one of the shields, which had a label of three points, or, with the arms of Colville, being, or, three torteaux, above a fess gules, and not those of Courtney as mis-stated by Glover. Sir William Mauleverer married Joan, sister and co-heiress of Sir John Colville, of Arncliffe, and the Dale, whose grandfather of the same name joined Hotspur and the archbishop of York, in their rebellion against Henry IV., and was beheaded at Berwick; he lives in Shakspere, (King Henry IV.); and their descendants have enjoyed the estate of Arncliffe from the reign of Henry V., till the

1585. The family of Mauleverer.

---

* *Arms.*—Gules, a chevron ermine between three goats' heads erased argent. *Crest.*—On a mount, vert, a ram couchant, argent, horned and hoofed, or.

A.D. 1585. present time.* The coat therefore was probably that of Sir William Mauleverer, and the lady Joan, his wife. The other with a coat argent, upon a chevron, three martlets, colours and owner unknown.†

A helmet, with a greyhound, Mauléver's crest, supported by a headless lance, fixed in the north wall of the old chancel, remained till 1779.

1593. Francis Kaye, M.A., vicar of Northallerton, 1593, died in 1624. This vicar left 20s. to the poor people of Northallerton, 10s. to Brompton, 5s. to Romanby, and 5s. to Deighton.‡ He is buried in the chancel of Northallerton church, a brass, bearing a Latin inscription, marking the place.

1594. A curious epistle.

William, lord Burghley, writes to his son sir Robert Cecil, the following epistle, concerning making sure of certain great annuities to the queen and her courtiers out of the bishoprics of Winton and Durham, before the new bishops (Day of Winchester, and Tobias Matthew § of Durham), be put in full possession:—

To my verie lovynge soune sr Robert Cecil, Kt.

1. I would wishe you to be carefull, touching the proceeding to be had for the nominated bps. of Winchester and Durham. That, before they be perfited, there be sufficient provision made and assurance to hir majestie, of such rents and annuities, as ought to be assured by them. As namely:

---

* William Mauleverer, esq., the late proprietor of Arncliffe Hall, son of col. Clotworthy Gowan, by his wife Anne, daughter of Thomas Mauleverer, esq., of Arncliffe; born in 1792, m. in 1812, Helen, daughter of the late sir George Abercromby, bart., of Forglen House, N.B., by the hon. Jane Orgilvie, his wife, daughter of Alexander, lord Banff, by whom (who survives him) he had two daughters.

Jane, m. in 1841 to Thomas Meynell, esq., of the Friarage, Yarm, and Kilvington, in the county of York.

Georgina Helen, m. in 1853, to Douglas Brown, esq., M.A., Barrister-at-law, of London, by whom she has issue a son and daughter.

Mr. Mauleverer was a magistrate and deputy-lieutenant for the North Riding. On the passing of the Reform Bill, he stood for the borough of South Shields, and although the defeated candidate, was chaired by the inhabitants, and presented with a diamond ring, as a mark of their esteem and regret. In 1835 he was solicited to become a candidate for the North Riding, and also for the borough of Northallerton. He died 26th March, 1857.

Arms.—Sa. three greyhounds courant, in pale arg.
Crest.—A maple branch arising out of the trunk of a tree.
Motto.—En Dieu ma. foy.

† Glover's visitation. The arms resemble those borne by Chessendon, Brisbon, Rode, Cobham, Cheldeword and Chedword, but I am unable to connect them with the Mauleverer family.

‡ Vide page 79.

§ Elected bishop of Durham, March, 1595; translated to York, 1606; ob. 1628. He was one of the most famous preachers of his time, and was ripe in

2. From the bp. of Winchester of a rent chardge of cccc£ (granted by the late bp. deceased) out of the manor of Taunton, and other manors.
3. As also of viii⁰ & iiij^xx £ yearlie rent, issuing out of the lordship of Allerton, and other lordships, within the bprick of Durham, payd to hir majestie. And further of cxi£ yearlie rent for the castle of Norham, and a fishing uppon the river of Twede, which my lord chamberlaine holds. Which rent was likewise answered to hir majesty by his lordship. 4. I pray youe therefore have a care to theise things touching hir majestie before any further proceding be had therein.
From my house at Westminster, the 14th Feb., 1594.*
Your lovyng father,
W. Burghley.

Northallerton suffered very considerably from the ravages of the "great plague," which devastated the country about this time. From the register of burials in the parish church we ascertain that over ninety persons of all ages died of the plague, and were buried in the churchyard, between July 16th and November 21st in this year.

Robert Grey, D.D., was born in the year 1610. He was younger son of Sir Ralph Grey, and was educated at Northallerton Grammar School, from which he went to Christ College, Cambridge. In 1617, the gentry of Northallerton and district assembled to pay their respects to James I, in his progress to Scotland, on which occasion young Grey, at that time seven years of age, was placed upon a table to deliver a loyal address to the king.

On the commencement of the civil war, Grey exchanged the "Sylvæ Academi" for the camp, and his gown for the sword, and attached himself to the cause and fortunes of the king. Subsequently he was ordained, and in 1652 collated to the rectory at Bishopwearmouth, and later in the year to the eighth stall in Durham cathedral. He was created D.D. in 1660. In king James's reign, riding on horseback from his rectory to Durham, Mr. J. Lamb, a popish justice of the peace, a busy, active and fierce man for that party, overtook the doctor, sneered at him, and told him he wondered he would ride on so fine a palfrey when his Saviour was content to ride upon a colt, the foal of an ass: the Doctor replied, "'Tis true, sir, but the king has made so many asses justices of the peace, he has not left me one to ride upon."

learning, eloquence, and wit. He kept an account of all the sermons he preached, by which it appears that while dean of Durham he preached 721 sermons, when bishop of Durham 550, and when archbishop of York 721. His widow gave his library, consisting of above 3,000 volumes, to the cathedral library at York.
* Peck's Desiderata Curiosa.

1610.　　　　He lived a pious and charitable life, was learned and well read in the fathers and councils; modest and grave; temperate, yet hospitable; constantly resided at his rectory or prebendal house by turns, and daily performed his office to the last week of his life. He lived a bachelor to above the age of 100 years, and was found dead at his devotions in his study at Bishopwearmouth.

1612.
The Codbeck.　　This comparatively large stream runs along the bottom of the Hambleton hills, three miles east of Northallerton. The following passage occurs in Drayton's "*Polyolbion*," published in 1612.

"*Northallerton*, by whom her honour* is increas'd,
Whose liberties include a country at the least,
To grace the wandering *Wiske*, then well upon her way,
Which by her countenance, thinks to carry all away;
Then having her receiv'd, *Swale* bonny *Codbeck*† brings,
And *Willow-beck*‡ with her two pretty revellings."

The Eshall Charity.　　By indenture dated 28th July, 1612, John Eshall and his wife conveyed unto John Chapman, his heirs, and assigns, all his estate at Catto, under a covenant that the said John Chapman and his heirs should yearly pay to the overseers of the poor of Northallerton the sum of 40s., by even and equal portions, at Christmas and Easter, to be by them distributed amongst the poor of Northallerton; and to the schoolmaster there, the yearly sum of 20s. in like even and equal payments; which said sums of 40s. and 20s. are now distributed by the churchwardens once a year, amongst the poor at Northallerton, at their discretion, and to the master of the Grammar School respectively.

1617.
Royal passage through the town.　　King James I. in his progress towards Scotland with a large retinue, passed through Northallerton. It was upon this occasion that young Robert Grey; then a scholar at the grammar school, was placed upon a table to deliver an address to the king.§

1623.
A religious debate.　　Two champions of the church of Rome, a secular priest and a Jesuit, having openly challenged the protestant clergy of the county of York to a public discussion on the controverted points of religion, found an antagonist equally willing and able to contend with them, in the person of the Rev. Richard Bramhall, a native of Pontefract, and afterwards archbishop of Armagh. Transubstantiation, and the denial of the cup to the laity, were the two great topics of

* The North-Riding.
† The word "Cod" is derived from the British word *Cottæ*, signifying *Woody*. The Sunbeck, which runs through the town, is a small tributary of the Cod-beck, and flows into the Wiske.
‡ Willowbeck is another larger tributary running into the town from the north, where it receives the Sunbeck.
§ Vide Raine's North Durham.

debate, in which Mr. Bramhall drove one of his antagonists to the necessity of asserting that "eating and drinking were synonymous terms," and victory was declared in Mr. Bramhall's favour. The contest took place at Northallerton.

1623. Victory for Mr. Bramhall.

The following is a copy of the will of the Rev. Francis Kaye, vicar of Northallerton, so far as relates to the charities left by him to this parish :—

"In the name of God, Amen, the one and twentieth day of June, A.D. 1624. I, Francis Kaye, of Northallerton, in the county of York, clarke, somewhat week in body but of very good memory God's holy name therefore be praised in regard of the certainty of death and the uncertainty of the hour thereof, revoking all former wills whatsoever do make this my last Will and Testament in manner and forme following. First, I bequeath my soul into the hands of Almighty God my heavenly Father, in full assurance of salvation through His mercy in the merits of Jesus Christ my only Saviour and Redeemer, and my body to be buried in the Queire* of North Allerton near my first wife at the discretion of my executor ; and for the goods wherewith God hath endued me withal, I give forty shillings to the poor of this whole parish of Northallerton in manner and form following, viz :— To the poor people of North Allerton, twenty shillings ; to the poor of Brompton, ten shillings; to the poor of Romanby, five shillings ; and to the poor of Deighton, five shillings ; * * * And for the land in Danby Forrest, called or known by the name of Sturmy Hall and Nook House with the appurtenances whatsoever thereunto belonging, lately purchased of Sir John Constable, knight, I give and bequeath unto my son John Kaye and the heirs of his body lawfully begotten and to be begotten for ever with this charge and trust that my son John and the heirs of his body and my next heirs for ever, shall pay out of the profits of the said land from the Feast of Saint Martin the Bishop in Winter, which shall be in the year of our Lord God one thousand six hundred and twenty, give the sum of eight pounds of lawful English money yearly for ever ; the one half thereof upon the first day of December, and the other half upon the twentieth day of May, unto four poor widows towards their maintenance, whereof two shall be of North Allerton and two of Brompton. Also the sum of forty shillings to be bestowed yearly from Martinmas come twelvemonth for ever in clothes to be equally divided, and given to the said poor widows

1624. Will of the Rev. Francis Kaye.

---

* There is no entry of Mr. Kaye's burial in any of the registers in Northallerton Church, but in the Chancel is the following inscription on a brass plate :— " Fran. Kaye, Vicarius hujos ecclesiæ obiit decimo quinto die Septembris A.D. 1624, annoque ætatis sexagesimo nono incumbentiæ tricesimo secundo."

1624.	yearly and every year for ever upon St. Bartholomew's Day out of the rents of the said lands,* and my mind is that widow Clarkson, widow Longbottom, widow Seamer, and widow Peacock, if they be then living, shall be the first four, and that when any of the said poor widows shall die that three other of the poorest shall be propounded by the overseers of the said townes * * out of which my son John Kaye * * shall choose one to succeed in the deads place * *
A pluralist.	John Cradock, M.A., vicar of Northallerton in 1624, collated to the fifth prebendal stall in Durham cathedral. He became archdeacon of Northumberland, and soon afterwards was appointed chancellor of the diocese. He was a
Mr. Cradock poisoned.	pluralist, being rector of Gainford and vicar of Woodhorn at one and the same time. He died by poison in 1627, for which his wife was accused, tried, and acquitted.
1626. A royal grant.	Charles I. granted his several fee-farm rents issuing out of lands in the county of Durham, in provision for his royal consort Henrietta Maria. A short extract from this curious record will show the portion the town bore:—

"Ac totum illum annualem redditum sive feodum firmum nostrum octingen' et octaginta librarum, de diversis terris, messuagiis, grangis, dominiis et maneriis de Allerton, alias Allertonshire, in comitatu Eborum, ac de dominiis et maneriis de Esington alias Esington Ward alias Esington Coronatorum, Sedburgh, Cotton-Monvile, Midleham, et Gateshed, in dicto episcopatu Dunelmensi, ac de terris et tenementis in Holden et Holdenshire in dicto comitatu Eborum, nobis heredibus et successoribus nostris execantium sive solubilium."

1628.	Thomas Blaikeston, M.A., vicar of Northallerton in 1628. He was forcibly ejected by the Rev. Thos. Mann in 1640.
	The following is an entry made at the end of the register of baptisms for 1626-29, in Northallerton church:—
Induction of Mr. Blaikeston	"Thomas Blaikeston, Mr of Arts was inuested into the vicaridge of Allerton (by John Crackanthorpe, clerk) and (sic) Mr of Artes, by vertue of a Mandate to him directed from the Venerable the Deane and Chapter of Durham upon Saturday beinge the 17th day of May, Anno D'ni 1628, and upon Sunday next after, beinge the 18th of the said month did reede his Artickles publicly in the church, in witnesse whereof we that were his auditors have set to our hands

George Metcalfe John Crackanthorpe, Clerke
Thomas Walb... ⎧ Richard Metcalfe
Rich. Scarlet *Churchwardens* ⎨ Anthony Lanchester
Anthon. Rymer ⎩ Tho. Lascelles
John Kaye ⎩ Geo. Staynes

---

* This sum of forty shillings is still given away every year equally between four poor widows, in acknowledgment of which the two resident in Northallerton are supposed to keep clean and bright the brass above alluded to.

Bishop Thomas Morton* prosecuted in the court of delegates his claim for dilapidations within his diocese, and recovered against archbishop Neile,† in the year 1634, no less than £500 with £50 costs of suit, notwithstanding the decorations and improvements that prelate had made at Durham and Auckland; also £60 was paid him by the representatives of bishop Howson.‡ By the sentence pronounced in the before mentioned cause, the castle of Craike, the houses of Whelhall, Howden, North Allerton, Middleham, &c., were decreed from thenceforth to be discharged from all account of dilapidations.§

A.D. 1634. Ecclesiastical litigation.

Thomas Burnet, LL.D., was born at Croft, 1635. His early education was acquired at the Northallerton grammar school, where he was usually proposed by the master as an example to the other scholars. In 1651 he was admitted at Clare Hall, Cambridge; elected fellow of Christ's College, 1657, and senior proctor of the University, 1661. He is the author of several valuable works, and there are few of our modern writers who surpass Dr. Burnet in the elegance of Latin composition. He took his degree of LL.D. in 1685, and died in a good old age.

1635. Dr. Burnet.

In the gallery of portraits, in the British Museum, is that of Dr. Thomas Burnet; another is in the master's lodge, at Charter House, and is one of Kneller's finest works.

Thomas Rymer, F.S.A., son of Ralph Rymer,‖ was born at Appleton Wiske, near Northallerton, in 1638, and educated at the Northallerton grammar school, in the same class as Dr. George Hickes, whence he was admitted at Sydney Sussex College, Cambridge, upon quitting which he entered

1638. Thomas Rymer.

---

* Translated from Lichfield, 1632. At his installation he gave twenty pounds to the library of the dean and chapter. He was dispossessed of his bishopric in the great rebellion, notwithstanding his great moderation and piety. He died 22nd Sep., 1659, æt. 95.
† Translated from Lincoln to Durham, Oct., 1617; to Winchester, 10th Dec., 1627; and to York in 1632; died 31st Oct., 1640. He was one of the most unprincipled flatterers of James I. Waller, the poet, one day went to see James I. at dinner, when he found Andrewes, bishop of Winchester, and Neile, bishop of Durham, standing behind the king's chair. The following conversation took place. The king—" My lords, cannot I take my subjects' money when I want it, without all this formality in parliament?" Neile—" God forbid, sir, but you should; you are the breath of our nostrils." The king to the bishop of Winchester—"Well my lord, what say you?" Andrewes —" I have no skill your majesty to judge of parliamentary cases." The king —" No puts off my lord; answer me presently." Andrewes—" Then, sir, I think it lawful for you to take my brother Neile's money, for he offers it."
‡ Translated from Oxford, 1628, died 6th Feb., 1632, æt. 75, and lies buried in St. Paul's.
§ Hutchinson, i. 499.
‖ This gentleman was trepanned into the Yorkshire Plot in 1663, and, upon very slight evidence, executed. But though he was cut short, his children lived long.

F

A.D. 1638. Gray's Inn. In 1692 he was made historiographer royal to king William III., a post which had been held by Shadwell and Dryden. His writings are numerous, those relating to our constitution are good; and his valuable collection of public records will be a lasting monument of his industry and ability. He died in 1713, and was buried in the church of St. Clement Danes, in the Strand.

1640. The rising of the Covenanters. On the rising of the covenanters in Scotland in 1639, king Charles I. came to York, accompanied by most of the nobility and general officers; after staying nearly a month in the city he proceeded with his army towards Scotland. At his approach the Scots submitted, laid down their arms, and swore obedience to their sovereign.

The year following, however, the Scottish army entered England. To put a stop to this bold invasion, the king set out from London on the 20th Aug., accompanied by the marquis of Hamilton and the duke of Lenox, and in three days arrived at York; on the 24th dined at the lord mayor's (Robert Belt) and knighted him; on the 29th rode to Northallerton, when he was informed of the defeat at Newburn, (where the Scotch artillery so frightened the English army, that Sir Thomas Fairfax, one of their commanders, did not A cowardly general. stick to own that till he passed the Tees, his legs trembled under him,)* and that the Scots had taken Newcastle. His majesty on receiving this intelligence returned to York.

Although the Scotch gained the victory on the 28th August, yet within a week they petitioned the king for redress. The king's forces had in the meantime rallied and concentrated at Northallerton.† The following letter from the unforunate earl of Strafford, K.G., lord-lieutenant-general of his majestie's army, to Sir George Radcliffe, speaks the language of the heart; it is a short but eloquent burst of indignation, from a brave and faithful man, heart-broken by the cowardice and treachery of all around him:—

" Cosin Radcliffe,

" Pitty me, for never came any man to so lost businesse. The army altogeither unexercised and unprovided of all necessarys. That parte which I bring now with me from Durham the worst I ever saw. Our horse all cowardly, the country from Barwicke to Yorke in the power of the Scott, an universal affright in all, a general disaffection to the king's service, none sensible of his dishonour. In one worde, here alone to fight with all these evils, without any one to helpe.

* Burnet.
† Fairfax correspondence.

God of his goodnesse deliver me out of this the greatest evil A.D. 1640.
of my life. Fare you well.*
"Your ever most faithfull and most
affectionate cosin and freind,
STRAFFORDE."†

North Allerton, 1st September, 1640.

In order to prevent the further advance of the Scots, the king agreed to a treaty, and named sixteen English noblemen to meet eleven Scotch commissioners; York and Northallerton were both suggested as the place of meeting, but it was finally fixed to be at Ripon, where the negotiations commenced on the 1st of October.‡ By this treaty it was agreed that the Tees should be the bounds of both armies, and that £850 a-day was to be levied out of Northumberland, Durham, and Westmoreland, for the subsistence of their army.§

Thomas Mann, vicar of Northallerton, possessed himself A disgraceful of the living during the interregnum; coming into church as scene. Mr. Blaikeston was reading one of the lessons, and producing a document by which he claimed the living under the then usurpation, he first turned Mr. Blaikeston out of the reading desk, and then getting up into the pulpit, made there a long prayer and a longer sermon.‖ Master Mann was either one of those puritan presbyterian ministers who took advantage of the disturbed condition of the nation, and the consequent jeopardy of the English church at that time; or, which is more likely, from the account of his subsequent induction, one of those elastic-minded clergymen of the "Vicar of Bray" type, who determined, "come what might" to get a living and keep it. But, whichever he was, the riot at Edinburgh on the introduction of archbishop Laud's liturgy in 1637 had probably emboldened Master Mann in his determination to dispossess Mr. Blaikeston when a convenient opportunity presented itself. Mr. Mann appears to have

* Life and correspondence of Sir George Radcliffe.
† This eminent statesman was born in London, in 1593; made custos rotulorum of the West Riding of Yorkshire, and represented the county in Parliament in 1621. Created Baron Wentworth of Wentworth, co. York, July 22, 1628; Visct. Wentworth Dec. 10 following; Baron Raby of Raby Castle, and Earl of Strafford Jan. 12, 1640; beheaded on Tower Hill, May 12, 1641, and being attainted, all his honours became forfeited. His body was afterwards embalmed, and appointed to be brought into Yorkshire, there to be buried amongst his ancestors, (see state trials). In Wentworth church there is a graceful figure of a man in armour kneeling, erected to his memory. He was succeeded by his son William; restored to all his father's honours in Dec. 1665; who died 16th Oct., 1695. A monument to his memory is placed towards the east end of the south aisle of the choir of York Minster, containing an effigy of the Earl and his Countess, separated by an urn.
‡ Fairfax correspondence.   § Rushworth.
‖ Vide Walker's "sufferings of the Clergy."

A.D. 1640. enjoyed undisturbed possession of the living until the induction of Mr. Neyle in 1669.

The Borough of North-allerton.

Little satisfactory information is to be obtained explanatory of the origin or nature of the English boroughs and burgesses. That boroughs existed in this country from the earliest period of our authentic history is confidently affirmed.

The Romans undoubtedly had boroughs,* (the word *borough* probably being of Roman derivation.) And as the actual existence of boroughs in this country from the time of Edward the Confessor is established beyond all controversy, this conjecture must not be considered as altogether unfounded; particularly as the boroughs existing in the time of king Edward are not spoken of as if then newly introduced, but as having been established so long, that they had become a part of the political institutions of the country. However, it is clear, that if we had the term from the Romans, they left us little but the name; for there appears no reason to suppose that the boroughs in England, during the Saxon and Norman times, had anything in common with the boroughs of the Romans.

Hume's assertion that "the boroughs were in the time of Domesday, little more than villages, and the inhabitants dependent on the king, or great lords, in a station little better than servile," is assumed without foundation, as an inspection of Domesday will show. Whatever their situation may have been, it is obvious that they stood in nearly the same relative position with respect to the rest of the country, as they do at the present time. If there has been any change, the probability is, that they possessed then a greater comparative importance than they do at present; "their burgesses being of free condition, which, at that time, was a distinguishing mark of no slight importance."†

At the time of the Domesday survey, there were in Yorkshire fourteen parliamentary boroughs, viz.:—York, Hull, Pontefract, Ripon, Beverley, North Allerton, Malton, Thirsk, Knaresborough, Scarborough, Richmond, Aldborough, Boroughbridge, and Hedon. Of these none are described in that record as boroughs, nor are the burgesses mentioned, excepting those of York. Of that place there is a long and minute entry, separate from the rest of the county, which it precedes.‡

" 5° die December. A motion was made for Malton and Allerton, two towns in Yorkshire, that have anciently sent burgesses to parliament, but for a long while have discontinued: It was desired, it might be referred to the committee

---

* Cod. Theod. vii. 13. Cod. Just. xi. 65.
† Merrewether & Stephens' Hist. of Boroughs.
‡ Fol. 298.

for privileges, to certify the state of that matter, upon view and examination of the record."*

A.D. 1640

"11º die December. *Ordered*.—That the towns of Malton and Allerton, in the county of York, which formerly (as appeared to the committee upon view of the record) sent burgesses, but for some time had discontinued, be restored and remitted to their ancient privileges of sending burgesses to parliament: and that a warrant issue forth under Mr. Speaker's hand, directed to the clerk of the crown in chancery, to send forth a writ for electing of two burgesses to serve in this present parliament for the said towns of Malton and Allerton."† Thomas Heblewaite, esq., and sir Henry Cholmeley, knt. *(et in vice unius*, Richard Darley, esq.) were chosen representatives.

The Franchise restored to Northallerton

Thus, notwithstanding the experience of James I., and his declaration of the difficulty he had found in managing the boroughs which then returned members to parliament, Charles I. had, at this time, either sanctioned or submitted to the restoration of no less than eight boroughs; two in the fourth year of his reign, and six in this year (1640); of the latter, three were in the north, and three in the south:— adding altogether 16 members to the House of Commons.

This course had been first adopted by Henry VIII., and afterwards followed by Queen Mary, Queen Elizabeth, and James I., in the beginning of his reign. Those, however, which were now restored, appear rather to have been adopted by the commons themselves, owing to the practice which the crown had before sanctioned, for the purpose of increasing their own power against the crown.‡

In six of the eight boroughs, the burgesses were defined to be the *inhabitant householders;* the right of election being decided to be in them. In the other two cases, Malton and North Allerton, the right was determined to be in the *burgage holders.*

King Charles I. passed through Northallerton on his way to York, and was entertained by the Metcalfes at Porch House.§

1641. Royal visit.

"In the name of God, Amen. I, George Metcalfe, of Northallerton, in the county of Yorke, Esq., sicke in body but of good and perfect memory, thankes be to God, doe make this my last Will and Testament in manner and forme followinge. First, I bequeath my soul to Almighty God my Maker, and to Jesus Christ my Redeemer, by whose meritts death and passion I hope to be saved, and my body to be buried in the Church of Northallerton. Item, I give and

1642. Will of George Metcalfe of Northallerton.

---

* Journal of the House of Commons.
† Journal of the House of Commons.
‡ Parl. Hist. xxi. p. 212.   § Vide page 70.

bequeath unto my nephewes George Metcalfe and John Bell, their executors, administrators, and assignes, all my houses, lands, tenements, and hereditaments scituate, lyinge, and beinge att Angram Grainge, in the parish of Welbury, in the county of Yorke; and allsoe all those my houses, closes, grounds, lands, tenements, and hereditaments scituate, lyinge, and beinge in Landmothe which I lately bought or purchased of Mr. William Greene and Richard Jackson, and now in the occupation of the said Richard Jackson; and allsoe all those my closes, grounds, lands, tenements, and hereditaments whatsoever, scituate and beinge in Romanby, which I lately bought or purchased of William Meade, now in the several occupations of Raiphe Lilly and Robert Wilson, for and during the tearme of fifteene years, for the raisinge and makinge portions for my daughters Elizabeth Metcalfe, Catheryne Metcalfe, and Mary Metcalfe, and for their preferment and education and the educatinge of my sonne Richard Metcalfe; and I doe give and bequeath unto my said sonne Richard Metcalfe, his heires and assigns for ever, all my said houses, lands, tenements, and hereditaments att Angram Grainge aforesaid, after the determination of the said fifteen yeares. Item, I give unto the poore people of Northallerton forty shillings yearely, for seaven yeares next after my death, to be paid att Christmas and Easter, by even portions foorth of one close on my back side called Pond Garth. Item, the residue of my goods and chattels, my legacies and funeral expenses deducted, I give and bequeath unto my said two nephewes George Metcalfe and John Bell, for the payment of my debts. And if my leases at Northallerton can be spared, over and above the payment of my debts, my will is that they shall come and accrue to my sonne William Metcalfe att his aige of one and twenty years, he payinge such sums of money to my said younger children as my said executors shall thinke fit. But my will is that my said sonne Richard shall have fifty pounds foorth of my said leases att Northallerton.

In witness whereof I have hereunto sett my hand and seale the eight and twentieth day of Maye, anno dni 1642.

GEORGE METCALFE." | L.S.

Sealed, signed, and delivered in the presence of William Pinkney, John Kaye, William Dinmore.

This will was proved at York the 14th day of May, 1647, by the oaths of George Metcalfe and John Bell, the executors therein named, to whom probate was granted, they having been first sworn duly to administer.

George Metcalfe, the testator, was a barrister of Gray's

Inn, and one of His Majesty's Justices of the Peace for the North-Riding. The nephew and executor named in the will was George Metcalfe, of Thornborough Hall, near Romanby, who married Anne, daughter and heiress of Henry Danby, of Romanby. His second son, Sir Gilbert Metcalfe, was Lord Mayor of York in 1695. Richard, the elder son, married Elizabeth Ogilvie, of the Earl of Findlater's family, whose grand-daughter and sole heiress, Elizabeth, married Nicholas Lambton, of Biddick Watervill, co. Durham, grandson of Sir William Lambton, of Lambton, by his wife, Catherine Widdrington. The only child, Margaret Lambton, died an infant, and the Thornborough Hall line of Metcalfe became extinct about 1747.

Elizabeth, grand-daughter of George Metcalfe, of Thornborough Hall, married Francis Proctor, of Thorpe-on-the-Hill, whose grand-daughter, Catherine Proctor, married Thomas Howard, 3rd Earl of Effingham, Deputy Earl-Marshal of England, Treasurer of the Household in 1782, and Master of the Mint in 1784.

The John Bell named in the will was a son of George Metcalfe's sister, Cecilie Metcalfe, who married Marmaduke Bell, of Elmer.

George Hicks, D.D., was born June 26th, 1642, at Newsham, in the parish of Kirby Wiske. Educated at Northallerton Grammar School, he was admitted a servitor at St. John's College, Oxford, in 1659, and elected a fellow of Lincoln College, 1664. He travelled with Sir George Wheeler, one of his pupils, through France and Switzerland. Soon after his return in 1675, he was presented to the rectory of St. Ebb's, Oxford, and became domestic chaplain to the Duke of Lauderdale. He obtained the degree of L.L.D. from the University of Oxford in return for some valuable Greek manuscripts which he brought back with him from Paris; and the degree of D.D. for his eminent services in ecclesiastical and state affairs. In 1680 he was installed Prebendary of Worcester, and vicar of Allhallows, Barking, in London. The following year he was appointed chaplain in ordinary to Charles II., and two years afterwards Dean of Worcester. In 1690 he was deprived of his Deanery for refusing to take the oath of allegiance and supremacy to William and Mary, and retired to London. Subsequently he espoused the cause of the Chevalier, and was actively engaged in the service of that unfortunate prince. He died December 15th, 1715, and was buried in St. Margaret's churchyard, Westminster. He was a man of universal learning, deeply read in the primitive fathers of the church, whom he considered the best expositors of scripture ;

A.D. 1642.   particularly skilful in the old northern languages and antiquities; and has given us some writings in this way, which will be valued when all his other works are forgotten.*

1644. Fatal skirmish at Northallerton.   Several matters of minor warfare took place in the early part of this year between the royalists of the north, and Leslie's army which came to the assistance of parliament. Gerard Salvin, son and heir of Gerard Salvin, of Croxdale,† esq., lieutenant-colonel of col. Tempest's regiment of foot, was slain at Northallerton, in the service of king Charles I.‡ The fatal battle of Marston Moor completed that unfortunate king's ruin in the north.

> "Where is that banner now?—its pride
> Lies whelm'd in Ouse's sullen tide;
> Where now these warriors?—in their gore
> They cumber Marston's dismal moor!"

Archbishop Palliser.   William Palliser, D.D., was born at Kirby Wiske, July 28th, 1644, educated at the Northallerton Grammar School, and afterwards at Trinity College, Dublin, which latter place he entered when fifteen years of age. He was successively elected fellow, medical fellow, and tutor of the University. In 1670 he took holy orders, and became regius professor of divinity in 1678, and shortly afterwards received the degree of D.D. In 1681 he was presented to the living of Clonfeacle, and in 1692 promoted to the see of Cloyne. In 1694 he was translated to the archbishopric of Cashel, and died in Dublin,

---

* On the feast of St. Matthias, Feb. 24th, 1693, the consecration of Dr. George Hickes and Thomas Wagstaffe was solemnly performed according to the rites of the Church of England, by Dr. William Lloyd, bishop of Norwich; Dr. Francis Turner, bishop of Ely; and Dr. Thomas White, bishop of Peterborough, at the bishop of Peterborough's lodgings, at the rev. William Giffard's house at Southgate in Middlesex: Dr. Ken, bishop of Bath and Wells, giving his consent.—*Notes and Queries*, 1st S. vol. ii. p. 355.

Thoresby, in his diary, May 18, 1714, says, "I visited Mr. Nelson (author of the Fasts and Festivals), and the learned Dr. George Hickes, who not being at liberty for half an hour, I had the benefit of the prayers in the adjoining church, and when the Nonjuring Conventicle was over, I visited the said dean Hickes, who is said to be bishop of———" [Thetford.] Both Nelson and Hickes resided at this time in Ormond Street; probably the conventicle was at one of their houses.

† William de Walton of the city of Durham, had lands in Northallerton, which belonged to Robert de Walton, in the 5th Edward III. His son Robert de Walton, of Durham, had lands in Old Durham, 1354, which were Joan Wyot's, eldest daughter and co-heir of John Wyot, of Old Durham. He had lands in Northallerton, 44th Edward III. His daughter Joanna, lady of Croxdale, died wife of William de Rissaby, seized of lands in Durham, &c., heretofore Robert de Walton's. Her only daughter and heiress Agnes, lady of Croxdale, married Gerard Salvayn, esq., in her right became "of Croxdale," in the county palatine of Durham, having had livery of his wife's inheritance on the 1st October, 1402.—*Burke's Commoners.*

‡ Surtees.

January 1st, 1726, aged 85 years, after a few days indis-   A.D. 1644.
position from a cold, and was buried in the parish church of
St. Andrew. The archbishop bequeathed his splendid library
of 4,000 volumes, which is still preserved and distinguished
by the name of "Bibliotheca Palliseriana" to Trinity College,
Dublin. He also gave £20 to the poor of the parish of
Northallerton.* His grace was an excellent Latin scholar,
an eminent divine, and a saintly christian. His memory will
ever be had in reverence by the people of Northallerton.

    King Charles I. having surrendered himself to the Scots,   1646.
was kept by them in close custody for six months, pending   Charles surrenders to the Scots.
negotiations for his release with the English parliament. At
first the two English houses of parliament passed a resolution
demanding the unconditional release of the king, but the
Scots remonstrated, saying that as Charles was king of Scotland as well as of England, both nations had an equal right
to be consulted regarding the disposal of his person; whereupon the English prepared for war. The Scots seeing that
they must yield up the person of the king or fight for it, at
length agreed to release him upon the payment to them by
the English government of £400,000 sterling, which was
acceded to.

    So early as the month of September, 1642, the memorable   The Episcopacy abolished.
long parliament had appointed a committee for the sequestration of the lands of all bishops, deans, and chapters,† and
subsequently proceeded to utterly abolish the name and title
of archbishops and bishops, by an act passed 9th October,
1646, by which they vested all their honours, manors, lordships, &c., all their charters, deeds, books, &c., in the hands
of trustees, for the payment of the just and necessary debts
of the kingdom.‡ The trustees were empowered to appoint
from time to time fit and able persons to survey the premises,
to hold courts of surveys, and to demand and receive all the
evidences and title deeds relative to the same. Pursuant to
the above act, an ordinance was issued for the sale of all the
bishops' lands and estates for the service of the commonwealth.§ By the same authority all purchasers were to have
letters patent under the great seal of England for these
grants, and to hold of the king in fealty only, according to
the tenure of the manor of east Greenwich. The attorneygeneral was authorised to prepare a bill for each grant or
sale, and the lord-chancellor empowered to pass it; whilst
the titles of the purchasers were to be defended at the public
charge. In addition to these securities, and in order to give
greater encouragement to their chapmen (as Walker calls

---

  * For further particulars of this benefaction, see entry under date 1687.
  † Whit. Mem. p. 63.   ‡ Scobell.   § Vide page 92.

A.D. 1646.

them), the estates were sold at an appraisement barely equivalent to the materials of the mansion-houses and timber on the ground; so that, as Dr. Bate truly remarks, "Episcoporum latifundia vili pretio sub hasta posuerint, unde sectores innumeri confluxerunt, qui materia ruderibusque palatiorum et silvis excisis pretium emptionis solventes, prædia ampla et integra maneria gratis fere adi piscuntur." It was further ordered that all surveys, particulars, contracts, &c., of the lands so sequestrated should be registered by a public officer, and catalogues drawn up of all evidences and writings touching the titles of the same.* The same steps, in regard to the lands of deans and chapters, were taken in April, 1649, in referring to which, and to the previous act, Walker says, "Having no information relating to the proceedings on that act, I can only assure the reader, that the lands, &c., were, in fact, sold or converted by the commissioners to their own private uses, but can give no particulars relating to these matters."

Accounts of the sale of episcopal lands, with the names of the purchasers, and price, are inserted under the respective years in which the sales took place, and will show to what an extent the proceedings in question were carried.

As a necessary prelude to the restoration, the two acts of sequestration were repealed in March, 1659-60; and, on the king's return, the subject of the restoration of these lands to the rightful owners, and the compensation to be made to the purchasers, became a subject of frequent deliberation in parliament, and produced several pamphlets on the side of the latter party.

The king had partly pledged himself to some equitable accommodation, and communicated his wishes on the subject to the parliament in September, 1660; and on the 7th October following, a commission was especially appointed, "To enquire into the pretended sales and purchases of crown and church lands."† These commissioners sat in the star chamber, and their proceedings are stated to have given the parties concerned general satisfaction.

1647.
Charles I. a prisoner.

Up to this time the Scots had detained the king (Charles I.) as a pledge for the £400,000 which they claimed. After many discussions it was agreed, that one half of the amount should be paid instantly;‡ but at the same time the king should be delivered up to the commissioners of the parliament of England, who were sent down to Newcastle-upon-Tyne to receive him. On January 5th, 1647, the money arrived at Newcastle from York, in thirty-six carts, under a strong escort. It was made up in bags of £1,000 each, and

* Scobell.   † Kennet's Register, p. 273.   ‡ Parl. Hist. XV. 236.

began to be counted into the hands of the Scottish receiver the same day, the counting being completed on Saturday, the 16th. On the 21st a receipt for the first half of the amount was signed at Northallerton, and on February 3rd a similar receipt was signed for the remainder. Lingard says, " the first payment of £100,000 of king Charles' ransom was made at Northallerton,* but this is doubtful. On January 30th, the king was committed to the care of the English commissioners, consisting of three lords, and six commoners, the earl of Pembroke being at their head. The commissioners of the English parliament, with their royal prisoner, arrived at Northallerton in February, and rested at the Porch House, which is situated on the east side of the town opposite the church. Tradition says he made an attempt to escape out of a window at the south end of the house.

Cromwell at this time was moving rapidly about in these parts, quelling the royalists, as will appear from the following letter :—

For his excellency the lord Fairfax,† general of all the Parliament's armies : These

Berwick, 11th September, 1648.

My Lord,

Since we lost lieutenant-colonel Cowell, his wife came to me near North Allerton, much lamenting her loss, and the sad condition she and her children were left in.

He was an honest worthy man. He spent himself in your and the kingdom's service. He being a great trader in London, deserted it to serve the kingdom. He lost much monies to the state, and I believe few outdid him. He hath a great arrear due to him. He left a wife and three small children but meanly provided for. Upon his death-bed, he commended this desire to me, that I should befriend his to the parliament or to your excellency. His wife will attend you for letters to the parliament ; which I beseech you to take into your tender consideration.

I beseech you to pardon this boldness to

Your excellency's most humble servant,‡

Oliver Cromwell.

---

* Vide Lingard VIII. 71.
† It is worthy of remark that, "while the civil war was at its height, Fairfax afforded a most useful protection to literature and literary institutions. By his care the libraries at York and Oxford were partially at least preserved from pillage." *(Guizot.)* After resigning the command of the army, he retired for awhile from public life, devoting his leisure hours to the encouragement and cultivation of letters, and left behind him a volume of poems and miscellanies, including an interesting account of his life. He died at Denton, 12th Nov., 1671.
‡ Carlyle's Letters and Speeches of Cromwell.

A.D. 1648.   The parliament on the 19th June, 1649, ordered that "widow Cowell" be paid her husband's arrears by the committee at Haberdashers' hall.*

Sale of Episcopal Lands.   The following bishop's lands belonging to the see of Durham were sold this year:—Lands in Northallerton, to John Wastell and James Danby, for £102 10s.; the Manor of Northallerton, to William Cave, for £1,453 6s. 8½d.; divers lands in Sowerby, Northallerton, and Osmotherley, to Richard Metcalfe, for £1,081 7s. 8½d.; four ox-gangs of land in Allertonshire, to Joseph Bell and George Burton, for £78 5s.†

1649.   A further sale of lands belonging to the bishopric of Durham took place this year, by virtue of the ordinance for the total abolition of episcopacy, which had been passed by both Houses of Parliament two years before:—A parcel of Wolsingham Manor, to Richard Marshall, for £158 11s. 8d.; lands in Northallerton Manor, to Thomas Lassels, for £553 17s. 3d.; several lands in Northallerton, to Robert Medcalfe for £289 0s. 3d.; Frankland Wood Park and colliery, with the meadows in Durham Moor and Gateshead, and tolls of the town of Gateshead, to Thomas Redger, for £2,559 2s.; Bishop Middleham Manor, to Thomas Hazelrigg, Esq., for £3,306 6s. 6½d.; and Sunderland Borough and the Manor of Haughton-le-Spring, to George Fenwick, of Brinkburn, for £2,851 9s. 6d.‡

1650.   The following possessions belonging to the See of Durham were sold by order of Parliament this year:— Durham Borough and Framwellgate, to the Corporation of Durham, for £230; two parcels of land near Durham to Richard Marshall, for £8 13s. 4d.; Northallerton Borough, to Henry Darley and John Wastell, for £237 3s. 2d.; and several parcels on Tyne Bridge, to Francis Alder, for £52 5s. 8d. Also, about the same time, Easington Borough, to Sir Arthur Hazelrigg, for £5,883 9s. 9d.; Bedlington Manor and Choppington Farm, to Robert Fenwick, Esq., for £1,296 0s. 5½d.; parcel of Northallerton and Whiston Cliffe, to Moses Jenkins, for £113 0s. 4d.; another parcel of Northallerton Manor, to Henry Darley, for £1,215 1s. 1¾d.; parcel of land in Rivehope (Ryhope), to George Fenwick, Esq., for £2,091 16s. 3d.; Wolsingham Manor, to Sir Arthur Hazelrigg, for £6,764 14s. 4d.; Howden Manor, to William Underwood and Thomas Caghill, for £5,192 15s.; and Easington Manor, to Walter Boothby, Esq., for £8,528 2s. 3d. The total sum realised by these and other sales of Church lands, during the five years from 1647 to 1651 inclusive, was £68,121 15s. 9d.‡

* Commons Journals, VI. 237.   † Brit. Mus. MSS. Add. 9049.
‡ Rawlinson's MSS. Bodleian Lib. B. 236.

John Radcliffe, M.D., was born at Wakefield, in 1650, received part of his education at the school of that town and part at the Northallerton grammar school. He was admitted at University College, Oxford, 1665, took the degree of B.A. in 1669, and that of M.A. in 1672, and then proceeded in the medical faculty. It is remarkable that he recommended himself more by ready wit and vivacity than by any acquisition in learning. He had few books of any kind, so few that when Dr. Bathurst, President of Trinity College, asked him where his library was, he pointed to a few files, a skeleton, and an herbal, and replied, " Sir, that is Radcliffe's library." In 1675 he resigned the fellowship of Lincoln College, (and was succeeded by his schoolfellow, John Kettlewell); proceeded M.B., and in 1682 M.D. Two years after he went to London, settled in Bow Street, and soon obtained an extensive practice. In 1686 he was appointed physician to Princess Anne of Denmark, and after the revolution he was sent for by William III. He attended Queen Mary in her last illness. *[margin: A.D. 1650. Dr. Radcliffe.]*

King William, after his return from Holland in 1699, sent for him, and showing him his swollen ankles, said, " What think you of these?" " Why truly," replied Radcliffe, " I would not have your Majesty's two legs for your three kingdoms;" this freedom lost the king's favour, and no intercessions could ever recover it. Soon after, he lost the favour of the Princess Anne, and when she came to the throne, the earl of Godolphin used all his endeavours to restore him to favour, but without success, " Because," said the queen, " he will send me word that my ailments are nothing but the vapors." In her Majesty's last illness, he was sent for, about noon, by an order of the council, but he replied, " I have taken physic and cannot come." " In all probability," says Ford, " he could have saved her life; for I am told, that the late lord Gower had often been in the same condition, and that Radcliffe had kept him alive for many years." *[margin: Amusing repartee.]*

In a letter to a friend, the doctor writes, " Ill as I was, I would have went to the queen in a horse-litter, had either her Majesty or those in commission next to her commanded me so to do." He died at the age of 64, and the following epigram upon him was written by Samuel Wesley:—

> " When Radcliffe fell, afflicted Physic cried,
> ' How vain my power!' and languish'd at his side;
> When Friend expired, deep-struck her hair she tore,
> And speechless fainted, and revived no more.
> Her flowing grief no further could extend;
> She mourns with Radcliffe, but she dies with Friend."

He bequeathed £5,000 to the college where he was first

A.D. 1650. educated, £40,000 to the University of Oxford, for building that noble library that bears his name, £150 per annum to the keeper thereof, and £100 for buying books into it perpetually: £600 per annum for maintaining two fellowships in St. Bartholomew's hospital in Smithfield, and made generous provision for all his relations and servants.

1653.
Rev. John Kettlewell.

John Kettlewell, M.A., was born at Low Fields, in the township of Brompton,* in the parish of Northallerton, on March 10th, 1653. He was educated at the Northallerton grammar school, and at the age of sixteen he became a student of St. Edmund's Hall, Oxford. He was successively elected fellow and tutor of Lincoln college, and gained universal esteem and veneration by his singular attention to the moral, religious, and literary improvement of his pupils. Dr. Marshall would often say, "God hath sent us a blessing in this young man." After entering holy orders, he became chaplain to the countess of Bedford,† and was afterwards presented to the vicarage of Coleshill, in Warwickshire. Refusing to take the oaths of allegiance and supremacy to king William III. and queen Mary, he was deprived of his vicarage, and retired to London, where he wrote several tracts on the times. Dr. Frampton, bishop of Gloucester, although adverse to controversial writings, had great satisfaction in reading those set forth by Mr. Kettlewell, and expressed admiration at so "worthy and pious an hero," as he called him. His books show him to be a very pious as well as a learned person, and will outlast any monument his friends can bestow upon him. He died of consumption at his lodgings in Gray's Inn, Holborn, at the comparatively early age of 42, and was interred in the parish church of Allhallows, Barking, in the same grave where archbishop Laud was interred. Dr. Hicks says, "His great piety, useful learning, and solid judgment, rendered him a public blessing, and a peculiar ornament of the church and age wherein he lived." Nelson says, "He was learned without pride; wise and judicious without cunning; served at the altar without covetousness or ambition; devout without affectation; sincerely religious without moroseness; courteous and affable without flattery or mean compliances; just without rigour; charitable without vanity; and heartily zealous for the interests of religion without faction."

* A stained glass window has recently been inserted to his memory in the south aisle of Brompton Church.

† Her son lord William Russell, who was beheaded in 1683, had a high esteem for him, which he did not fail to express, even in his last moments, by sending a message to him from the scaffold in token of his kind remembrance of him.

The *Mercurious Politicus* contains the following advertisement, showing not only the slow pace at which our ancestors were content to travel, but also the cost of the tardy infliction.

A.D. 1658. Slowness of travelling.

"From the 26th day of April, 1658, there will continue to go stage coaches from the George Inn, without Aldersgate, London, unto the several cities and towns, for the rates, and at the times hereafter mentioned and declared :—

"Every Monday, Wednesday, and Friday, to Salisbury in two days for xxs. To Blandford and Dorchester in two days and a half for xxxs. To Burput in three days for xxxs. To Exmaster, Hunnington, and Exeter, in four days for xls. To Stamford in two days for xxs. To Newark in two days and a half for xxvs. To Bawtrey in three days for xxxs. To Doncaster and Ferribridge for xxxvs. To York in four days for xls.

".Mondays and Wednesdays, to Ockington and Plimouth for ls. Every Monday to Helperby and Northallerton for xlvs. To Darneton, Ferryhill, for ls. To Durham for lvs. To Newcastle for iii£. Once every fortnight to Edinburgh for iv£ a piece, (Mondays). Every Friday to Wakefield in four days for xls."

This palace is described by a singular traveller little more than twenty years afterwards as "demolished with age, and the ruins of time," and serving "as a receptacle for bats and buzzards, owls and jackdaws."* A good piece of the gatehouse was standing about one hundred years ago, but through the injuries of time, and the violence of illiterate hands, not the smallest vestige now remains.†

The Bishop's Palace in ruins.

> "Of high embowed roof,
> With antique pillars, massy proof,
> And storied windows richly dight,
> Casting a dim religious light."

The moat which surrounded the palace is still in existence; a small but elegantly laid-out cemetery occupying the site of the palace. Great interest attaches to this moat, now filled with trees, on account of a prophecy of "Mother Shipton"‡ connected with it, to the effect that it would successively be filled with water, trees, and blood, which prophecy, it is said, has been literally fulfilled; the reception of dead bodies being an allowable fulfilment of the last decade.

Mother Shipton.

In one of the registers for 1653-63 is found the following entry :—" September yᵉ Twenty second one thousand six hundred and sixty Thomas Man minister of yᵉ Gospell by

1660. Induction of Mr. Mann.

---

* Northern Memoirs by Richard Franck.
† The site is now used as the cemetery.
‡ Mother Shipton was born near the Dropping Well at Knasbrough, in 1487.

96   ANNALS OF

A.D. 1660. vertue of a Mandate from John Neile Archdeacon of Cleeve-land Batchelor of Divinity was inducted into ye Parish Church of North Allerton; Reall, Actuall & Corporall pessession being given him to ye whole & every Member of ye same parish of North Allerton by Christopher Foster Vicar of Leeke."

CHR. FORSTER cler.*

The Restoration.   The commonwealth may be said to have been practically at an end when Richard Cromwell signed his abdication, but it was not until General Monk's submission that the king was recalled and the monarchy fully restored. Lingard says that Lambert, one of Cromwell's ablest generals, on hearing of Monk's submission, "disbanded his army and parted with his officers at Northallerton with tears."† Lambert died in banishment.

The army disbanded at Northallerton

Bishop Cosin.   John Cosin, S.T.P., was elected bishop of Durham, 2nd Nov., 1660; consecrated 2nd Dec., and the temporalities restored 14th of the same month. He died 15th Jan., 1671, aged 77; in April his remains passed through Northallerton to be interred at Bishop Auckland.‡ He left by will £2 to the poor of this town. The following amusing letter refers to his domestic affairs:—

DARLINGTON, July 29th, 1662.

Amusing letter.   Sir,—I am come as farr as this place to meet the judge, who lay last night at Allerton, but is not come yett. We are prepared to entertaine him nobly at Durham castle.......Pray will you go to the Woolsacke in the Poultre near the Compter, Mr. Turford's shop, and there buy a gallon of his best oyle, and barrel of his Luca olives, if he has any fresh and very good come in; buy them in the same long and slender barrills they came in, and tell him the last oyle I had of him was none of his best. You may please to pay him out of my lord's money, and account it with me. If you can find any large good damaske prunes, which are not easily got, we want some for my lord, which pray gett for him. These things you may send any day from Billingsgate to Newcastle. Direct them to Mr. Jo. Blackiston's, at his house in Pilgrim-Street, *but not towne clerke*, sir Jo. Marley giving him £300 for it, to conclude all disputes, who intends it for his sonne. Sam Davison§ says, his brother

---

* Vide page 83.   † Vide Lingard VIII. 293.
‡ See Appendix.
§ Steward of the Halmot court, married Elizabeth, dau. of bishop Cosin, and widow of sir Thomas Burton.

Cosin* shall not want. I have a great minde to send his truncke with his clothes, if you know whither I may direct it. If you see him my service to him; tell him if he will but go to church with us, and doe as others doe amongst them, he may goe to heaven in good company without borrowing the keyes of the gates at Rome. My service to your wife. Your affectionate, humble servant, EDW. ARDEN.—For his hon'ble friend Mr. Myles Stapylton, at Mr. Hinde's house in the new buildings in Lothbury.

On the fly leaf at the end of the third register of baptisms are the following memoranda :—

Licenses granted 1661 for eating of flesh to y^{ose} sick persons,—

Elizabeth ye daughter of Mr. Patrick Ogilvy } Feb. 18, 1661.
Frances ye daughter of Mr. Patrick Ogilvy }

William Flower, sonne of Thomas Flower, deceased, went to Camebridge the eightene day of May, in the yeare of our Lord one thousand six hundred fiftie eight.

The Rev. John Hickes, M.A., a younger brother of Dr. Hickes, was born at Newsham; educated at the Northallerton grammar school and Trinity College, Dublin. He was first minister of Stoke Damerell, Devonshire, which living being in the gift of the crown, he was obliged to quit at the restoration; when he removed to Saltash, in Cornwall, where he was ejected by the Act of Uniformity in 1662. In 1675, having published a pamphlet complaining of the Conventicles Act, and of the oppression of many honest men in Devonshire, two king's messengers were sent to apprehend him as a state criminal. "It happened," says Dr. Calamy, in his Noncomformists Memorial, "that upon the road John Hickes fell into the company of these messengers, having no suspicion of them. He travelled all the morning and dined with them, when they talked with great freedom against one John Hickes, as an ill man and a great enemy to the Government. He bore with their scurrility till dinner was over, and then going to the stable to his horse, of which he was always tender, he there gave them to understand that he was the person they had so vilified, and to teach them to govern their tongues better in time to come, took his cane and corrected them till they begged his pardon. He then mounted his horse and rode to London." Upon his arrival he procured

A.D. 1660.

1661.
Curious entries.

1662.
John Hickes.

An amusing adventure.

---

* John Cosin, the bishop's only surviving son, whom he laments in his will as his *lost and only son* John Cosin, twice forsook the protestant religion, having been perverted by the Jesuits, and at last took orders in the church of Rome. He, in fact, left England under his maternal name of (Christopher) Blackiston, and professed himself in a convent at Paris. No threats or intreaties could persuade him to return, and his subsequent history is unknown. —*Longstaffe's Darlington.*

G

A.D. 1662.

an introduction to the king (Charles II.) with whom he pleaded so successfully, that he not only obtained indemnity for himself, but for all the Devonshire Noncomformists. In the ensuing reign he unhappily joined the duke of Monmouth's army, and escaping from Sedgemoor, sought refuge at the house of lady Alice Lisle. On account of this kindness in receiving him, her ladyship was accused of comforting and assisting rebels, and was tried at Winchester, August 27th, 1685. The jury thrice brought her in "Not guilty," but Jeffreys expostulated with them so vehemently, and threatened an attaint, that after another consultation, they gave a reluctant verdict of "guilty." Jeffreys sentenced her ladyship to be burnt alive the next day. This excess of cruelty moved the pity and indignation even of devotees of the crown. The clergy of Winchester cathedral remonstrated with the chief justice, who, brutal as he was, was not mad enough to risk a quarrel with them; he consented to put off the execution five days, during which time many applications for pardon for her were made to the king, who said, that he had given Jeffreys a promise not to pardon her; and the utmost that could be obtained was commutation from burning to beheading. Her ladyship was executed in the market place of Winchester, in her seventieth year, declaring, with her dying breath, that the judge omitted to recount her defence to the jury. Hickes himself was soon afterwards convicted, and in a letter written just before his death, he says, "my brother, the dean, has gone up to London to see what could be done for me." He was, however, hanged shortly afterwards at Glastonbury.

The font in Northallerton Church.

The original font seems to have been destroyed or made away with in some other way during the great rebellion, in common with many others in this neighbourhood; and the same hand appears to have been employed in restoring them. The present font, which is figured below, is a plain and tasteless piece of work, supported on the same column which sustained the former one. It is octangular and on four of its sides contains the following legends:—T. M. [Thomas Mann, vicar], 1662.—R. C.—I. S.—G. W.—T. D.—These latter being the initials of the four churchwardens of the time. A wooden pyramidal cover was formerly suspended from the roof beneath the gallery, and worked with a pulley, upon which there was some carving of no very remarkable character.

1663.
The Castle Soke Mills.

A short distance from the moat stood the Castle Mills, for the repairing of which a great part of the stone from the ruins of the episcopal palace or manor house was, by the following grant, bearing date the 26th day of September, 1663, by Dr.

John Cosins, bishop of Durham, given to Thomas Lascells, A.D. 1663. esq., of Northallerton:—

"To John Danby, gent., tenant of the Hall Garth, North Allerton.

"Whereas I am informed there is a great decay in the Castle Mills of North Allerton; and that without some speedy remidie one of them is likely to fall to the ground, whereby a considerable rent due to the bishoprike of Durham would be extinguished; and in regard I am informed that the stone in the mannour house there will be very convenient to supply those ruins and defects aforesaid:

"These are therefore to require you to suffer Thomas Lascells, or some appointed by his order, to take downe and carry away from the said mannour house, one hundred and twenty fother, for the works aforesaid; as also for repairing some other defects in the markett place in North Allerton.

"And this shall be your sufficient warrant herein. Given under my hand and seal manuel, this 26th September, in the year of our Lord God, 1663.

"Jo. DURESME."

In the following year, bishop Cosins gave orders to John Danby, his steward of the manor, to enforce all the inhabitants of Northallerton, and its parish or vicinity, to have their corn ground at these mills, as being the soke mills of the manor. Little is known of the subsequent history of these mills, and not a vestige now remains.

1664.

> 'Tis gone, and merely left a name,
> Gone like the meteor's rapid light.

From the reign of queen Elizabeth to that of king Charles II., tradesmen coined small money or tokens, for convenience of trade; the figures and devices were various, and the materials of lead, tin, copper, or brass. Every tradesman who issued this useful kind of specie, was obliged to take it again when brought to him. In large towns where many were in circulation, tradesmen kept a sorting box, into the partitions of which they put the money of the respective tradesmen, which at stated periods they exchanged either for their own tokens or silver. In this manner they proceeded until the year 1672, when Charles II. ordering a sufficiency of copper coin to be issued for the exigencies of commerce, these practices of the tradesmen were no longer useful or necessary. The following tradesmen's tokens were struck at Northallerton:—

1667. Tradesmen's tokens.

A.D. 1667.
1. O. EDMVND . BAVSTOW . IN ⁎ *A Coat of Arms between the letters* E $^B_.$ I.
   R. NORTH . ALLERTON . 1667 ⁎ *In the Field.* HIS HALF PENY.
2. O. THO. REDMAYNE . KINGS ⁎ *A Post Boy on Horseback, at full speed.*
   R. ARMS . NORTHALLERTO$^N_.$ ⁎ *In the Field.* T $^R_.$ M.
3. O. WM. HUTTON . OF NORTH. ⁎ ....
   R. ALLERTON . HATTER . 1669 ⁎ ....HIS HALF PENY.
4. O. FRANCIS . RYMER . OF . NORTH ⁎ *The Mercers' Arms.*
   R. ALLERTON . MERCER . 1670 . *In the Field.* HIS HALF PENY. F ⁎ R.

1669.
John Neile.

John Neile, D.D., became vicar of Northallerton in 1669. He was formerly scholar and fellow of Pembroke Hall, Cambridge, and rector of Beeford. He became archdeacon of Cleveland in 1638, but was deprived of his preferments because he would not comply with the prevailing party against the king and church. After the siege of York he fled from place to place until reduced to the utmost poverty; but when Charles II. ascended the throne he was restored to all his preferments, and became chaplain to his majesty. When he came to Northallerton, he exchanged his living of Beeford for that of Sigston, and was thus vicar of Northallerton and rector of Sigston at the same time. He became dean of Ripon in 1675, and died there.

1671.
Funeral of
Bishop Cosin.

The following certificate from the College of Arms, of the death and funeral ceremonies of John Cosin, bishop of Durham, may be interesting to Northallerton readers:—

"The Right Reverend Father in God, John, Lord Bishop of Durham, departed this life at his lodgings in the street called Pell Mell, within the suburbs of Westminster, upon the fifteenth day of January, anno 1671, being then lxxvii yeares of age, had, in order to his funerall at Auckland in the Bishoprick of Durham (as by his last will and testament was appointed), his corps wrapt in cere-cloth, and coffin'd with lead: and upon Friday 19° Aprill next ensuing thence conveyed in an herse drawn by six horses, with banner-rolls on each side, borne by gentlemen of quality, through the Strand and Chancery-lane to the end of Gray's Inn-lane: a solemne proceeding made by seventy-seven poore men in mourning gowns, led by two conductors with black staves; and after them his servants, with divers gentlemen, &c. Then his Chaplains. Next the great banner borne by Miles Stapylton, esq. After him Rougedragon, Pursuivant at Armes. Then York Herald, bearing the crosyer, and Norroy King of Armes, the miter; the chief mourner and his assistants all in their gowns and hoods following in coaches. Whence it was carryed the same night to Welling in Hertfordshire, and so by several stac'ons to Northallerton in Yorkshire, and upon Saturday xxvij° Apr: to Durham, the greatest part of the gentry, with many of the clergy of that county Palatine, meeting it at the river Tese, and attending thereon to that city, into which a solemne proceeding on horseback was made from Farwell-Hall (a mile distant), the Mayor and Aldermen standing within the West-gate in their liveries, and following it to the castle; whence after a short stay, a new proceeding being form'd on feet, it was borne to the Cathedrall a little before evening prayer-time in this manner:

A.D. 1671.

" First, two conductors with black gowns and staves. Then the poore of those his two Hospitalls of Durham and Auckland by him founded. Next servants to gentlemen. Then his owne servants. After them gentlemen, esquires, and knights (all in mourning), with many clergymen of that Dioces in their canonicall habits. Next to them five of his chaplains. Then Sir Gilbert Gerrard,* bart., Shireeve of the same county Palatine. Next to him the bishopp of Bristoll. Then the great banner, crosyer, and myter (carryed as before expressed), and the corps by eight men in gowns, under a large pall of velvett supported by four prebends of that cathedrall. On each side thereof the banner-rolls were likewise born, as abovesaid. After which the chief mourner and his assistants in close mourning, and after them the Mayor and Aldermen of Durham with a multitude of chief gentry thereabouts, the whole quire in their surplices falling in next to the chaplain at the entrance of the church-yard. And thus coming to the upper end of the middle isle of that cathedrall, the poore people, conductors, and servants dividing themselves, the rest entered the quire, and placed the corps in the midst thereof, where it conntinued till Munday ensuing, and then was carryed to Bishopp Auckland (about seven miles distant) in the like manner as into Durham, at which place the poore of the hospitalls before menc'oned attending, were added to the proceeding made again on foot from the markett crosse there to that sumptuous chapell adjoyning to the castle by him totally built, where, after evening service regularly compleated, and a sermon preach'n by the learned Dr. Bazier, one of the prebends of Durham, it was solemnly interr'd in a faire vault prepared under a large stone of black marble, the bishopp of Bristoll performing the office of buriall.

" This worthy prelate was sonn of Giles Cosin, sometime citizen of Norwich in Norfolk; and having been educated in Caius colledge, in Cambridge, became at length so eminent for his learning, that he was advanced to the degree of Doctor of Divinity, afterwards Prebendary in the cathedrall church of Durham, then to the archdeaconry of the East-Riding of Yorkshire; next to the rectory of Branspeth in the county

* M.P. for Northallerton, 1661 to 1681. See Appendix.

A.D. 1671. Palatine of Durham, where he beautified that parochiall church in an extraordinary measure. After which he was constituted master of St. Peter's colledge (com'only called Peter-house) in Cambridge, and vice-chancellor of that university; then dean of Peterborough and chaplain in ordinary to king Charles the First, of blessed memory, as also of king Charles the Second; in all of which places and employments his deportment was with such gravity and exemplary piety as that at the beginning of the late unparalleled rebellion raysed by the schismatiques of this kingdom, he was miserably persecuted and oppress'd, by plunder of his goods, sequestrac'on on all his estates, and seventeen years exile.

"Upon the restaurac'on of our present Sovereign king Charles the Second, this venerable person being consecrated bishopp of Durham did amply repaire the castles of Durham and Auckland, and likewise the bishopp's house at Darlington, which then were very ruinous, and enrich'd the chapells belonging to those two castles with divers pieces of faire gilt plate, books and other ornaments, with purpose that they should remain to his successors in that bishoprick for ever; the cost thereof amounting to twenty-six thousand pounds. He likewise built and endowed two hospitalls, the one at Durham for eight poore people, the other at Auckland for four, the annual revenue of the first being lxx^{li} and the other xxx^{li}. And neere to his hospitall of Durham rebuilt two schoole-houses to the charge ccc^{li}. He likewise built a faire library neere to his castle of Durham, the charge whereof, with the pictures wherewith he adorned it, amounted to eight hundred pounds, and gave books thereto to the value of two thousand pounds, as also an annuall pension of xx marks for ever to a library keeper there. Moreover upon the building of the bishopp's courts exchequer and chancery, and towards the erecting of two sessions houses at Durham he gave a thousand pounds. He likewise gave to the cathedrall at Durham a faire carved lectern and litany deske, with a large scallop-patten, silver and gilt, for the use of the communicants there, which cost xlv^{li}. Also the college of dissolved prebends at Auckland, purchased by sir Arthur Haselrigg and by him forfeited to the king, which his majestie thereupon gave to his lordship in fee, he hath given to his successors for ever, the value thereof being cccxx^{li}."

* * * * * *

"He took to wife Frances, daughter of Marmaduke Blakeston, son of sir William Blakeston, of Blackston in com'. Palat. Dunelm, knt., by whom he had issue John his only son, and four daughters, viz.: Mary wife of sir Gilbert Gerrard of Fickerton in com'. Linc. bart. 2. Elizabeth, first married to Henry Hutton, a younger son to sir Ricard

Hutton of Goldesborough in com'. Ebor, knt. one of justices of the court of common pleas; next to sir Thomas Burton of Brampton in com'. Westmorl. knt. and lastly to Samuell Davison of Wingate-grange in com'. Palat. Dunelm. son to sir Alexander Davison late of Blakeston in the same county Palat. knt. 3. Frances, marryed to Charles Gerard, brother to sir Gilbert Gerard, bart. before mentioned : and fourthly, Anne, wife of Dennis Greenvile (a younger son to sir Beville Greenvile of Kilkhampton in com'. Cornwl. knt. brother to John, earle of Bathe) now archdeacon of Durham, rector of Easington and Elwyke in com'. Palat. Dunelm, and chaplain in ordinary to king Charles the Second." *[A.D. 1671.]*

William Neile, M.A., son of the former vicar of Northallerton, succeeded his father in 1675. He was a fellow of Jesus college, Cambridge. He died in 1685. *[1675. William Neile]*

The following letter is preserved in the British museum, entitled " A congratulatory Leter of Thanks from the Corporation [Borough] of Northallerton in the county of York, to their two Representatives in Parliament upon the advice of the late Prorogation ; published for an Example to the Kingdom in general." *[1680. Letter of thanks to Members.]*

To Sir Gilbert Gerrard, Bart., and Sir Henry Calverly, Knt.

Northallerton, January 14th, 1680.

The unexpected and suddain News of this day's post preventing us from sending those due acknowledgements which the greatness of your Services, for the publick good have merited from us ; We have no better way (now left us) to express our Gratitude and the high Resentments of your actions, before and in your last Sessions of Parliament, then to manifest our approbation thereof, by an assurance that if a dissolution of this present Parliament happen, since you have evidenced so sufficiently your affections to his Majestie's Royal Person, and endeavours for the preserving the Protestant Religion, our Laws and Liberties ; We are now resolved, if you are pleased, to comply with us, to continue you as our Representatives ; and we do therefore beg your acceptance thereof, and farther that you will continue your station during this Prorogation, faithfully assuring you that none of us desire to give, or occasion you the Expence or Trouble of a journey in order to your election (if such happen), being so sensible of the too great Expence you have been at already in the careful discharging the trust and confidence reposed in you by Gentlemen,

SIRS,
Your obedient, faithful friends and servants,
THOMAS LASCELS, RICHARD LUMBLY,
with sixty more.

A.D. 1680.   The above letter is thus spoken of in "An address to the Honourable City of London and all the Shires and Corporations, concerning their choice of a New Parliament, &c." "Give me leave to insert a President worthy both the consideration and imitation of all the Shires and Corporations in England; it is a most generous letter written since this late Prorogation from the honest burgesses of Northallerton, to their representatives whose Worth and Loyalty deserve Immortal Fame, and to be recorded as an honourable example both now and hereafter, for all other Boroughs."

1686.
John Harper.   John Harper, M.A., became vicar of Northallerton in 1686. He was formerly vicar of Berwick-upon-Tweed. He died in 1694.

Thomas Smelt   On November 19th, 1686, Mr. Thomas Smelt, master of the Northallerton grammar school, was buried in the parish church-yard. "He was," says Dr. Hickes, "the best master the school ever had; and, although he had not received a university education, he was an excellent grammarian, both of Latin and Greek, diligent in his office, and vigilant in his care and observation of the boys. He was, nevertheless, much given to drink. Sometimes he would drink two days together; but he kept his school in such excellent order, and his scholars made such proficiency under him, that the town overlooked this fault in him, and valued him as a blessing sent from God, there being in those parts none comparable to him for the instruction of youth. He was also a great loyalist and cavalier, though he concealed his principles, which upon some occasions, however, would discover themselves in the school. North Alverton being a noted thoroughfare on the northern road through which part of the army of those times, both horse and foot, did often march; and we observed that as soon as he heard the sound of a drum or trumpet, his countenance did always fall, and it usually was a good while before he could recollect himself and reform his disordered looks. The officers would sometimes come to beg play-days, but he would never grant it; and once one of Cromwell's great commanders, whose name I have forgot, lying in the town, he sent one of the officers in his name to beg a play-day, but as I remember he would not grant it, and coming to the knowledge of the boys, who went to petition the major-general (Lambert) to make that request to him (Mr. Smelt), chastised them in a most severe manner, and had like to have turned them out of school."*

1687.
Archbishop
Palliser.   By an entry in the register book of charities, copied from another book of accounts, it appears that the sum of £20 which was subsequently increased to £100, by several

* Vide Dr. Hickes' Life of Kettlewell,

charitable benefactions from archbishop Palliser and others, A.D. 1687.
to the poor of this parish, after being laid out in a turnpike
security, was, by a resolution of the select vestry in 1788,
again called in, and expended in re-building the hospital
called *Maison Dieu*.

The entry runs as follows :—

Memorandum.—Wee the minister, churchwardens, and over- Palliser's
seers of the poor of the parish of North Allerton, in the North Charity.
Riding of the county of Yorke: doe hereby acknowledge that
we have the day and yeare above mentioned received from the
hands of Mr. James Whiston, of Beedall, in the said Riding, the
sum of twenty pounds, being the guift of Dr. William Palliser,
now the most Reverend Father in God his Grace the Lord-
archbishop of Cassell, in the kingdom of Ireland, to the poore
of the parish of Northallerton, which had the honour to have
the said archbishop instructed in his first school education in
it, whose will and pleasure is that the said sume of twenty
pounds should be putt out to interest in a safe hand, and the
person who borrows the sume to finde two sufficient bonds-
men for the greater security of the said money till it can be
secured upon land, which the said archbishop desires may be
done as soone as conveniently it can by the said minister,
churchwardens, and overseers of the poore, or their successors, who are also to receive the interest of the said twenty
pounds yearly, and every year ; and to distribute the same
every Christmas Day to the most needfull poore of the said
parish, according to their discressions. The said sum of
twenty pounds to remain a fund for the use of the said poore
for ever.

And we beseech Allmighty God who takes such charity
as done unto himselfe to recompense it an hundredfold into
the donors bosome."

Amongst the churchwarden's accounts for 1687, the Curious entry.
following entries appear :—Given to a poore gentlewoman,
2s. 6d. ; paid the spirituall men their fees, 2s. 6d.

At the general quarter sessions of the peace for the North- 1688.
Riding, held at Northallerton, by adjournment, the 17th July, A loyal
1688, the justices there assembled addressed king James II., address.
to express their joy and gratitude "for the great blessing God
Almighty had bestowed on his sacred majesty and the
kingdom, by the happy birth of his royal highness the prince
of Wales." They not only congratulate with him, as they
say, for this blessing, but pray and wish for his long life and
health, and the increase of his royal family ; that after ages
might know and enjoy an equality of that peace and plenty ;
in which they, through his wise and just government, (to
the envy of their neighbours), then flourished.* A few

* Gazette.

A.D. 1688.   months after the presenting of this loyal address, the king, with his queen and infant son, was compelled to desert his throne and kingdom. The pretender, introduced by Swift in lines on the prayer prepared by the bishops of Chester, (Thomas Cartwright,) Peterborough, (Thomas White,) and Durham, (the hon. Nathaniel Crewe,)

> Two Toms and Nat, in council were sat
> To rig up a new thanksgiving,
> With a dainty fine prayer, for the birth of an heir,
> That's neither dead nor living.

The Lord Wharton Charity.   Philip, fourth lord Wharton, by deed appropriated the clear yearly rents, issues, and profits, arising from time to time out of Synithwaite and other lands in the county of York, as a perpetual fund for the purchasing yearly 1050 bibles for the use of the poor of Northallerton, Bedale, Thirsk, and Boroughbridge. The ninth clause recites "That there be 10 catechisms and as many bibles delivered each year to so many poor children in the above-mentioned places, and that on the day of delivery of the bibles there shall be sermons preached." The child, before it shall receive, or be entitled to receive the book, shall be taught to read and be able to say by heart the catechism and some of the prayers therewith sent, according to the establishment of the church of England, as well as the 1st, 15th, 25th, 37th, 101st, 113th, and 145th psalms; the name and age of the child to be written in the book.

1694. **Charles Neile.**   Charles Neile, M.A., was instituted to the vicarage of Northallerton, in 1694. He was a minor canon of Durham; and died in 1718.

The Kettlewell Charity.   By an indenture of lease, dated March 9th, 1694, John Kettlewell conveyed to Leonard Smelt and five others a messuage and farm commonly called "Low Fields," situate within the township of Brompton, in the parish of Northallerton, upon trust, from time to time, to suffer the minister for the time being of the town and parish of Northallerton, and two good and substantial inhabitants of the town and parish of Northallerton and Brompton to receive the rents and profits of the said premises, and to dispose of and apply the same as follows :—

Religious Books.   "To lay out yearly, or as often as need shall require, the sum of £2 10s., part of the said rent, in buying bibles, common prayer books, or such like books of practical divinity as the minister and incumbent for the time being should think most convenient, to be distribuied among such poor inhabitants of the said towns as could read, and by reason of their poverty could not buy such books for themselves; and after the poorest and most indigent were furnished therewith, then for providing the like for others of the said towns that might want them, and who should be thought persons likely to make a good and proper use of such books. To employ, if there should be occasion, a yearly sum of £5 in physic, and things necessary in the recovery of the health of such poor persons of the said townships, as by reason of their poverty were exempt from payment to the church and poor, or for such other persons of the said townships as were really poor and sick, and not able to be at the charge of physic and things necessary. To employ the yearly sum of £5 for clothes for such poor widows or widowers, or other poor housekeepers within the said townships as were in want, and had been industrious, and constantly frequenters of the church, and of sober and peaceable demeanour, such clothing to be provided and delivered before November 1st, yearly. To employ £4 yearly in teaching and instructing the children of such poor people aforesaid; the girls to read English intelligibly, and to knit and sew so as to render them capable of getting an honest livelihood; and the boys to be taught to read and to write, and cast accounts so as to qualify them for being bailiffs or servants to gentlemen, or to be set out to some honest trade. To employ the yearly sum of £6 for setting out yearly one boy, the son of some poor person inhabiting within one of the said townships, such as should be fatherless or motherless, if both, to have the preference, and always one who could say the church catechism, and could read, write, and cast accounts as aforesaid, and upon further trust, that in case there should be any surplus of the said rents, after the several trusts aforesaid should have been performed, or in case there should not be occasion yearly to lay out so much on any one of the particular purposes aforesaid, to lay out and employ the same to such other of the purposes aforesaid, as the said minister and said two inhabitants, or any two of them, should think fit, or else in furnishing some apprentice in one of the said townships, or one who had served his apprenticeship out of one of the said townships, if he was set out by virtue of that trust towards setting him up in his trade, and buying him work tools, so as the sum of any one apprentice did not exceed 40s.: and upon further trust, that if it should happen, that if there were any youth of either of the said townships, of piety, parts, and good improvement in school learning, whose friends of themselves were not able to maintain him at either of the universities of Oxford or Cambridge, but who might be educated there by the help of such a sum yearly as this charity might supply, the said minister and trustees when they should see cause, should employ part, or the whole, as need should be, of the yearly rent and profits of the said premises towards

A.D. 1694

Physic.

Clothes.

Education.

Sundry objects.

University education.

A.D. 1694. the maintenance of such youth at either of the aforesaid universities, for the full space of four years and no longer."

The above directions, however, are not now strictly adhered to by the trustees, but the money is distributed more in accordance with the advanced requirements of the times.

1695. In the fourth register of burials of the parish church under date December 15th, 1695, is entered the burial of a Dutchman's child.

1697. Petition to Parliament. On the 15th February, (10 Wm. III.) a petition of the ancient borough of Northallerton, in the county of York, was presented to the house, and read: setting forth, That quantities of lead, butter, and other commodities are daily carried from thence to Burrough-Briggs; and thence by water upon the river Ouze to several parts of this kingdom, and beyond the seas; but in case the rivers Ayre and Calder be made navigable as is intended by a bill now in this house, it will drain the river Ouze, and deprive the petitioners of the benefit they receive thereby: And pray, that the said rivers may not be made navigable. *Ordered*, that the consideration of the said petition be referred to the committee to whom the said bill is committed.*

Northallerton Ale. "The town," says Langdale, "was never incorporated, neither is there any particular manufactory carried on therein. But it appears formerly to have enjoyed a distinguished reputation for the particular manufacture, if we may be allowed the expression, of *Strong Ale*, which we are sorry to find, says Langdale, both here and everywhere else, very much on the decline. The following couplet occurs in a poem by Giles Mornington in praise of Yorkshire Ale, published in York in this year :—

> " Northallerton, in Yorkshire, does excel,
>   All England, nay, all Europe, for strong ale,"

and the person it seems most celebrated at that time for making this "*humming stuff*" was Mrs. Bradley. †

1698. Quakers buried in the churchyard. In the fourth register of burials of the parish church under date 1698, the following entry appears :—June ye 5th, 1698.

James Whitehead, buried } Quakers, both.
Elizabeth Metcalfe, buried

Another petition. On the 7th March, (11 Wm. III.) a petition of the shoemakers in and about this borough was presented to the house and read: setting forth, That some attempt had been made to export tanned leather, which, if permitted, would impoverish and ruin the petitioners, and especially the dealers in thin work, there being persons buying up great quantities of

* Commons Journal.   † Vide Appendix.

calves' skins to send beyond sea, so that the petitioners would not be able to furnish themselves at any rates to carry on their trades, which by the duty on leather was brought so low that they could scarce live; and praying that the exportation of tanned leather might be stopped effectually. *Ordered*, that the said petition do lie upon the table.*

Entry in parish books :—Paid to ringers when the quene was proclaimed, 5s.

Entry in parish books :—To ringers on coronation day, 5s., oyle for bells, 3d.

Ralph Thoresby, the antiquary, visited Northallerton, which he thus records in his diary—

A.D. 1698.

1701.

1702.

1703. Thoresby, the Antiquarian.

" May 17. Along the banks of Swale, are the very pleasant gardens of sir William Robinson,† lately lord mayor of York, but a few miles after a more doleful object of Mr. Busby hanging in chains, for the murder of his father-in-law, Daniel Anty, formerly a Leeds clothier, who having too little honesty to balance his skill in engraving, &c., was generally suspected for coining, and other indirect ways of attaining that estate which was the occasion of his death, even within sight of his own house. Thence through Sand Hutton, and both the Otteringtons to North Alverton, where we lodged. Upon the road we had a distant prospect of Ounsberry or Rosemary Toppin, a remarkable height, being a mark for the mariners, and a nigher for the growing market town of Thresk, which sends burgesses to parliament, as also does North Alverton—witness ' Parliamentarius ' upon a tomb in the church, for the inscriptions whereof *vide* the later book of my collections. Was pretty much out of order by the excessive heat, and too unadvisedly drinking a hasty draught of new milk ; but after prayer and a tolerable night's rest, was better in the morning, blessed be the God of my mercies ! "

" 18. Went to view the town ; found an hospital, called the earl of Carlisle's,‡ but was the benefaction of another family they matched into, and is only paid by them ; it is for four persons, who have each fifty shillings per annum ; transcribed some epitaphs in the church, of which Mr. Francis Kaye was thirty-two years vicar, who left £10 per annum to four widows. I inquired after Mr. George Meriton, an attorney of North Alverton, who writ ' Anglorum Gesta,' ' Landlord's Law,' ' Nomenclatura Clericalis,' and somewhat of the northern dialect, &c., but could not hear anything

* Commons Journal.
† M.P. for Northallerton, 1688 to 1695. Vide Appendix.
‡ The earl of Carlisle formerly nominated the poor people to the Maison Dieu, as a descendent of Leonard, son of lord Dacres of Gilsland, who married the heiress of the Strangways family.—*Tanner.*—*Gale.*

A.D. 1703. further, than that he removed into Ireland, where he was said to be made a judge, but whether alive or dead, unknown. From North Alverton, we passed by several country villages, but of no great consideration, till we passed the river Tees."

"On his return, May 21, the river Tees not being fordable by reason of the late rains, we went about by Croft bridge. We baited at North Alverton; thence we rode by Sand Hutton, Topcliffe, &c., to Burrowbridge; had wet weather, and one smart thunder-shower, but blessed be God, without any prejudice."

Thoresby often passed through North Allerton. On April 6, 1680, at the age of 22. "Thence to North Alverton, and so to Darlington, expecting there to have met with captain Widdrington." May 22, 1680. "From thence [Durham] to North Alverton, and having dried us there (it being a most stormy rainy day), to Buroughbridge, where we lodged all night." Sept. 6, 1681. "We rode to Burrowbridge, and thence to Topcliffe, where, supposing we should not stay long, left my charged pistols in the bags, which at my mounting again, being gone, caused a great jealousy of some design against us; and the rather, because Mr. H. and his debtor had come to high words, and the landlord took the debtor's part, and denied to send for the ostler, till upon some brisk compliments, we were just for riding to depose upon oath before sir M. Robinson, and then in the very same straw we had sought carefully before, they were found, and one of them where the horse could not get to; which more fully manifested the knavery, as also their leaving, for a pretence, the red bags in the holster; but we got very well, though late, to North Alverton that night."

July 7, 1707. Thoresby sets down "Received a kind visit from Roger Gale, esq., of Scruton, a learned and ingenious gentleman, eldest son of the excellent dean Gale, and parliament-man for North Alverton."

The following letter from Dr. John Sharp, archbishop of York, is fraught with interest.

Bishopthorpe, Sept. 7, 1708.

GOOD MR. THORESBY,

I received your letter, and because I could not answer it myself, I sent it to Mr. Nelson,* whose answer (which I

---

* Robert Nelson, esq., a pious and learned writer, the reverend friend and executor of the rev. John Kettlewell, was born in London, in 1656; educated at St. Paul's school, and Trinity College, Cambridge. He was author of many popular works—"A Companion to the Festivals and Fasts of the Church of England;" "The Practice of the True Devotion;" "The Whole Duty of a Christian;" &c. He died in 1714; buried at St. George the martyr, Queen's Sq., London.

received this morning) I here send you. I likewise here send A.D. 1703.
you an original letter of Mr. Kettlewell's, which I had from
Mr. Nelson a post or two before. I had told him likewise
that I must have an autograph of Dr. Hickes's, in case you
had not any before. But in answer to this, Mr. Nelson tells
me that that very post dean Hickes was a-writing to you.

I did not know before I read this letter of Mr. Nelson's,
that Dr. Palliser, archbishop of Castells, [Cashel] was a
Yorkshireman. So that now we have a list of six archbishops
(five of them primates), and that within the compass of thirty
years, viz., from 1662 to 1692, all born in Yorkshire; and, I
believe, all of them having their education there (I mean as
to school learning), viz., archbishop Bramhall, primate of
Ireland, who was born at Pontefract, and trained up at school
there till he went to Cambridge. He was one of the most
learned divines of the age, and none ever better defended the
church of England against papists, fanatics, and hobbists
than he did. 2. Archbishop Margetson, his successor in the
archbishopric of Armagh, who was born at Drighlington, in
the parish of Birkstall, or Birstall, and who there founded
and liberally endowed a school for the education of boys in
grammar learning. .3. This archbishop of Cashel, Dr. Palliser,
who, whether he be now living or dead, I do not know.
4. Archbishop Lamplugh, my immediate predecessor, who
was born at Thwing, in the East-Riding of Yorkshire. The
other two I need not name to you.

I know you delight in these sorts of memorandums. But
if I have now told you nothing but what you knew before, I
beg your pardon.

I truly thought that our famous Dr. Ratcliffe had been
bred at Wakefield school, as Dr. Bentley was, but this
account of Mr. Nelson's says otherwise.*

I have no more at this time, but only to beg of you to
present my service to all friends at Leeds, Mr. Thornton,
Mr. Killingbeck, &c., and to assure you that I am,

Your sincerely affectionate friend,

J. EBOR.†

* Vide page 93.
† Archbishop Sharp was himself a Yorkshireman, being born at Bradford,
in 1644; educated at the grammar school there and at Christ's coll., Cambridge. He was a man of considerable piety and learning, and distinguished
himself by preaching against popery in the reign of James II., which gave
such offence to the court, that an order was sent to the bishop of London to
suspend him; but the bishop having refused on the ground of its being contrary
to law, he as well as Dr. Sharp were suspended by the ecclesiastical commission.
After the revolution he became dean of Canterbury Cathedral, and in 1691
archbishop of York. He died 2nd Feb., 1714; bur. in his cathedral, where a
monument with Corinthian columns is erected to his memory. (See plate in
Drake's Eboracum.) He was the father of Dr. Thomas Sharp, archdeacon of
Northumberland, and the learned Granville Sharp.

112 ANNALS OF

A.D. 1703. [Dr. Samuel Pullen, archbishop of Tuam, was also a Yorkshireman; he was born at Ripley, and was schoolmaster at Leeds. R. T.]

1704. Entry in Parish Books. The following entries appear in the churchwardens' accounts for 1704:—"Paid Mary Brown, for ale, on Easter day, 2s.; paid for a tar-barrell when Tallard* was taken, 1s. 2d.; paid to ye ringers at ye said time, 10s., in ale, 3s.; paid for ringing on gunpowder treason, 13s."

1705. "Paid to ringers when the news came that Ld. Marleborough had obtained the victory over the French at Brabant, 5s."

1706. Viscount Northallerton. On the 9th November, her majesty queen Anne, was pleased to sign a warrant for creating George Augustus, prince electoral of Hanover, a peer of England, by the style and title of baron of Tewksbury, viscount Northallerton, earl of Milford Haven, and marquis and duke of Cambridge; created prince of Wales, 22nd Sept., 1714, K.G.; and ascended the throne as king George II., 11th June, 1727, when all these dignities became merged in the crown.† He married, 2nd September, 1705, the princess Wilhelmina Charlotte Caroline, daughter of John Frederick, marquis of Brandenburgh Anspach, by whom he had two sons, Frederick Lewis,‡ prince of Wales, K.G., born 1709, died *vita patris* 1751; and William Augustus, duke of Cumberland, K.G., born 1721, died 1765, *sine prole*; and five daughters, Anne, princess royal, married to William Henry, prince of Orange; Mary, m. Frederick, prince of Hesse-Cassel; Louisa, m. Frederick V. king of Denmark; and Amelia, and Caroline, who were never married.§

Through some private uneasiness which had subsisted between himself and his father (George I.) this prince, for a considerable time, had been a stranger at court. It is evident, however, that this could not have arisen from any dissension in opinion, as to public measures, for, on his

---

* Marshal Tallard was defeated at the battle of Hochstadt and taken prisoner by the duke of Marlborough, on which occasion he said to the duke, "Your Grace has beaten the finest troops in Europe." The duke answered, "You will except, I hope, those who defeated them." Tallard was brought to England, with 26 other officers of rank, 121 standards, and 179 colours, and remained till 1712, when he returned to Paris, and was created a duke; he died in 1728.

† Nicolas's Synopsis of the Peerage.

‡ This prince mar. in 1736, Augusta, princess of Saxe-Gotha, by whom he had issue five sons—George Augustus, afterwards George III.; Edward Augustus, duke of York, K.G., died in 1767, s.p.; William Henry, duke of Gloucester, K.G., died in 1805; Henry Frederick, duke of Cumberland, K.G., died in 1790, s.p.; Frederick William, died young; and four daughters—Augusta, duchess of Brunswick; Eliza Caroline; Louisa Anne; and Caroline Matilda, queen of Denmark.

§ Smollett. Nicolas.

NORTHALLERTON. 113

ascending the throne, he retained the same ministers and pursued the same system of government which had distinguished his father's reign. That no doubt might remain on the minds of his subjects, as to the religious and political principles by which he intended to be guided, his majesty on the 14th June, 1727, declared in council, that he was decidedly friendly to the protestant succession, and was resolved to maintain inviolable the religion, laws, and liberties of the kingdom, and to adhere to the alliances which his late father had contracted, and which had in no small degree contributed to the tranquility of Europe.

A.D. 1706. Events of his reign.

Actuated by these principles, he determined to espouse the cause of the injured queen, Maria Theresa, whom the king of France, and other continental powers, had combined to deprive of her inheritance. With this view, he sent an English army to the continent, which was joined by a large body of Hanoverian troops, the whole being commanded by the earl of Stair. The next day his majesty followed his soldiers, and, at the battle of Dettingen, fought at the head of his own regiment with peculiar bravery, and his arms were crowned with success. In the following year, war was declared against France; and commodore Anson returned from his voyage round the world. In 1745, the English and their allies were beaten at the battle of Fontenoy, through which the French obtained the ascendancy in Flanders. Encouraged by these events, the grandson of James II. renewed his pretensions to the crown; and, aided by the partisans of the papal faction, effected a landing on the Scottish coast. Success at first seemed to favour their enterprise. A battle was fought at Preston-Pans, in which the English forces under the command of sir John Cope were completely routed, all the infantry except 170 being either killed or made prisoners. In this engagement the brave and pious colonel Gardiner fell on the field of battle. Animated with these favourable omens, the pretender, at the head of his victorious highlanders, determined to push his fortune; and the rapidity of his march threw all England into a state of alarm. But the duke of Cumberland, returning from Flanders at the head of a few regiments, took the command of the forces, and on the 15th of April, 1745, so completely vanquished the rebel army at the battle of Culloden, that the pretender never more became an object either of terror or apprehension.

Although the early part of the reign of George II. was much agitated by a foreign war, by the efforts of rebellion raised by the pretender, and by distracted councils, which much embarrassed the measures of his government, the tide took a decided turn in his favour. The earl of

H

A.D. 1706. Chatham being called to his council, gave a vigorous impulse to public opinion ; and the successes which attended his administration, confirmed the favourable sentiments which his talents and virtues had inspired. It was in no small degree owing to his superior talents, that the French power in the East Indies was nearly annihilated; that their colonies in the western Archipelago were reduced to the dominion of Britain; that Canada was conquered; and that the victory of Minden exalted the reputation of the British soldiery to the highest pitch of military glory. The successes of England upon the ocean were equally triumphant. The victories of her fleets corresponded with the conquests of her armies. Both by sea and land the pride of France was humbled; and the boasted power of that ambitious nation reduced to a state of comparative insignificance, which it has hitherto striven in vain to recover.

"But while the arms of Great Britain," says Smollett, "still prospered in every effort tending to the real interest of the nation, an event happened which for a moment obscured the splendour of her triumphs. On the 25th of October, 1760, George II., without any previous disorder, was in the morning suddenly seized with the agony of death, at the palace at Kensington. He had risen at his usual hour, drank his chocolate, and enquired about the wind, as anxious for the arrival of the foreign mails ; then he opened a window of his apartment, and perceiving the weather was serene, declared he would walk in the garden. In a few minutes after this declaration, while he remained alone in his chamber, he fell down upon the floor; the noise of his fall bringing his attendants into the room, who lifted him on the bed, where he desired in a faint voice, that the princess Amelia might be called; but before she could reach the apartment he had expired. An attempt was made to bleed him, but without effect ; and indeed his malady was far beyond the reach of skill : for when the cavity of the thorax or chest was opened, and inspected by the court-surgeons, they found the right ventricle of the heart actually ruptured, and a great quantity of blood discharged through the aperture into the surrounding pericardium ; so that he must have died instantaneously in consequence of the effusion. Thus died George II., at the age of seventy-seven, after a long reign of thirty-four years."

Character of George II. By the writers of contending factions, his character and talents have been variously estimated. In his temper he is said to have been rather violent. But these momentary impulses rarely occasioned any variation in his conduct, which seems to have been guided by more permanent principles. His attachment to his continental possessions was strong; but through the whole of his life he appeared more friendly to the useful virtues, than to the decorations of external splendour. Rectitude and integrity were conspicuous in his character; and his noble declaration, "there shall be no persecution for conscience sake in my dominions, during my reign," will be transmitted to posterity, to his immortal honour, when his personal courage, and the many splendid events of his reign, shall cease to be remembered, or shall be perused in the pages of history without exciting any particular interest. *A.D. 1706.*

The following entry occurs in the parish books :—" On king Charles's restoration, for ringing, 6s. *1710. King Charles's restoration.*

This nobleman was born at Northallerton in a house on the west side of the main street, exactly opposite to the old Tollbooth, then in the possession of a Mr. Midford. The woman who nursed his grace died a few weeks before him. She said that every time the good old duke passed through the town, he always used to leave a sum of money for the use of the old nurse and her sister. The duke's family name was Smithson —sir Hugh Smithson, of Newby, near Northallerton, father of the duke, was High Sheriff of York in 1738.* *1712. Duke of Northumberland.*

The Rev. Charles Neile, vicar, gave to Northallerton church in this year a crimson pulpit cloth and cushions. *1714. A gift to the Church.*

Cholmley Turner, esq., M.P., and Leonard Smelt, esq., M.P., members for Northallerton, gave to the town a public clock to be placed in the tower of Northallerton church. *Gift of public clock.*

Lady Mary Calverley, widow of sir John Calverley, by her will dated May 10th, 1715, gave the sum of £1500 to be invested at interest, the yearly dividends to be paid amongst any of the poor people residing in any of the parishes between, and including Northallerton and Darlington. The acting trustees are the incumbents for the time being of Northallerton, Brompton, and Darlington, and the charity is distributed towards the relief of the most deserving poor, sick, and infirm people, not receiving parochial relief, in any of the parishes aforesaid ; including (if there should be, in the judgment of the trustees, special circumstances to call for it), any inhabitant or inhabitants of the parishes of Northallerton and Darlington, to be applied in the discretion of the said trustees in medical attendances, provision, fuel, blankets, clothing, or money. *1715. Dame Calverley's Charity.*

Christopher Hunter, M.A., became vicar of Northallerton in 1718. He was formerly curate of Sedgefield. He married Mrs. Mary Metcalfe, of this parish, and died in 1725. *1718. Christopher Hunter.*

* Mann-Dowson Todd's MSS.

A.D. 1718.
Petition to Parliament.

On the 16th January, (5 Geo. I.) a petition of the skinners of this borough was presented to the House of Commons, and read: setting forth, "That great abuses are committed by butchers and others, in flaying sheep-skins and lamb-skins, by cutting holes therein, and gashing and scoring the same, and otherwise; by reason of which abuses such skins are rendered unfit for service, to the great prejudice of the public and all dealers therein; and the revenues are avoided, or lessened, by the abuses aforesaid; and praying, that the said abuses may be redressed." *Ordered*, that the said petition do lie upon the table.*

1720.
Quarter Sessions.

The Quarter Sessions commenced to be held this year at the Vine House, now used as the Cottage Hospital, and continued to be held until 1770.

1721.
Longevity.

On the 14th September, Mrs. Ann Stringer, widow, was interred in the Northallerton churchyard, having attained the advanced age of 108 years.

1722.
Parish records

"Paid ye ringers for ringing on king Geo. birthday, and K.C., birth and return, £1; spent king Geo. cor. 5s."

1726.

In the fifth register of burials of the parish church, under date January 11th, 1726, the following entry appears:—"Robert Smith, some time servant to Mr. Neile, vicar, whose niece and heiresse he marryed."

Thomas Rudd

Thomas Rudd, M.A., became vicar of Northallerton in 1726. He was formerly vicar of S. Oswald, Durham, and resigned the living of Northallerton for the rectory of Washington in 1729.

Registers of Deeds.

The following is an extract from the *Newcastle Courant*, of May 14th, 1726:—"The office for registering of deeds or conveyances for the North-Riding of the county of York, will be kept at Mrs. Lowery's, Fleece Inn, at Thirsk, where attendance will be given every Monday, from ten in the morning till four in the afternoon, by Mr. John Close, of Oulston, near Easingwold; and after the 1st day of June next, attendance will also be given for the like purpose every Wednesday, at the house of Mr. Straker, innholder and postmaster, King's Head, Northallerton."

1727.
The Hartlepool tragedy.

In July, William Stephenson, grocer, Northallerton, was tried at Durham, and sentenced to death, for the murder of Mary Farding (or Fawden), whom he threw into the sea, when pregnant by him, at Hartlepool, near the Maiden's Bower.† A small rock detached from the Town Moor, a few yards to the north of what is called the East Battery, cannot fail, from its singular situation, to attract the notice of a

---

* Commons Journal.

† The name "Maiden Bower," was not derived from this circumstance, as it occurs frequently in the parish register previous to this period.

stranger. The yawning span which separates this rock from the mainland is known by the name of 'Maiden Bower,' and many a tale of 'plighted faith and broken vows' is associated with it.* A ballad called "The Hartlepool Tragedy"† is still remembered and sung by the old inhabitants, founded on "the confession and dying words of William Stevenson (or Stephenson), merchant, late of Northallerton, in the county of York, aged 27 years, who was executed at Durham, on Saturday, the 26th of August, 1727, for the barbarous murder of Mary Fawden, near Hartlepool, in the bishopric of Durham; taken from his own mouth the night before his execution, by a person that went to visit him while in gaol." One of the verses represents him as having lashed the girl to her death :—

A.D. 1727.

> She dreading her fate, alas! when too late,
> Did call out for mercy, whilst I did her beat,
> With the whip in my hand. She, not able to stand,
> Ran backwards, and fell from the rock to the strand.

From another verse we gather that he was a married man, and was thus led to the commission of the crime :—

> I feared she'd breed strife 'twixt me and my wife,
> And that all my friends would lead me a sad life,
> Then Satan likewise did join each surmise,
> And made me a hellish contrivance devise.

In the present century, tradition pointed to a grass-grown rock as the scene of the murder, said to have been separated from the mainland by the action of the sea long after the time of George the First. In the closing week of this reign (June 7th), the sexton was "making Mary Farding's grave," for which, as the churchwardens' accounts set forth, there was paid 1s. 10d. The entry with regard to the above atrocious and premeditated murder relates that " Mary Farding, a stranger, who, by the coroner's inquest was found to be murdered by William Stephenson, merchant in Northallerton, to whom she was pregnant, was buried June 7th, 1727.

In the fifth register of burials of the parish church, under date 1728, we find the following curious entries :—" Mrs. Katharin Conyers, an old maid; Robert Sayer, the bishop's bayliff; Mr. John Romans, attorney (fever); a stranger woman, whose name we could not learn, going to her husband, a soldier."

1728. Entries in the Parish Books.

"To ringers, king George II. proclaimed, 5s.; ditto coronation, 7s. 6d.; ditto birthday, 7s. 6d."

* Vide Sir Cuthbert Sharp's History of Hartlepool.
† Vide Appendix.

A.D. 1729.
Rev. John
Balguy.

The Rev. John Balguy, M.A., son of Thomas Balguy, by his wife Sarah Hathornwhite, a lineal descendant of Dr. Thomas Westfield, bishop of Bristol; was born at Sheffield, 12th Aug., 1686. In 1702 he was admitted at St John's coll., Cambridge; took his B.A. in 1706, and in 1708 entered the family of Joseph Banks, esq., of Scofton, as tutor to his son; in 1710 admitted to deacon's orders, and in 1711 ordained priest. He was introduced to the Liddell family by his friend Mr. Banks, and resided for a time with sir Henry Liddell at Ravensworth castle. In June, 1715, he married Sarah, dau. of Christopher Bromhead, esq., of Sheffield, master cutler in 1696; in 1726 he was admitted M.A.; in 1728 collated by bishop Hoadley to the prebend of south Grantham, in the church of Sarum, and in 1729 obtained the vicarage of Northallerton. He bore a distinguished part in the Bangorian controversy, which ensued on the publication of a sermon preached before George I., in 1717, on the text, "*My kingdom is not of this world*," wherein the bishop of Bangor, Dr. Benjamin Hoadley, advanced opinions regarding the constitution of the church which excited strong opposition from the zealous advocates of ecclesiastical authority. He was the able, but polite, adversary of lord Shaftesbury and other deistical writers. His writings, which were voluminous, were chiefly controversial. For the first four years of his incumbency in North Durham, he never intermitted one week without composing a sermon; but fearing that his son, who was in orders also, might not follow his example, he destroyed almost his whole stock, and committed at one time two hundred and fifty sermons to the flames. His works, independently of his tracts on the Bangorian controversy, occupy four octavo volumes. His remaining sermons, twenty in number, went through at least three editions. His Life was communicated by his son to the "Biographia Britannica." He died at Harrogate, on the 21st September, 1748.

1734.

In the sixth register of baptisms at the parish church under date 1734, the following entry may be seen:—" Ann, bastard daughter of Ann Sherington, bedrid, and about fifteen years of age, baptised privately."

1735.
A female
fanatic.

On Sunday morning, July 20th, Ann Flower, of Northallerton, incited by her husband, a quaker, went into the church during the time of divine service, to the great consternation and confusion of the congregation, or as she termed it "assembly," and though cautioned, nay positively forbidden by the vicar to talk, or as they call it, speak in the church, began to hold forth. The vicar, without further remonstrance, than that it was the apostle's command that a woman should not be suffered to teach in the church, directly led her out, thereby preventing a mob from cooling her frenzy in a neighbouring brick-pond, which they began to threaten, although she said she was sent by the Spirit.*   A.D. 1735.

In pursuance of an Act of Parliament (8 George II., c. 2), the magistrates of the North-Riding selected Northallerton as the place for establishing an office for the registration of deeds for the North-Riding of Yorkshire.   Registration of Deeds.

By indenture of lease dated October 15th, 1737, Elizabeth Raine, widow, conveyed two closes called "Yarn Acres," to George Prissick and others, upon trust, out of the rents and profits thereof, to distribute amongst the poor people of Romanby, the sum of 20s. upon Christmas-eve in every year; and upon further trust, to pay and apply the yearly sum of 40s. to and for four poor children of the township of Northallerton, such as should be thought most deserving, that is to say, 10s. for each of such poor children, 5s. thereof for teaching such to read and write, and 5s. towards providing him with clothes, for three years together, and no longer; upon further trust, to pay and apply the yearly sum of £6 4s. 6d. as follows :—30s. thereof to be laid out in loaves of bread, to be given and distributed by the minister and churchwardens, to each poor family in Northallerton on Christmas-eve; 15s. to be laid out in loaves, and distributed in like manner on Easter-eve: 15s. more on Whitsun-eve; and 52s. to be laid out in bread, and distributed by the said minister and churchwardens twelve pennyworth thereof on every Sunday in the year, among such poor people of Northallerton and Romanby, as should duly attend divine service in the parish church the same day; and 12s. 6d. to be laid out in gloves for the minister and churchwardens, 5s. for the minister, and 2s. 6d. for each of the churchwardens for Northallerton, for their care and trouble in the several distributions aforesaid.   An inscription upon Mrs. Raine's tombstone, on the south side of the church, directs that the bread should be distributed in equal quantities upon her grave-stone and that of her husband, every Sunday, and upon the eves of Christmas, Easter, and Whitsuntide, for ever.†   1737. Raine's Charity.

Since May, 1762, marriages have ceased to be solemnized in York minster. In a list of marriages, extracted from the registers of the minster, by Mr. R. H. Skaife, of York, the following entry appears :—   Marriage in York Minster.

"(1059.) 1737. Aug. 14th. Thomas Carver, of Northallerton, and Mary Brearey, of St. Mary's, in Castlegate. (Lic.)"

If there are any descendants of Mr. Carver now in North-

* Sykes's Local Records.
† It is to be regretted that the provisions of the deed are not now carried out in their integrity.—J. L. S.

A.D. 1737.   allerton, it may be interesting to them to know that this is the only marriage of a Northallerton person in York minster recorded in the registers of the cathedral.

1739.
Right of Election.

The right of election as previously stated was vested in the owners of burgage houses. Oldfield* says, "They were distinguished by the appearance of a certain number of chimneys. The greater part of the burgage-tenures here front the street, and now exist in the form of stables or cow-houses, in which a chimney is preserved as the memorial of the right; others are let out to poor persons at a small annual rent, on the condition of their keeping them in repair; and many are totally ruinous and uninhabited. The vote is in some instances separated from the house, by the practice of granting a lease of the latter for the term of 999 years, subject to an annual peppercorn rent; in either case the vote is considered as being worth £100 more in the purchase than the value of the property."

In 1739 there were in number but 194 houses and a half, and were distinguished from other houses in the town by their having had a right of common on the North-moor, as appears by the deed of partition thereof, which is still extant. Subsequently the houses claiming votes increased to about 204, and it not being known which of them had crept clandestinely into this privilege, it is presumed they who had done so retained the privilege; but the number was then so settled that it could not afterwards be increased. Most of these houses pay a small fee-farm rent to the crown. Boroughs that had obtained this privilege were said to be enfranchised or made free, and were called free boroughs, or *Liberi Burgi.*† It has been supposed by many writers, and sometimes in the courts of law, that every grant of a borough at fee-farm to the burgesses, made them a corporate body; because otherwise their successors could not be bound to pay the rent, and the king might therefore lose his intended profit of the land.‡ But this doctrine has been most successfully combated by Mr. Madox, who expressly states, that many of the king's towns which were not, as well as others which were, corporated, were charged to pay the king yearly a firm for their town, that is to say,—"Towns not corporated might and did hold their town at firm, in like manner as the corporated towns were, by the king's favour, wont to hold." He cites many examples from the great rolls to establish this point.§

1742.
A singular suicide.

On the 27th February, 1742, Mr. Hayes, one of the free porters of Newcastle, set out on a journey to London, and on the next evening arrived at Northallerton; after supper he

* Hist. of Parliament.   † Maver's Arch.
‡ Bro. Abr. tit. Corporations.   § Mad. Fir. Burg. 54.

went to bed in seeming good spirits, but when the servant went to bring away the candle, he was shocked to find him with his belly ripped open and several parts cut away! On being asked the reason for so rash an act, he replied, "*If thine hand offend thee cut it off,*" and immediately expired.

The Castle Hills,* are generally thought to have been Roman works, but as some antiquaries, who have viewed them, have had doubts whether they were of Danish or Roman origin, on account of the interior entrenchment being of a circular form, it may not be uninteresting to insert the observations of that judicious antiquary, Roger Gale, esq., in his letter to Mr. Place:—

"The Romans did not always observe to make their camps square, as Vegetius tells us in his first book, c. 23, ' Interdum Romanorum castra finisse quadrata, interdum trigona, interdum Semirotundo, prout loci qualitas et necessitas postulabat;' and we have several camps in England, undoubtedly Roman from their coins found there, of a round form, some with a double vallum, as Yanesbury, in Wiltshire, and others with a triple, as Camolet, in Somersetshire, and which I believe you have often viewed, Hogmagog, in Cambridgeshire, which, though generally believed to be Danish, is certainly Roman, for I myself have some coins of Valentinian and Valens, dug up there in the year 1685. Perhaps when the Roman discipline was strictly kept up under their commonwealth and first emperors, they might still observe the exactness we read of in setting out their camps ; but when they relaxed in the Bas empire, and their armies were composed of several barbarous nations, negligence crept upon them, and they grew remiss in their encampments, as well as in other parts of military science; and where an army consisted of the greatest part not Romans, they might easily fall into that method of fortifying their camps which was most usual to the country where those troops were chiefly levied."†

This encampment consisted of a circular mound in the centre, and high embankments below at some distance, with deep trenches and ditches, altogether occupying an area of at least 20 acres, and was considered by those competent to form an opinion, to have been one of the finest Roman encampments in this country. The name of Castle Hills does not imply (as some suppose) that the castle formerly stood there, as this name is very commonly applied to spots where no such building ever stood, but from its vicinity to the castle. It has been the opinion of some antiquaries, that the Romans had here a *castellum exploratorium*, or watch-tower,

A.D. 1742.

1743. The Castle Hills.

---

* Vide poetical description by Miss A. Crosfield, appendix.
† Bib. Top. Brit. No. 2, pt. 2.

A.D. 1743. Discovery of ancient relics. whence they might look out and observe any hostile foe from the surrounding country. Numerous relics have been found at these hills, not only Roman, but Danish and Saxon. The duke of Leeds sent to the exhibition of works of art at Ripon, in 1840, a pair of spurs in good preservation, such as the Saxons wore, with rowels almost the size of a crown piece, dug up at these hills. The late Francis Smyth, esq., F.A.S., of New Building, near Thirsk, frequently paid these remains a visit, and possessed Roman coins, which had been dug up on the summit, in perfect preservation. The Rev. John Balguy, vicar, wrote the following lines " From the ashes of a Roman urn dug up at the Castle Hills, near Northallerton, A.D. 1743."

Trifling mortal, tell me why
  Thou hast disturbed my urn;
Want'st thou to find out who am I?
  Vain man, attend and learn!

To know what letters spelt my name,
  Is useless quite to thee:
An heap of dust is all I am,
  And all that thou shalt be.

Go now, that heap of dust explore,
  Measure its grains or weigh;
Can'st thou the title which I bore,
  Distinguish in the clay?

What glitt'ring honors or high trust
  Once dignified me here,
Were characters imprest on dust,
  Which quickly disappear.

Nor will the sparkling atoms show
  A Claudius or a Guelph:
Vain search! if here the source thou'dst know
  Of nobles or thyself.

The mould will yield no evidence,
  By which thou may'st divine,
If lords or beggars issued thence
  And fill'd the ancient line.

Learn then the vanity of birth,
  Condition, honors, name:
All are but made of common earth,
  The substance just the same,

Bid av'rice and ambition view,
  The extent of all their gains,
Themselves and their possessions too,
  An earthen pot contains.

Haste, lift thy thoughts from earthly things
  To more substantial bliss,
And leave that grovelling pride to kings,
  Which ends in dirt like this.

Let virtue be thy radiant guide
  'Twill dignify thy clay;
And raise thy ashes glorify'd,
  When suns shall fade away.

The following entry appears in a register of burials in the parish church-yard, under date 1744:—" Mr. Peter Deburine, alias Dubern, captain of a French privateer, who was taken prisoner off Scotland, and died of grief, on his journey to London." A.D. 1744.

Northallerton, in common with Thirsk and Osmotherley, was early favoured with Mr. Wesley's preaching. His visits, however, were but few and far between. This may be accounted for on the ground that his chief resting-place on his journeys north, and when returning, being within about eight and a half miles, would induce him to push forward to his old quarters, the Buck Inn, Sand Hutton. On this supposition, it is not at all unlikely but that he passed through Northallerton more frequently than he has recorded. His first visit to the town was in 1745, on the evening of Easter Monday; he writes,—" April 15th, I preached at the Inn (Old Golden Lion) Northallerton." In a letter to his brother Charles, bearing the same date, Mr. Wesley says:— " About six, I preached at Northallerton in the house; but it should have been (as I afterwards found), at the cross; for the people there are, most of them, a noble people, and receive the word with all readiness of mind." The term " *a noble people* " is doubtless, in allusion to the Bereans, whose nobility consisted in readily receiving the word and searching the scriptures.*   [1745. John Wesley at Northallerton.]

The following entry appears in a register of burials in the parish churchyard, under date 1745:—" A sergeant of one of ye Dutch regiments that was marching into Scotland, and his name not known."   [A curious entry.]

During the rebellion in Scotland, the English army under the command of William Augustus, duke of Cumberland,† K.G., G.C.B., second son of George II., (viscount Northallerton,) passed through this place on their way to the north; pitching their temporary camp at the Castle Hills, a short distance west of the town. Robert Simpson, of the Pack Horse inn, many years ostler at the Old Black Swan, during the time of this rebellion, rode express from North-   [Movement of troops. Robert Simpson.]

---

* Ward's Methodism in Thirsk Circuit, pp. 33, 34.

† His royal highness entered the army at an early age. At the battle of Dettingen, in 1743, he was wounded, while fighting by the side of his father; in 1745 he distinguished himself, when commander-in-chief of the British army in Flanders, at the battle of Fontenoy, though defeated. On his return to England he took the field against the Scotch, reduced Carlisle, and finally defeated them at the battle of Culloden. Upon this occasion both houses of parliament voted their public thanks to his royal highness; and the commons, by bill, added £25,000 per annum to his former revenue. In 1748, he again set out for Flanders, to take the command of the allied army, during the continental war; after the convention of Cluster-Seven, he returned to England, and shortly afterwards resigned all his military commands.

124   ANNALS OF

A.D. 1745. allerton to Newcastle-upon-Tyne, with dispatches from general Wade, whose army was then encamped at the Castle Hills.* Simpson died at Northallerton, Dec. 28th, 1812, aged 90. George Spooner, who died in 1816, aged 84, formerly an assistant ostler and postboy at one of the inns in this town, frequently during this rebellion rode post with the many expresses that passed through. A few years afterwards he enlisted into the Scotch highlanders, who were passing through the town southward, in which regiment he served his king and country many years. In 1786, a relation, who died at Newcastle, bequeathed him a handsome legacy, which enabled him to end his days in ease and comfort.†

George Spooner.

1747.
A Cattle-plague Psalm.

The following is part of a psalm, sung in Osmotherley church, near Northallerton, above a century ago. It was composed by the parish clerk on the occasion of the murrain, a severe distemper that raged among the horned cattle in the year 1747. It was sung and chorused by the whole congregation in the church. The four first stanzas contained an account of the cattle that died, and the names of the farmers to whom they belonged. The remaining verses were as follows:—

"No christian's bull nor cow, they say,
But takes it out of hand;
And we shall have no cows at all,
I doubt, within the land.

The doctors, though they all have spoke,
Like learned gentlemen,
And told us how the entrails look
Of cattle, dead and green.

Yet they do nothing do at all,
With all their learning's store;
So Heaven drive out this plague away,
And vex us not no more."

This piece was so well received, that after the service it was desired again by all the congregation, except five farmers, who wept, declaring that the lines were too moving. The minister, on going out, said to the clerk, "Why, John, what psalm was that we had to-day, it was not one of David's?" "No, no," quoth John, big with the honour he had acquired, "David never made such a psalm since he was born; it's one of my own."‡

1748.
Robert Pigot

Robert Pigot, M.A., formerly fellow of Peter House, Cambridge, became vicar of Northallerton in 1748. He was also a minor canon of Durham, and died in 1775. He is buried in the chancel of Northallerton church, where may be seen a slab, bearing an inscription.

* Gent.'s Magazine.   † Ibid.
‡ Town and Country Magazine for 1800.

In the book of excommunications in the parish church, under date 1752, appears the following entry :— *A.D. 1752. Excommunication for incest.*

"Jan. 12th. Thomas Powles and Mary Robson his pretended wife (niece to him by his own sister), were publicly declared to have been and to be excommunicated, by virtue of a process from ye ecclesiastical court at Durham, and for ye causes therein mentioned, and particularly for continuing to cohabit with each other as man and wife, and persisting in ye crime of incest, by me Robert Pigot, vicar."

On the 17th March, it was ordered, "that Mr. Speaker do issue his warrant to the clerk of the crown, to make out a new writ for electing a Burgess to serve in this present Parliament, for the borough of Northallerton, in the county of York, in the room of Henry Lascelles, esq., who, since his election, had accepted of a place." *Parliamentary order.*

In this year a remarkable convulsion took place near the ridge of mountains called Black Hamilton, and close to Whiston-white-mare. The Rev. John Wesley visited Osmotherley shortly afterwards, and rode over[*] and made a personal inspection of the place. In his Journal, Mr. Wesley says, "I walked, crept, and climbed round and over a great part of the ruins * * * one part of the solid rock was cleft from the rest in a perpendicular line, and smooth, as if cut with instruments. It is split into many hundred pieces; an oval piece of ground thirty or forty yards in diameter, had been removed, without the least fissure, whole as it was, from beneath the rocks." The explosion, which resembled the sound of many cannon, and the oscillation of the ground, was distinctly heard and felt at Northallerton. That part of the cliff from which the rest is torn, lies so high and is now of so bright a colour, that it is plainly visible to all the country round, even at the distance of several miles. *1755. Earthquake.*

In his Journal, Mr. Wesley briefly writes :—"Monday, May 12th, we (my wife and I), rode to Northallerton." Mrs. Wesley accompanied her husband on many of his journeys, and was with him at Northallerton.[†] *Mr. and Mrs. Wesley at Northallerton*

The following entry appears in the book of excommunications in the parish church, under date 1755, 24th August. "Mary Jackson, of this parish, was publicly denounced and declared to have been, and to be excommunicated, by virtue of a process from the ecclesiastical court at Durham, for her contumacy in not appearing, upon a citation, to answer for the crime of fornication by her committed, by me, Robert Pigot, vicar." *Excommunication for the crime of fornication.*

[*] Ward's Methodism in Thirsk Circuit, pp. 57, 60.
[†] Ibid, p. 34.

A.D. 1756.
Lieut.-Col.
Lambton.

William Lambton was born of humble parents, at Crosby Grange, near Northallerton, in 1756. His early rudiments of learning were received at the Northallerton grammar school, and finished under the celebrated Dr. Charles Hutton. He was for twenty years a lieutenant-colonel in India, where he distinguished himself by conducting a trigonometrical survey, and died while proceeding on his duty from Hyderabad to Nagpoor and Hingin Ghaunt, in the 67th year of his age. For twenty-two years he carried on his operations in that ungenial climate, with unabated zeal and perseverance, and the annals of the Royal and Asiatic Societies bear ample testimony to the extent and importance of his labours.

1758.
Raising of the 15th Hussars.

During the German war, colonel Ainslie and major sir Wm. Erskine raised the regiment called Elliot's light dragoons, (now the 15th hussars), at Northallerton; William Squire, esq., was their banker—all the horses were contracted for by Mr. John Carter, of Northallerton, and Mr. Harry Turner, of London. Leave was given to the officers by the then tenant of the Castle Hills, to have the horses and men trained on those grounds, previous to being sent to head quarters.* Colonel Ainslie and sir William Erskine seldom passed through this town without taking a walk to these hills; on one occasion sir William had a draughtsman with him, who took a plan of these grounds, and the high mound and entrenchments. George William, duke of Argyll, always either in going to or returning from London, used to go and see the "Roman encampment," as he used to call it.

The late Miss Lambton, of Biddick, then owner of the Castle Hills, had in her possession many coins that had been dug up in the time of her grandfather, William Metcalfe, esq., some of which were found at the time of levelling and making the ground ready on the south-east side of the hill, for the purpose of planting that beautiful clump

"Of old trees, with trunks all hoar,
But light leaves young as joy,"

which were cut down in 1838, during the construction of the Great North of England railway.

1759.
The Romanby Tragedy.†

In the village of Romanby, near Northallerton, there resided a desperate band of coiners, whose respectability and cunning concealment precluded all possibility of suspicion as to their proceedings. The victim of their revenge was Mary Ward, the servant of one of those ruffians. Having obtained an accidental view of some secret apartments appropriated to

---

* Todd's MSS.
† The above date is the most reliable, but not absolutely certain. A ballad founded upon this remorseless tragedy is given *in extenso* in the Appendix.

their treasonable practices, she unguardedly communicated A.D. 1759.
her knowledge to an acquaintance, which reaching her
master's ears, he determined to destroy her. The most
plausible story, time, and means were selected for this
purpose. On a Sunday evening after sunset, an unknown
personage on horseback arrived at her master's mansion,
half equipped, to give colour to his alleged haste, and stated
that he was despatched for Mary, as her mother was dying.
She lingered to ask her master's permission, but he feigned
sleep, and she departed without his leave. On the table of
her room was her bible, opened at these remarkable words in
Job, "*They shall seek me in the morning, and shall not find me; and
where I am they shall not come.*" Her home was at the distance
of eight miles from Romanby, and Morton bridge hard by
the heath where she was murdered, is the traditionary scene
of her nocturnal revisitings. The impression of her re-
appearance is only poetically assumed, for there is too much
of what Coleridge would term "the divinity of nature"
around Morton bridge to warrant its association with super-
natural mysteries.*

Died at Northallerton, in Trinity vacation, 1 Geo. III., 1761.
the hon. sir Richard Lloyd, knt., baron of the exchequer, on Sir Richard Lloyd, Bart.
his return from Newcastle-upon-Tyne, where he had been to
try some rebels against the militia. Sir Richard was made a
serjeant-at-law, and baron in 1759, upon the death of the
hon. Mr. baron Legge.†

The following excommunication is recorded in the book Excommuni-
set apart for that purpose in the parish church, under date cation for incest.
1761:—" 24th May. George Pattison and Ann Wass his
pretended wife, both of this parish, were publicly denounced
and declared to have been and to be excommunicated, by
virtue of a process from the ecclesiastical court at Durham,
for their contumacy in not appearing, upon a citation, to
answer for the crime of incest by them committed, the said
Ann Wass being sister to his former wife, by me Will.
Peacock, curate.‡

Miss Ann Allan's expenses of a journey to and from 1762.
London, extracted from her household book, will give some Cost of travelling and provisions.
idea of the great cost of travelling in those days, in a post

---

* Vide Ingledew's Songs and Ballads of Yorkshire.
† Wilson's Reports.
‡ Although the Affinity Table of the Church of England distinctly forbids marriage with a deceased wife's sister, great efforts are now being made to legalise such marriages on the ground that only a judicial and not a blood relationship exists between a man and his deceased wife's sister; that marriages of cousins which *is* a blood relationship is legally permissible, and that marriage with a deceased wife's sister has been already legalised on the continent and in America.—J. L. S.

128 ANNALS OF

A.D. 1762. chaise. The journey up was performed in nine days. "Jan. 29. Paid bill at Darlington for chaises and horses, £1 2s. 7d.; at Northallerton, £2 1s. 0½d.; Boroughbridge, all night, £2 3s. 5d.; Wetherby, breakfast, 10s. 7d.; Aberforth, dinner, £1 5s.; Ferrybridge, all night, £3 1s. 1d.; Doncaster, dinner, £1 13s. 5d.; Barnbymore, all night, £2 14s. 1½d.; Tuxford, breakfast, 6s.; Carleton, dinner, £1 9s. 8d.; Newark, all night, £2 18s. 7½d.; Grantham, dinner, £1 13s. 5½d.; Cotesworth, all night, £2 14s. 0½d.; Stamford, dinner, £2 10s. 8d.; Stilton, all night, £2 16s. 1d.; Bugden, dinner, £2 6s. 5½d.; Biggleswade, all night, £3 2s. 4d.; Stevenage, breakfast, £1 1s. 9d.; Hatfield, dinner, £1 18s. 5d.; Barnett, all night, £3 4s. 9d.; fifteen days hire of six coach-horses, coachman, and postillion, from York to Darlington and from thence to London, and return to York, at £1 15s. a day, £26 5s.; paid coachman extra present, £2 2s.; paid postillion, ditto, £1 1s. May 17, coach and six horses from London to Grange, £28 14s.; road expenses from London to Grange, £51 6s. 3½d. Total cost of journey, £150 1s. 9½d.

The rev. Sydney Smith, in a letter to the countess Grey, thus writes, " I shall be glad to hear that you are safely landed at Portman-square, with all your young ones; but do not set off too soon, or you will be laid up at the Black Swan, Northallerton, or the Elephant and Castle, Boroughbridge, and your bill will come to a thousand pounds, besides the waiter, who will most probably apply for a place under Government."*

1763.
A depraved female.

Margaret Middleton, alias Coulson, was executed at Durham. She had been employed by a township in Durham to take a pauper child, called Lucy Elliott, alias Curry, to Northallerton, its place of settlement. She received the wages of her journey beforehand, and carried the child only as far as the river Browney, not two miles from Durham, where she drowned it on the 24th June. She was hanged on Monday, the 1st of August, and dissected by Mr. Richard Hopper, surgeon.†

1765.
Horse races established.

About this time the Northallerton horse races were established, the site selected for the course being opposite the railway station, on the east side.

Robin Horton

In 1765, there lived at Northallerton one Robin Horton, a chimney-sweeper, who had two club feet, and what was more remarkable, his wife had also a club foot, and he had an old grey horse who likewise had one club foot. Robin Horton was a man who was held in no great repute by his neighbours; for his manners were revolting, his person tall and ruffianly, and his countenance extremely unprepossessing.

* Lady Holland's Memoir and Letters of Sydney Smith.   † Sykes.

His wife was also a woman of the most disgusting appearance A.D. 1765.
and depraved habits, and he had three sons and two daughters, whose characters were dishonest and dissipated. Yet, singular as it may appear, Robin Horton did business for all the nobility for miles around his dwelling. His horse and he were seldom seen apart, and it had been often noticed, that every night after dark they went out together, no one knew whither, though they had often been met returning home long after midnight, and by the most unfrequented paths. This excited considerable suspicion of the actions of Robin, but as no proof of crime could be substantiated against him, every one wisely kept their surmises locked within their own breasts, fearful of a sound drubbing from the father or the sons.

Things went on in this way for several years, when one His career.
morning the mansion of a wealthy gentleman in the neighbourhood was discovered to have been broken into during the night, and plate and other property to a considerable amount carried away. This happened in the depth of winter, when the snow was lying thick upon the ground, and in hope of discovering the road the burglars had taken, the officers examined the ground minutely around the mansion. There in the snow, they distinctly traced the impression of three club feet, and suspicion immediately falling on Robin, from this circumstance, the officers proceeded to track the footmarks, and actually did track them right to the residence of Robin. The property was all discovered in a cellar underneath his abode, and in consequence, the father and his two sons were apprehended, and finally committed to York Castle to take their trial for the same. One of the sons turned king's evidence against his father and brother, and they were transported for life. The horse had been employed by them to convey the stolen property to their residence.

After this affair, Robin Horton's wife and the son continued to follow the sweeping profession, though now their characters were so well known, it was very little business they could get to do. Still they seemed more prosperous than ever, and never appeared in want of money. At last they were discovered breaking into the residence of Lady ——. The mother, son, and two daughters, were all apprehended in the act, while the old grey horse was found at a distance, waiting to carry home the fruits of their plunder. For this burglary, the whole of this infamous and singular family were transported for life, and the horse was shot.

Died at Northallerton, March 22nd, aged 42 years, Miss Miss Crosfield
Anne Crosfield, only daughter of Thomas Crosfield, esq., solicitor, of Northallerton, by his wife Mary, daughter of Robert Raikes, esq. Miss Crosfield composed the poetical

130   ANNALS OF

A.D. 1765. description of the Castle Hills (given in appendix), and the following epistle to Allan Ramsay, written in 1751:—

> Fain wad I join the blythsome lay,
> And pou a sprig of Scottish bay;
> For Scotland has sic rowth of wit,
> She weel can spare a friend a bit.
> Sing then my muse in lilting strains,
> The glory of the British plains,
> Wha fra auld Thames, to silver Spey,
> Excels and bears the gree away
> When on his Forth, as flowery braes,
> He warbles fast his tuneful lays.
> See! how the lads and lasses thrang
> To listen to his blithsome sang:
> When dorty Bell begins to mane,
> What wooer wad na turn agane?
> Or wha but hings his lugs to hear,
> Of scornfu' Nancy's biting jeer?
> While Bessy Bell and Mary Grey
> Split a' the laddies hearts in twa;
> And bra Locharber, warlike swain,
> Mak's ilka listning lass his ain.
> But ah! what heavenly concert springs,
> Whene'er the Gentle Shepherd sings.
> The pastoral muse ower lang mistain
> Now shows us how she ought to reign;
> And busk'd in natur's sweetest flowers,
> Fra cowslip glens and hawthorn bowers,
> O'er all the glaring tinsil flowers.
>   Oh Ramsay! lang may ye be found
> The ferlie of the nations round!
> Lang may ye shine (alas from far!)
> The rising poet's northern star!
> And when ye break the mortal chain,
> Ascend to music like your ain.

1767. A public absolution.

The following entry appears in the book of excommunications in the parish church, under date 1767:—

"March 22nd. Margaret, otherwise Mary Robson, late pretended wife of Thomas Powles, lately deceased, was publicly declared, in time of divine service, to have been and to be absolved, by virtue of a process from the ecclesiastical court of Durham, from her contumacy therein mentioned, and from her excommunication consequent thereupon, by me Robt. Pigot, vicar."

1768. Entries in Parish Books.

The following entry occurs in the parish books:—"For wine and ale to ringers, 15s.; for oil for bells, 3s. 2d."*

1770.

In the sixth register of baptisms of the parish church, under date 1770, may be seen the following entry:—"William, son of parents unknown, put to nurse with Grace, wife of George Pearson, joyner, by Mr. John Reed, surgeon, who ordered him to be registered by the name of Stockdale."

* Upon what occasion both the ringers and bells of Northallerton were indulged so liberally, we cannot conjecture.

NORTHALLERTON.   131

The Quarter Sessions commenced to be held this year in the Toll Booth, now pulled down, and continued to be held until the erection of the present Court House in 1783. *A.D. 1770. The Quarter Sessions.*

The following entry occurs in the parish books:—"For ringing king's birthday, 7s. 6d.; Nov. 5th, ringers, 11s.; barrells and candles, 5s. 10d." *Entry in Parish Books.*

The following is a verbatim copy of a lease of tolls and premises connected with the fairs and markets held during the year at Northallerton:— *1772. Grant of Tolls*

"Whereas, our Sovereign Lord King *Henry* the First, in the Twenty-seventh Year of his Reign, in the Year of our Lord 1127, Did Grant to *Robert*, then Lord Bishop of *Durham*, and his Successors, the Manor of *Allertonshire*, with a Market every *Wednesday* at *North Allerton:* Also, a Fair on *Candlemas* Day, and a Fair to be held there every Two Weeks till *Easter:* Also, a Fair to be held there on *Bartholomew* Day and the Day after.—Also, King *Philip* and Queen *Mary*, in the First Year of their Reign, 1554, granted to *Cuthbert*, then Bishop of *Durham*, and his Successors, One Fair at *North Allerton* aforesaid, upon Saint *George* Day and the Day after, with a Fair every Two Weeks till *Lamass*.—Also, King *James* the First, in the Eighth Year of his Reign, *Anno Domini* 1610, granted to *William*, then Bishop of *Durham*, and his Successors, one Fair to be held at *North Allerton* aforesaid, on Saint *Matthew* Day, and the Day after, with a Fair every Two Weeks till *Christmas*, with Tolls for Cattle Bought and Sold at these Fairs, &c.

And Whereas, The Right Reverend, *John*, now Lord Bishop of *Durham*, hath granted to *George Dowson* and *Dorothy Dowson*, of *North Allerton* aforesaid, under his Episcopal Seal, a Lease of the same Tolls and Premises, with full power and Authority to Collect and Receive the same. All Persons therefore, buying Cattle at the said Fairs, are hereby required to Pay the Tolls for the same, to the said *George Dowson* and *Dorothy Dowson*, or to whom they shall appoint, except such as shall shew a sufficient Exemption.

"*July* 20, 1772."

About one o'clock this (Sunday) morning, the inhabitants of Northallerton were alarmed by the appearance of a large ball of fire, that passed with great velocity from the west to the east; several houses were greatly agitated, and many doors and windows were forced open. *1773. A Meteor.*

Benjamin Walker, M.A., became vicar of Northallerton in 1775. He had a family of eighteen children, and died in 1814. He was interred in the church, where a monument is erected to his memory. *1775. Benjamin Walker.*

In this year it was decided to take down the old Grammar School, which was then in a dilapidated condition, and rebuild it in a substantial manner. The work was commenced *1776. Rebuilding of Grammar School.*

A.D. 1776. and finished the same year. The following entry appears in an old record of parish affairs preserved in the parish church: "Be it remembered, that after building the school, having a considerable sum to spare, it was agreed on between Rev. Mr. Benj. Walker, vicar, and W. Squire, to build a room to the west of the school to serve for punishing scholars in, or to let as might hereafter be thought proper, and being a supernumerary edifice, is intended for the benefit of the master of the school for the time being, in order for a fund wherewith to keep the school in repair,—Will. Squire."

1779. Rebuilding of Chancel.

The chancel of the parish church of Northallerton being considered in a dangerous state, was in 1779, pulled down and rebuilt, and roofed with slate; and in 1786 the roof on the western end was taken down and a new one, though much inferior to the former in the beauty of its construction, erected and covered with the same material as the chancel. The pews in the church, being in bad condition, were in the following year taken down, and replaced by oak ones, which made it much more comfortable and commodious. During the building operations, one of the workmen fell from the roof, through the scaffolding, into the interior, and was instantly killed. Blood-stains were visible upon the altar steps for several years, until they were taken up and replaced with new ones.

Fatal accident

1780. Sir J. S. Byerley.

John Scott Byerley, F.R.S.L., was born at Brompton, near Northallerton, on the 16th October, 1780, having sat and "conned his book" at the same black oak table, then in use at the Northallerton grammar school, at which so many Northallerton worthies had acquired their elements of greatness. At the age of 18, young Byerley went as clerk into the office of Francis Walker, esq. (son of the Rev. B. Walker, vicar of Northallerton), solicitor, Ripon; and about two years afterwards he removed to a similar situation at Stockton-on-Tees, where he addressed himself so sedulously and successfully to mathematical studies, that the well-known Mr. Friend invited him to London. Here he published various prose works on ethical, political, and chemical subjects. He was made a knight of the Russian order of St. Wladimir, by the emperor Alexander, and received an annual pension of £200 from the prince Regent, (afterwards George IV.) Sir John is best known as the patentee of Oleagine, a composition of importance to woollen manufacturers. He died suddenly at Farm Hill, near Stroud, aged 57, and it is said, "Those loved him most who knew him best."

The Lascelles Family.

The family of Lascelles is of ancient standing in the county of York, and has for some centuries been intimately connected with Northallerton.

"Roger de Lascelles was summoned to parliament 23rd

June, 30th September, and 2nd November, 23 Edward I. (1295), and 26th August, 24 Edward I. (1296). He was also summoned 8th June, 22 Edward I. (1294; but it is doubtful if that writ was a regular summons to parliament.* He died about 1297, without male issue, leaving his four daughters his co-heirs, among whose descendants and representatives this barony is probably in abeyance."†

A.D. 1780.

John de Lascelles, of Hinderskelf (now Castle Howard), was living in 1315, and from him was descended Francis Lascelles, of Stank Hall, which estate he obtained by marriage with Elizabeth, daughter and co-heir of John Charter, of Northallerton. He died in 1628, seised of Stank, alias Winton Stank, and of the manor or Grange of Thormanby. His grandson and heir, Francis Lascelles, of Stank Hall and Northallerton, was a colonel in the army of the parliament; M.P. for the North-Riding 1653, 1654, and 1656, and was elected for Northallerton in 1660, but having sat three times as one of the judges at the trial of king Charles I., though he did not sign the warrant for the king's execution, was, on the 12th of June, 1660, discharged from being a member of the House of Commons. He married Frances, daughter of sir William St. Quintin, of Harpham, baronet, by whom he had a numerous family, five sons and eleven daughters.

Daniel Lascelles, son and heir, of Stank Hall and Northallerton, born 6th November, 1655, M.P. for Northallerton in 1702; J.P. and high sheriff of Yorkshire in 1719; died 5th September, 1734, aged 78, and was buried at Northallerton. He married first 22nd August, 1672, Margaret, daughter of William Metcalfe, esq., of the Porch House, Northallerton, (by his wife Anna, daughter of sir George Marwood, of Little Busby, bart.,) by whom (who was buried at Northallerton, 20th December, 1690); he had issue George Lascelles, of Stank Hall, and of St. Michael's in Barbadoes, who continued the line which failed in the year 1800; and Henry Lascelles, baptised at Northallerton (with his twin sister Hannah) 20th December, 1690, the same day on which their mother was buried.

Henry Lascelles was sometime collector of customs at Barbadoes, where he laid the foundation of a very large fortune, a director of the East India Company, and M.P. for Northallerton 1745-52. In 1739 he purchased the Harewood estate from the trustees of John Boulter, esq., the spendthrift relative of the miserly sir John Cutler. He died in London, and was buried at Northallerton, 19th October, 1753. Henry

* Vide Sir Harris Nicolas's Synopsis of the Peerage under "Clyvedon."
† Vide Ingledew's History of Northallerton.

A.D. 1780. Lascelles was succeeded by his eldest son Edwin, first lord Harewood, of Harewood Castle, Stank Hall, and Northallerton, born in 1712-13. M.P. for Scarborough; for Northallerton in 1754, and again from 1780-90. Created baron Harewood, of Harewood, 9th July, 1790; died 25th January, 1795, s.p., when the dignity became extinct, but it was in the year following revived in the person of his cousin, Edward Lascelles, of whom hereafter. He married first Elizabeth, daughter of sir Darcy Dawes, bart., and secondly Jane, daughter of Wm. Coleman, of Garnhay, county Devon, esq. In March, 1759, Edwin lord Harewood laid the foundation of the princely Corinthian edifice, named Harewood House, which has since been the residence of the successive earls of Harewood.

Daniel Lascelles, brother to the first lord Harewood, was M.P. for Northallerton from 1752 to 1780. He purchased the Goldsbrough estate about the year 1756, and in 1760 the manors of Plumpton and Rofarlington. Goldsbrough Hall, a large and noble Elizabethan house, is generally the residence of some members of the Lascelles family. He died in 1784, s.p.

Mary, daughter of Daniel Lascelles, by his wife Margaret Metcalfe, was married at Northallerton 27th August, 1706, to Cuthbert Mitford, esq., of Northallerton, from whom is descended the Venerable Archdeacon Cust, M.A., now rector of Danby Wiske, near Northallerton, son of the Rev. Daniel Mitford Peacock, senior wrangler, 1791.

Elizabeth, another daughter of Daniel Lascelles and Margaret Metcalfe his wife, was married at Northallerton, 10th September, 1713, to George Ord, of Longridge, county Northumberland, esq.

Edward Lascelles, first earl of Harewood, grandson of the first-named Daniel Lascelles, of Stank Hall and Northallerton, by a second marriage, born 1740, succeeding to the large estates of his cousin Edwin, first lord Harewood, was raised to the peerage as baron Harewood (second creation), 1796, and viscount Lascelles and earl of Harewood in 1812. He was M.P. for Northallerton 1790-96. In 1761 he married Anne, daughter of William Chaloner, esq., of Guisborough, by whom he had issue Henry, second earl, lord-lieutenant and custos rotulorum of the West-Riding, and high steward of Allerton, grandfather of Henry Thynne Lascelles, fourth and present earl of Harewood.

A branch of the family of Lascelles descended from Cuthbert Lascelles, second son of Francis Lascelles, of Stank Hall and Northallerton, by his wife Elizabeth, daughter and co-heir of John Charter, of Northallerton, resided at Sowerby and Breckenbrough for several generations.

On Saturday, June 3rd, Mr. Wesley writes in his journal: —" At noon I preached to a large congregation at Northallerton; the sun shone full in my face when I began, but it was soon overcast, and I believe this day, if never before, God gave a general call to this careless people." Thus during the twenty-five years from his former visit, his hearers had degenerated from a "noble" to a "careless" people. In the interval, many of the former had gone into eternity, and a new generation had risen to fill their places. The service was held in Jackey Wren's yard, which then included the yard of the present Buck Inn, near the grammar school. Mr. Wesley's text on this occasion was "*If the salt have lost its savour, wherewith shall it be salted*"? Mrs. Sheppard, who died on Dec. 18th, 1867, at the age of 93 years, said she remembered very distinctly Mr. Wesley preaching here in 1780. She was then a little girl, between five and six years old; she had a most vivid recollection of the sun shining in his face while preaching, and the sorrow her young heart felt whilst thinking it would inconvenience him. The yard was full of people, and she sat on her mother's knee. She remembers also walking by his side in his black gown and cassock, and taking hold of a hem of his flowing robe. The Jackey Wren, mentioned above, was a pious and useful man, and by trade a weaver. The preaching for some time was held in his cottage. A gentleman of the town, who had more waggery than religion, used to frequent Jackey's house during the services; and being a great ventriloquist, he took delight in making strange noises, and then urging Jackey to go and see what it was. Mr. Wesley's home, while here, was at a Mr. Atkinson's, tanner, who lived at the north end of the town. They were a devotedly pious family, and lived in comfortable circumstances. At their house all the preachers were entertained; and they felt it a great honour to take in those despised and persecuted servants of the Lord.*

A.D. 1780. Rev. John Wesley at Northallerton

The following entries occur in the parish books:—" To ringers on news of surrender of Charlestown, 5s.; on lord Cornwallis's† success over the rebels in South Carolina, 5s."

Entry in Parish Books.

The following is a copy of the answers to the articles enquired of at the ordinary visitation of the Most Reverend Father in God, William, by Divine Providence Lord Archbishop of York, held at Thirsk, the 17th day of September, 1781, by the churchwardens of Northallerton :—

1781. Episcopal visitation.

* Ward's Methodism in Thirsk Circuit, pages 35-37.
† He greatly distinguished himself at the battle of Brandywine, and at the siege of Charlestown; in 1786 he was made governor-general and commander-in-chief in India; created marquis Cornwallis in 1792; lord-lieutenant of Ireland in 1799, K.G.; in 1804 he was again made governor-general of India, and died at Ghazepore in 1805.

A.D. 1781.

[COPY.]

Tit. 1.—Concerning Churches, &c.

Ans.—We think our Church is in decent repair in the roof, windows, and floor. So are the seats in general; but some few are deficient, whose owners are not certainly known.* Nothing further on this title to present.

Tit. 2.—Concerning the Living and the Minister's House.

Ans.—We deliver a Terrier along with this, wherein these particulars are explained at large. (*vide Appendix.*)

Tit. 3.—Concerning the Clergy, &c.

Ans.—Our Minister resideth constantly upon his Living, and is regular in his deportment respecting the other inquiries under this Title. We have a Curate in our Parish who is of sober life and diligent in the discharge of his duty. We know not whether or no he is licensed to the Cure, neither what is his salary. We have no Lecturer in the Parish.

Tit. 4.—Concerning Hospitals, Schools, &c.

Ans.—We have no Hospital or Alms-house in Northallerton. We have Grammar School endowed with about three acres of land, and the sum of five pounds and twenty pence a year. Taught by the Curate of our Parish. Under this head nothing further to report.

Tit. 5.—Concerning Parish and Church Officers.

Ans.—In the whole of this title we have nothing presentable.

Tit. 6.—Concerning the Parishioners.

Ans.—We have nothing to present.

Tit. 7.—Concerning Ecclesiastical Officers.

Ans.—We know nothing of the Fees due to any of them; neither do we know anything of their conduct that is amiss. We have the Articles of Visitation and the Offices of Public Prayer upon special occasions delivered in due time, and we pay what is demanded for them.

Tit. 8.—Concerning peculiar Jurisdictions.

Ans.—These we are not able to give any satisfactory account of.

Northallerton, Sep. 14th, 1781.

Will. Squire,
Ed. Dawson, } *Churchwardens.*
Ja. Langdale,

---

* At this time nearly all the church pews were rented, and their repair devolved upon their owners for the time being. The sittings are now free, the churchwardens being responsible for their good condition, &c.

NORTHALLERTON.   137

A.D. 1781.

The following entry occurs in the parish books:—" Paid ringers on news of taking of St. Eustatia, till 9 at night, 7s. 6d."

Sunday school

The first Sunday school in Northallerton was opened in May, 1780, when upwards of thirty poor children were entered upon the roll. The Wesleyans of Northallerton were the first to introduce into the town the laudable scheme of Robert Raikes, but to the Rev. Mr. Benson, M.A. (Glasgow), pastor of the Independents, may be given the credit of imparting to the local movement a genuine and lasting impetus. Mr. Benson's exertions doubtless laid the foundation of the Zion Sunday school's past and present prosperity, and also stimulated the hitherto dormant churchpeople into action. May the movement go on and prosper, and it *will* if the love of Christ constrains all its promoters and teachers.

1782. The Register Office.

The present Register office, for the public registering of deeds, wills, conveyances, and other incumbrances, was erected in 1782, near the site of an older building in Zetland street; and additional buildings were added to the old office so as to render the same a residence for the Registrar. There are only four Register offices in England, at the following places:—Wakefield, Beverley, Northallerton, and London. It would seem, however, that there was a local office for the registration of deeds at Thirsk, previous to the passing of the Act constituting public Register Offices, as appears from an advertisement in the *Newcastle Courant*, dated May 14th, 1726.*

1783. Ill-mated.

On August 25th in this year, it appears from one of the registers of the parish church that George Lumley, of Northallerton, was married at the exceeding ripe age of 104 years to Mary Dunning, of the same parish, a maiden of 19 summers. The officiating minister was the Rev. Jas. Wilkinson, curate; and the witnesses of the ceremony Thomas Robinson and W. M. Gibson. The aged bridegroom affixed his mark to the registers and the bride her signature in very tremulous caligraphy, and well she might when we remember that it is said—

"Crabb'd age and youth cannot live together."

What could possibly have induced the young lady to entrust her charms to the keeping of decrepit old age is best known to herself, but

"Sad is the sight when money's power controls
In wedlock's chains the fate of human souls."

Certain it was that love was dead, for May cannot, under any circumstances, mate with December; the chilly embraces of

---

* Vide pages 116, 119.

A.D. 1783. the one would shrivel with a deadly blight the tender blossoms of the other. We remember, however, that Abishag cherished king David in his old age, and we would fain believe that such was Mary Dunning's laudable object, if so

> "Remember, I do not pretend
> There's anything perfect about it :
> But this I'll aver to the end,
> Life's very imperfect without it."

Whether the happy (?) couple continued to reside in the town cannot be ascertained, but if they did no entry of the patriarch's death and burial can be found in the parish registers, and we may infer that they lived happily together for many years, either dying together in some far off parish, or parting to meet in

> "Some world far from ours
> Where music, and moonlight, and feeling are one."

Ballooning extraordinary. "The following notice appeared the *York Chronicle*, for January 10th, 1783:—"Whereas the air balloon has been found to be of such singular advantage in France, in conveying people in an easy and expeditious manner from place to place: this is to give notice, that for the accommodation of people in the neighbourhood of Whitby, &c., a large one is now completed there, with every advantage equal to those in France, which will be found the best and cheapest conveyance from thence to meet the fly, &c., at Northallerton; as the innkeepers have of late been so extravagant in their charges. It will set off every morning at eight o'clock, from the "Robin Hood," in Northallerton, and be at Stokesley about half-past eight, at Guisborough about nine, at Whitby to dine, and will return to Northallerton the same evening, to meet the fly, diligence, &c., from the north and south the next morning.

N.B.—It will be very convenient on the Mondays to convey the gentlemen of the law, &c., from Stokesley to Guisborough market; and on its return to bring them home again: it will also be very useful for the posts, if they should happen to get drunk or tire their horses, as there will be pockets, &c., (and every other convenience) in the balloon carriage, for putting parchments, letters, and pocket bottles, &c., &c."

The House of Correction. The House of Correction is situated at the east end of Zetland-street, on a piece of ground formerly waste. The site was granted by the bishop of Durham to the justices of the North-Riding, conditionally, that the bishops' courts should be held in the Court House to be erected thereon in perpetuity. The land was low and swampy, and was, up to the time of being built upon, the receptacle for the rubbish of the town; about the middle was a pond used for the washing of posting and coaching horses, called the Horse Pond, and at the south-east corner was the pinfold. The House of Correction was erected in 1783, since which time considerable alterations and enlargements have taken place. *A.D. 1783.*

In this year the town of Northallerton suffered very severely from epidemic small pox, as the register of burials testifies. *1784. Small-pox.*

In his journal, Mr. Wesley writes,—" Monday, June 14th, about noon, I preached at Northallerton, and, I believe, God touched many hearts." This was his last visit to the town.* *Wesley's last visit.*

The first foundation of the present Court House and governor's residence for the House of Correction for the North-Riding of Yorkshire, was laid on a vacant close of ground at Northallerton called the "Priest Garth," situate at the east of the town, on Saturday, April 16th, 1785. The buildings were designed to be occupied by the governor below, and for the Sessions House above. *1785. Court House.*

The old London and Edinbro' mail-coach was established, and commenced running on the second Monday in November of that year, and came by way of Leeds to Newcastle, it was worked by Mr. North, of the King's Arms Inn, Briggate, Leeds; Messrs. Goodlad & Thackway, Harrogate; Mrs. Alice Haddon, Unicorn Inn, Ripon; Mr. William Smith, Black Bull Inn, Northallerton; Mr. James Trenholme, Darlington; Mr. Thomas Wrangham, Rusheyford; and Mr. Matthew Hall, Cock Inn, Head of the Side, Newcastle. After running by that route for two or three months, it was changed to go by way of York instead of Leeds (being much nearer to London), and continued until 1841; except from May 6th, 1825, to May 6th, 1827, it ran by way of Boroughbridge. *London and Edinbro' Mail Coach.*

The late Mr. Jonathan Wigfield, of Northallerton, stated before he died, that he recollected distinctly going to hear Mr. Wesley preach at Thirsk in 1786, and his text was, "*The King's business requires haste.*" Mr. Wigfield was then six years old.† *Mr. Wesley at Thirsk.*

The following is a copy of a notice served on John Marshall, one of the overseers of the highways, within the township of Northallerton: *1786. Overseers warned.*

To John Marshall, John Dixon, and John Wallis.

"You being the present Overseers of the Highways within this township of Northallerton; we, whose names are subscribed, do hereby give you notice, that if you expend either

---

* Ward's Methodism in Thirsk Circuit, page 35.
† Ibid, page 37.

A.D. 1786. labour or money on behalf of the township in amending any Way that does not lead from town to town, the same or any part of it will not be allowed in your accounts."
Dated this 13th day of May, 1786.
B. WALKER, Vicar.
WILL. SQUIRE.
WILL. WAILES.
JOHN WALKER.

1787. A suicide.
On May 17th, died at Northallerton, wife of John Ward, schoolmaster, at the age of 46 years. She starved herself to death in a fit of insanity, through fear of being poisoned! This hallucination was created by a dream, in which she declared her husband had attempted to poison her in three successive meals.

Wholesale spoliation.
In 1787, the high-pitched roofs of the nave, aisles, transepts, and chancel of the parish church were lowered in order to obtain the lead. Instead of the three distinct roofs which covered the nave and aisles, one monstrous slated roof was substituted. The churchwardens' accounts about this time afford a very remarkable instance of the reckless manner in which churchwardens were in the habit of dealing with edifices, upon which their forefathers spared neither expense nor skill. For instance 19 tons 16 cwt, 3 qrs. 24 lbs. of old lead, stripped from the roof, produced £320 15s.; and this wholesale spoliation and vandalism reduced a debt of £332 10s. 5½d. to £7 17s. 1½d. The churchwardens might have been capital managers for the then parishioners, but as wardens of the church, to use a mild term, their mode of action was injudicious.

1788. Thomas Byerley.
Thomas Byerley (brother of sir John) was born at Brompton, Nov. 11th, 1788, and educated at Northallerton grammar school. At an early age he evinced a great aptitude for knowledge, and going to London, soon found employment for his talents. He became editor of the *Literary Chronicle*, *Percy Anecdotes*, *Evening Star*, *Mirror*, &c. He died at the early age of 38 years, deeply regretted by a numerous circle of literary friends.

Discovery of an urn of coins
In a field close to the Castle Hills, a large urn was dug up by one Lawrence Leadley, containing an innumerable quantity of coins, chiefly of the later Roman emperors; a few were corroded, but the greatest part were in good preservation; the urn was made of coarse blue clay and porous. So numerous were the coins, which amounted to several hundreds, that they soon got into circulation as farthings, and went by the name of "Lawrie's farthings." Curiosity is naturally excited as to why Roman coins are found secreted in so great abundance. With regard to such coins as are

NORTHALLERTON. 141

discovered enclosed in urns and buried in the earth, it has been supposed that it was a custom with the Romans to hoard their money in such a situation. Among the military it seems likely that the method of burying money would be pursued in general, for as the Roman forces were paid in copper money, called therefore *Æs Militare*, a service of any duration would occasion such an accumulation of this ponderous coin as could not be carried about by the soldier in his numerous marches ; the surest method, therefore, would be to deposit it in a spot known only to himself ; but as it frequently happened that these veterans died before they had an opportunity of re-visiting their hoards, the knowledge of them would be necessarily lost with their owners, and they would continue in the place where they were originally deposited, until accident or curiosity again brought them to light.* {A.D. 1788.}

On the east side of the town, against the side of the house called *Vine House*, formerly the property of Robert Raikes Fulthorpe, esq., now used as the Cottage Hospital, grew the largest vine in the kingdom, which in 1789 contained 137 square yards, and had it been permitted, when in its greatest vigour, would have extended over three or four times that area. The circumference of the trunk a little above the surface of the ground was 3 feet 11 inches, but from its great age and from an injudicious management, the greater part of it is now gone to decay. It is supposed to have been planted upwards of 200 years. There is another vine of smaller dimensions in the yard of the "King's Arm's Hotel," the tendrils of which at one time are said to have extended to the bottom of the yard, a distance of forty or fifty yards. This vine was most probably reared from a cutting taken from the old original vine. {1789. Large Vines.}

The following entry occurs in the parish books :—" Paid ringers for his majesty's recovery,† 7s. 6d." {Entry in Parish Books.}

A person when at work ploughing in a field about a mile south of Northallerton, turned up a silver coin, rather larger than a shilling, but somewhat thinner, which, on cleaning, proved to be a coin of king Alfred, in a fair state of preservation. {1792. Ancient coin.}

In the churchwardens' accounts, the following entry is made :—" Ringers, at taking of Valinceons [Valenciennes] 5s., ale 2s. {1793.}

In the summer of this year, some of the officers of the duke of Gloucester's regiment (115th Foot), whilst passing through Northallerton, created an alarming disturbance, {1795. A disturbance}

* Brewer's Introduction.   † George III.

A.D. 1795 which was likely to have been attended with serious consequences, but was happily frustrated by the magistracy. The grand jury at the ensuing Quarter Sessions for the North-Riding found a true bill of indictment against certain of the said officers, but the matter was subsequently settled by the officers agreeing to pay a sum of money for the use of the poor of Northallerton.*

An adult baptism.

The following baptism is recorded in a register in the parish church, under date 1795:—"John Thomas, an adult, native of the coast of Guinea, and late a slave in Antigua."

1796. Wesleyan Chapel.

The old Wesleyan Methodist Chapel built. It is now used by the Baptists, who bought it when the present Wesleyan chapel was erected.

Remarkable discovery.

About the latter end of the year 1796, a few pennyworth of turnips were bought from George Wood, a Northallerton gardener, by an old lady, and in cutting through one of them, the knife grazed against something hard in the middle or heart of the turnip, which proved to be a gold wedding ring. The gardener's wife was sent for, and was asked if she had, during the time they had rented the garden in which the turnips were grown, ever lost, or knew of any other person having lost a gold ring. Upon which she replied that, being one day weeding, or doing some other work in the garden, she remembered having lost her wedding ring from off her finger, which was then about fourteen years ago. From the description she gave of the ring, the old lady was certain this was the same ring. Upon its being shown to her, and the question asked if she had ever seen that ring, the poor woman immediately knew it to be the identical one which she had dropt from her finger about fourteen years before, which was then about a year after she was married to her husband George Wood. It appears that the turnip must have grown through the ring, and at last enclosed it.†

1797. Instrumental music in the Church.

In the churchwardens' accounts for 1797, the following entries appear:—" For soldiers playing band of music in ye church, 5s.; ringing twice on duke of York's passing through the town, 8s. 10d.; ringing on admiral Duncan's‡ victory over the Dutch fleet, 7s. 6d.

1798.

The following entries occur in the churchwardens' accounts:—" Ringing for beating the French in Ireland,

---

* Mann-Dowson Todd's MSS.

† Vide Gentleman's Magazine, Sept. 24th, 1799.

‡ Admiral Duncan totally defeated the Dutch fleet, off Camperdown, and captured 8 sail of the line, for which service he was created visct. Duncan of Camperdown, and baron Duncan of Lundie, co. Perth, Oct. 30th, 1797, with a pension of £3,000 per annum to himself and the next two heirs of the peerage; died 1804.

7s. 6d. ; ditto for admiral Nelson's* victory, 7s. 6d ; ditto, sir J. B. Warren's victory, 10s. A.D. 1798.

Inserted in churchwardens' accounts :—" Ringing for taking the Dutch fleet, 10s." 1799.

In this year a small theatre was established in Northallerton, but was discontinued in 1832. Charles Keen, the celebrated dramatist, frequently appeared before attentive and appreciative audiences therein. The building is now used as a Primitive Methodist Chapel. 1800. Northallerton Theatre.

On the 23rd March, 1800, William Sturdy, of Romanby, was buried in Northallerton church-yard, aged 100 years. Longevity.

The following lines were originally written upon a square of glass, in the bar of a public house, at a small village on the post road between Northallerton and Boroughbridge:— A genial parson.

> "Here in my wicker chair I sitt,
> From folly far, and far from witt,
> Content to live, devoid of care,
> With country folks and country fare ;
> To listen to my landlord's tale,
> And drink his health in Yorkshire ale.
> Then smoak and read the *York Courant*,
> I'm happy, and 'tis all I want ;
> Though few my tythes, and light my purse,
> I thank my God it is no worse."

The lines are said to have been written by the late parson of that parish, who was a daily customer there, and a good type of the clergy at that time.†

In the year 1800, there resided in the town of Northallerton, a worthy, pains-taking hair-dresser, &c., named Ramble,‡ called in his day "a Jack of all trades." Were he now living and pursuing his various avocations, he would, doubtless, be styled " a genius," for, like Bob Handy, he could do everything. Well may I say could ; for, alas ! he has long slept in his peaceful grave, in the church-yard of one of the now quietest country towns of the north of England. The rail-road has removed its traffic, and covered its pavement with grass. The church, which stands in the centre of the town, surrounded by its elevated burial-ground, is no longer agitated by the passing to and fro of the " Wellington," " Highflyer," or " Victoria " coaches, or the " Royal Mail " ; the guard's horn or coachman's whip no more disturbs the devotion of the assembled congregation. The barber of Northallerton

---

* At the battle of Aboukir, Nelson gained a glorious victory ; all the French vessels, with the exception of two men-of-war and two frigates, were taken or destroyed. He was rewarded with the title of baron Nelson of the Nile, and of Burnham Thorpe, co. Norfolk, Nov. 6th, 1798, and an additional pension of £2,000, besides the estate and dukedom of Bronte, in Sicily.

† Mann-Dowson Todd's MSS.

‡ By "Ramble" is meant Gamble, a late Forensical Wig-maker at Northallerton.

A.D. 1800. Poor Ramble! in thy day Northallerton was a town of importance, and could boast of the "Royal Charlotte," six inside, four-horse coach, passing through on its way from London to Newcastle, the journey being generally performed in fifty-six hours, exclusive of remaining one night in York. Passengers occasionally remained in Northallerton on business, and at times required the aid of the tonsor's art; and as surely as the sound of coaches was heard, so surely was Ramble seen to pop his bald pate over the closed half of his little shop door, from which he could command a clear view "up street and down street," and gain the earliest intelligence, if not as to who, certainly as to what was coming. The "Royal Charlotte's" arrival brought him hope, but hope deferred; for, as regarded customers from or by it, he must wait the boot's or porter's summons to "dress a traveller just come by t' 'Charlotte.'" Not so when a lighter rattling sound was heard, and a travelling carriage was seen entering the town, drawn by two or more horses. Then were Ramble's hopes raised to the highest pitch of expectation. On such occasions he flew to the door of the inn, thinking his appearance there with his shaving and his dressing apparatus might gain him an order, as he said; and certainly his clean apron, cravat, and shoes, his smooth grey locks, his bright pewter shaving-jug, his white napkin, and his smiling countenance, free from "superfluous hairs," gained him many a customer. * * * It was Ramble's boast that he once dressed the wig of Judge ——, the very wig he wore when he passed sentence upon the notorious ——, for murder, the superior dressing of which was such, as Ramble was wont to boast, "that niver a single air of it was ruffled when he pulled hof his condemnation cap; na, I did hear say as how he did'nt have his wig dressed again for half a year after I had put it properly into friz, I had done it so well." Ramble's talents were not confined to comb, puff, or razor,—no, he could play a little upon the fiddle, did beat the big drum in the volunteer band, and occasionally, when John Stockwell's little boy was ill from an over-ripe plum affection, played the triangle. Nor did his acquirements cease here. He invented a superior blacking, could varnish fishing-rods and walking-sticks, mend wooden clocks, put a new spoke in the wheel of a wheelbarrow, paint a sign-post, make a three-legged stool, hoop a washing-tub, repair broken china, make a mouse-trap, mend a watchman's rattle, (no new police in his day), put up a four-post bedstead, fill up a broken window-pane with wood or glass, remove rheumatic pains, loose teeth and warts, carve an odd figure or face on the head of a walking-stick, re-cover umbrellas, gild oak-apples for school boys for Royal Oak Day, or the tips of constables' staves, prepare the chairing-chair for elections, post placards for the rival candidates (covering his morning's work with the evening's), distribute bills for the theatre, missionary meetings, assizes, races, or auctions, officiate for the bellman; was a supernumerary in processions on the stage, and, from long service, cleanliness, and attention, was a leader in such; an extra constable at the hustings, a *locum tenens* for the watchman, an additional waiter at the race ordinary dinner, a tipstaff at the sessions, and the only dealer in cork soles in the town. The loss of Ramble was sincerely regretted; for in such a town he was indeed a treasure.*

A.D. 1800.

In this year the high embankments on the south side of the Castle Hills were cut down, and the deep trenches filled up and levelled, thus destroying all traces of their antiquity.

1801. Destructive improvements

The following entry occurs in the parish books:—"Oct. 4th. Paid ringers when the preliminaries of peace were signed, 10s. 6d."

Entry in Parish Books.

The following is a copy of a small hand-bill printed by Langdale, of Northallerton, in 1802:—

1802. Association for the Prosecution of Felons.

NORTHALLERTON ASSOCIATION FOR THE PROSECUTION OF FELONS, &c.

We, whose Names are hereunto subscribed, having entered into an Association for the Prosecution of Felons, &c., DO HEREBY GIVE NOTICE that any Person who shall commit any Robbery, Felony, Theft, or Larceny upon the Persons or Property of any of the Members of the said Association, will henceforth be immediately prosecuted and brought to Justice.

And whoever will give such Information to Mr. H. HIRST, Solicitor to the said Association, as may be the means of detecting, apprehending, or convicting any Person or Persons guilty of any of the said Offences, shall receive a suitable Reward from the Committee of the said Association.

Rev. B. Walker	Jackson Parker
Godfrey Hirst	Thomas Walton
Henry Todd	John Dixon
Henry Hirst	John Readman
John Carter	George Clark
John Tennant	Thomas Watson
Joshua Pannel	John Wallis
Cuthbert Marshall	Ralph Wilson
Robert Reed	John Marshall
Richard Dighton	Joseph Watson
Thomas Dowson	John Smith
William Bulmer	Thomas Mothersill
Jonathan Peacock	Thomas Simpson

February 5th, 1802.

* Bentley's Miscellany.

A.D. 1802.
Mount Grace Bell.   The bell which was said to have come from Mount Grace was broken about this time. It was remarkable for the sweetness of its tone.

Entry in Parish Books.   Entry in parish books:—"Paid ringing for the definitive treaty being signed, 10s. 6d."

Captain Peat.   Died at Northallerton, October 17th, 1802. Captain Peat, before his death, was an enthusiastic promoter of the local Volunteer corps in Northallerton, the captain of which he ultimately became.*

1803.
An eccentric character.   On the 6th of July in this year, died at Northallerton, one Daniel Frazer, a travelling tinker. He travelled about from village to village in a small wooden house on wheels, known as "Noah's Ark," a name probably given thereto because "Dan" was in the habit of pulling up his house when he came into Northallerton, in the middle of the Sun-beck. He was found dead in the "Ark," at the comparatively ripe age of 68 years, and it is said that he was worth upwards of a thousand pounds at the time of his death.

1804.
Gunpowder Plot.   On Nov. 5th, 1804, general Hewgill being stationed at Northallerton with his regiment, endeavoured to suppress the bonfires, an interference which highly enraged the populace. Being unable to read the Riot Act, on account of the stones and mire which were thrown at him, he was glad to abandon the attempt. God grant that neither we or ours may ever live to see the 5th of November forgotten, or the solemnity of it silenced.

A Pony Race   A match for 100 guineas a side was decided between Mr. Tennant's chesnut galloway, and Mr. Hawman's black pony, ridden by the owners, 100 miles, on the road between Northallerton and York, which was won by the galloway. They set off from Northallerton at eight o'clock in the morning, and the winner returned, after completing the 100 miles, at half-past eleven at night. The pony kept the lead for eighty-two miles, and was then passed by the galloway, which won

---

* Near the tower in Northallerton Church, a marble tablet erected to his memory, bears the following inscription :—

To the Memory of
SAMUEL PEAT, ESQUIRE,
Late Captain commanding the Northallerton Volunteers,
He departed this life 17th October, 1802,
Aged 47 Years.

Why hallowed dust, should friendship seek to tell
That merit here ! thy life has spoke so well :
Thy powers departed now with " here he lies,"
Points to the spirit wafted to the skies !
Teach us to follow dear departed worth,
To rise with him above the grovelling earth.
Eternal Father ! at whose awful throne
We bow, let " Thine Almighty will be done."

easily, beating the pony by six miles. They were ridden once A.D. 1804. to York and back, and twice to Thirsk and back, round Northallerton cross each time. In going back to Thirsk, the pony gave up at Thornton-le-Street, when about a quarter of a mile behind the galloway.

On January 30th in this year, died at Northallerton, 1805. Elizabeth York, daughter of Eugene Aram, schoolmaster, of Eugene Aram Lynn and Knaresborough, and murderer of the old man Lockey. Hood's poem entitled "*The Dream of Eugene Aram*," written in 1843, is so well known to our readers that it is unnecessary to quote it *in extenso*, suffice it to say that Aram, though married, was a comparatively young man when he committed the crime for which he suffered the extreme penalty of the law. Auromania or gold madness was the evil power which suggested the foul deed, and impelled its perpetration. The pathos of Hood's poem is very touching, and his description most graphic. Mrs. York was considered quite a celebrity.

John Herring was sexton of the parish church in 1805. John Herring. The following anecdote is related concerning him:—An illiterate person coming into the church whilst John was dusting, caught sight of the letters I. H. S. on the pulpit cloth, and enquired what they meant; to which John replied, "A'll assure tha, they stan' for John Herring, Sexton."

The following entries occur in the churchwardens' Entry in accounts:—"Ringing lord Nelson's victory,* 15s.; ringing Parish Books. on account of sir Robert Strahan taking 4 sail of the line,† 15s."

Ann Harris, formerly Hedley, a native of Northallerton, A martial was married to a private of the 51st regiment during their woman. stay in this town. When the regiment left, she accompanied her husband, who was soon afterwards sent abroad, and served in the army under the duke of Wellington and sir John Moore. At the battle of Corunna, where sir John lost his life, she also lost her husband, and notwithstanding, she was one of those females who gave their assistance in paying the last sad office to the remains of that gallant and much lamented general.

The following entry is made in the parish books:— 1806. "Ringing on account of the victory of Martinico, 15s." Entry in Parish Books.

* The ever-memorable battle of Trafalgar, in which the undaunted hero lord Nelson was slain. The last signal he hoisted was "England expects that every man will do his duty," and the last words he spoke, upon being informed of the victory were "Thank God I have done my duty."

† Sir R. Strahan captured after the battle of Trafalgar, the Formidable, 80 guns; Mont Blanc, 74 guns; Scipion, 74 guns; and Duguay Tronin, 74 guns.—*Nelson's Despatches.*

A.D. 1807
Fine for Sunday trading.

The following entry appears in the churchwardens' accounts for 1807:—" Paid Thomas Bradley, for 30 loaves to be given to the poor, for Wm. Williamson's fine for selling meat on the Lord's Day, 5s."*

Further discoveries at Castle Hills.

About this time whilst the embankments and trenches on the east side of the Castle Hills were being taken down and levelled, a few coins, an antique silver buckle, and a glass ornament, undoubtedly Roman, were turned up by the spade.

General Election.

On the dissolution of parliament by the Canning and Castlereagh administration, William Wilberforce, esq., lord Milton, the hon. Henry Lascelles, and Walter Fawkes, esq., offered themselves as representatives for the county of Yorkshire. Mr. Fawkes withdrawing, the two great families of Harewood and Wentworth, representing the two great parties in the county, were thus directly opposed to each other, and the contest was one of the most memorable and costly in the history of elections. Money was expended in great profusion during a fifteen days' poll; and, according to the ancient custom, all the freeholders went to York to vote. The following went from Northallerton and voted as follows: 54 for Lascelles, 13 for Wilberforce, and 3 for Milton. The greatest activity and excitement was manifested. At the final close of the poll (5th June), the numbers stood thus:— Mr. Wilberforce 11,806 votes, lord Milton 11,177, and Mr. Lascelles 10,789.

1808.
Castle Hills.

In this year the Castle Hills were enclosed, and formed into neat small fields.

Hutton, the Historian.

Hutton,† the historian, visited this town on his road to Coatham; after a brief description he says, "this town, two hundred years ago, was the residence of my family. My grandfather's grandfather was a native, and enjoyed the *capital* honour of furnishing the place with hats. Walking in the churchyard, it occurred to my thoughts that I might be treading upon the dust of my ancestors; and, being indisposed while there, thought I might possibly leave my dust to mix with theirs. I enquired after my relations, but found the name was extinct.

"While I lay indisposed at Northallerton, a gentleman,

* This was a contravention of the Lord's Day Act, (3 Chas. 1, cap. 2, sec. 1,) which is still unrepealed.—J. L. S.

† William Hutton, F.A.S.S., was born at Derby, in 1723. In 1750 he opened a shop for the sale of old books, to which was added a circulating library, at Birmingham; soon afterwards he embarked in the paper business, and by frugality and industry arrived at opulence. He took up the pen, at the advanced age of fifty-six, a period in which most authors lay it down. He drove the quill thirty years, in which time he wrote and published fourteen books, the principal of which are the histories of Birmingham, Blackpool, Derby, Battle of Bosworth Field, Hundred Court, Roman Wall, Tours to London, Scarbro', Coatham, &c. He died in 1815, aged 92.

his lady, and daughter, in a chaise and four, attended by his servant, stopped, changed horses, and flew away in a moment. I was sorry when I heard they were for Coatham, and would want three beds. I had no doubt but they would apply to our inn. As I knew promise and profit were at variance, and that the bird in hand was worth two in the bush, I considered the chance was against me. We set off early the next morning, made a double stage, and arrived one hour before noon. The landlady had kept her promise, and the gentleman was obliged to hire four shabby rooms at £2 12s. 6d. a week, and wait a fortnight before room could be made at the inn, by which he lost five guineas besides being incommoded.

"This gentleman's family and ourselves afterwards contracted an intimacy, which grew into that friendship which cost a tear at parting. He had brought two or three books; one of which was Hargrove's History of Knaresborough, much used. I liked the book, 'Pray what was the price?' 'Two shillings I believe.' I looked into the title-page and found it was four. 'The book,' said I (holding it in one hand, and four shillings in the other,) 'was written at Knaresborough, and printed at York, neither of which places are in my return. But both lie in your neighbourhood; you can procure, and I cannot. Which hand will you have?' He afterwards put the book into my hand, with 'When you see this book, think of me.'

"I found written upon a blank leaf:—

'Mr. Hutton, of Birmingham,
  The Gift of
John S............s,
  of B............ Hall,
As a token of his regard.'"

The following records of national events are found in the churchwardens' books:—"Aug. 17th. Ringers paid for sir A. Wesley,* [Wellesley] 15s.; ringers for good news, 12s."

During our conflicts with France in the matter of Portugal about this time, the "Combat of Coa" stands forth conspicuously as one of the most brilliant exploits of the war; and, although the result was glorious to the troops engaged, it was an ill-considered conflict which might have seriously compromised the deep-laid schemes of the commander-in-chief (Lord Wellington). How this was so, will be gleaned

---

* Sir Arthur Wellesley gained on the 28th July, the victory of Talavera, when the British troops were opposed by double their number of picked French veterans. This was the first great engagement during the Peninsular war; and for this victory he was created visct. Wellington of Talavera, &c., with a pension of £2,000 a-year for two generations.

from a private letter written by Lieutenant (afterwards Lieutenant-Colonel) Henry Booth, of Northallerton, to his brother, in England:—

Letter from Lieut. Booth of the 43rd, to his brother.

"Camp at Celorico, July 30th, 1810.

"We are both (alluding to his brother Charles, in the 52nd), as well as possible, quite clear out of all the scrapes, thank God! But to the point. Our gallant, I wish I could say *wise*, General Crauford, after having been driven from his position near Gallegos, about three leagues in front of Almeida, posted his division a little to the right of that fortress, amongst rocks, walls, and vineyards, on the slope of the hill which descends to the river Coa—a worse position, every one allows, could not have been chosen. However, after a dreadful stormy night, with incessant rain, thunder, and lightning until day-break, our men and officers thoroughly drenched—I may say half-drowned—and fire-locks nearly unserviceable, we waited patiently the attack of the French on the morning of the 24th. Our pickets were soon driven in, and the French fired on our line with musketry, shot, and shells; we returned the fire, and were ordered to retire *in line*—*very wisely and properly ordered!* But unfortunately, from the vast quantity of high walls, six feet high generally, the number of rocks, vineyards, and broken ground which continued down to the water's edge, our *line* was very soon broken, past all chance of being formed again, till we had crossed the bridge. In this manner the whole division retired down this tremendous hill. This was fine fun for the French skirmishers, who were following us closely from rock to rock, pelting us pretty handsomely down to the river. However, in all this confusion, our fellows behaved nobly, and retired fighting inch by inch, which in the end proved our misfortune; for had we made the best of our way over the bridge, and occupied the hills on the other side as soon as possible, we should have suffered less, and precisely the same position would have been gained. But why did our general wait for the attack in so infamous a position? It was impossible for us to keep our ground, nor was it intended that we should. We remained, as it were to be fired upon, without the means of defending ourselves till we could cross the bridge. Would it not have answered the purpose if general Crauford had *at first* occupied the hills on the other side of the bridge, advancing his pickets some distance in front, which could have retired on the approach of the French, covered by the fire of our line on the hills, and then defend the bridge, as we might have done against a much superior force? Every one asks the same question. The general is universally blamed, and Lord Wellington is said to have expressed to him his disapprobation. In proof he has given sir Brent Spencer the command of the Light Division, which has caused no little satisfaction amongst us. To continue my tedious, and I am afraid, confused account, we defended the bridge against three attempts of the French to force it, in all of which they failed, suffering heavy loss. At last the firing mutually ceased, on account of the torrents of rain that fell, after five hours' hard peppering at each other. Towards night we retired, and have been gradually falling back on this place. The main body of the army is still more in rear, and we have only a few cavalry in our front. We *must* retire when the French advance. Where the army will halt and fight, of course we are ignorant. It depends entirely on the force they bring against us. We have had a good share of fag, and shall be glad to have a reprieve. Things are now, I assure you, coming to a crisis. All depends on the force of the French. It is the general opinion that the enemy will bring on such numbers as to leave little doubt of the issue of a battle. Happen what may, we have lads who will do their duty. The people of England, I dare say, are looking to us. Well they may. Now, my dear Tom, with much sorrow, I lay before you a long list of killed and wounded of the 43rd. Killed—Colonel Hull, who had joined us to take command the preceding day; Captain Ewen Cameron; and Lieutenant Nason, a fine young lad of seventeen. Wounded—Captains Lloyd, J. W. Hall, W. Napier, Shaw, Deshon, the first four severely; Lieutenant M'Diarmid, Harvest, Johnston, Stevenson, Frederick, Hopkins. Poor Frederick, a fine young boy, has since lost his leg; it was amputated yesterday. Hopkins commanded the company I am attached to, and was wounded in the first fire. The command afterwards fell to me. I was not so unfortunate; I came clear off. Sergeants, drummers, and privates killed, wounded, and missing, 130.

The 95th has suffered almost as severely as ourselves in officers and men. The loss of the 52nd, I am happy to say, is comparatively trifling. Two officers wounded, and a few men killed. They were not so much exposed as ours and the 95th. We regret the loss of Colonel Hull; in short, of all who fell. Major M'Leod, who has succeeded Colonel Hull in the command, distinguished himself. Is not this a pretty loss for one regiment, owing entirely to the blunders of——? I hope we shall be better managed for the future. We only wish for a fair chance; there is then no fear of our lads gaining distinction. Is it not a pity such fine fellows should always be obliged to fight *retiring?* Yet this must be the game now for a while. The French force in our front, in the neighbourhood of Almeida and Rodrigo, is stated to be about

A.D. 1810.

Battle of Busaco.

Letter from Lieut. Charles Booth of the 52nd.

80,000. It is said they were advancing in other directions. This is a camp letter; pray excuse faults."*

The following letter, written by Lieutenant Charles Booth, brother of Lieutenant Henry Booth, of Northallerton, both of whom fought in this battle, is replete with interest:—

"Camp, near Aruda, about fifteen miles from Lisbon, 9th Nov., 1810.

"Never did a military man commit so great a blunder as Massena in attacking the position of Busaco. Without any previous reconnoissance of our force or the nature of our position, he attacked what was far from being its weakest points with a force unequal to make the slightest impression. We lost certainly some brave fellows, but, compared to their loss (especially in *killed*), ours was a mere trifle. In the part of the line occupied by the Light Division and about 200 yards immediately to its front two columns of the enemy—supposed about 5,000 each—were met by the two left-hand companies of the 43rd, and the right two of the 52nd. The front of their columns alone—chiefly composed of officers—stood the charge; the rest took to their heels, throwing away their arms, pouches, &c. Our men did not stand to take prisoners; what were taken were those left in our rear in the hurry of pressing forward in the charge. The flanks of the 43rd and 52nd in their charge met only the enemy's skirmishers, who had, by superior numbers, driven in the 95th Rifles but a few seconds before the charge of the division. These poor fellows were all glad enough to give themselves up as prisoners, our men not being allowed to fire a shot at them. The advanced part of the charging line—the four companies first mentioned—after throwing themselves into the midst of the enemy's retreating columns, killing, wounding, and in short felling to the ground lots of them, were with great difficulty halted, and then commenced from the flanks of the whole division the most destructive flanking fire that I believe was ever witnessed. Not a tenth part of their whole force would have escaped had not the four companies, by precipitating themselves too far in front of the general line, exposed themselves to the fire of their comrades, and thus prevented more than 300 firelocks on each flank of the division from being brought into action. The flanks, and in fact every other part of the division (except the four centre companies), had to pass over in the charge some very steep rugged ground, where, not meeting with anything but the enemy's skirmishers, they pushed on head-over-heels, until the descent became almost perpendicular. At this time

---

* Vide Historical Records of the 43rd Regiment.

they were halted, and had a fine view of what was going on in the centre.

"I was in the left wing of the battalion, and am sure, though we were not five minutes in the charge down the hill, it cost us more than half-an-hour to get up into our first position again. I have often had described to me what is called a '*hot business*,' and where confusion 'tis said 'reigns triumphant on all sides.' If this be true, then I have only to say that I have never been in a general action, or what is termed 'hot business.' It must indeed be a terrible sight if it exceeds what we saw at Busaco, where, to all those who had their eyes open and not poking their way with a bayonet, everything appeared to be carried on with the greatest possible regularity, considering the ground we had to act upon. Orders, to be sure, could only be communicated by sound of bugle, or by the stentorian voice of a company officer. Great was the screech set on foot by our fellows during the charge. Poor Barclay was shot twice in front of the four companies, at a very few paces from the enemy; he was cheering the men at the time.

"You will see by the '*Gazette*,' that the 52nd took General Simon, two or three field officers, and some of inferior rank. Some one has had the audacity, rascality, I should say, to contradict this in the newspapers; if this gentleman is wise, he will not give the slightest hint of his name to any of the Light Division. It was said too, that he was actually engaged with the division on that day. General Simon was both wounded and taken by the same person — a private soldier of the 52nd. He had been much in advance and on the right of their column in coming up the hill, and at the time he was wounded was reconnoitring in their line of skirmishers. Harry I reckon as having narrowly escaped on several occasions during the retreat. At Busaco he was in Captain Lloyd's — the left-hand company of the 43rd — in one of those who met the head of the French column in the charge. His captain, who was close to him at the time they reached the enemy's columns, was on the point of being bayoneted, but knocked down the fellow attempting it. Harry must have had a shave or two, as he could not prevent himself from being in the very thick of them, but he speaks only of the actions of the others. At the Coa, near Almeida, his was one of the companies that covered the retreat of the division across the bridge; and had it not been for the gallant manner in which this detachment — principally 43rd — behaved, most of the division would certainly have been taken prisoners, or forced into the river, where they must inevitably have perished. Lieutenant Hopkins, in command of this company, had been wounded in the early part of the

A.D. 1810. day, whilst in conversation with Harry respecting their unfavourable position. Harry, of course, took command of the company for the rest of the day, which was by far the most trying part of it, having been amongst the last of the few who escaped over the bridge after the retreat of the principal body of the covering party. Had any person of interest been inclined to have taken proper notice of his conduct, and that of a few others on that day, and represented it properly to Lord Wellington, a company would have been the least he could have rewarded them with.

"The day of the retreat to our present position, Harry's (Captain Lloyd's) company was on the rear-guard on the most stormy disagreeable day I ever witnessed. The enemy had come upon us rather unexpectedly whilst snug at our dinners at Alemquer. Considerable confusion ensued on our leaving the town, for the enemy's riflemen were actually entering it before the 43rd had assembled. Harry was in rear of all with a section of the company, and obliged to blaze away in all directions in order to keep them in check, so great was their impudence and spirits at seeing us retreat in so confused a manner. The town withal contained excellent plunder, and what they most wanted, shelter for the day."*

1812.
Soke Mills.

The foundations of the dam of the ancient Castle Soke Mills at Northallerton discovered, and many loads of good useful stone carted away for various purposes.†

Entry in Parish Books.

Entries in churchwarden's' accounts:—" Paid ringers for the victory of Sellenancos [Salamanca] 15s.; ditto, at Madrid, 15s.

An incident in church.

At this time the church of England was degraded by that intolerable mode of accommodation known as the rented pew system, and which still lingers in many nonconformist places of worship. By this system pews were bought and sold, bequeathed and transferred much in the same way as a house or piece of land, so that the gospel was very often at a premium; to the poor only it was " *without money and without price.*" In Northallerton this description of simony flourished in rank luxuriance, the pews in the parish church being high hideous boxes effectually hiding the members of the congregation from each other, and making a glimpse of the minister in his "three decker" an incident for a week's table-talk.‡

* Vide Historical Records of the 43rd Regiment.
† Mann-Dowson Todd's MSS.
‡ The origin of high pews is generally attributed to Bishop Burnett, who complained that the ladies of the princess Anne's establishment did not look at him while preaching, but were looking at other objects. He, therefore, after much remonstrance on this impropriety, prevailed on the queen Anne to order all the pews in St. James's Chapel to be raised so high that the "fair delinquents could see nothing but himself," when he was in the pulpit. The

NORTHALLERTON.

The doors of each pew bore a brass plate upon which was inscribed the name of the owner, whilst the poor people were doomed to sit in humble ranks along the sides of the walls, or down the centre of the aisles, and were expected to rise, tug the front lock and curtsey in token of servility as the "quality" left their luxuriously furnished seats. Thus, although "*the rich and the poor met together*," it might easily have been imagined that the same God did not make them all. Indeed, St. James's sarcastic picture was vividly and graphically reproduced in Northallerton church whenever the fashionable stranger, conspicuous by his splendid dress and jewelled fingers, entered the sacred edifice. Eagerly welcomed by the wardens, he was ushered forthwith into a good place or pew; while "*the poor man in vile raiment*,"—some broken hearted wanderer, possibly the victim of his own folly and vice, who had timidly strayed in to see whether it be true that "*Christians love one another*," and have a gospel for the poor,—was left shivering by the door, and pointed to a vacant spot on the floor. It chanced one Sunday morning about this time that a private in a Highland regiment then, passing through the town came into the church, and not being able to find a seat, or the door of a pew hospitably opened to admit him, unceremoniously vaulted over the top of one of the pews and descended into the midst of its startled occupants saying in a loud voice, "*God is no respecter of persons.*"*

"Entries in churchwardens' accounts:—" Paid ringers on account of lord Wellington's victory, 15s.; paid ditto of news from Holland, 15s."

Reginald Gideon Bouyer, L.L.D., archdeacon of Northumberland and rector of Howick, became vicar of Northallerton in 1814. He died in 1826, and was interred at Durham. Shortly after his induction to the living, he published a pamphlet entitled "A Friendly and Serious Address to the labouring poor within the parish of Northallerton, and more especially to those who inhabit the townships of Northallerton and Romanby." From this pamphlet several interesting extracts are here inserted, which will give the readers of the "Annals" some idea of the religious state of Northallerton at that time. Mr. Bouyer says, "I suppose it must be known to you, that for a twelve-month past the care of your immortal souls has been committed to my charge, and that during the last half-year I have resided and discharged the duties of my ministry amongst you.'

A.D. 1812.

1814. Entry in Parish Books.

Reginald Gideon Bouyer.

---

princess laughed at the complaint; but she complied when Burnett told her that the interests of the church were in danger. The whim of bishop Burnett was imitated in many places which had not been pewed before, and high pews are at this day to be seen in remote country parishes.

* This incident was related to me by an eye-witness, Marmaduke Jaques, the clerk of Northallerton church.—J. L. S.

A.D. 1815.

Religious indifference of the poorer classes.

After explaining the object of his pamphlet, the worthy vicar says, " I was much encouraged by observing the large size of our parish church. Great, therefore, were my grief and disappointment to find that there were scarcely any attendants in the worship of Almighty God, except those whose habitations entitled them to the property of a pew, or, who, by easy circumstances, were enabled to purchase or hire seats. Upon enquiring into the cause of this scandalous and lamentable absence, I found that it was wholly imputed to the want of accommodation for the poor. I most sincerely lament that there should ever have been any ground for such a complaint, and it is with the greatest satisfaction I have to inform you that measures are now being taken to provide a great number of very commodious seats, to be open to all that will occupy them; and upon this great improvement, I do most cordially congratulate all aged, lame, and weakly persons." Mr. Bouyer then proceeds to rebuke those who absent themselves from the house of God, "under idle or frivolous pretences." The most common of these excuses, he says, " is that of not having clothes sufficient to make a decent appearance, and as this excuse has been sometimes pleaded, not only to account for absence from church, but to justify the withholding children from school, it deserves a separate consideration. For these necessaries the poor in general knew where to apply, several valuable legacies having been left to the poor of this parish." Passing on to the subject of education, the vicar reminds his readers that " within the last four years a most respectable society has been formed, under the patronage of the prince Regent, and under the active care of all the bishops, and of a great number of the most respectable nobility and gentry of the realm, to forward a new plan of education, by which instruction is conveyed more quickly, more certainly, and to a far greater number of children, than have ever before been made partakers of the great benefit of charity schools. In which short period an almost incredible number of schools have been built all over the kingdom, and many thousand children have been taught in them, who, but for that most valuable institution, would still have been left an unguarded prey to ignorance, vice, and misery. That salutary plan has been adopted in this parish, where it has been gradually improved, and is now advancing fast to perfection. A hundred children of each sex, will now be admitted into it, and since the fitting up of the new room for the boys, every convenience has been provided in the old one, to train the female scholars to such employments, as are most likely to be

Want of church accommodation.

Free seats provided.

Charities.

An Education Society.*

Additional school accommodation.

---

* The National Society for the education of the poor.

useful to them during their lives, besides their instruction in religion, reading, writing, and accounts.   *   *   *   I am sorry to say, that the profanation of the Sabbath has been lamentably observable in carrying on trade,* and doing worldly business on the Lord's-day, or wholly consuming it in amusements, and recreations, which however innocent and lawful they may be in themselves, must always be considered as highly criminal, if they occupy any part of the time, which is, by our excellent church set apart for the solemn and devout worship of Almighty God."

A.D. 1815. Prevailing profanity.

The people of Northallerton collected during the month of October, the paltry sum of £60 1s. 8d. for the wounded heroes and families of those who fell in the dreadful battle of Waterloo, whilst the little village of Hutton Bonville sent £215 2s.†

Battle of Waterloo.

An old inhabitant of the town‡ says that the first day-school instituted in Northallerton was originated by the Rev. Gideon Bouyer, L.L.D., Vicar. The children used to assemble in the vicarage coach-house, where was a large table with a small ledge all round it, the top of which was sprinkled with sand; this was called the "sand-desk," and the rudiments of writing and arithmetic were invariably taught to the younger children upon it, who formed their letters and figures with a stick. "*Hoo far 'es thoo gitten?*" was the frequent enquiry of many a fond parent; and, "*Wha ah's at t' sand-desk yit,*" was the equally frequent reply. Thus the sand-desk supplied the place of the then more expensive slate and copy book, with the latter of which the children were only supplied when considered proficient in the arts of reading and arithmetic. Connected with this day-school was a condition and a privilege. The condition was that all the children attending it should also be regular attenders at the church and Sunday school; and the privilege was the use by the boys, whilst they remained scholars, of a uniform Sunday suit of clothes, which was given out by the vicar to each boy on Saturday evening, and returned by him on the following Monday morning.

Day School.

William Hutton, esq., the venerable historian, died at Birmingham this year at the ripe age of ninety-four. Mr. Hutton's ancestors were hatters in Northallerton.

Death of Hutton.

The following records appear in the churchwardens' books:—" Paid ringers on account of Blucher's victory, 15s.; paid ditto, of Allied army's entering Paris, 15s.; June, ringers

Entries in Parish Books.

---

* The sale of butchers' meat and fish was regularly carried on in Northallerton, the latter being hawked in carts on Sunday morning before church-time.
† Mann-Dowson Todd's MSS.   ‡ Mr. Edward H. Reed.

A.D. 1815. on proclamation, 15s.; ringers illumination by order, £1 1s.; candles for church, 1s. 7½d.; ringing on peace with America, 15s.; 25 June, ditto on good news, 15s.; 28th ditto, on more good news, 15s.

1816. An imperial visit.
On the 12th December, 1815, the grand duke Nicholas and Constantine, of Russia, accompanied by sir William Congreve, and a numerous suite, in four carriages and four, and two outriders, arrived at Mr. Francis Hirst's, Golden Lion Hotel, Northallerton, from York, and stayed all night, and proceeded the next morning at eleven o'clock, on their tour to the north. Mr. Hirst set the whole off, with first rate horses, and eight post-boys, all dressed alike in scarlet and jockey caps. In the churchwardens' accounts for 1816, the following entry appears :—" Ringing on the arrival of duke Nicholas and suite, 10s.

Inspection of skins.
During the wars which disfigure the pages of English history about this time, there was a large demand for good leather for the use of the army. But it was found that the hides and skins were much injured by the carelessness of the butchers, and strict regulations were made by government for the inspection of skins in each market town. John Melsonby held the office of inspector in Northallerton. He was afterwards master of the old workhouse.

1817. Escape of prisoners from the gaol.
In August, 1817, five felons, though heavily ironed, made their escape from the house of correction at Northallerton. One of them named West, by taking up some of the flags in his cell, made a hole large enough to admit him into the adjoining passage; he then wrenched off the handle of the pump, with which he forced off the locks of the cells of several other criminals, by whose assistance the doors leading into the area were forced ; and by blankets and rugs tied together, and attached at one end to a large stool, which they threw over the outer wall, made their escape.*

Entry in Parish Books.
Entry in church books :—" Ringing (tolling) for Princess Charlotte, 16s. 6d."

1818. Trial of Queen Caroline.
Readers of English history will be familiar with the incidents which led up to the trial of queen Caroline, instigated by her jealous consort George IV. When the news of the queen's success in vindicating her character reached Northallerton, the bells of the church were rung and all the windows of the town illuminated with lighted candles. There were, however, three men in the town who did not agree with the verdict of the jury, believing the queen to be guilty, and accordingly they refused to illuminate their windows, which were quickly smashed by the indignant populace. The names of the gallant (?) three were captain Fife, Fletcher Rigg, esq.,

* Vide Ingledew's History of Northallerton, page 361.

NORTHALLERTON.   159

and the rev. Robert Macfarlane, curate of the parish. The latter resided at the Vine House. When the work of destruction commenced, Mr. Rigg hastily lit up his windows and so, to some extent, saved them from the stones of the mob.   A.D. 1818.

Entry in church books:—" Ringing for prince Coberg, 10s. 6d. ; tolling for the queen (Caroline) 2s. 6d."   1819.

Mr. James Langdale, bookseller, author of a small History of Northallerton, and a Topographical Dictionary of Yorkshire, died this year in the 72nd year of his age. His death was occasioned by a cart, in which the driver was asleep, running against his gig, which produced so severe a shock, as to rupture a vessel in the region of the heart.   1823. James Langdale.

The organ in the parish church first played by hand. Previous to this the instrument which is small, and very old, contained three barrels, each barrel being capable of producing ten tunes, extracted therefrom by the grinding process.* In still earlier times, the singing of the worshippers in Northallerton church was led by an orchestra of stringed instruments.   The Parish Church Organ

Early in the year, General Foissac le Tour, the general commanding the French army in Spain, came to Gibraltar. Colonel Haverfield being absent on leave, Major Booth offered to show him the regiment. He replied he should be delighted, and came on the ground in full dress, a large crimson saddlecloth embroidered in golden fleurs de lys, and attended by his aide-de-camp, nearly as richly caparisoned. On the conclusion of the field day, General Foissac said, " Major Booth, you have well commanded your well-instructed regiment. This day has disabused me of an error of twenty years. I always thought the French infantry the quickest to move in Europe, but they are nothing to you, you move like cavalry ! "   1825. A compliment to Major H. Booth.

Singularly enough the French General thus unwittingly parodied the old Shorncliffe *refrain*—

"No cavalry in England can form a line so quick,
As the 43rd Light Infantry—at the double quick ! " †

George Townsend, D.D., was formerly chaplain to the bishop of Durham. He became vicar of Northallerton in 1826, and resigned the living through ill health in 1839.   1826. George Townsend.

This year will be memorable in the annals of history on account of the partial destruction, by fire, of the venerable minster of York. The incendiary, Jonathan Martin, was a religious enthusiast of the puritan type, and amongst other things which incurred his dislike was the magnificent organ   1829. The incendiary of York Minster.

---

* Being worn out, and having served the church of Northallerton well and faithfully for many years, the old organ has recently been sold, like a worn-out horse, for the very small sum of £11.

† Vide Historical Records of the 43rd Regiment.

A.D. 1829. in York minster. The day before the fire, he concealed himself during evening service behind archbishop Grinfield's tomb, in the north transept, muttering to himself as the organ played, "*Buzz, buzz,—I'll teach thee to stop thy buzzing.*"* After the service he coolly made a heap of bibles, prayer-books, and hangings, set fire to them, and escaped, praising God for having "*strengthened him to do so good a work!*" Martin left the minster a little after three o'clock in the morning, proceeding to Easingwold, thence to Thirsk, and from Thirsk to Northallerton, arriving about three o'clock in the afternoon of the day following the fire. He appeared to be quite exhausted, and remained with his brother-in-law, who resided at Northallerton, until the evening. He left the town at nine o'clock the same evening in a coal cart, and was arrested at Hexham a few days later, at the house of a friend, whilst reading a hymn-book. In the course of his defence before baron Hullock, he detailed the particulars of his journey from York to Northallerton, during which time he said he had very little food, but "*t' Lord refreshed my soul on t' road wi't snow on t' ground.*" He was brought in "not guilty on the ground of insanity," and ordered to be kept in close custody during the king's pleasure. That Martin was afflicted with religious mania cannot be doubted, indeed his whole life presents one string of eccentricities and strange notions culminating in arson and sacrilege.

1830.
Chairing the Members.

It was the custom before the passing of the Reform Bill, after the two members had been elected, to carry each member in a chair on the shoulders of men from the Toll Booth round the market cross, to the 'Golden Lion.' This was called "chairing the members," and on several occasions, the last being in 1830, after the members had been chaired, an old man called Duke Flower, who was popular with the mob, was also chaired round the cross with much cheering.

1832.
Coal Supply.

Prior to the introduction of railways and for a short time afterwards, the inhabitants of Northallerton were supplied with coals by carts and wagons, which journeyed to and fro, between the coal-fields of South Durham and Northallerton. Every Wednesday and Saturday long rows of thirty or forty coal-laden carts might be seen standing in the market-place, from which purchasers supplied their wants. Asses also in considerable numbers were employed in this trade, and it was no uncommon sight to see a drove of twelve to twenty asses toiling along, laden with sacks of coal, on their way to the moor-villages amongst the hills and dales, for the convenience of those who were unable to afford the more expensive mode of transit. This method of conveying fuel was continued

* Yorkshire Oddities, vol. 2, page 165.

some time after the carts had found it unprofitable to compete with the railway. The last person engaged in this business was "Geordy Harland," whose soot-begrimed features, and long stick with which he belaboured his unfortunate beasts of burden, will be remembered by many now in middle life.

The year 1832 is a memorable one in the annals of Northallerton for the Reform Bill, which was passed in June of that year, awakened amongst all classes in the borough a deep interest in political life. The electors newly admitted to the franchise, fired with zeal, determined to make an effort to shake off the influence of certain powerful landowners, who had previously done very much as they liked, nominating and returning members of their own families to Parliament, which was facetiously termed "the action of a free and independent electorate." With this object in view, a deputation consisting of R. Davison, esq., J. Horner, esq., and John Metcalfe, esq., waited upon Capt. Boss, R.N., of Otterington Hall, and invited him to become a candidate at the election which was shortly to take place; at the same time pledging themselves to use every effort to secure his return, and assuring him that in their opinion his chance of success was very great, a prediction which, after events, proved correct. The gallant captain was quite willing to comply with their request, for the sole purpose of opening the borough, provided they could shew him that there was a reasonable probability of success, and steps were at once taken to test the feeling of the electors. A memorial was got up requesting Capt. Boss to stand, which was signed by two-thirds of the electors, and a demonstration to celebrate the passing of the Reform Bill and introduce the candidate to the electors was arranged to take place on Brompton green, a description of which, taken from a local newspaper of that date, will not be out of place here. It must, however, be remembered that by the Boundary Act,* were included "the respective townships of Northallerton and Romanby, and the chapelry of Brompton."

"Monday, June 25th, was the day appointed to commemorate the passing of the Reform Bill,—and as soon as the midnight of Sunday was past, a fat ox was put down to spit to be roasted entire, a spectacle that attracted numerous visitors during the morning from Northallerton and the surrounding country. A half-moon battery was also erected, and six pieces of cannon, provided for the occasion, fired repeated volleys during the day. The 'Royal George' and 'Union Jack' floated from the masts purposely erected for

* 2 & 3 Wm. IV., c. 64.

A.D. 1832. their reception, and several other banners, public and private, adorned the houses of the inhabitants.

About eleven o'clock a procession left Brompton, headed by a band of music, with colours flying, and banners bearing devices of various kinds. Each person in the procession wore an orange ribbon in his coat, the members of the committee being distinguished by a rosette of white silk tied with blue ribbon. The most striking feature of this interesting exhibition, was a stage erected upon a wagon, on which a flax dresser, stripped, with tucked-up sleeves and paper cap, was adroitly combing the flax before him; upon a form sat a weaver, throwing quite at his ease, the swiftly gliding shuttle, ever and anon receiving his supply of bobbins from a fair maiden, who, calmly and deftly turned her wheel to keep him in continual action; whilst an aged dame, attired in a blue gown of ancient make, sat with the utmost composure against the jovial flax dresser, drawing out the lengthened thread, an employment that conferred the appellation of *spinster* upon the unmarried ladies of antiquity, and which, in law terms, is still in existence, though the practice itself is now no more. The spinning jenny was intended as an emblematical representation of the linen manufacture of Brompton, and afforded considerable enjoyment to the assembled crowd around. In front of the stage before-mentioned, an enormously large broom (also an emblematical design) was elevated, wherewith to sweep the rotten borough influence out of Northallerton, and so purify a constituency of which the inhabitants of Brompton now formed a part. After moving through the town in the highest style of order, the procession halted in the main street of Northallerton, where the band played several patriotic airs, after which the cavalcade returned to Brompton to dine.

Derivation of the word "Spinster."

The Dinner. Captain Boss's approach was hailed with acclamation, waving of hats, and firing of cannon. Three extensive ranges of tables were erected on the village green, and presented the appearance of a long oval, having a triumphal entrance arch in the middle of each side, formed of oaken boughs, ornamented with flowers. Mr. Wilford presided, and Mr. Pattison was the vice. The dinner consisted of the ox which had been roasted entire, also another cooked in joints (roast and boiled), three hams, and fish, &c., with the usual accompaniments, and a copious supply of good ale. The greatest order and harmony prevailed, and every one seemed to enjoy the feast with the highest degree of satisfaction. About 500 sat down to dine.

The dinner being concluded, the worthy chairman rose to propose the health of his Majesty and the other members of the royal family, which were drunk with three

times three, answered by the battery firing a royal salute. After the health of earl Grey and his colleagues (who had fought in the cause of the people, and gained for them their glorious victory), had been duly honoured, the chairman proposed the health of captain Boss, which was drunk amidst the most deafening applause and salvoes of artillery. After the cheers had subsided, the gallant captain rose and said:—
"I rise under a considerable degree of embarrassment— as in the first place this is my maiden speech, and in the second place I am a sailor,—to return you my best thanks for the honour you have done me. The beautiful regularity, the well organised arrangement, the unanimity you have displayed throughout this day's proceedings, reflect the highest degree of credit upon every person concerned, and I can truly say the warm heartedness I have experienced from the inhabitants of Brompton, merits my grateful thanks, and will remain engrafted upon my heart to the latest hour of my existence. (Cheers.) Gentlemen, in coming among you on this occasion, the honour is not conferred by me, but upon me. (Cheers.) I have been in all quarters of the globe, but never did I behold a sight equal to this (cheers); in short you act, emphatically speaking, as though you were a little colony of yourselves, having but one object and one voice. (Much cheering.) It is not the glitter of rank or title, nor is it the dazzling splendour of wealth that makes the man—no, it is the spirit and independence, it is the ardent love of liberty, the consistency of principle; in one word, it is worth that constitutes the man, and confers upon him the noblest of all distinctions. I have been requested by a number of gentlemen to offer myself as a candidate for the borough of Northallerton, in order to burst asunder the galling fetters that have so long enthralled the inhabitants of that place. In becoming member of parliament, I have no wish for personal aggrandisement, no towering ambition to gratify, and should I come forward, it will be for the sole purpose of throwing open the borough and (now that the right is conferred) of enabling free men in a free country to express their sentiments fearlessly and openly. (Cheers.)

"Whether I shall come forward or not, it is not for me now to say; I am a gentleman of small independence, and it might, perhaps, be no difficult matter for the earl of Harewood and sir John Beresford combined, by their purses and influences, to crush captain Boss of the navy into the dust, but my spirit they could never conquer; the noble love of liberty which warms the breast of every true-born Englishman, and particularly that of a sailor, will accompany me to my grave, and though I may not become your representative, yet I will never cease to honour you."

A.D. 1832.

Speech by Capt. Boss.

This speech was received throughout with repeated cheers, and the festivities being over, captain Boss and his lady took their seats in the carriage, which was drawn through the village by members of the procession, amidst the firing of cannon, cheers, and waving of hats, which the gallant gentleman acknowledged in the most gracious manner by standing in his carriage, uncovered, and frequently bowing. The carriage was then drawn by men from Brompton to Northallerton, where horses were attached to it.

After the dinner, about 300 females sat down to an excellent cup of tea, plum cake, &c., which concluded the day's rejoicings.*

The following is the second address put out by captain Boss soon after his introduction to the constituency:—

Address of Captain Boss.

NORTHALLERTON ELECTION.

TO THE INDEPENDENT ELECTORS OF THE BOROUGH OF NORTHALLERTON.

GENTLEMEN,

The opportunities which I have had of laying before you my opinions, render it unnecessary for me further to allude to them; they are the opinions of Freedom and Independence, and as such have met with your approbation. Nothing could have so much surprised me as the circumstance of another candidate being brought into the field, and asking your support, when that support had been nobly and freely disposed of, to one whom I am sure, no undue influence will ever cause you to desert. I have ever been anxious that a fair opportunity should be given to my opponent as well as myself, for stating those reasons which have induced us, but for widely different causes, to seek your approbation; and I disclaim any discredit which is attempted to be thrown upon me by the injudicious conduct of those who court popularity without resorting to the only honourable means of obtaining it. And though I have never had the honour of a seat in parliament, other honours, not less important, have been conferred upon me by my country; and because I have attained them in opposing the foes of our country, and the enemies of Britain, so am I confident that they are a pledge that my conduct in the House of Commons will be such as you may with safety rely upon, as tending to the prosperity and advantage of the nation, and particularly of that part in which I live, and desire to make myself useful, and the people free, independent, and happy.

The *Reform Bill* has added to Northallerton the constituency of Brompton and Romanby, disfranchising the electors of those townships as far as regards their voice in

* York Herald, June 26th, 1832.

the choice of county members, with the intention of conferring upon them a greater benefit, by enabling them to return one member for the three townships, and thereby effectually to destroy *all nomination* in the borough. But what will be the practical result of this sound piece of legislation if the borough of Northallerton should not be able to return a member of its own choice, in opposition to the interest and influence of those who have so long nominated the borough members? The result will be, that the new electors will be deprived of a right which they once enjoyed and exercised, but which would be for ever effectually taken from them by nomination and coalition. That you should submit to such a contrivance, much more aid in carrying it into execution, would be to produce your own destruction, and treat with ingratitude and contempt the exertions of the brave defenders of your liberties, who have wrested from the hands of your oppressors the second Magna Charta, and who, in accordance with their pledge, must now proceed to curtail the dishonest and wasteful expenditure of the public money, and by that means be enabled to remove those burthens of taxation, which corrupt and nomination parliaments have unsparingly laid upon you, and which a reformed and free parliament alone can displace.

In accepting your requisition and standing forward to represent you, I have sacrificed all minor considerations, but I consider no sacrifice too great, and no exertions too laborious to *open the borough*—the chief object of our united efforts. Will you choose *Mr. Wrightson* as a more approved candidate, because he is supported by a whig and tory coalition,—by the interest of Miss Pierse—or by any other interest opposed to that of the people? and let me ask you, will you desert our noble and praise-worthy object? and that too in the hour of victory?

My opponent says "That the success of his canvass has exceeded his most sanguine expectations." Gentlemen, the major part of you have had the opportunity of witnessing the reception which must have produced these "sanguine expectations." The promises of support which you have individually and personally given to me on my canvass, and since, are so numerous, that I should not be speaking with candour and fairness, if I did not at once declare that it is impossible for either Mr. Wrightson, or any one else, to secure one third of the number of votes which are promised to me by the most honourable pledge. Can I then doubt of ultimate success! Can I refuse to stand to the last as the champion of your cause!! No—I will never, never desert you; an opportunity shall be afforded to you of shewing your numerical strength at the day of election, and the mutual confidence which I find

A.D. 1832. to exist between us, will I say, in the face of the whole world, place me as your independent representative, where alone independence ought to be found—at the top of the poll.

I have the honour to be, gentlemen, with every feeling of gratitude and respect,

Your very obedient servant,

J. G. BOSS.

Committee Room, July 17th, 1832.

Mr. Wrightson's views. It must not be forgotten that Mr. Wrightson was a liberal in politics, having voted as member for Hull, for the Reform Bill, but the objection to him was his coming under the support of the old nomination influence.

The contest. The contest began in June, 1832, and continued, without intermission, to the day of election, the 10th of December the same year. During this long period the greatest excitement prevailed, and each side using its utmost exertions, intimidation and pressure being freely exercised. The Reform Bill had set the country wild with expectations of the benefits to come from it, and a spirit of independence strongly manifested itself. The chief thing talked about day by day was the contest, each side declaring their confidence of success, whilst conjectures were freely expressed how each elector would give his vote.

The election was appointed by the returning officer, J. S. Walton, esq., to take place on Monday, the 10th December. After the usual preliminaries were gone through, Mr. Wilford, of Brompton, proposed captain Boss as a fit person to represent the borough of Northallerton in the next parliament, Mr. Lancelot Marshall seconded the nomination; Mr. Henry Sedgewick then came forward to propose Mr. Wrightson, and Mr. Isaac Thompson seconded. On the show of hands being taken, the returning officer decided in favour of captain Boss, when Mr. Wrightson demanded a poll. At six o'clock the polling for the day ceased, when the numbers stood—

Captain Boss............... 108
Mr. Wrightson............ 97

Majority for captain Boss... 11

Captain Boss then addressed the people from the window of his committee room, thanking them for the support they had given him that day, and during the evening it was announced that Mr. Wrightson did not intend to resume the polling on the morrow, and that consequently captain Boss was the successful candidate.

Next morning the chairing took place; the chair, which was covered with cloth of an orange colour, and tastefully ornamented with laurel, &c., was placed upon a temporary A.D. 1832. platform in the captain's open carriage. The procession was preceded by Mr. Marshall, the chairman of the commitee, and Mr. Davison,* solicitor, each mounted; then the band, accompanied by flags and banners ; next the members of the committee ; and lastly the captain, followed by some thousand spectators. The procession moved round the market cross three times, then went forward to Romanby, and returned through Northallerton to Brompton. After leaving Brompton, the procession again returned to Northallerton, where the captain and his committee dined. The committee consisted of Mr. Lancelot Marshall, chairman ; Messrs. Davison, Metcalfe, Horner, E. Hare, Tesseyman, Smith, Ainsley, and others of Northallerton ; Mr. Wilford and his three sons, Aaron, John, and Bartholomew ; William and John Pattison, George Suggett, and others of Brompton. The general committee held their meetings at the Black Bull Inn once or twice every week. Mr. Davison, solicitor, was the agent of captain Boss, and to his untiring attention and skilful management, the success of the contest was mainly due.

Mr. Wrightson's committee was composed of Mr. Sedgewick, chairman ; Messrs. Hamilton, Thompson, Jefferson, Clemishaw, Marshall, and others. Mr. T. Fowle, solicitor, was the agent for Mr. Wrightson.

A singular feature of this election was the exhibition of a large gilded key, exhibited by captain Boss from his carriage when prosecuting his canvass, and invariably excited great attention. This was emblematical of opening the borough.†

On a change of ministry, a dissolution of parliament took place. The candidates were captain Boss and W. B. Wrightson, esq. Captain Boss only canvassed two days, and then retired in favour of Mr. Wrightson, who was elected without further opposition. 1835. General Election.

* Robert Davison, esq., only son of Robert Davison (who died in 1812) by his second wife Ann Elgie, (who died 16th Feb., 1857, æt. 78) ; born at Great Smeaton, near Northallerton, 25th Jan., 1806. Upon the death of his father he went to reside with his honoured guardian, Henry Foggy, esq. ; educated under Mr. York, of Northallerton; studied law under Henry Harrison, esq., of the same place, and in 1827 was duly admitted a member of that profession, in which he practised at Northallerton until the time of his death, which took place 27th March, 1846, æt. 40. Unimpeached in his integrity, consistent, honest, and firm in his principles : he was undoubtedly the most eminent lawyer of his day between York and Durham. His mortal remains were deposited in the church-yard of Great Smeaton.

† Of those who formed the committee of captain Boss, and took the chief part in the management of this memorable election, all have passed away with the exception of one or two. From one of them now surviving (J. Horner, esq.,) I have received my information. Several of their descendants, however, are still remaining, and may feel an interest in the event.—J. L. S.

A.D. 1836.
The See of Ripon.

His Majesty's ecclesiastical commissioners having made certain suggestions in a report, an act (6 & 7 Will. IV. cap. 77) was passed this year, by which an episcopal see was established at Ripon. Among the various endowments of the see was the manor of Northallerton and Allertonshire, which was now transferred from the bishop of Durham* to the bishop of Ripon,† after the former had held it uninterruptedly for the space of seven centuries and a half. It remained attached to the see of Ripon during the episcopate of bishop Longley only.

Tithe Commutation Act.

The "Tithe Commutation Act of 1836," was a wise settlement of a question of the greatest importance to the agriculture of the country. Previously tithe owners and farmers were generally at variance on the subject; the tithe owner had the right, in law, to take from the farmer one-tenth of the corn crop, and remove it to his own barn. A contributor‡ of information on the subject, witnessed the way in which the matter was carried out. He was staying at the house of a gentleman in the locality, who was owner and occupier of his farm; it was harvest time, and a fine crop of wheat in a field near the house was cut and standing in stook, and the farmer wishing to have it secured in his stackyard, sent a messenger to the tithe owner requesting him to send some person to tithe the crop; an answer came back that it was not convenient to send any person that day, but that the farmer was to tithe it himself, which he proceeded to do by placing a green bough on every tenth stook, and in due course the tithe owner's wagons took away one-tenth of the crop. In this case the tithe owner was a neighbouring squire, on friendly terms with the farmer, and no discord arose; but the farmers of that day were in a much worse position than those who cultivate under commutation, which has secured to them all the advantages which result from increased industry and improved farming.

1837.

On the occasion of sir Archibald Campbell's resignation of the government of New Brunswick—the conqueror of the Burmese Empire—issued the following farewell address, after reviewing the 43rd for the last time :—

* William Van Mildert, D.D., consecrated bishop of Durham in 1826, and was the last who enjoyed the dignity and revenues of the palatinate; he died in 1836, and was succeeded by Edward Maltby, D.D., F.S.A., consecrated bishop of Chichester in 1831; translated to Durham in 1836; resigned (by act of parliament) in 1856.

† Charles Thomas Longley, D.D., first bishop of Ripon, consecrated in 1836; formerly head master of Harrow school; translated in 1856, on the resignation of bishop Maltby, to the see of Durham, and was succeeded by Robert Bickersteth, D.D., late rector of St. Giles's, and canon of Salisbury; consecrated in 1857 to the see of Ripon.

‡ Mr. Edward H. Reed, of Northallerton.

General Order.   A.D. 1837.
"Head-Quarters, Fredericton,   Another compliment to
19th May, 1837.   Col. H. Booth

"His Majesty having been graciously pleased to accept Major-General Sir Archibald Campbell's resignation of the government of New Brunswick, His Excellency cannot leave the province without intimating to Lieut.-colonel Booth, the officers, non-commissioned officers, and privates of the 43rd Regiment, the high opinion he entertains of the perfect discipline, general good conduct, and efficiency of that distinguished corps.

"Of no regiment with which it has been His Excellency's fortune to serve, during a long and varied course of service, has he had occasion to express himself more favourably, with none certainly has he ever parted with more sincere regret; and on making his report of the half-yearly inspection of this day, His Excellency will not fail to convey these sentiments to the General Commanding-in-chief.
"By command,
"J. CAMPBELL, Captain, A.D.C."*

In consequence of the death of king William IV., a General dissolution of parliament took place, when W. B. Wrightson, Election. esq., again (21st June), became candidate on the reform interest, and the hon. Edwin Lascelles, fourth son of Henry, 2nd earl of Harewood, became candidate (3rd July) in the conservative interest. The canvass continued until the 18th July, when Mr. Lascelles retired. The writ arrived 20th July, and was immediately proclaimed, and the election holden 25th July, when Mr. Wrightson was returned without further opposition.

On the 12th October, the North-Riding Liberal Registration Association was formed at Northallerton, for the purpose of attending to and promoting the due registration of persons qualified to vote for members to serve in parliament for the said Riding, and of supporting the liberal interest. The hon. Thomas Dundas, M.P., was elected president; Mark Milbank, esq., and Peter Consett, esq., vice-presidents. The hon. J. C. Dundas, M.P., sir Edward Dodsworth, bart., sir B. R. Graham, bart., sir C. Style, bart., M.P., John Bell, esq., Samuel Crompton, esq., M.P., F. Cholmeley, esq., E. Copley, esq., C. H. Elsley, esq., rev. P. Ewart, col. Hilyard, John Hutton, esq., (Sowber Hill), John Hutton, esq. (Marske), Wm. Lawson, esq., Wm. Mauleverer,

---

* Sir Archibald Campbell was succeeded by sir John Harvey, K.H., and soon after the rebellion broke out in Lower Canada. (Vide Historical Records of the 43rd Regiment, pages 234, 235).

A.D. 1837 esq., Thomas Meynell, esq., Thomas Meynell, jun., esq., rev. J. J. T. Monson, L. Marshall, esq., Wm. Rutson, esq., H. V. Straubenzie, esq., Martin Stapylton, esq., Edmund Turton, esq., John Wormald, esq., Henry Witham, esq., rev. E. Wyvil, captain Wyvil, committee; Robert Davison, esq., solicitor, principal secretary.

The following district associations were formed, to act in concert with the above central association, viz. :—York; Easingwold; Thirsk; Helmsley and Kirbymoorside; Pickering and Malton; Scarborough; Whitby; Guisborough; Stokesley and Yarm; Northallerton; Bedale and Masham; Leyburn, Askrigg, and Hawes; Richmond, Bowes, and Romaldkirk.

A conservative association was formed at York a few months previous, but both the associations were dissolved in 1843.

Peculiar of Allertonshire. In the course of a charge to the clergy and churchwardens of the peculiar of Allertonshire and its neighbourhood, delivered on the 30th of August, 1837, in the parish church of Northallerton, the Rev. George Townsend, D.D., vicar of Northallerton and canon of Durham, made the following observations :—

"Because we are so few in number, it has been our custom in former years to meet only in the vestry, and there to speak to you on any point which might be worthy of consideration. I have, however, determined on the present occasion to speak to you in this more formal manner, because the other mode of addressing you, personally and individually, as the churchwardens delivered their papers, and as the names of the clergy were being called over, not being sufficiently public, it has pleased those who are on the watch to observe, and who have misunderstood our more quiet proceedings, to affirm, in the newspapers of the neighbouring districts, that the duty of the visitation was neglected and disregarded. We live in days when it is especially necessary that '*our good shall not be evil spoken of;*' and, therefore, I have resolved to conduct the visitation in this more open and public manner, that all may see our proceedings, and hear the reflections which I may deem it right to submit to you. It was the custom in former ages, when the bishops of their respective dioceses visited the churches and clergy at certain seasons, to inquire whether the statutes and laws of the church were properly observed. When, however, it so happened, that a parish or a manor belonged to another bishop, he, and not the diocesan, was accustomed to visit his own parish or manor. We are in the diocese of York. The archbishop of York, therefore, would have been the proper person to hold a visitation in this place, as well as in the other parts of his diocese. The parish or

Visitation of Clergy and Churchwardens.

History of the Peculiar of Northallerton

manor of Northallerton, however, was granted, from the very earliest times of our history, to the bishops of Durham, who were accustomed therefore to superintend this district, and certain other places in the neighbourhood.* One of the bishops of Durham, many centuries ago, gave to the convent of Durham a part of his jurisdiction. The dean and chapter of Durham, as their successors, possess the same power; and it is by virtue of that power, as their representative, that I am enabled to require the churchwardens to bring in their papers, and the clergy of the peculiar also to be present in the church this day. I mention these things because some have inquired by what authority the visitation was held here. I believe that the laws respecting this kind of peculiar ecclesiastical jurisdiction are about to be either materially altered or entirely abolished.† When that is done, the authority of the master keeper of Northallerton, as the representative of the dean and chapter of Durham, will cease. Until, however, the law is altered, the duty I am fulfilling will remain: and it rests, you will perceive, on the same foundation with any other authority of a similar kind, whether of a dean and chapter, of a bishop, or of an archbishop, which may be exercised elsewhere. It rests upon the foundation of a prescription and custom, and therefore of law; which may be traced with more or less exactness, for nearly a thousand years, to the period before the Norman conquest."

The Northallerton Poor Law Union was formed in this year, under the provisions of the Act 4 and 5 Will. IV., cap. 76. The Union now comprises an area of 67,000 acres, comprehending 43 parishes and places, with a population of 11,884. The old workhouse was situated on the west side of the town, near the Sun Beck, and was formerly the Guildhall. There sir George Bowes and others sat to receive the submission of offenders, who had been concerned in the rising of the north in 1569.

On the 28th March, the workmen of the Great North of England railway commenced digging the foundation for the first bridge, a little south of the hill, and on the second day part of an urn, supposed to be Roman, was dug up; it was of dark blue clay. At the foot of the hill portions of foundations of freestone were dug up, but of no great magnitude; and several Roman coins. Further in the hill was found a "*Votive Altar*," and from an inscription upon it, plainly showed that this had been a station occupied by the sixth Roman

A.D. 1837.

Abolition of the Peculiar.

Northallerton Poor Law Union.

1838.
N.E. Railway commenced.

Discovery of Roman relics.

---

* For the parishes originally included in the Peculiar of Allertonshire, see page 2.
† The visitatorial power has since been transferred from the Dean and Chapter of Durham to the Archbishop of York.—J. L. S.

A.D. 1838. legion. The inscription reads that "Being present, Flavius, Hyronimianus, of the Sixth Legion, Victorious."

> INSTANE
>
> FLA. HYRO.
>
> LEG. VI. V.

Many other curious and interesting stones were discovered, but immediately broken by the workmen to fill up the abutments of the bridges.* Near the centre, and about a yard from the summit was discovered a *well*, about a yard in depth, of neatly dressed freestone; and a little to the south was another well or pit, nearly two yards square, of oak wood, quite black, but perfectly sound, strongly bound together, and dove-tailed at the corners. When the men came to the level on which the railway was to pass, they had not got to the bottom of either the well or pit by several yards, and previous to filling them up, a good quantity of stone and wood was taken out; the latter, visitors were anxious to procure for snuff boxes, walking sticks, &c. A drain of freestone running from the centre hill to the north-east was also exposed. Besides the relics already mentioned, Roman spurs were found, and the coins of Antoninus Pius, Marcus Aurelius, Commodus, Severus, Geta, Constantius, Chlorus, and Constantinus, a sufficient proof that this was a Roman encampment, the only remaining part being the rampart or terrace on the east side.

Fall of a bridge.

On Wednesday evening, July 18th, about six o'clock, the massive bridge over the Willow Beck, being the second on the line of the Great North of England railway, south of the Castle Hills, Northallerton (then nearly finished), suddenly came down with a tremendous crash, by which three workmen were most severely injured. Most of the workmen had left a short time previous to its fall, or the consequence might have been fatal to many of them. It is somewhat remarkable that many of the workmen dined under the arch on the noon of that day, so that its fall was not anticipated.

* It is greatly to be regretted that some arrangement was not made with the company for the preservation of these ancient remains.—J. L. S.

Theodosius Burnett Stuart, M.A., was formerly a fellow of Queen's college, Cambridge, and became vicar of Northallerton in 1839, but resigned it in 1849 for the vicarage of Wookey. _{A.D. 1839. Rev. T. B. Stuart.}

In this year the pulpit which had stood from time immemorial on the north side of the transept arch, was removed to the south side. _{1841. Removal of the Pulpit.}

On the opening of the Great North of England railway from London to Darlington, in March, 1841, the stage coach was compelled to give place to _{Opening of the Great-Northern Railway.}

"The fierce engine with outrageous speed,
Swifter ten-fold than hoof of the Arab steed,"

and the huge wagons disappeared from the roads; whither they are gone no one knows, and unless specimens are preserved, in a short time it will not be known what they were like, for those who travelled in them will also have gone into oblivion, together with the lively notes of the guard's key-bugle, and the crack of the postillion's whip, which made merry the hearts of Pickwickian travellers in days gone by. _{Disappearance of the Stage Coach.}

This gallant soldier, after passing safely through many battles and much hard service, died peacefully at Northallerton, May 6th, 1841, and was buried in Northallerton churchyard.* _{Lieut.-col. Henry Booth.}

The conservatives coming into office, a general election took place. W. B. Wrightson, esq. and the hon. Edwin Lascelles again presented themselves. After a severe contest Mr. Wrightson was returned by a small majority. _{General Election.}

---

* A marble tablet is erected to his memory on the north transept of the Northallerton church, bearing the following inscription:—
    Arms. On a field three boars' heads couped erect, two and one.
Near this place is interred the body of
LIEUT.-COL. HENRY BOOTH, K.H.,
Of the 43rd Regiment of Light Infantry,
Fifth son of the late William Booth, esq., of Brush House, in the parish of Ecclesfield, in the county of York;
He died at Northallerton, May 6th, 1841, aged 51.
His military life was passed in the 43rd Regiment, he entered it as ensign, March 6th, 1806, was promoted to be lieut.-colonel June 29th, 1830, and retained the command of it until the day of his death, he served with the armies in Spain and Portugal under sir John Moore and the Duke of Wellington, and was present at Vimiero, Corunna, the passage of the Coa, Busaco, Salamanca, Vittoria, and the attack on the heights of Vera.
This tablet was erected by the Officers, Non-commissioned Officers and Privates of the Regiment, who had served under his command, to record their respect for his character, and their esteem and affection for his gallant, generous, and amiable qualities, by which he won the hearts of all who served under him, and infused through every rank a high and honourable feeling.

Lieut.-col. Booth, married 13th April, 1826, Miss Mary Ann Monkhouse, of Northallerton, by whom he had issue, Charles, Henry Jackson Parkin, and William Henry.

A.D. 1842. Captain Leighton.	Thomas Richard Leighton, grandson of Richard Dighton, esq., surgeon, of Northallerton, was killed in the fatal retreat from Cabul, in 1842.*
1843. Major-general Walker.	Major-general Forster Walker, the eighth son of the rev. Benjamin Walker, vicar of Northallerton, died at Calcutta, 19th Jan., in this year.†
Encouragement of Horticulture.	In this year the Rev. T. B. Stuart, vicar of Northallerton, granted to the industrious poor persons of the town a large field, which is now divided into allotments, at a moderate rent, for the encouragement of horticulture. He also laid out a part of the large field called the "Vicar's Croft," on, or upon part of which the National School was afterwards erected, to be made into neat gardens, to accommodate tradespeople and other industrious inhabitants of the town. The first year no rent was asked for.
Erection of the National Schools.	The erection of the present National Schools was commenced in the summer of this year, on a site granted upon the glebe land called the "Vicar's Croft," at a cost of £917 2s. 2d. The vicar of Northallerton, for the time being, is the sole trustee; the managers being selected by him annually. The schools are in union with the National Society, and are open to Government inspection. A record

* A small marble tablet is erected to his memory in Northallerton church, with the following inscription :—
In Memory of
CAPTAIN THOMAS RICHARD LEIGHTON,
Of Her Majesty's 44th Regiment of Infantry,
Who was killed in action in the fatal retreat from Cabul, in Afghanistan,
January the 10th, 1842, in the 32nd year of his age.
The deceased was eldest son of the late Thomas Leighton, esquire,
of Richmond, Yorkshire,
and grandson of the late Richard Dighton, esquire, Surgeon, of this place.
He was a dutiful and affectionate son, a kind husband and father,
and greatly beloved by all his relations and friends.

Capt. Leighton, eldest son of Thomas and Anna Leighton, married 16th July, 1834, at Chinsurale, Bengal, Emily Cornelia, only daughter of the late captain De Waal, and had issue, Miss Leighton, of Northallerton.

† His memory is preserved by a handsome marble tablet erected in Northallerton church, with inscription as follows :—
Arms. Arg. a chevron betw. three crescents sa.
To the Memory of
MAJOR-GENERAL FORSTER WALKER,
Colonel of the 1st Regiment of European Light Infantry, in the army
of the Honble. East India Company;
He was the eighth son of the late Rev. Benjamin Walker, M.A.,
Vicar of this parish during 39 years.
After 40 years of active and distinguished service, he died in peace, in the hope of a blessed resurrection through the mercy of his God and Redeemer,
at Calcutta, the 19th of January, 1843, aged 61.
This tablet was erected by his afflicted widow.

Major-general Walker married Lydia Sophia, daughter of James Pattle, esq., of Calcutta.

of the erection of these schools is found in an old register of A.D. 1843. parish affairs deposited in the parish church. The record is in the handwriting of the the rev. Theodosius Burnett Stuart, through whose instrumentality the schools were built; and at the foot of the record, also in the handwriting of Mr. Stuart, is the following sentence: "*Remember me, O my God, for good.*"

A gentleman in Northallerton had for some time in his possession a tame lion, which had always been considered perfectly harmless, till a few nights previously to Christmas, when he broke his chain, and perambulating the town, he came in contact with a ferocious bull-mastiff belonging to a butcher; a battle instantly commenced, when the roaring of the lion, and the howling of the dog, called forth a large party of all sorts of people, who, as is customary, encouraged the two combatants to worry each other. For some time the victory was doubtful, but at length the dog by a singular manœuvre threw the lion on his back, and made a furious grasp at the poor animal's throat, and would have despatched him, had he not been rescued by the spectators.* *A singular conflict.*

The separation of the chapelry of Brompton from the mother church of Northallerton, and its constitution into an independent benefice, was effected under the Act 1 & 2 Vict., c. 26, and the order in council was registered in the registry of the archbishop of York, in October, 1843. The patronage is vested in the dean and chapter of Durham, and the nett value of the living, according to Crockford, is £350 and a house. The separation was effected on the recommendation of the rev. Theodosius Burnett Stuart, B.D., vicar of Northallerton. The rev. William John Middleton was the first incumbent of Brompton. *Brompton constituted a separate benefice.*

Colonel Walker, sixth son of the rev. Benjamin Walker, vicar of Northallerton, died at Madras, 4th Dec., in this year.† *Lieut.-colonel Walker.*

---

* Vide Schroeder's "Annals of Yorkshire," vol. 1, page 345.

† A large and handsomely carved marble tablet is erected in Northallerton church to his memory, bearing the following inscription:—
Arms. Arg. a chevron betw. three crescents sa.
Sacred to the Memory of
GEORGE WARREN WALKER,
Sixth son of the Rev. Benjamin Walker, M.A., formerly vicar of this parish;
Lieut.-colonel of the 41st Fusiliers, and Major-general
upon the Staff in East Indies.
He served honourably under Lord Lake and General Gillespie, and after
44 years of distinguished service, died in the hope of a blessed
resurrection, through the merits of his Saviour, at St. Thomas's Mount,
Madras, 4th Dec., 1843, aged 65 years.
This tablet was erected by his much afflicted widow and family.

Lieut.-colonel Walker married Miss Patten, daughter of general Patten, governor of St. Helena.

A.D. 1844.
Grammar School enlarged.

On July 20th, Mr. Jonathan Horner was appointed to the mastership of the Grammar School, which at that time was in a very dilapidated condition, and very inconvenient. Mr. Horner at once set to work to rebuild that portion of the house between the school and the kitchen, and to thoroughly restore and repair the other parts, at an expense to him of nearly £300. At the time also of Mr. Horner's appointment the school had fallen away both in tone and numbers, but Mr. Horner's genial manner, and educational tact and ability soon restored the school to its old standing. The initial letter H and the figures 1844, forming the centre piece on the entrance ceiling of the dwelling-house, mark the date of these alterations.

On October 6th, the lord bishop of Chester (Dr. Graham) preached in Northallerton parish church.

1847.
Re-seating of the Church.

On the 28th of January, a faculty was granted by the ecclesiastical court at York, on the suit of the Rev. T. B. Stuart, vicar, and the churchwardens of Northallerton, for reseating the whole area of the church, repairing and altering the west gallery, for removing the organ gallery and a small gallery on the north side, and for other minor alterations. A citation had been previously published, calling upon all who supposed themselves possessed of rights to pews, to shew cause, if they were able, against the issuing of the faculty. It was found that no claims could be maintained in law, either on the ground of the general faculty of 1788, or of prescription, gift, sale, or inheritance. All opposition therefore being abandoned, the faculty was carried into execution during the summer and autumn of 1847; the whole of the seats in the church (except the chancel) were removed, and others were erected on an entirely different plan, the seats in the west gallery were cut down, divested of their doors, and otherwise altered. *Thus all vestige of private right being for ever obliterated, all the seats without exception, belong now to the parishioners generally to be freely used and enjoyed by them according to law.*

The Parish Church made free and open

A considerable addition was made at the same time to the accommodation in the church, the number of sittings being increased from 780 to 1011. On the work being completed, the churchwardens, using the power with which the law invests them (under the control of the ordinary), allotted certain sittings to those families and individuals who constantly attended the church, *but no right of property was thereby conferred, or could be conferred in any case:* the undisturbed occupancy of those sittings is secured to those to whom they are thus allotted, *while they use it;* on their ceasing to do so, the sittings are either allotted to others, or left free to the use of all. Such is the present state of the parish church of Northallerton in respect of all the sittings contained in it. The churchwardens therefore and their successors are hereby solemnly charged to preserve it inviolate for ever, to the benefit of the inhabitants; resisting every attempt to encroach upon their ancient rights as parishioners now restored to them, doing justice in this matter equally to all, without fear, partiality, or prejudice; remembering that the souls of all are of equal value in the sight of Him who redeemed them; and regarding their office as a sacred trust, for the discharge of which they will have to give an account at the judgment seat of God.* {A.D. 1847. The office of Churchwarden a sacred trust.}

At the general election this year, W. B. Wrightson, esq., being the only candidate, was duly elected in the liberal interest. {General Election.}

This year an Act of parliament was obtained to form a railway from Melmerby to Northallerton, and thus complete the necessary connecting link in the chain of the new northern line. {1848.}

John Clarkson, a native of the town, became a soldier in the 3rd regiment of the king's (George III.) foot guards, and served under general sir Ralph Abercromby during the campaign in Egypt of 1801. He lost his sight from opthalmia, and in consequence became an out-pensioner of Chelsea hospital, and returned to his native place and family, living in comfort and respectable circumstances until the 9th of February, 1849, when he died at the good old age of 86 years. Although he was deprived of sight, he was able for some time to discharge the duties of town crier, having a good voice, together with a clear and distinct utterance, in which respect he has not been equalled by any of his successors in office. The veteran used to sit on fine evenings outside his house, and relate to listening neighbours his recollections of what had happened during his military days in the valley of the Nile. Amongst others he related the following circumstance:—" On one occasion he was placed on duty as an out-post sentinel, where he had to pace to and fro a certain distance on the sandy plain, with nothing in sight but a French sentinel placed on corresponding duty. This was no doubt weary work to both, and the French soldier first showed signs of weariness by making friendly signs to Clarkson, showing a drinking flask and advancing some distance towards him; but Clarkson with "John Bull" suspicion did not respond, until the Frenchman plunged his gun, with fixed bayonet, into the sand, and advanced beyond it toward Clarkson: this gave our countryman confidence, and he advanced until they met. The Frenchman being able {1849. A worthy townsman.}

---

* The faculty above referred to is preserved in the archives of the Parish Church. The Seats are now free and unappropriated.

A.D. 1849. to converse in English, said they might discharge their lonely duty as sentinels without personal enmity; he had some brandy and Clarkson had some bread, so they partook of each other's fare, had a brief parley, shook hands, parted, and resumed their respective duties, having run some risk by this departure from strict discipline."

Leave of absence.
The following document, in the hand-writing of the then archbishop of York (Dr. Thos. Musgrave), is preserved in the parish church:—

"We, Thomas, archbishop of York, hereby license you Theodosius Burnett Stuart, clerk, vicar of Northallerton with Deighton, in the county of York, within our diocese, to be absent from your benefice until the thirty-first of March, one thousand eight hundred and fifty, on account of the ill health of your wife.

"And you having provided for the duty of your said benefice to our satisfaction.

"Given under our hand this third day of April, in the year of our Lord one thousand eight hundred and forty-nine.

"T. Ebor."

An interesting discovery.
On Monday, the 16th June, a man while at work ploughing in a field about a mile south of Northallerton, turned up a silver coin, rather larger than a shilling, but somewhat thinner, which, on cleaning, proved to be a coin of king Alfred, in a fair state of preservation, considering that it was over 900 years old.

This year a branch railway was made from Northallerton to Bedale, joining the Great North of England at the Castle Hills.

Mechanics' Institute.
The Mechanics' Institute was established here in 1849. The library contains upwards of 2,000 vols. of books. The institute is in union with the Society of Arts and the Yorkshire Union of Mechanics' Institutes.

1850.
Thomas Warren Mercer, M.A., was formerly rector of Weeley, Essex. He became vicar of Northallerton in 1850, and died on Christmas Day, 1876.

Death of Mr. Geo. Wombwell.
On November 16th, 1850, Mr. George Wombwell, the celebrated menagerie proprietor, died at Northallerton, aged 73 years. Single-handed and by dint of extraordinary tact, Mr. Wombwell maintained and enjoyed up to the day of his death, the distinguished position of being the largest proprietor of wild animals in the world. Mr. Wombwell was a native of Essex, and the strict integrity which ever marked his conduct through a long and arduous career, gained him the sincere respect of all who knew him.

1851.
Local Board of Health.
The Northallerton Local Board of Health was constituted in this year. Its Bye-Laws were duly made and ordained at

a meeting of the Board on the 9th of February, and on the 3rd of June in the following year, and confirmed by Her Majesty's principal Secretary of State for the Home Department, pursuant to the "Public Health Act, 1848," and the "Common Lodging House Act, 1851." The Surveyor of the Board at that time was Mr. France; the Inspector of Nuisances, Mr. Joseph Heslington; the Collector, Mr. Wm. Smithson; and the Clerk, Mr. Fowle, solicitor, in whose offices the meetings of the Board were held. *A.D. 1851.*

The last interment which took place in Northallerton parish church was that of Mary, wife of F. Bedingfield, esq., of Thornton Lodge. She was the only daughter of Fletcher Rigg, esq., of Northallerton. Mrs. Bedingfield was interred in the chancel of Northallerton church, on April 12th, 1851, where a stone bearing an inscription to her memory formerly marked the place. *Last interment in parish church.*

This year a man working in a field adjoining the Standard Hill grounds, found a silver coin of king Stephen in good preservation. The head appears in profile, with the sceptre in his right hand, and the name oddly spelt, viz., "Steifne, R." On the reverse is the name of the supposed moneyer of that day, and a cross, with the date 1137. A similar coin was found near the same place about twelve years ago, and near it also the silver hilt of a sword.* *Discovery of coins.*

On August 28th, Her Majesty the Queen, the Prince Consort, the Prince of Wales, and the rest of the royal family and suite passed the Northallerton railway station, *en route* for Scotland, about a quarter to eleven o'clock. The royal procession, however, did not pass very quickly, which gave the numerous persons assembled at the station, and on the eastern rampart of the Castle Hills, a good opportunity of viewing Her Majesty and the royal party. *An interesting event.*

On scraping the north wall of the nave of the parish church, the armorial bearings of Henry, Lord Percy, were discovered, though much mutilated. From an old register it is ascertained that letters of fraternity were granted by the prior and convent of Durham to his widow, "the lady Alianor de Percy, and Henry and William her sons, for benefits to our priory of Finchale and to our church of Northallerton, which had been burnt and destroyed by the Scots." This will account for the arms of Percy being found in Northallerton church, where they were probably placed (perhaps with an inscription), as a memorial of the circumstance. *1852. The Percy Arms.*

W. B. Wrightson, esq., was again elected at the general election in this year without opposition. *General Election.*

* Vide *Illustrated London News*, May 3rd, 1851.

A.D. 1852.
Dr. Townsend visits the Pope

Soon after his collation to residentiary canonry in Durham cathedral, Dr. Townsend, vicar of Northallerton, visited Rome to interview his holiness Pio Nono, relative to certain reforms in the Romish church ardently desired by the worthy doctor.

The following is from the *Augsburg Gazette* of May 8th, under date, Rome, April 30th:—" Dr. Townsend, canon of the cathedral church of Durham, lately presented to the Pope a memorial. The doctor was the bearer of a letter of recommendation from the archbishop of Paris. The Pope gave him a most cordial reception, and promised to examine the memorial. Dr. Townsend recommends Pius IX. to convoke a council, composed of ecclesiastic and secular deputies from the different christian countries, whose object should be to devise the means of uniting all the christian sects. Dr. Townsend received a message from the Holy Father, inviting him to a second interview. But the doctor being on the point of departing for Naples, requested the Pope to put off the audience until his return."—The Roman correspondent of the *Daily News*, writing on May 2nd, gives the following details:—" One of the most interesting occurences of last week was the interview of the Rev. Dr. Townsend with the Pope. The reverend doctor's object was to endeavour to induce his holiness to do away with the bickerings, animosities, and polemical discords which keep the various denominations of christians separate and at enmity; and, by a general council, to establish the basis of an universal creed. It was certainly a bold attempt for a protestant clergyman to convert the Pope himself: but the doctor was determined to beard the lion in his den, and on Friday last he went to the encounter in full dress canonicals. After having knelt to kiss the Pope's hand, Dr. Townsend was invited by his holiness to take a chair, and an animated conversation commenced in Latin, a fit language for controversy, and one in which the disputants might be presumed to be a match for each other. The Pope was, upon the whole, very tolerant, as may be imagined from his having not only listened with calmness to Dr. Townsend's arguments in favour of releasing the catholic clergy from their vow of celibacy, but also assured him that he entertained serious ideas of adopting such a plan in the early part of his reign, especially after having received pressing letters upon the subject from Germany, but that, in the present state of Italy, and indeed of the whole continent, any innovation on his part would be dangerous, even if he had the power to act freely, which he had not, being by no means the free agent that he was on his first accession to the throne. The same objection would prevent him from calling a general council, or attempting to unite the great and divided family of christians, although he fully admitted the grandeur of the scheme, protested his own desire for peace and harmony and wept at Dr. Townsend's enthusiastic picture of England recognising in Pio Nono the head of a universal church. After three-quarters of an hour's discussion, the reverend canon took his leave, placing in the hands of his holiness a document containing the principal heads of his argument, which appears to have made some impression on the pontiff's mind, judging from the fact of his having sent to the doctor's residence on Sunday last, only two days after the interview, requesting to be made acquainted with the period of Dr. Townsend's return (he had just gone to Naples), as he should then like to have some more conversation with him."

A.D. 1852.

The Northallerton and Melmerby railway was completed and opened for traffic on the 15th May, this year, having occupied two years in construction. The engineer was J. T. Naylor, esq., and the contractors Messrs. Faville and Maxfield.

Melmerby Railway.

About this time a somewhat unusual circumstance occurred in the village of Silton. The Wesleyans applied to the clergyman of the parish for permission to have their Sabbath school sermons preached in the established church, which was granted. Mr. Dowson, draper, of Northallerton, independent, officiated on the occasion. This affair may be considered as unique in the religious world; a dissenter and (Independent) layman, preaching Sabbath school sermons for the Wesleyan Methodists from a Church of England pulpit!*

A unique proceeding.

Whilst encamped at Keiskamma Hoek, Kaffir Land, on the 1st of December, during a tremendous thunderstorm, two men of the 43rd were killed, and 19 others injured, owing to the explosion of ammunition in the pouches. The day had been very sultry, even for tropical midsummer. Just after dark the temperature suddenly changed to chilly cold, and large hailstones fell. A flash and detonation broke simultaneously, followed by the immediate ignition of ammunition, amid yells and shrieks of the men, imprisoned in their now prostrate tents, from which they could not extricate themselves. Lieutenant Booth (of Northallerton), and Captain Dick rushed out, and managed to drag up the pegs, and haul the soldiers—absolutely mixed up with the exploding pouches strapped to the poles—out, notwithstanding the terrific fury of the elements. Of all the 19 injured, few or none permanently recovered, although several served on for some years.†

A startling incident in camp.

* Ward's Methodism in Thirsk Circuit, page 101. Mr. Dowson informs me that he did not enter the pulpit but preached from the reading-desk. His text in the morning was Luke xv, 10; in the afternoon, Matthew xiv, 35, 36.—J. L. S.

† Vide Historical Records 43rd Regiment, page 269.

182   ANNALS OF

A.D. 1853.
A curious epitaph.

Upon a tombstone in Northallerton churchyard may be seen the following curious inscription :—

"Hic jacet Walter Gunn,
Sometime landlord of the 'Sun,'
Sic transit gloria mundi!
He drank hard upon Friday,
That being a high day,
Then took to his bed and died on Sunday." *

1856.
Establishment of Police Force.

Previous to this year the peace of the town had been preserved by parish constables, elected annually by the ratepayers in vestry assembled, and confirmed by the magistrates in Petty Sessions. But on the establishment of the county police force in the town, the ancient and honorary office of parish constable, although it did not immediately die out, became a merely nominal one; and it was not until the death of Richard Nicholson, "the last of the watchmen," that these relics of antiquity vanished into oblivion. Not that Northallerton needed a stronger staff of peace-preservers, for seldom was the pacific surface of public life ruffled by any thing more alarming than the song of a midnight inebriate; and even if it had, the united courage of "Dickey, the watchman" and three parish constables, invested with official dignity and armed with the "terrors of the law," would have been more than sufficient to quell even a small riot. But like their blue-coated and brass buttoned successors, these official ornaments were seldom to be found upon the scene until the storm was over. The three gentlemen who last fulfilled the onerous duties of parish constables, were Messrs. Akers, Hardy, and J. Fairburn in or about 1875.

Captain Hill.

Thomas Hill, esq. (late captain North York Militia), appointed chief constable of the North-Riding, October 4th, 1856.

The Shepherd family.

The members of the Shepherd family were remarkable for the satisfactory discharge of their duties as governors of gaols. Thomas Shepherd was governor of the gaol at Northallerton, and his sons respectively governors of York castle, and the gaols at Wakefield, Beverley, and Northallerton. For many years all these important county gaols continued to be in charge of these good Shepherds; a grandson becoming governor of Wakefield gaol, and a son-in-law governor of York castle.

Closing of the Churchyard.

Consecration of the Cemetery.

The churchyard being ordered to be closed by the Secretary of State, the site of the castle, west of the church, was purchased and laid out in a suitable manner for a cemetery; the southern half was consecrated on the 20th September, 1856, by bishop Spencer (acting for Dr. Musgrave, archbishop of York), and appropriated to the members of the

* *Home Companion* of December 10th, 1853.

established church; the northern half to the dissenters. A.D. 1856.
Two chapels were erected, in which the funeral services are
respectively performed.*

At the general election, this borough was contested by 1857.
W. B. Wrightson, esq., and the hon. Egremont Lascelles, General Election.
second son of Henry, third earl of Harewood, and brother to
the present earl. The election took place on Friday, the 27th
March, the proceedings being opened by W. T. Jefferson,
esq., the returning officer. Mr. Hare proposed Mr. Wrightson,
and J. Pattison, esq., seconded the nomination. F. R. Gibbs,
esq., then came forward and proposed Mr. Lascelles, who
was seconded by C. J. D. Ingledew, esq. A show of hands
was taken, and declared to be in favour of Mr. Wrightson,
when a poll was demanded by the friends of Mr. Lascelles,
which took place the following day (Saturday) and closed as
follows:—

  Wrightson................. 129
  Lascelles.................... 126

On the 6th of May, an order in council was made transferring, among other portions of the revenue of the see of
Ripon, the manor of Northallerton, from the see of Ripon to
the ecclesiastical commissioners, in whose possession the
manor now remains.

In or about this year, the right hon. J. Evelyn Denison, Mr. Wrightson appointed
Speaker of the House of Commons, having expressed his Deputy
intention to go abroad during the recess, it became incumbent Speaker.
that a deputy should be appointed. Previous to the prorogation this responsible office was conferred on W. B.
Wrightson, esq., M.P. for Northallerton, of Cusworth Park,
Doncaster. This distinguished honour to the veteran member afforded much gratification to the inhabitants of
Northallerton and district.

This year a workhouse for the Northallerton Poor Law The Workhouse.
Union was erected on the east side of the town.

On June 20th, 1857, a handsome piece of plate was An interesting presentation.
presented to James Pulleine, esq., of Crakehall, valued at
£480. The subject is taken from the "Battle of the Standard."
The principal figure is David, king of Scotland, mounted on
a magnificent war horse, and engaged in mortal combat with
two warriors on foot, the king wielding a battle axe, and his
assailants attacking him with spears. On the right of the
king there are two other figures representing prince Henry
wounded, and supported by a courtier. The king and his son
are represented wearing coats of mail, and the former is

---

* By the "Burials Act, 1880," one chapel only is now necessary, permission being given alike to all to inter in any part of the cemetery, on complying with the conditions of the Act.

A.D. 1857 warding off the blows of his assailants with a massive shield. On the battle ground are some pieces of broken swords and several arrows, which appear to have recently pierced the ground. The whole is composed of bronze work with an undulating surface, and is mounted on a large circular block or pedestal of wood, upon which there are two silver plates; the one bearing Mr. Pulleine's coat of arms, with the motto "*Nulla pallescere culpa;*" and on the other is inscribed "This piece of plate was presented to James Pulleine, esq., chairman during sixteen years of the Quarter Sessions of the North Riding of Yorkshire, by justices, attorneys, and other friends, in token of their grateful thanks to him for the care and attention with which he protected the interests of the rate-payers, and for the unwearied zeal and ability with which he discharged the business of the court, and upheld the dignity of the bench, A.D. 1857."

1859. General Election. At the general election on April 30th, 1859, W. B. Wrightson, esq., and C. H. Mills, esq., came forward as candidates. The contest was a keen one throughout, both parties being confident of victory up to the declaration of the poll. At the close of the poll, the numbers stood—

        Wrightson 138
        Mills 136

1860. South Parade. In this year the town of Northallerton began to exhibit signs of increasing vitality, houses being erected in the direction of the railway station. The first house of a new street called the South Parade was erected by Mr. Miles Soppet.

1862. A tragic event. Early on the morning of January 26th, 1862, a man named Johnson Metcalfe, watchmaker, of Northallerton, whilst under the influence of liquor, entered his house, procured his gun, returned into the street and shot at another man named William Parker, of Brompton, inflicting a wound from which he died a few hours afterwards. For this crime Metcalfe was tried on the charge of wilful murder at York Assizes, convicted of manslaughter, and sentenced to ten years' penal servitude, from which he was released on a ticket-of-leave after the expiration of seven years. It may interest our readers to know that Metcalfe died eighteen years afterwards within a few hours of the time when the crime was committed. Shortly before his death, Metcalfe expressed a desire to be buried "in an upright position, in order that he might be prepared "to run at the sound of the last trump."

The Savings' Bank. The new Savings' Bank was opened in this year. It stands on the site of the old Guild Hall.

George Gardner, esq., (late captain 13th Hussars), appointed governor of the North-Riding House of Correction, at the Midsummer Sessions in this year.

The foundation stone of a new Wesleyan Chapel was laid on June 23rd, 1864, by Thomas Sadler, esq., of Bedale. The site of the chapel was for many years occupied by the "Pack Horse Inn." A jar was placed in the cavity under the stone by the rev. D. Williams, containing a roll of parchment, on which was engrossed the names of the trustees of the new chapel, ministers of the circuit, treasurers, corresponding secretary, and the secretary of trustees' meetings; also the names of the architects and builders, a preachers' plan for circuit, and a copy of the *Northallerton and Bedale Times* newspaper. The trowel and mallet were presented to Mr. Sadler by Mr. R. M. Middleton on behalf of the trustees.

A.D. 1864. New Wesleyan Chapel.

This was by far the most important engagement of the Maorie war, and perhaps the most disastrous to the British troops, for in it Lieutenal-colonel H. J. P. Booth, of Northallerton was dangerously wounded, subsequently dying from the wounds then received. The following is a detailed account :—

Assault of the "Gate Pa."

Lieutenant-general Cameron, commanding the forces, having made a reconnaissance of the rebel intrenchments at Puke-hina-hina (Gate Pa), an attack was organised. On the highest point of a neck of land, a quarter of a mile wide, of which the slopes fell off on either side into swamp, the Maories had constructed an oblong redoubt, well palisaded and surrounded by strong post-and-rail fence, difficult to bowl over with artillery, and an almost invulnerable obstacle to an assaulting column. The intervals between the side faces of the redoubt and the swamp were defended by an intrenched line of rifle-pits. The 68th Light Infantry, with a mixed detachment under Major Ryan, 70th regiment, encamped on the 27th, twelve hundred yards distant, and on that and the following day the guns and mortars intended to breach the position were brought up to the camp, augmented by a large force of seamen and marines from the squadron of Commodore sir William Wiseman. Head-quarters and five companies of the 43rd, under command of Lieutenant-colonel Booth, joined.

After dark a feigned attack was made on the front of the enemy's position, to divert their attention from a flank movement by the 68th, who had received orders to gain the rear and so surround them, which it was conjectured could be effected at low water by passing along the beach and outside the swamp on their right. The manœuvre succeeded perfectly, and in the A.M. the 68th, in extended order, was in rear of the enemy. The guns and mortars opened soon after daybreak, their fire being principally directed against the left angle of the centre work, regarded as the least impregnable point. At twelve o'clock a six-pounder Armstrong gun was taken across the swamp on the enemy's left to the high ground on the opposite side, from which its fire completely enfiladed the left of the position. The bombardment continued, with short intermissions, until 4 p.m., when a portion of the fence and palisading being destroyed and a practical breach made, the assault was ordered. One hundred and fifty men of the 43rd, with an equal number of seamen and marines under Commander Hay, of H.M. ship 'Harrier' formed the assaulting column, led by Lieut.-colonel Booth. Major Ryan and his detachment were extended as close to the work as possible, to keep down the fire from the rifle-pits. The remainder of the 43rd, seamen, and marines, amounting to 300 in all, followed as a reserve.

As Colonel Booth gave the word "inward face," the 43rd to the right, the Naval Brigade to the left, advanced by double files from the centre to where the breach had been made, which protected in a measure by the nature of the ground, was gained with little loss, and an entrance effected into the main body of the work. A fierce conflict then ensued, in which the natives fought with the greatest desperation. Lieut-colonel Booth and Commander Hay, who led into the work with Captain Glover and Ensign Langsland, fell mortally wounded, and in a few minutes almost every officer of the column was either killed or disabled. Up to this moment the men, so nobly led by their officers, struggled gallantly and carried the position; but, finding themselves beset on all sides by a withering fire, which had already laid low so many comrades, they suddenly wavered, and upon a shout being raised by the sailors, "they are coming into us in thousands, retire!" in spite of all Lieutenant Garland's entreaties to persevere, they fell back upon the nearest cover; he and three or four others alone remaining, until forced to make their escape from the Pa. These men were afterwards specially thanked by H.R.H. the commander-in-chief, and one of them Colour-sergeant W. B. Garland, received a medal for distinguished service in the field, along with an annuity of £15. This disastrous retreat, commenced by the Naval Brigade, the Lieut.-general could only attribute to the confusion created amongst the men by the intricate nature of the interior defences, and the panic which the sudden fall of so many of their officers inspired, added to darkness setting in. Under these circumstances, the General hesitated to renew the assault by ordering up the reserve, and contented himself with throwing up a line of intrenchments within a hundred yards of the redoubt, intending to resume operations next day. An orderly was despatched to Tauranga for a reinforcement of all available men, and another company of the 43rd joined the same evening. The Maories, however, availing themselves of the extreme darkness of the night, abandoned their hold, and escaped through the lines of the 68th.

A.D. 1864.

On taking possession of the work in the morning, Lieut.-colonel Booth and some privates were found still breathing, and, to the credit of the natives, had not been maltreated, neither had any bodies of the killed been mutilated. The loss of the enemy must have been very heavy, although not more than twenty bodies and six wounded were found in and about the position. The prisoners avowed that a large number of killed and wounded had been carried off during the night.

In General Cameron's despatch he wrote :—

"I deeply deplore the loss of many brave and valuable officers who fell in the noble discharge of their duty on this occasion. The 43rd regiment and the service have sustained a serious loss in the death of Lieut.-colonel Booth, which took place on the night after the attack. I have already mentioned the brilliant example shown by this officer in the assault ; and when I met him on the following morning, as he was being carried out of the work, his first words were an expression of regret that he had found it impossible to carry out my orders."

After Lieut.-colonel Booth was mortally wounded, he was carried into camp, and immediately surrounded by sorrowing comrades ; addressing General Cameron, who stood by the wounded officer, said, "I am sorry I have not been able to carry out your orders, sir ; but I have done my best," to which the General replied in terms of commendation and praise, which must have been very dear to the dying soldier. Lieut.-colonel Booth * was interred in the naval and military

* A marble slab is erected to his memory in Northallerton church, bearing the following inscription :—
Sacred to the Memory of
HENRY JACKSON PARKIN BOOTH,
Lieutenant-Colonel of the 43rd Light Infantry, the second son of
Lieutenant-Colonel Henry Booth, K.H., of the same regiment,
and Mary Ann his wife, and grandson of William Booth, esq., of Brush House,
in the parish of Ecclesfield, in this county,
Born July 19th, 1830, died April 30th, 1864.
His military life, like that of his father, was passed in the 43rd Regiment, in which he became ensign, June 11th, 1847, and lieutenant-colonel, February 11th, 1862.
He served his country in Africa during the Kaffir wars in 1851, 1852, and 1853; in India, and in New Zealand, in the rebellion in 1864, when he was mortally wounded at the head of his men, while leading the attack in the storming of a fortification at Tauranga, April 29th, 1864. His services were acknowledged by a memorandum from the war office, dated November 3rd, 1864, that had he survived he would have been recommended to Her Majesty for the distinction of Companion of the Military division of the Order of the Bath.

A.D. 1864. cemetery, at the end of the Te Papa, Peninsula, where an obelisk is erected to the memory of the officers and men of the 43rd regiment.*

Richard Booth. Richard Booth, esq., of Warlaby, master of the celebrated Warlaby herd, died October 31st. A handsome white marble monument is erected to his memory in Ainderby parish church.

1865. The rev. T. M. Netherclift, B.A., was appointed chaplain of the North-Riding House of Correction, on April 4th. Mr. Netherclift was formerly curate of Northallerton parish church.

The surprise at Warea. Towards the close of the Maorie war in New Zealand, a patrol of the 43rd Regiment, in command of captain Close, on turning a corner of the road was surprised by a heavy volley from the natives, when captain Close fell mortally wounded. Ensign O'Brien immediately ordered " fix bayonets," and " charge," but the aborigines escaped through the bush. On receipt of the intelligence at New Plymouth, colonel Warre, C.B., ordered out a party of the 43rd regiment, under command of lieut.-colonel Colville, for the purpose of chastising the Warea rebels. Various moves took place before October 22nd, when a party of the 43rd left Warea to lay an ambush for the rebel Maories. About fifty were drawn on, and fire being opened, they were soon forced to retire, but the regiment lost several valuable lives. On this occasion sergeant J. Dyer (afterwards drill-instructor of the Northallerton rifle volunteers) was dangerously wounded.†

An Election incident. On the 8th of July, Mr. Jasper Wilson Johns, a candidate for the representation of the borough of Northallerton, in the liberal interest, addressed the electors from the window of the " Black Bull Hotel." Whilst listening to the candidate's harangue, Abraham Peacock, jun., fell down and directly afterwards expired.

General Election. The two great political parties in the state are pretty evenly represented in the borough of Northallerton ; the elections being nearly always hotly and narrowly contested. In this year, however, the conservatives registered a victory by the comparatively large majority of 49 votes,

Mills 239
Johns 190

This majority the liberals declared to have been obtained by illegal practices, and a petition to unseat Mr. Mills, the conservative member, was accordingly instituted by Mr. Johns, the defeated candidate. The petition was heard before a committee of investigation in London, and Mr. Mills was unseated on the ground of bribery, treating, and undue

* Vide Historical Records of the 43rd Regiment, pages 283—287.
† Ibid, page 291.

influence. This necessitated a bye election, and in the following year Messrs. Lascelles and Wrightson came forward to solicit the suffrages of the Northallerton people, but the conservatives again carried the seat:

Lascelles 224
Wrightson............ 201

A.D. 1865.

This society which for many years had ceased to exist, was, this year resuscitated, through the efforts of the late T. C. Booth, esq., of Warlaby, and Messrs. J. Vasey and F. Hutchinson, appointed hon. secretaries. Mr. Booth who took a great interest in the prosperity of the society, acted as chairman of the committee, until his death in 1878, when John Hutton, esq., of Solberge, succeeded him in that capacity. When Mr. Hutchinson left the town, Mr. John Kirby, of Barstow Hall, was appointed co-secretary with Mr. Vasey. Each year the society has been increasingly appreciated, and it is now a settled and prosperous institution.

1867. Northallerton Agricultural Society.

The right hon. earl Cathcart resigned the chairmanship of the North-Riding Quarter Sessions, and was succeeded by John Richard Westgarth Hildyard, esq., of Hutton Bonville.

1868. Lord Cathcart

The rev. Edwards Cust, vicar of Danby Wiske and Hutton Bonville, appointed archdeacon of Richmond. Mr. Cust shortly afterwards resigned the living of Hutton Bonville.

The year 1868 will ever be remembered as an important one in the annals of Irish ecclesiastical history, as the year in which the liberal government then in power disestablished and disendowed the Irish church. Whilst the bill was passing through the House of Lords, the rev. Tennison Mosse (himself an Irishman) vicar of Smeaton, was preaching one Sunday evening in Northallerton parish church : of course it was natural to suppose that the reverend gentleman would call attention to the impending spoliation of his " darlin' " church, but his feelings gaining the mastery, eloquence quickly gave place to clamour and violent gesture, the consequence being that the sleeves of the reverend gentleman's surplice caught fire by coming into contact with the lighted candles in the pulpit, to the consternation of the congregation, but the flames were extinguished before any mischief was done. This startling occurrence evaporated Mr. Mosse's ardour, who afterwards declared it to be an evil omen for the church of Ireland.

An alarming incident.

John Hutton, esq.,* was elected M.P. for Northallerton, November 17th, after an exciting contest. Mr. Jasper W. Johns was the liberal candidate.

General Election.

* Mr. Hutton's ancestors purchased Sowber Gate in 1684, where his family resided until 1824, when his father built Sowber Hill (Solberge) ; we have been unable to obtain the block of Mr. Hutton's arms.

190   ANNALS OF

A.D. 1868. Nomination of Mr. Hutton

At eleven o'clock in the morning of November 16th, the nomination of candidates took place. This was the last occasion on which nominations took place on the "hustings," and for this reason the proceedings are given *in extenso*. After the reading of the proclamation writ by Mr. W. T. Jefferson, solicitor, the returning officer, the oath was administered by the rev. T. W. Mercer, J.P., and Mr. Jefferson called upon any elector to propose a candidate.

Mr. J. Yeoman, of Osmotherley, proposed Mr. Hutton as a fit and proper person to represent the borough in parliament, and expressed a wish that every speaker should have a fair hearing. He had been asked to propose that gentleman to-day, which was his apology for being present, and the duty lay lightly on his shoulders. The gentleman he had to propose was the son of a Yorkshire sire, who was an open-hearted, open-handed, and truthful man, the late John Hutton. (Cheers.) Mr. Hutton had for his opponent a gentleman whose acquaintance they had made in a hurry, and his proposer and seconder could give no account of him. He advised them to send an independent man to parliament, and to let that man be Mr. Hutton. Mr. Loane, who seconded the nomination of Mr. Hutton, said he had much pleasure in performing that duty, especially as he thought Mr. Hutton was a man who would assist in carrying out great constitutional principles. He condemned Mr. Gladstone's Irish church policy, and advised the electors to read Mr. Gladstone's former writings on church and state. He described Mr. Gladstone as a comet that had crossed the horizon and shewn his light and then gone out in total darkness. He next censured Mr. Gladstone in reference to the bankruptcy act. Speaking of working men as members of parliament, he referred to the treatment Mr. Odger had received, and said it was not aristocratic prejudice but liberal flunkeyism. He called upon them to return Mr. Hutton to parliament.

Nomination of Mr. Johns.

Mr. Edward Hare, of Northallerton, then came forward to propose Mr. Jasper Wilson Johns as the representative of the borough. He said he would not inflict upon them such a speech as had been delivered by the last speaker, and hoped that after the excitement and turmoil of the election was over, they would all be as good friends as before. He said at the last election it had been objected to Mr. Wrightson that he was too old; and did they not think that the tories had gone to the other extreme, and brought out a candidate who was too young? He had previously discharged a similar duty to the one he was now doing with pleasure, but now there was this drawback, that he was opposing the son of a gentleman of honour and of liberal principles, from which he never deviated. The name of John Hutton ought to be dear to many, especially to the liberal party. Personally, he had the greatest respect for his son, and had he come forward as a liberal, he should have been glad to have voted for him, but he could not cast away the principles of forty years like an old garment. (Great cheering.) He hoped the question of the Irish church would be discussed in a christian spirit, and that England would do to Ireland as she would like Ireland to do to her in similar circumstances. Mr. Pattison, of Brompton, seconded the nomination of Mr. Johns, and said, that Mr. Johns, if returned, would do them credit. He challenged his opponents to say anything against the character of Mr. Johns, and said if anything could have been brought forward against that gentleman, Mr. Yeoman would have found it out. Mr. Johns had kept all his promises, and was entitled to their support. A fortnight ago he thought they would have had Mr. Hutton as a supporter of the liberal party. Mr. Pattison, who declared himself a churchman, argued in favour of disestablishing the Irish church, and supported the policy of Mr. Gladstone as more favourable to the country than that of Mr. Disraeli. He called on the electors of Northallerton to do their duty, as they would do theirs at Brompton, and then he assured them they would place their candidate at the head of the poll.

Mr. Hutton was received with great cheering from the conservatives. He had, he said, much pleasure in coming before them that day, and that they were called upon to decide upon one of the most important questions that ever came before the people of England—a question whether the constitution should remain as it was, or whether it should be "squashed." There were many statements made respecting the Irish church which were not true. That church was established by St. Patrick, and the pope was not its acknowledged head until 1152, and the property given to the church between those periods was the property of the protestant church of Ireland. Mr. Pattison had told them that the Irish church should go because it was in a minority, but he would ask Mr. Pattison who were in the minority in the time of Jesus Christ? Why, the christians. Mr. Hutton contended that the Irish people did not contribute one farthing towards the establishment, and then read part of the coronation oath, and stated that they could not ask Her Majesty to break the oath she had taken. The people of Ireland were not in favour of disestablishment, and that act would be one of robbery and sacrilege. He next compared the expenditure of liberal and conservative governments, and contended that the latter were more economical. He spoke favourably of the increased pay to soldiers, and the measures for providing them with better arms. He eulogised the foreign policy of

A.D. 1868. the present government; Mr. Gladstone had professed to
have a large majority in the House during last session, and
since then he had stated that the rating clauses of the reform
bill must be repealed. 'Why, he asked, did not Mr. Gladstone
prevent them being carried? He then stated that Mr.
Disraeli had saved Northallerton from disfranchisement. He
asked what had the liberals done for the people? They had
talked about a reform bill for many years, and other measures,
but had never carried them. He denied that he was a turn-
coat, and said the liberal party were the turn-coats as
instanced in their policy on the Irish church. He thanked
the electors for the courtesy shewn him during the canvass.
He was sorry that any misunderstanding should have arisen
with the noncomformists, and asked the electors to give him
their confidence, which he would not betray, and he had
confidence that on the morrow they would place him at the
head of the poll. (Cheers.)

Speech of Mr. Johns.   Mr. Johns was received by the liberals with loud and
enthusiastic cheering. He said Mr. Hutton had told them
Mr. Disraeli had been the preserver of the borough of Northallerton, but he feared Mr. Hutton had not read the debates,
but was drawing his inspiration from friends behind him. In
the bill introduced, Northallerton was dropped, but during
the debate an amendment was made by Mr. Bouverie, a
liberal, which decided that only seven instead of ten
boroughs should go, and therefore they had to thank the
liberals for its preservation. They had had two speeches
from the other side, with the foul-mouthed roarer who began
at first. (Interruption.) He had heard him with that contempt he most worthily deserved, and left him to be judged
by his fellow townsmen. He had at last had the advantage
of hearing Mr. Hutton speak, and had seen him several times
down in the street listening to him, and had hoped he would
in this way have been brought back into the proper fold, but
he had been seduced to leave the traditions of his house.
They knew pretty well his views, and he should, therefore,
endeavour to make his remarks more general to-day. Most
of them knew the facts and figures of the Irish church, but
how could they deal with the question that the Irish people
were paying nothing for the Irish church. Why, Mr. Hutton
knew that the tithe commutations increased the rental of
many farmers 25 per cent. What had the conservatives
done? They had refused to give the people cheap bread.
They had refused to throw open the universities. They
would not increase education, and yet, forsooth, they can
talk of being the preservers of the church of Ireland. He
would just touch upon education. He held broad and extended views on the matter, and he would like to see this

country equal to Prussia and America. Contrasting the expenditure of the liberals and conservatives, he said the liberals had saved £3,000,000 a year, and the tories had spent £3,000,000 more than they got,—a difference of £6,000,000 in two years. He (Mr. Johns) expected to hear why his opponent had changed his creed, but he had not. They had all heard of mermaids and probably of syrens. He had heard that their young friend was being lured away by a young syren. Well, he was young once, and would do a great deal, perhaps, for the clasp of a beautiful hand; but he would never turn away from his political principles. Mr. Johns said his cause was that of the people, and of their children after them, and if he went to parliament he should do all he could for the benefit of his fellow men. He would be in the ranks of Mr. Gladstone and Mr. John Bright, who were trying to advance their interests. He asked them to be early at the poll, and not to let their opponents get one a head of them. (Great applause.)

A show of hands was then taken, and declared to be in favour of Mr. Johns. A poll was demanded by Mr. Yeoman on behalf of Mr. Hutton, and the proceedings terminated after lasting over three hours.

The result of the election which took place on the following day was as follows :—

Hutton 385
Johns 373

The following is an abstract of the detailed statements of the election expenses incurred by or on behalf of John Hutton and Jasper Wilson Johns, esquires, candidates at the election held for the said borough, on the 16th and 17th days of November, 1868, as made out and signed by the respective agents, who have paid and delivered the same, with the bills and vouchers relative thereto, to the returning officer :—

As to the Election Expenses of John Hutton, Esq.

	£	s.	d.
W. T. Jefferson, Returning Officer — Payments and Disbursements by him	21	2	10½
Advertising, Printing, Stationery, and Postages	43	7	6
For Room for the despatch of business	12	2	0
Amount paid for Inspectors, Poll Clerks, Clerks, Lists of Voters, Telegrams, and Messengers	24	7	9
Horse Hire, &c.	1	15	0
Mr. Hutton's personal Expenses	26	17	7
	£129.12		8½

(Signed)
JOHN S. WALTON, M.D.,
Northallerton,
Agent for Election Expenses for the said John Hutton, Esq.

A.D. 1868.

As to the Election Expenses of Jasper Wilson Johns, Esq.

	£	s.	d.
W. T. Jefferson, Returning Officer — Payments and Disbursements by him	13	0	1½
T. T. Trevor, Esq.—Professional Services	12	3	0
J. Vasey—Printing and Stationery, &c., as per voucher	29	3	2½
Payments to Messengers, Clerks, Telegraph Messages, Copies of Lists of Voters, Postage Stamps, Use of Committee Rooms, Candidate's personal Expenses, including Cab Hire on Canvass, Lodgings, Servants, &c., &c.	55	6	3
	£109	12	7

(Signed)
J. METCALFE,
Agent appointed by Jasper Wilson Johns, Esq.,
for Election Expenses.

The foregoing abstract of statements of election expenses is prepared and published pursuant to Statute 26 and 27 Vic., c. 29, s. 4, entitled "An Act to amend and continue the Law relative to Corrupt Practices at Elections of Members of Parliament."

W. T. JEFFERSON,
Bailiff and Returning Officer
12th Jan., 1869.   of the said Borough.

Brompton Church. The parish church of Brompton, near Northallerton, was re-opened for divine worship, after a complete and handsome restoration, December 21st. The archbishop of York and the bishop of Ripon were both present on the occasion. His grace preached the morning sermon, and bishop Bickersteth in the evening.

1869. Election Petition. On Saturday evening, April 10th, 1869, judge Willes arrived in Northallerton to try the election petition, which had been lodged by the liberals against the return of Mr. Hutton, the conservative member. On the following Sunday morning, his honour attended divine service at the Northallerton parish church. The trial commenced on Monday, April 12th, and on the following Thursday the decision of the constituency was sustained, and Mr. Hutton declared elected. The election had taken place on the 17th of November previous, and the contest (as is nearly always the case at Northallerton) was sharply and hotly maintained, resulting in the return of Mr. Hutton by an exceedingly narrow majority. This gave the liberals, who were represented by Mr. Johns, an excellent opportunity of trying to reverse the decision of the electors, and they immediately set up a charge of bribery, treating, and corruption against the conservatives, with the result above stated.

Adoption of the Highway Act. A large and influential meeting of County Justices was held at Northallerton, October 15th, 1869, previous to the usual business of the Quarter Sessions, to discuss the question of adopting the Highway Act throughout the North-Riding of Yorkshire. Mr. Harcourt Johnstone moved that the provisional order of the Easter Sessions, varied by the provisional order of the Midsummer Sessions, for the adoption of the Highway Act in the North-Riding, be now confirmed, by a final order dividing the Riding into sixteen highway districts. Lord Zetland seconded the motion. Lord Feversham proposed as an amendment that the Court having regard to the strong and very general expression of opinion on the part of the ratepayers in the North-Riding against the adoption of the Highway Act, does not deem it expedient to put it in force at the present time. Mr. Milbank, M.P., having seconded the amendment, a division took place, when 63 voted for the motion, and 31 for the amendment. The decision in favour of the Act was confidently anticipated.

A.D. 1869.

Thomas Fowle, esq., the eminent conservative lawyer and agent, died February 11th.

1870. Thos. Fowle.

Mr. George Howard, deputy chief constable of the North-Riding, died May 20th. Mr. Howard was greatly esteemed, a staunch churchman, and an enthusiastic Sunday school teacher, having been superintendent of the Northallerton boys' Sunday school for several years. The Rev. Ansell Jones, curate, preached Mr. Howard's funeral sermon, founding his discourse upon the words, "*he was a good man, and a just.*"

On June 16th, a cricket match was commenced, and continued on the two following days, between eleven of All England and twenty-two of Northallerton and district. The weather was most unpropitious, rain falling incessantly on the two first days, consequently neither the ground or players were in their best form on the occasion. Nevertheless a goodly assemblage of spectators were present on the third day, the match ending in a draw in favour of Northallerton.

All England Cricket Match

John Clay, formerly landlord of the "Golden Lion Hotel," Northallerton, was accidently run over on the Northallerton railway station crossing, and sustained such serious injuries that he died the same evening. Mr. Clay served for eighteen years in the Royal Horse Guards.

Railway accident.

On March 23rd, a charter was obtained, and a new lodge of Freemasons consecrated at Northallerton by John Pearson Bell, esq., M.D., Deputy Provincial Grand Master of the North and East Ridings, and Past Grand Deacon of England. It was named the "Anchor Lodge," and John S. Walton, esq., deputy coroner for the North-Riding, was elected first Master. An old masonic lodge formerly met at an Inn called the "Pack Horse," which stood where the Wesleyan Chapel now stands. This lodge was probably a moveable lodge, as

1871. Masonic Lodge.

A.D. 1871. no record of a charter being granted can be found in the archives of the Grand Lodge.*

New Bells. On April 25th, two new bells which a few days previously had been added to the original peal of six in Northallerton church tower, were solemnly and joyously inaugurated. All the shops in the town were closed at five o'clock p.m. There was a morning service, but the inaugural service was held at half-past six in the evening. The rev. J. C. Raw, vicar of Ainderby Steeple, was the preacher.

1872. Thomas Masterman, esq., of Little Danby, a prominent local gentleman, died February 4th. The name of Masterman will not soon be forgotten in the district, for he was a man who left behind him many tangible proofs of genuine liberality, of which the Yafforth National School is not the least.

The Shambles On March 14th, the demolition of the unsightly old shambles which had for so long disfigured the centre of the town was commenced, thus disconnecting another link which bound us to the stagnant lethargy of the "good old times."

Local Will Case. The great "American Johnson" will case commenced on Friday, April 26th, and ended May 1st. Johnson, who was a native of Brompton, went to America, and after accumulating a large fortune there, returned to England, made purchases of property in and about Northallerton, residing and dying in a house in the market place which he had purchased from the representatives of the late Mrs. Booth. He had made a will which, however, could not be found, and a suit-at-law was instituted between a nephew (Johnson's heir-at-law) who claimed the real property, and the nearest of kin of the deceased. After four days trial the court allowed the draft of the will to be proved, whereby the heir-at-law failed to establish his claim to the estate.

Attempt to create a Military Depôt. On July 12th, a meeting was held at the "Golden Lion Hotel," to discuss the desirability of memorialising the Home Secretary in favour of the proposed establishment of a military depôt at Northallerton. After an exciting discussion, an amendment was carried against the proposal, and Richmond recommended to the Home Secretary as the best centre.

Capt. Peirse. Captain R. W. Peirse, registrar of the North-Riding, died in London on July 24th, and was buried at Hutton Bonville, near Northallerton, on August 1st.

Election for Registrar. On November 12th, the election for the office of Registrar of Deeds and Probate of Wills was commenced. Messrs.

* Mr. J. S. Walton informs me that he found two very old masonic aprons, possessing tool pockets at the right and left hand corners near the top, and bearing the following inscription :—" Masons' Lodge, Pack Horse, Northallerton."—J. L. S.

G. A. Cayley and R. S. Crompton had been nominated, and A.D. 1872. on the following day Mr. Crompton retired, and Mr. Cayley was declared duly elected.

The foundation stone of the new Town Hall was laid in Town Hall. this year on the site of the old butchers' shambles. There was no elaborate ceremonial upon the occasion. The right of collecting the tolls of markets and fairs was previously purchased from the Ecclesiastical Commissioners by Messrs. Jefferson and Fowle on behalf of the shareholders of the Market Company. Messrs. Ross & Co., of Darlington, were the architects, and Messrs. A. Peacock & Son, of Northallerton, the principal contractors.

On Thursday evening, December 12th, the celebrated Rev. Newman rev. Newman Hall preached to a large congregation in the Hall. Zion Congregational Church, Northallerton.

The rev. William John Middleton, first vicar of Brompton, 1873. died June 25th.

The old Toll Booth, which had for several generations Toll Booth. occupied a prominent position in the centre of the town, was on the 20th August, 1873, sold by auction to Mr. Percival Hindmarch, of Northallerton, for £18, who, at the same time, purchased the Market Cross for £5, which is now in the possession of W. T. Jefferson, esq. The Toll Booth had Market Cross. for some time previous to the erection of the Lock-up, been used as a receptacle for prisoners, as a Court House, and place of assembly for public meetings. It was removed in the following month, and thus disappeared one of those ancient land-marks which sever our connection with the days that are past.

The rev. S. R. Coxe, M.A., the new vicar of Brompton, Rev. S. R. came into residence on December 13th. Coxe.

On December 22nd, the Town Hall, erected on the site Opening of of the old shambles, was inaugurated with a concert, and Town Hall. opened to the public.

Whilst the workmen were digging gravel out of the pits Interesting on the site of the Friarage, at the east of the town, they relics. came upon several large pieces of curiously painted glass, in good preservation. The pattern was the *Fleur de lis*, and most probably had fallen from one of the windows of the ancient Friarage. Without a doubt also, many of the stones used for the internal repair of the Vine House were obtained from the same source.

John S. Walton, esq., M.D., coroner for the North-Riding, 1874. died January 12th. He was succeeded by his son. Dr. John Stamford Walton. Walton was the first medical attendant for the Northallerton ford Walton. District of the Poor Law Union, and registrar of births, deaths, and marriages for the same district.

A.D. 1874.
General Election.

On Tuesday, February 3rd, the first parliamentary election by ballot was commenced in the Town Hall. As was anticipated, the proceedings were of a much more pacific nature than on former occasions. The nominations took place three days earlier, and the candidates were Mr. G. W. Elliot (C), only son of Sir George Elliot, bart., M.P. for North Durham, and Mr. W. B. Wrightson (L.) Mr. Elliot was returned by the narrow majority of nine votes, the numbers being—

Elliot 387
Wrightson 378

Queen's Prizeman.

The Queen's Prize offered at Wimbledon for the best marksman of the year was won by corporal William C. Atkinson, of the 1st Durham Rifle Volunteers (Stockton). Mr. Atkinson was born and educated at Northallerton. Having served his apprenticeship to Mr. George Chapman, joiner, he left the town and went to Stockton, where he commenced business as a builder. He subsequently joined the volunteers there, and soon became a crack shot, carrying off the coveted distinction at Wimbledon, in 1874, with a score of 64 points. Corporal Atkinson tied in the second stage with sergeant Rae, of the 1st Renfrew Volunteers, who won the Queen's Prize in 1878. Atkinson also won the Olympic in 1874, a money prize of £52.

1875.

Mr. Walker Stead elected bridgemaster of the North Riding, January 5th.

Freemasons' Hall.

The brethren of the masonic craft who had previously held their lodge meetings in a room behind the Golden Lion Hotel, met for the first time in the large assembly room of Durham House, now known as the Freemasons' Hall, on Thursday, January 12th.

Gas Explosion

On the evening of Sunday, February 14th, an alarming gas explosion took place in the Baptist Chapel, Northallerton. It appears that the rev. W. Stubbings, the pastor, went into the chapel as was his wont, late in the evening, to turn the gas off at the meter, and see that everything was safe. When Mr. Stubbings, who carried a lighted candle in his hand, reached the vestry door, an explosion took place, by which the roof was blown off, the windows shattered, and Mr. Stubbings thrown violently to the ground, where he was found in a state of unconsciousness. It is supposed that one of the jets had by some means been left turned on, the escaped gas having accumulated. The report of the explosion was heard at Lovesome Hill, a distance of three miles from Northallerton.

Re-opening of Appleton Wiske Church

Appleton Wiske church was re-opened for divine worship, after undergoing an internal and external restoration, on May 27th. The morning sermon was preached by the right rev. Bishop Ryan, vicar of Bradford, the evening preacher being the rev. T. M. Netherclift, B.A., chaplain of the North Riding Gaol. The restoration was carried out under the able direction of Walker Stead, esq., of Northallerton, who also defrayed a great part of the expense. *[A.D. 1875.]*

On Tuesday afternoon, July 18th, H. R. H. the Duke of Connaught arrived at Northallerton, *en route* to Edinburgh, in command of a detachment of the Connaught Rangers (Hussars). The men were billeted in the town, the illustrious duke putting up at the Golden Lion Hotel. The people of Northallerton, as might be expected, were not wanting in manifestations of loyalty towards the prince. His Royal Highness left the town next morning. *[1876. Royal visit.]*

The greyhound dog "Coomassie," trained by Mr. John Shaw, of Northallerton, was this year the winner of the Waterloo Cup, valued at £500. *[1877. The Waterloo Cup.]*

Benjamin Charles Caffin, M.A., was appointed by the Dean and Chapter of Durham to the vicarage of Northallerton, soon after the death of Mr. Mercer, and was inducted in March, 1877. Mr. Caffin is the Rural Dean of the Deanery of Northallerton, and a late Fellow and Tutor of Worcester college, Oxford. He is also a surrogate for granting marriage licences. When appointed to the living of Northallerton he was second master of Durham Grammar School, and one of the Theological Examiners of Durham University. Whilst at Oxford, Mr. Caffin was one of the select preachers to the University, and Rector of St. Martin-Carfax. He took several prizes, and came out in the 1st cl Lit. Hum. *[New Vicar.]*

On the 27th March, the rev. W. F. N. Allen, master of the Northallerton Grammar School died. After his death it was discovered that Mr. Allen, whose movements during life had been somewhat eccentric and mysterious, was a priest of the Roman Catholic communion. Among his personal effects was found a box containing conclusive documents, and a full set of papal vestments. Mr. Allen, however, never assumed a clerical garb, or ventured to officiate in any priestly capacity, but it was generally thought that he was in some way connected with the Order of Jesuits. He was formerly an assistant master at the Mount School under the rev. E. Bittleston, the then head master. *[A strange discovery.]*

The rev. B. C. Caffin, M.A., the newly appointed vicar of Northallerton, preached his first sermon in the parish church on Sunday, April 22nd. Mr. Caffin is the forty-eighth vicar of Northallerton. *[Rev. B. C. Caffin.]*

The present Post Office was opened October 1st, previous to which time the postal business had been transacted at the Vine House. *[New Post Office.]*

A.D. 1877.
Another worthy townsman.

Of the many worthy inhabitants of Northallerton who deserve to be remembered, Robert Blackett was undoubtedly one. He was the first rural letter carrier appointed in this district under the regulations of the Penny Postage Act. His duty was to take charge of, and deliver all letters sent from the Northallerton post office, to Warlaby, Ainderby, Morton-on-Swale, Thrintoft, and Great and Little Langton, on every day of the week except Sundays, being a daily round of sixteen miles. This duty he faithfully discharged on foot in all kinds of weather, for twenty years, without a single intermission. During this period he was so much and deservedly respected, that he received many marks of kindness from the families in his district. Lord Teignmouth who resided at Langton Hall, presented him with a bible, which contains the following inscription :—

"Robert Blackett, the gift of Lord Teignmouth, Nov. 30th, 1863, on his completing the sixteenth year of his round, as postman for this district, daily, without a single intermission (Sundays excepted).
Langton Hall, Northallerton, Nov. 30th, 1863."

And in 1867 the ladies of Langton, on the completion of his twentieth year of service, presented him with a silver tea pot, sugar basin, and cream jug; the following inscription is engraved on the tea pot :—

"Presented to Robert Blackett, by the ladies of Langton-on-Swale, 1867, as a mark of respect and esteem during 20 years' service as postman."

These testimonials to his worth are highly valued and preserved by his family. The complete and faithful performance of this duty for so long a period, under the trying influences of sun, rain, frost, and snow, is most remarkable, as it involved the walking of nearly one hundred thousand miles. He retired in 1867 on a well deserved pension, and with his son and daughter, occupied a small farm near this town, until September, 1877, when he died widely respected, aged 83 years.

The Cottage Hospital.

The Vine House, after undergoing internal repair, was opened as a Cottage Hospital for Northallerton and district, October 11th, mainly through the liberality and exertions of John Hutton, esq., of Solberge.

1878.
The Waterloo Cup.

The Waterloo Cup again won by the dog "Coomassie," trained by Mr. John Shaw, of Northallerton. Mr. Shaw's reputation as a trainer is now well established, as was testified by the hearty welcome which the sporting public accorded him on his arrival at Northallerton railway station with his canine hero.

Edward Hare.

Mr. Edward Hare, an old and respected townsman of the borough, died July 18th. Mr. Hare, who was possessed of considerable oratorical ability, was invariably to be seen during election times upon the hustings, upholding the principles and proclaiming the merits of the liberal candidate. He was a whig of the old type.

On August 6th, the Yorkshire Agricultural Show was commenced on the race course, Northallerton, and was continued for three days.

A.D. 1878
Yorkshire Show.

Mr. Thomas C. Booth, a noteworthy agriculturist, and owner of the celebrated herd of short-horns, at Warlaby, near Northallerton, died September 7th, 1878, after a short attack of typhoid fever. No man could be more respected in the neighbourhood of Northallerton, or by the whole agricultural world, than he was. From the time he became the possessor of the Warlaby short-horns, they fully maintained the great reputation in which they were held during the time of his predecessor, Mr. Richard Booth*; and those who had the privilege of seeing the herd during the Yorkshire Show held at Northallerton will never forget the treat or the kindness of its owner. Mr. Booth's loss was most keenly felt by his neighbours, as a truer friend or better neighbour never existed. Land-owners, tenant farmers, and the poor were all indebted to him for his innumerable acts of kindness. In public affairs he always took an active part, and from the establishment of the Highway Act he was chairman of the Northallerton Highway Board, and it was chiefly through him that the Act was so well administered in the district, and the irritation caused by the adoption of the Act smoothed down. He was also for many years an active member of the Board of Guardians. In political matters he was a strong conservative, and the mainstay of the party at Northallerton. He represented the Royal Agricultural Society on the Lords' Committee on the Cattle Diseases Bill in 1878, and all agriculturists are greatly indebted to him for the part he then took. It was mainly through his exertions that the Yorkshire Agricultural Society's show was held so successfully at Northallerton, the local show at this place having been one of the best in Yorkshire, and for many years under his presidency. He was a good churchman, and was selected to represent the rural deanery of East Richmond at the Leeds congress. In 1874, when presented with a testimonial by his neighbours and breeders of stock throughout the country, as a recognition of his liberality in various ways, he replied, "In what I have done, I only feel I have done my duty; and if God spares my life, I hope to continue to do my duty to every man."†

T. C. Booth.

---

* For a portrait and long sketch of him see the *Agricultural Gazette* for July 17th, 1875. In the chancel of Ainderby Steeple church is a memorial window erected to the late Richard Booth, esq., of Warlaby, by his friends and neighbours.

† Vide "Old Yorkshire Worthies," xxxviii, 250. For a sketch of T. C. Booth, esq., see *Live Stock Journal Almanack* for 1879, by Cassell's.

A.D. 1879. Battle of Isandula. On January 22nd, 1879, the British camp at Isandula, in Zululand, was suddenly attacked by a horde of infuriated savages, who advanced in overwhelming numbers, brandishing their assegais, sending up the most deafening yells, and completely annihilating the 24th regiment before either an alarm could be given or succour obtained. Sergeant Milner, of Hutton Bonville, near Northallerton, was amongst the slain.

Weston. On Tuesday, February 11th, 1879, Weston, the champion pedestrian of the world, walking from Land's End to John O' Groat's, passed through Northallerton. His fame as a pedestrian of extraordinary speed and endurance had naturally preceded him, and the inhabitants of the town were on the *qui vive*. Weston entered Northallerton at midnight, and was escorted out of the town on the following morning by an enthusiastic crowd of admirers, and proceeded on his way, doubtless much encouraged by their vociferous shouts of hilarity and good-will.

A singular coincidence. An old couple named George and Hannah Metcalfe, of Northallerton, were interred together in the Northallerton cemetery on March 21st. They had lived very happily together until the old man died, but his faithful wife declined to remain behind, and followed him three days afterwards. They were laid to rest together, "lovely in their lives, and in death not divided."

Mr. James Holmes, sexton of the parish church for twenty-three years, died on September 8th.

Accident in hunting field. Whilst hunting, John Hutton, esq., of Solberge, was thrown from his horse and very much hurt.

1880. Educational meeting. On January 6th, 1880, an influential meeting was held at the Court House, Northallerton, presided over by the Marquis of Ripon, K.G., to take steps for the formation and erection of a public school to be called the "North-Eastern Counties School."

Mr. Richard Mayne, auctioneer, died at Northallerton, March 9th. His bills of sale were frequently masterpieces of auctioneering composition, which even the celebrated George Robbins might have envied.

General Election. On April 1st, the election for the parliamentary seat, rendered vacant by the dissolution of Lord Beaconsfield's administration, took place. Mr. G. W. Elliot (C) and Mr. Albert Rutson (L) were the nominated candidates. Notwithstanding the liberal reaction which had set in throughout the country, the electors of Northallerton again returned Mr. Elliot by a hundred votes, the largest majority ever obtained at any previous election, the number of votes being,—

Elliot 484
Rutson 384

On Sunday afternoon, June 13th, an adult inmate of the Northallerton Cottage Hospital named Samuel Whittaker, aged 69 years, was publicly baptised in the parish church of Northallerton, by the rev. J. L. Saywell, curate. Whittaker was a Brompton man, and died there shortly afterwards.

A.D. 1880. An adult baptism.

During the months of May, June, and July, the various Sunday schools in the town celebrated the centenary of Sunday schools with treats, special services, and sermons. On July 25th, special sermons were preached in Northallerton church in aid of the Northallerton church Sunday schools, on the subject of the centenary, that in the morning by the rev. B. C. Caffin, vicar, and that in the evening by the rev. J. L. Saywell, curate. In the afternoon a children's service was held, and was addressed by the rev. W. C. Barwis. During the following week the centenary was celebrated by a treat to the day and Sunday scholars, and a cricket match. Centenary medals were also distributed to the children. May the name of Robert Raikes, the founder of Sunday schools ever remain dear in the memory of all engaged in Sunday school work.

Sunday School Centenary.

On Sunday morning, February 27th, the British troops engaged against the Boers, in South Africa, were repulsed with considerable loss, in an attempt to storm the Dutch position on the Majuba Hill, on which occasion Lieutenant Hill, of Romanby, near Northallerton, was severely wounded, in a gallant effort to rescue a brother officer, who was subsequently shot dead in his arms. Laying down his dead comrade, Lieutenant Hill, beneath a galling fire, picked up another wounded soldier, and carried him safely into the British camp, for which heroic conduct he was honourably mentioned in the despatches by General George Colley.

Battle of Majuba Hill.

On Whitsun Tuesday, June 7th, the foundation stone of a new church-of-ease for Romanby was laid by John Hutton, esq., (late M.P. for Northallerton) of Solberge. The clergy robed in the schoolroom, and proceeded to the site, where the choir and a large company were assembled. The rev. W. C. Barwis, curate (in the absence of the vicar), having explained the need of a church, and of a service of prayer and praise to Almighty God for his blessing on the building of this christian temple, then led the appointed service of hymns, prayers, creed, and psalms. The rev. T. M. Netherclift read the lesson. The architect then handed to Mr. Hutton the trowel provided for the ceremony, with the mallet and plumb, who then laid the stone "in the faith of the Lord Jesus Christ, and in the name of the Father, the Son, and the Holy Ghost." He also placed a bottle containing a few coins of the date, and a newspaper within a cavity of the stone, which was then sealed up, only to be

1881. Laying foundation stone of Romanby Church.

A.D. 1881. opened when the withering hand of time shall have crumbled to dust the smaller stones which bind it, and the voices of successive generations shall have been lost along the distant corridors of the misty future. The company then adjourned to the school-room, where Mr. Hutton delivered an excellent and heart-teaching address, saying what a blessing a new church would be to Romanby, as another witness to Almighty God, in this age of scepticism and religious indifference. The rev. J. L. Saywell, curate, concluded the prayers for the builders and masons. It was a day of foundation promise and strength for Romanby. There had been, hundreds of years before, a chapel here, but its very site and name have been lost. The name of St. James for this church is taken from the ancient hospital in Thirsk road.

Reception of Lieut. Hill. On August 7th, Lieut. Alan Hill was met at the Northallerton railway station on his return from South Africa, by the Northallerton volunteers and a large crowd of enthusiastic and patriotic inhabitants, and escorted with musical and military honours, to his home at Romanby.

The Salvation Army. For some years past, the religious world had been kept in a state of ferment by the doings of a somewhat eccentric body of Christians, styling themselves the "Salvation Army." They came into notice not long after the departure of the American evangelists, Messrs. Moody and Sankey, and had increased so rapidly both in numbers and influence, that hardly a village of any importance was without a "corps." Each detachment was commanded by one or more male or female officers, who wore a distinctive uniform, and claimed the power of "enlisting" as many privates as possible by all legitimate means, such as mission marchs, outdoor preaching, singing, and praying, followed by devotional meetings. The army is supposed to be contending against the powers of darkness, and as such chiefly invades the haunts of the abandoned and depraved which as a rule are out of the reach of the usual christian influences. The army is undenominational, and its tactics eminently calculated to accomplish the objects which it has in view. "General" Booth is the commander-in-chief, and his head-quarters are at London. On September 10th, a detachment of the salvation army invaded the town of Northallerton, since which time many converts have been made, chiefly from the "lowest of the people."

On October 10th, the 209th corps, commanded by "captain" Close and "lieutenant" Wessberg, marched to the parish church, to hear a sermon by the rev. George Body, rector of Kirby Misperton, the celebrated church revivalist.

Presentation to Lieut. Hill. On September 15th, a very handsome and highly engraved sword bearing a suitable inscription, was presented to Lieutenant Alan Hill by the superior officers of the North Riding

Constabulary, as a mark of admiration and esteem for his bravery in the Transvaal War. A large party of justices and friends were entertained at dinner by Captain Hill on the occasion. The presentation was made to the young soldier by Deputy-Chief Constable Walmsley in appropriate and felicitous terms. Several eulogistic speeches were afterwards made in Lieutenant Hill's honour, to which he responded in a modest yet manly manner.

On Tuesday, November 1st, an adjourned meeting of parishioners was held in the vestry of the parish church, for the purpose of further considering the question of restoring the church, which, during the last few years, had fallen into a very dilapidated condition. It was resolved to thoroughly restore the whole building, and to invite C. Hodgson Fowler, esq., F.S.A., of Durham, to confer with the committee as to the execution of the work. Mr. J. I. Jefferson was appointed secretary, and Mr. W. Emmerson, treasurer of the restoration fund.

The rev. S. R. Coxe, vicar of Brompton, resigned, February 2nd.

On March 11th, the rev. A. Maclennan, D.C.L., was appointed by the dean and chapter of Durham to the living of Brompton, vacant by the resignation of the rev. S. R. Coxe, M.A. Dr. Maclennan is the third vicar of Brompton, and was formerly fellow of the University of Durham, and incumbent of St. James, Edinburgh.

On the morning of March 15th, the people of Northallerton were agreeably surprised with the official announcement that her Majesty Queen Victoria had been graciously pleased to signify her intention of conferring the Victoria Cross upon their gallant townsman, Lieutenant Alan Hill. This honourable distinction is the one most coveted by Englishmen, and signifies that the possessor has distinguished himself in military action by conspicuous bravery and heroism. The cross is a bronze one, and bears the inscrption "For Valour." We congratulate Lieut. Hill, V.C., and trust that he may be long spared to enjoy his well merited honour, and that the spirit of Wellington will urge on the young "hero" to further deeds of heroism and glory.

On Sunday morning, March 26th, the 209th corps of the "Salvation Army" stationed at Northallerton, attended at the parish church to receive the Holy Communion. The celebration was at 8 o'clock, and everything was done decently and in order, the "soldiers" being devout and well-behaved. It was a bright, happy, and strengthening service. There were forty eight members of the army present, augmented by forty regular communicants. The revds. B. C. Caffin, vicar, J. L. Saywell, curate, W. C. Barwis, Romanby, and A. L.

A.D. 1882.

Presentation of oil-painting.

Manby, Yafforth, officiated. Application for admission to the Sacrament, was made by the captain (Miss Wessberg) to the vicar, who obtained the consent of his grace the archbishop of York.

At the fortnightly meeting of the Northallerton Board of Guardians held in May, the clerk read the following letter, received by the chairman, together with an oil painting, from the rev. G. T. Townsend, D.C.L., formerly curate of Northallerton, and now incumbent of St. Michael's, Bishopgate Street, London:—" This picture was painted about fifty years ago by Mr. Wheldon, a clever self-taught artist, an inhabitant of Northallerton. This was painted at the cost of the rev. George Townsend, at that time the vicar of the parish. It represents the interior of the Northallerton workhouse, previous to the passing of the new poor law. The old workhouse stood close to the bridge (in the causeway), over the beck nearly opposite Vine House. All the figures in the picture are portraits of persons at that time inmates of the house in the year 1832. The woman smoking was an Irishwoman, and the woman behind her was an idiot woman. The fisherman, named Simpson, was at that time a well known character in the borough, and was therefore introduced by the artist. It is probable that some of the older inhabitants may yet remember, and be able to identify some of the other figures. Dr. Townsend, the present owner of the picture, has much pleasure in presenting it to the board of guardians. He trusts that it will be valued by them as an interesting memorial of past times."

GEO. TYLER TOWNSEND,.
Incumbent of St. Michael's,
May 3, 1882.   Bishopgate St.

The painting, which is a perfect work of art, was exhibited to the Board, and it was resolved to hang it in the present Board Room. It was also resolved that the best thanks of the Board be given to Dr. Townsend for his most valuable present, and that it would give them great pleasure to preserve it, as a memorial of olden times.

Consecration of Romanby new Church.

The new church of St. James, Romanby, was consecrated by the archbishop (Dr. Thomson) of York, on Whit-Tuesday, May 30th, the anniversary of the laying of the foundation-stone. The usual formalities were followed by morning service. The prayers were said by the rev. W. C. Barwis, curate in charge of Romanby. The first lesson was read by the rev. J. L. Saywell, curate of Northallerton, and the second by the rev. B. C. Caffin, vicar. The archbishop delivered a powerful and eloquent sermon from the words " *And they were all amazed and were in doubt, saying one to another, What meaneth this ?*" In the evening the rev. C. Camidge, vicar of Thirsk, preached a stirring sermon on the words "*And I saw no temple therein.*" The total amount collected during the day was £41, which nearly cleared off the entire debt.

Whilst lying in Northallerton gaol, Mrs. Quinton, the wife of a Whitby doctor, made a second attempt to commit suicide, by suspending herself by the neck to some gas-piping, using her garters for the purpose; fortunately she was discovered before death could ensue. She was subsequently removed to York castle, there to await her trial on the charge of having thrown a quantity of corrosive liquid at Mrs. Mary Jane Bowers, whom Mrs. Quinton had suspected of having had criminal intercourse with Dr. Quinton. Soon after throwing the vitriol, Mrs. Quinton attempted to poison herself by taking a dose of laudanum. If there was the slightest foundation for Mrs. Quinton's jealousy, she is entitled to our sympathy, although her rash act was not thereby justified.

Dr. Alexander Maclennan, the newly appointed vicar of Brompton, read himself into his benefice on Sunday morning, July 2nd. In the evening the reverend gentleman preached his first sermon as vicar of Brompton, to a crowded congregation, founding his discourse upon the text, "*I have an errand unto thee, O captain.*"* Dr. Maclennan's popularity as an eloquent preacher had preceded him, and the church was filled to overflowing by an attentive and appreciative audience.

The removal of accumulated earth on the south side of the church, preparatory to its restoration, was begun on Monday, July 3rd. The work was entrusted to Messrs. Bendelow & Sons, of Northallerton, whose tender had been selected by the restoration committee. The first six spadesful disclosed a skull, almost perfect, and before the day's work was done large quantities of bones had been unearthed and carefully re-interred in another part of the yard. On the third day several large stone coffins were exposed to view, which had been built into the outside wall of the south aisle, thus proving the existence of a very early burial ground. Only one recent grave was materially interfered with, whilst the loose bones which were continually thrown up, had doubtless been repeatedly unearthed on previous occasions to make way for new graves.

In July, Mr. G. W. Elliot, M.P. for Northallerton, had the honour of being appointed a deputy-lieutenant for Monmouthshire by the Duke of Beaufort, lord-lieutenant of that county.

* 2 Kings, ix, 5.

A.D. 1882.
Rare birds.

On Saturday, August 19th, some workmen captured in a plantation near Northallerton a sparrow, which was perfectly white. They were unable to take the old birds and remainder of the brood, all of which were white.

Archæological Excursion.

On Wednesday, August 30th, the members of the Yorkshire Archæological and Topographical Association had their sixteenth annual excursion, their destination being Northallerton and Mount Grace Priory. The party numbered about two hundred ladies and gentlemen, including some of the most eminent antiquarians and archæologists of the day.

History of the Priory, and description of ruins.

Mount Grace Priory is the first ruin of the kind visited by the members of the association. The Carthusian order was founded in 1080 by St. Bruno, a native of Cologne, and the first house was built at Chartreuse, near Grenoble. According to the rules of the founder the Carthusian monks had to wear a hair cloth next to their body, a white cassock, and over it a black cloak; they were never to eat meat, to fast every Friday on bread and water, to eat alone in their chambers except upon certain high festivals, to observe an almost perpetual silence, and they were never allowed to go out of their apartments except to church without leave from the superior. At Mount Grace Priory there were about twenty monks, whose houses, each with its garden, formed three sides of a large enclosure, the fourth side being formed by the church and probably the prior's residence. Some of the cells, two storeys high, are in a very fair state of preservation, and the curious hatch through which food was given to the monks can still be plainly seen. The ruin lies at the foot of a high and well-wooded hill on the Hambleton range of the Cleveland series, whence a very fine view of the surrounding country is obtained. On approaching the ruin the first object that attracts attention is a house which has been altered and adapted from its original purposes as part of the Priory buildings, the date, as indicated by the inscription, being 1654, and the owner at that time Thomas Lascelles. The Priory, or "House of Mount Grace of Ingleby," was founded in honour of SS. Mary and Nicholas, in the year 1397, by Thomas de Holland, Earl of Kent and Duke of Surrey. It was not completed, however, until some years later, when the work was finished by the liberality of King Henry V. At the time of the dissoluton of the monasteries, the revenues were valued at £382 5s. 11d., and the site, with the adjacent property, was granted in 1541 to Sir James Strangways, Kt., to hold *in capite* for military service. Sir James devised it to the Dacres, and from them it descended to the Hon. Conyers Darcy, who in 1653 sold it to Thomas Lascelles. In 1744 the rev. Robert Lascelles sold the property to Mr. Timothy Mauleverer, who added it to the

THE MOUNT, NORTHALLERTON.

MOUNT GRACE PRIORY.

Arncliffe estate, to which it is now attached. The party having gathered together in the enclosure, Mr. William Brown, of Ingleby Arncliffe, read an interesting historical paper, in the course of which he said Mount Grace was situated in the parish of East Harlsey, about eight miles E.N.E. of Northallerton. The position of the ruins, at the foot of a steep hill covered with oak woods, was very beautiful, and the grey stone tower of the church, standing out against the dark green foliage, exhibited a very pleasing landscape. Before the foundation of the priory, at the end of the 14th century, Mount Grace was known by the names of Bordlebi, Bordelbia, or Bordelby. At the time of Domesday it was included in the king's land, and held for him by Malgrin, who was also lord of the neighbouring manors of West Harlsey, Morton, Ingleby, and Arncliffe. Shortly after the survey, the king granted Bordleby to Robert de Brus, the ancestor of the Scottish kings, and who was supposed to have come over to England about 1086 or 1087. This was the same as the Robert de Brus who founded Guisborough Priory in 1119, fought at the battle of the Standard in 1138, and died about 1141. At the beginning of the 13th century Bordleby was held of the Bruses by a branch of the Lascelles family, who also held East Harlsey, Siddall, and Sawcock. He was unable to connect them with the baronial house of the same name, who, besides other property in Lincolnshire and Yorkshire, owned Scruton, in the North Riding. Members of the Bordleby and Harlsey Lascelleses were benefactors to Rievaulx and Guisborough. They retained possession of the place until 1301, when Edmund de Lascelles settled the Manor of Bortleby on Robert de Fourneus and Matilda his wife. In 1316 it belonged to Galfri de Hothum, after which they found no mention of it until the close of that century, when the priory was founded by Thomas de Holland, Lord Wake, and Earl of Kent by descent, and afterwards by creation Duke of Surrey, who was the grandson of Joan Wake, called the Fair Maid of Kent. She married secondly the Black Prince, and by him became mother of Richard II. It was in 1397 that the Duke of Surrey founded the Priory of Mount Grace. In the foundation he stated that the reason he chose the Carthusian Order was the "admiration and love he had had from his earliest youth for their holy and peculiar rules, and for the persons living in them, and also from the affection he bore to the festivals of the Assumption of the Glorious Virgin and of St. Nicholas." With the assent of the Prior of the Chartreuse, he nominated Robert Tredewy the first prior, and ordained that the monks of the house should always in their orisons recommend to God the good

A.D. 1882.

Interesting Description.

Foundation of the Priory.

A.D. 1882. estate of King Richard II, his Queen Isabel, himself and his wife Joan and their heirs, his brother, John de Holland, Duke of Exeter, John de Ingelby and Ellen his wife, and others.

Royal grants. In 1398 the Duke of Surrey got the King to grant to Edmund Prior of Mount Grace, the alien priories of Hinckley, in Leicestershire, Warham, in Dorsetshire, and Caresbrooke, in the Isle of Wight, belonging to the Abbey of St. Mary de Li(y)ra in Normandy, to hold as long as the war continued between England and France. The revolt during Richard II's absence and the accession of Henry Duke of Lancaster as Henry IV, had a very disastrous effect on the fortunes of

Burial of the Duke of Surrey. the Duke of Surrey, who, with his brother, the Duke of Exeter, engaged in plots to assassinate Henry, and was afterwards shot with an arrow in a fight in the streets of Cirencester. His body was buried in the Abbey of Cirencester, and remained there until 1412, when his widow, Joan, obtained leave to remove his bones to Mount Grace, and re-inter them there. On March 13th, 1400, his widow was allowed to take her husband's head down from London Bridge, where it had been placed after his death, and to bring it where she liked. Within the walls of Mount Grace were the memorials of another person who died in rebellion against Henry IV,

Archbishop Scroope. namely Archbishop Scroope, whose arms were to be found in the south-east corner of the inner quadrangle, where they formed the terminations of the dripstone of one of the cell doors. In consequence of the Duke's death in rebellion no grants were made during Henry IV's reign, and no mention of the Priory occurred until 1415, when Henry V, on the petition of his uncle Thomas, Earl of Dorset, confirmed to Nicholas, Prior of Mount Grace, the alien Priory of Hinckley for the support of five monks to pray for his good health and that of the said Thomas during their lifetime, and for their souls after death. As a reparation for his father having seized the Priory of

Benefactions. Ware, Henry V, in 1421, granted the monks an annuity of £100, and in addition the alien priories of Long Bennington in Lincolnshire, and Feildalling in Norfolk, belonging to the Abbey of Savigney in Normandy; that of Hagh in Lincolnshire, belonging to the Abbey of Cherbourg; and the alien Priory of Mintington, in the same county, belonging to the Monastery of St. Benedict on the Loire. In 1440 parliament confirmed the grant of the manor of Bordelby to the monks, but the confirmation did not seem to have been very efficacious, as in 1508 Henry, Prior of Mount Grace, accepted from John, Prior of Guisborough, a lease for a term of fifty years at a yearly rent of £8 of the Chapel of East Harlsey, and lands which included the whole manor of Bordelby. In 1456 Sir James Strangways obtained leave to appropriate the Church of (B)Deighton to Robert, prior of Mount Grace, and in

1462 the monks received a grant of the manor of Atherstone, in Warwickshire, belonging to the alien Priory of Great Okebourne, in Wiltshire. In 1471 the Prior of Mount Grace received the last royal benefaction recorded on the rolls—the manor or alien Priory of Beggar, in Derbyshire. This was granted to the monks in consideration of their poverty. In consideration for this gift they were to pray for the king's health whilst alive and for his soul when dead; and for the souls of Richard, Duke of York, "of glorious memory, his father, true heir of the realms of England and France and Lord of Ireland, and of his brothers and sisters and all faithful persons deceased." To carry out this object, they were required to celebrate "three masses daily to the Blessed Virgin, the undivided Trinity, and the holy and glorious martyr Erasmus." Nothing further was heard of this house until the Reformation, when its net revenues amounted to the respectable sum of £323 2s. 10½d. At the dissolution the convent consisted of a prior, sixteen priests, three novices, six conversi, and one donatus—in all twenty-seven persons. An annual sum of £194 was divided amongst the inmates by way of pension, of which the prior, John Wilson, received £60, together with the house and chapel called the Mount. At the Reformation the site of the priory was granted to Sir James Strangways the younger, of Harlsey Castle, to hold *in capite* by military service. On his death (April 20th, 1540), without issue, his extensive estates became divisible between his cousin, Robert Roos, of Ingmanthorpe, and his aunt, Joan, wife of Sir William Mauleverer, and widow of Sir John Bigod, of Settrington. By an Act of Parliament passed in 1544, Mount Grace, with other properties forming part of the inheritance of the Strangways, was allotted to Roos. Shortly after he sold the manor of Mount Grace to Ralph Rokeby, sergeant-at-law, whose son, William Rokeby, of Skiers Hall, in 1616, settled Mount Grace, with other lands, on his grand-daughter Grace on her marriage with Conyers Darcy, son and heir of Sir Conyers Darcy, of Hornby Castle. In 1653, Conyers Darcy, described as the Hon. Conyers Darcy, of Hornby Castle, sold the capital messuage at Mount Grace, with the site of the late dissolved monastery, to Thomas Lascelles, for £1,900. Thus, after an interval of 350 years, a person bearing the name of Lascelles again became settled at Mount Grace. Thomas Lascelles was most probably a cadet of the Lascelles of Stank and Northallerton, who have since been ennobled with the Earldom of Harewood. His descendant, William Lascelles, used arms very similar to those of the Harewood family, namely, a cross flory; and by his will, which was made in 1722, in case of the failure of former devises, he left his estate at Mount Grace to Daniel Lascelles, of Northallerton, the grandfather of the first Lord Harewood. Shortly after completing his purchase, Lascelles came to reside at his newly acquired property, and enlarged or remodelled the present dwelling-house, which occupies a considerable portion of the south side of the first or outer court. His initials, with the date 1654, are placed over the doorway. The purchase of Mount Grace seemed to have crippled him very much. In 1654 he was forced to mortgage part of his property at Mount Grace to raise £200, and the creation of a trust to raise £2,000 out of other lands there for his children, followed, as it was, by a chancery suit, dealt a blow to the family from which it never recovered. Towards the end of the century the Lascelles ceased to reside at Mount Grace, and lived entirely in Durham. They did not, however, part with the property until 1744, when the rev. Robert Lascelles sold the Priory and 500 acres to Timothy Mauleverer, esq., of Arncliffe, from whom it had descended to its present owners. This property was until lately entirely surrounded by a mound, with a ditch on either side, probably cast up by the monks. In the uncultivated parts it is still quite perfect, and can be easily followed. At the top of the hill behind the Priory are the remains of a small chapel called "Lady Chapel." The pathway leading to it is called Lady's Steps, but the stones with which it was formerly paved have disappeared. It is said to have been founded in 1515, and to have been the burial place of the monastery. Tombstones were to be seen there within the memory of persons now living, but the remains now are insignificant. In James I's reign it became notorious for the pilgrimages made to it by adherents of the old faith, who, notwithstanding the severity of the laws against Papists, flocked to it by night from great distances. With a view of enforcing the law and putting a stop to these "Popish, idle, and superstitious pilgrimages, and like vanities," a document was issued by the Commission for Ecclesiastical Causes at York, entitled "Commission for Pilgrims," which was as follows:—

"Whereas it is enformed that diverse and sundrie superstitious and popishlie affected persons have frequented and still doe frequent (in manner of pilgrimage) to repare unto a certaine Chappell or Hermytage, nere unto the late dissolved Monasterie of Mount Grace, in Cleveland of the dioces of Yorke, especiallie upon the ladies, and other saints' eves, and certaine other sett, and appointed tymes by the people of that countrie observed and noted, att which place and tymes, the saide persons flockinge together, doe observe and practice diverse superstitions and popishe ceremonies, and have certaine unlawfull Conventicles for the actinge and performing of sundrie suche popishe, idle, and superstitious pilgrimages and like vanities : And forasmuch, as those persons that doe repare thither, come secretlie and closelie and for the moste parte in the night tyme, whose names are not knoune certainlie, the rather for that some of them are thought to come from farr : Therefore to meet with the delinquents in that kynd, and to take away that superstitious use and meetinge, not to be tolerated, we doe in the Kynges Majesties name and by virtue of his Highness Commission for causes ecclesiasticall within the Province of Yorke to us and others directed, will and command you, that you or one of you not omitting for any libertie, priviledge, or exemption, doe attache and apprehend, or cause to be apprehended, not onlie all and evrie suche person and persons as have frequented the saide pilgrimage, but alsoe all and everie suche person and persons, as you or any of you shall take at the saide Chappell or Hermytage at any tyme hereafter, and to sett doune their names, surnames and qualities and other circumstances which maye tend to the siftynge owt of the cause and purpose of their comynge thither. And upon their apprehensions to bring them forthwith before us, or else take them bound with good sureties in the some of fiftie poundes apeece to his Majesties use to be and personallie appeare before us or three or more of his Majesties saide Commissioners, whereof one to be of the quorum, at the Cittie of Yorke, in the Consistorie Churche of Saint Peter, uppon the next generall session or High Commission Court there to be held and kept after their apprehension, then and there to make personall and several unto suche matters as all their cominge shall be objected against them, and upon their appearance not to departe withoute licence first obtained of the saide Commissioners or three of them, willinge and comaundynge all and singular his Majesties Justices of Peace, Maires, Sherifs, Bailifs, and Constables, and all other his Majesties Officers and lovynge subjectes within the Province of Yorke to be ayding and assists. to you in the exeqution hereof. Faile you not hereof as youe will answer the contrarie at your perills. Given at Yorke under his Majesties signett used in this behalfe the fift daie of September ano. 1614.

TOBIAS EBORACEM	PHINEAS HODSON
JO. BRISTOL	H. BARKER
GEO. LUDWORTHE	H. SWINBURN
W. INGRAM	

Mr. J. T. Micklethwaite, F.S.A., then said that the members of the society had thrashed out the Cistercian monasteries, and now they had come to a totally different place. The Cistercians had a very hard rule indeed, and seemed to make themselves as uncomfortable as they possibly could. In this

Régime of Cistercian and Carthusian monks.

A.D. 1882.

respect they were beaten by one order, the Carthusians. The members of the Yorkshire Archæological Society were then within the most perfect Carthusian ruin we had in England. The chief peculiarity of rule in which the Carthusian differed from all the other abbeys was that every man lived in a separate dwelling by himself. They never went out except to church or to the chapter-house, or to till their gardens. Each man's house contained everything that he wanted for his own daily life, and the monk filled up his time by digging his little garden or copying manuscripts. The Carthusians at Mount Grace had a very small church, and a very large cloister, which latter was simply a passage connecting the little houses of the monks. They had, however, a large kitchen for entertaining their guests. The monk's house consisted of an entrance passage, a living room, small bedroom, and a little pantry. Then there was a staircase two feet wide, communicating with a room in the roof, used as a store room or a workshop.

After a minute inspection of the ruins had been made, the party returned to Northallerton, where the members and friends lunched together at the Golden Lion Hotel, under the presidency of Mr. John Hutton, J.P., of Solberge (late M.P. for the borough). After dinner, a numerous company proceeded to the ancient Parish Church of Northallerton, the special features of which were pointed out and described by Mr. Hutton.

Provincial Grand Lodge of Freemasons.

The Provincial Grand Lodge of Freemasons for the North and East Ridings of Yorkshire was held at Northallerton on Thursday, October 5th, under the presidency of the Right Hon. and Right Worshipful the Earl of Zetland, P.G.M. The invitation had been given by the brethren of the Anchor Lodge, Northallerton, and accepted by the Provincial Grand Lodge at its annual meeting. No expense or effort was spared by the Northallerton brethren to give a right loyal and fitting reception to the Provincial Grand Lodge, which for the first time was honoring our ancient town with its presence, and right heartily was the good-will thus evinced appreciated. At the banquet which followed, the Psalmist's observation was verified to the letter, " Behold, how good and pleasant a thing it is brethren to dwell together in unity." There were nearly three hundred brethren present, among whom we noticed Sir George Elliot, bart., M.P., P.G.M., Eastern Division, South Wales; Sir James Meek, P.P.S.G.W., York; the Hon. W. T. Orde Powlett, P.P.S.G.W.; G. W. Elliot, M.P., P.P.S.G.W. On this occasion two Northallerton brethren were appointed Provincial Officers, viz., C. Waistell, P.M., to be P.G.R., and J. Fairburn, P.M., to be P.G.P. The procession from the Masonic Hall to the Town Hall was a most imposing one.

A very rare visitor to our shores was captured on October 27th, in the shape of an American bittern. It was shot by the Hon. W. Dawnay, near Northallerton, and forwarded by that gentleman to the York Museum. The scientific name of the bird is *Ardea lentiginosa* or *Botaurus moloko*. The last bird of this species seen in England was shot near Frome, in 1804, and is preserved in the British Museum. A.D. 1882. Rara Avis.

On Sunday, October 29th, the two last services were held in the old parish church, previous to its being closed for restoration. Large congregations were present both morning and evening. The morning sermon was preached by the rev. J. L. Saywell, curate, from the text, "*Here we have no continuing city, but we seek one to come.*"—(Heb. xiii, 14.) Alluding to the sacred memories and associations connected with the old church, which rendered its familiar features in wood and stone, pulpit and pew, so dear to many of those present; the preacher said the pain of parting, although intense, was alleviated by the thought that at some future time not far hence, they hoped to meet on the same spot, with feelings of joy and gratitude, to re-dedicate to God a cleansed and beautified temple, in which to worship the Lord in the beauty of holiness. In the evening the vicar, the rev. B. C. Caffin, occupied the pulpit, and preached an eloquent and impressive sermon from the words, "*After these things I beheld, and lo, a great multitude, which no man could number, of all nations, and kindreds, and people, and tongues, stood before the throne, and before the Lamb, clothed with white robes, and palms in their hands.*"—(Rev. vii, 9.) Having referred in touching terms to the impending divestment of the old parish church, the reverend gentleman solemnly reminded his hearers of the uncertainty of life, and how that, in all probability, some of their number would be called to their account before the work was completed. Closing of the Parish Church

Early on the following morning the work was commenced, and the sound of axe and hammer reverberated through the sacred edifice. The chancel was boarded off, and fitted up for the services held during the restoration of the nave. The contractor for the stone-work was Mr. J. Dodgson, of Northallerton; for the wood-work Mr. Joseph Wilson, also of Northallerton. The work of Church restoration commenced.

On the evening of October 30th, the curious old custom of " riding the stang " was observed, on the occasion of the return home of a couple who had eloped a short time previously. A conveyance was procured, and in it were placed effigies of the unfaithful pair, and a procession was formed, those taking part in it carrying torches. On the following evening the farce was repeated, and on the third Riding the Stang.

A.D. 1882 evening, the effigies having been carried to the residences of the delinquents, were burnt amidst the hoots and yells of the indignant crowd.

Discoveries in Northallerton Church.
The workmen engaged in restoring the parish church, found, in several places on removing the plaster from the walls, water-colour inscriptions, apparently texts of scripture. The capital letters are red, and the rest black old English text. It is impossible to say how long the inscriptions had been covered, or when they were originally laid on, but in places the letters appear quite fresh. In the south transept, near the tower, on the east wall, an archway of considerable dimensions was exposed, the back of which was painted. From its position it is generally supposed to be an old English altar, in use in pre-reformation times; the south east pier cuts through the left hand side of the arch. In the west wall of the church outside, a well plastered arched recess was discovered behind a monumental slab, in which was probably placed the effigy of some saint. This conjecture is confirmed by the position of the niche, which is close to the west entrance of the church on the right hand side. These discoveries prove the parish church of Northallerton to be one of very considerable antiquity. The oldest monumental slab in the church bears date 1593.*

An ancient Oil-painting.
In an upper room, over the mantel-piece of the house now occupied by Mrs. Hide, is an ancient oil painting supposed to represent the episcopal palace of the bishops of Durham, which once occupied the site of the present cemetery. The draw-bridge and moat, in which two swans are gliding, are shewn in the painting, together with several houses in the vicinity of Castle Hills. The picture, apparently the work of an amateur, is painted on a panel, and as such is a fixture, but it no doubt represents something of the appearance which that interesting portion of the town presented in the painter's time.

Removal of Stone Tablets
The inscriptions upon the two stone tablet insertions under the window of the south transept having become illegible, the tablets were removed from the wall by order of the architect undertaking the restoration of the church.†

1883. The North-Riding Record Society.
This society was formed in January, for the purpose of publishing a calendar and index of the important documents deposited with the Clerk of the Peace at Northallerton. They include miscellaneous sessions oaths and declaration rolls from the thirtieth year of Henry VIII., and information relating to local history, the social status and condition of the people, the prevalence and nature of crime at various periods, obsolete statutes and usages, archaic words and phrases,

* Vide illustration on last page. † Vide page 69.

curious place-names, together with a complete record of the numerous prosecutions of Roman Catholic recusants, and also of members of the Society of Friends.*

On Friday Evening, February 16th, the bishop of Sodor and Man (Dr. Rowley Hill), preached a most eloquent sermon in the parish church, from the words, "*What is that in thine hand?*" On the following day Dr. Hill administered the rite of confirmation, afterwards addressing the newly confirmed from the words, "*I will not let Thee go, except Thou bless me.*"

On the removal of the plaster from the walls of the south aisle by the workmen engaged in the restoration of the parish church, the following inscription was exposed:—

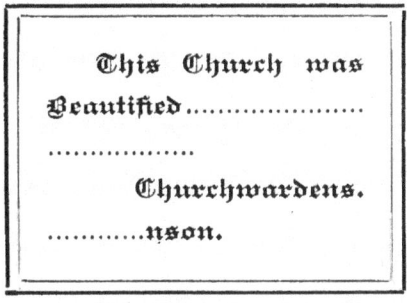

A.D. 1883.

Bishop of Sodor and Man.

Inscriptions on Church Walls.

> This Church was
> Beautified......................
> ....
> Churchwardens.
> ....nson.

The beautifying above referred to was found on the further removal of plaster to be texts of scripture in old English characters, surrounded by floral and grotesque devices, covering the walls all round the inside of the church. The date of the above inscription was obliterated, but beneath one of the texts was found the names—

William Allenson,
171—
.........duke Bell.

On the north wall of the north aisle, under the gallery, a nearly obliterated name and date were exposed.

For the third time in six years this cup has been won by a dog trained by Mr. John Shaw, of Northallerton.† On Saturday, February 24th, when the three o'clock train from the south arrived at Northallerton station, it was met by several hundred people from the town and surrounding district to do honour to the return of "Wild Mint," the winner of the Waterloo Cup, "Waterford," another successful dog, and Mr. John Shaw their trainer. As soon as Mr. Shaw

The Waterloo Cup.

---

* A list of the items relating to Northallerton, extracted from the published Records of the Society by the compiler, will be found in the Appendix.

† Vide pages 199, 200.

A.D. 1883. alighted from the train he was loudly cheered, and speedily conveyed to a carriage, in which he and the canine winner were placed. A procession was formed, headed by a brass band, the carriage being drawn by a number of men. On the route down the station-road and throughout the town the band played "See, the Conquering Hero Comes." On arriving at the Golden Lion Hotel, loud and repeated cheers were given, an adjournment made to the house, and the evening spent in harmony.*

Further Discoveries in Northallerton Church.

As the work of restoring the parish church progressed, the following interesting discoveries were made:—a copper half-penny of William (III.) and Mary, 1696; a small piece of Roman pottery, and a large quantity of carving and tracery of various periods, including several fine pieces of Saxon work. On scraping the walls, the private marks of the masons by whom the stones were worked were found upon the face of the ashlar. It is customary now to put these marks upon the bed of the stone.

A Relic.

During the excavations for the new gas-works one of the workmen turned up from a considerable depth a small antique spur in good preservation. Whether it had fitted the boot of a doughty knight who had fallen whilst escaping from the Battle of the Standard, or from its size indicates the age of small heels and large overhauls worn by the cavaliers of the Stuart period, cannot be decided, but it is nevertheless an antique and valuable relic. Northallerton was in byegone days celebrated for the excellence of durability and finish of the spurs manufactured in the town. The last spurrier in Northallerton was Robin Richardson, who died in 1811 or 1812. Spurriers were always to be found in towns through which troops were frequently passing.

Visit to Littlethorpe Museum.

A large party of the members of the Ripon Naturalists' Club, and Scientific Society, availed themselves on Saturday, October 6th, of the kind invitation of Mrs. Rothery, of Littlethorpe Hall, to visit the museum of the late Charles Rothery, esq. It consists of a large entrance hall, and two or three smaller rooms adjoining, strewn with objects of curiosity and interest, such as the art of byegone generations, and the fossils of the past eras of the world's history. There is the grand old oak bedstead, beautifully carved and inlaid, in which James I. slept at Northallerton, with the rest of the furniture of the bedroom *en suite;* and a suit of fluted armour of the time of Henry the seventh, of fine Milanese steel, with broadswords, and Highland claymores, by Andrea

---

* The readers of the "Annals" must not suppose that because the compiler has inserted the above he therefore approves of coursing and its attendant evils.

Ferrara. The stuffed birds are real works of art, and are all A.D. 1883.
by the celebrated Greenwell. The fossils are numerous, and
there are two or three ichthysauri, splendid specimens, and
the ganoid fishes and ammomets are in great variety. The
contents and arrangement of the museum shows the judgment and talent of a collector who never spared his means
to obtain a worthy object. Unfortunately, the late Mr.
Rothery did not live long to enjoy the contemplation of his
work. After partaking of the generous hospitality of their
kind hostess, the party returned to Ripon in the rosy glow of
an autumnal sunset, charmed with their visit to the museum,
and the kindness of Mrs. Rothery.*

Whilst pulling down the east wall of the north transept of Discoveries.
the church which had been condemned by the architect, the
foundations of the Norman aisles and tower were exposed,
which will enable archæologists to fix the lines and exact
position of the Norman church. Two pieces of carved stone
in excellent preservation were also discovered,—the one late
Runic, and the other Norman.

Marmaduke Jaques, for over thirty-two years parish clerk Marmaduke
of Northallerton, died after a short illness at the advanced Jaques.
age of eighty years, September 4th. He had been a good
and faithful servant to the church throughout his term of
office, never having once missed a service or neglected a duty,
unless prevented by indisposition. When a young man he
was an enthusiastic campanologist and musician, and the
author of several vocal and bell compositions of considerable
merit,—one, a chorale, entitled "Wolverhampton," is set to
the words, "While shepherds watched their flocks by night,"
and is sung with great enthusiasm every Christmas by the
waits and carol singers in Northallerton and vicinity. With
the death of old Jaques, another link connecting us with the
ancient days has been snapped. He possessed an excellent
memory and could remember incidents connected with the
now extinct stage-coach, and orchestra of stringed instruments
formerly used in neighbouring churches, in which he himself
very frequently played the bass viol. He could also
remember the Manchester Bread Riots, the Liverpool Cotton
Famine, and the Birmingham Chartist Disturbances. His
white head will be missed from its accustomed place in the
old church which he loved so much.

The newly restored nave, aisles, and south transept of the Re-opening
parish church were re-opened for divine worship with solemn of the Nave
rejoicings, September 6th. The principal alterations were and Aisles.
the raising of the roofs to their original height, the cleaning
and pointing of the stonework both inside and outside the

* Bedale and Northallerton Times.

A.D. 1883.

building, and the insertion of new stone where necessary; the piercing of the lancet windows in the north transept, and the general beautifying of the church throughout. There was a celebration of the Holy Communion at eight o'clock, followed by morning service at eleven. The prayers were read by the rev. J. L. Saywell, curate, the first lesson by the rev. Canon Camidge, and the second by the rev. B. C. Caffin, vicar. The sermon was preached by the ven. Archdeacon Yeoman, from the words, "*I will fill this latter house with glory, saith the Lord of Hosts.*" There was a large attendance of the local clergy, and the offertory amounted to £27. In the evening there was an overflowing congregation to hear the celebrated rev. George Body, canon missioner of the diocese of Durham. The prayers were again read by the rev. J. L. Saywell, the first lesson by the ven. Archdeacon Cust, and the second by the vicar. Canon Body took for his text the words, "*By the grace of God, I am what I am,*" from which he preached a sermon of rare eloquence and power, holding the immense congregation spell-bound from beginning to end. The amount collected was £25 5s., which with £3 15s. collected at the Holy Communion made a total of £56.

Burial of Marmaduke Jaques.

In the afternoon of the same day the old parish clerk, Marmaduke Jaques, was laid to rest, thus fulfilling his own prediction that he should not live to see the old church re-opened. After the burial several dumb peals were rung in honour of his memory, and the choir habited in their surplices attended the funeral and sung two hymns, one in the chapel and the other at the grave. The burial service was conducted by the revds. B. C. Caffin and J. L. Saywell.

The re-opening services were continued on the following Sunday, September 9th, the preacher in the morning being the ven. Archdeacon Cust, and in the evening the rev. S. R. Coxe, rector of Baconsthorpe, and late vicar of Brompton. The amount collected was £22.

Archdeacon Cust.

In consequence of advancing age, the ven. Archdeacon Cust resigned the livings of Danby Wiske and Yafforth, and was succeeded by the rev. R. Connell, B.D.

1884.
Re-opening of the Tower and North Transept.

Another section of the parish church restoration work, consisting of the tower and north transept, was re-opened for divine worship on February 22nd. The service was intoned by the rev. W. H. Robertson, minor canon of Durham cathedral, the first lesson was read by the ven. archdeacon Cust, and the second by the rev. B. C. Caffin, vicar. The sermon was preached by his grace the archbishop of York, from the text, "*Be not conformed to this world, but be ye transformed by the renewing of your minds.*" The offertory taken after the sermon was £36 10s. In the evening the prayers were

intoned by the rev. H. C. Holmes, rector of Birkby, the first A.D. 1884.
lesson was read by the rev. J. L. Saywell, and the second by
the vicar. The preacher was the ven. archdeacon Hamilton,
whose text was, "*I will pray with the spirit, and I will pray with
the understanding also; I will sing with the spirit, and I will sing with
the understanding also.*" The amount collected was £20 10s.,
making a total of £57 for the day. The re-opening services
were continued on the following Sunday, the prayers being
intoned by the rev. J. L. Saywell, and the lessons read by the
vicar. The preacher in the morning was the rev. Dr. Pearce,
professor of mathematics, and subwarden of the University
of Durham, his text was, "*Whose faith followed.*" The preacher
in the evening was the rev. canon Pulleine, who preached a
telling sermon on the cleansing of the temple at Jerusalem.
The amount taken during the day was over £14.

Robert W. Hodgson, esq., M.D. (London), F.R.C.P. Dr. Hodgson.
(Edin.,) died at Northallerton, on February 29th, and was
interred at the west end of the cemetery.*

On Monday, March 10th (no cause having been shewn Demolition of
why the faculty should not issue), Mr. J. Dodgson, assisted the Chancel.
by a gang of fifteen workmen, commenced to excavate the
church-yard, remove the tombstones, and cut down the rank
brushwood surrounding the chancel of the parish church,
previous to its demolition. Happily the accumulation of soil
was not great, so that no human remains were disturbed
except such as had been turned up by former interments.
On the following Monday the work of taking down the
chancel was commenced, but was unfortunately marred by
an accident, the first since the commencement of the work
of restoration. One of the workmen engaged on the roof
missed his footing, and fell through the ceiling, carrying with
him a large quantity of the plaster, covering two men at work
underneath; one was slightly injured, the other two seriously.
The same day, a small bottle tightly corked, was found
imbedded in the mortar near the apex of the east gable,
containing a slip of parchment, much discoloured, bearing
the following inscription :—

"Anno Mundi, M.M.M.M.M.D.C.C.L.X.X.V.II., Anno Domini,
M.D.C.C.L.X.X.V.III. in the XVIII year of the reign of Georgius
III., Dei Gratia de Anglis, Scotia, Frances, et Hibernia Rex.
In the III^D year of the commonwealth of America, the Chancel
of this Church was entirely taken down and rebuilt at the sole
expense of the Rector."

* The compiler would gladly have written a memoir, but he felt that the
late respected doctor's modesty would have prompted him to decline the
honour, could his wishes have been consulted.

A.D. 1884.

REVERSE.

* * Esq., and Benj. Walker, vicar. Dan. * Wm. Henry Peirse, Esq., representatives of the borough. Stephen Bennison, architect.

◊ Sit Lux et Lux Fuit. ◊

The most high, most puissant, and most illustrious Prince George Montague,* Duke of Manchester, Right Worshipful Grand Master of England."

Further Discoveries.

A large quantity of carved stonework was also discovered, including the head of a fine Saxon cross in good preservation (another proof of the existence of a Saxon church at Northallerton), a smaller cross of later date, and a number of Early English crosses and mouldings, the latter proving the insertion of an Early English east window, in the place of the Lancet one, after the destruction of the chancel by fire.

Laying the Corner Stone of the new Chancel.

Another link in the sequential history of the ancient parish church was added to the historical chain of the town on Tuesday, July 1st, in this year, by the laying of the corner stone of the new perpendicular chancel to be erected in the place of the old grotesque, barn-like structure which was built in 1778. The old chancel was taken down and the foundations of the new one put in by Mr. James Dodgson, of Northallerton. The work of erecting the new chancel was entrusted by the building committee to Mr. George Grange, who, with a large and competent staff of workmen, superintended by Mr. Thomas Carse, clerk of the works, quickly made the necessary preparations for the laying of the chief corner stone. It was decided that the ceremony (like that which accompanied the placing of the copestone of the old

---

*George Montague, Duke of Manchester, was Grand Master of the southern or London Grand Lodge of Freemasons, which was then known as the Grand Lodge of England. He was appointed in 1777. The northern or York Lodge was designated the Grand Lodge of all England, and although the representative lodge of northern Freemasons, its prime authority was recognised by the Grand Lodge. There was a sort of provincial lodge held at Halifax at this time. Each Grand Lodge enjoyed independent privileges, such as granting of warrants for new Lodges, choosing its own Grand Master, &c. The two Grand Lodges continued to work amicably together, until a shyness arose between them in consequence of the southern Grand Lodge having granted warrants out of its prescribed jurisdiction; from which time the progress of Freemasonry was rapid in the south, and gradually declined in the north. In 1790 the Grand Lodge of all England held at York became defunct. From the fact of the name of the Duke of Manchester appearing upon the scroll, it would appear that the workmen employed at the building of the chancel belonged to the southern Grand Lodge, and held a charter which constituted themselves an itinerant lodge. It is known that a lodge did exist about this time, which held its meetings at the Pack Horse Inn (vide page 195). The title "Prince" was commonly given to Dukes at that time, and does not imply Royal affinity or connection in any way.

chancel) should be a masonic one, and the Earl of Zetland, Deputy Provincial Grand Master of the North and East Ridings of Yorkshire, was accordingly invited to perform it. His lordship cordially accepted the invitation, but regretted his inability to lay the corner stone in person, and commissioned Dr. Bell, his deputy, to conduct the ceremony. Whereupon the Anchor Lodge at Northallerton undertook to make arrangements for the holding of a special Provincial Lodge on Tuesday, July 1st, for the purpose of laying the stone. The day, which was a brilliant one, was commenced with an early celebration of the Holy Communion, the Rev. B. C. Caffin, vicar, and the Rev. J. L. Saywell, curate, being the officiating clergymen. At twelve o'clock the special Provincial Grand Lodge met in the Assembly Rooms of the Golden Lion Hotel, and marched in procession to the church in the following order:—

A.D. 1884.

Masonic Ceremony.

Northallerton Borough Band (under the leadership of Mr. T. Jenkinson); Two Tylers, with drawn swords; Visiting Brethren; Officers and Brethren of the Craft Lodges of North and East Yorkshire, under their respective banners; Provincial Grand Officers of other Provinces; Officers of the Provincial Grand Lodge of North and East Yorkshire, each bearing the emblems of their office.

The children of Northallerton National Schools were arranged in lines on each side of the pathway leading to the church, through which the procession passed, and on reaching the west door of the church the Tylers halted, the brethren dividing and forming an avenue facing inwards, through which the officers and past officers of the Provincial Grand Lodge passed into the church in order of seniority. All having taken their seats, a short service was held, the sermon being preached by the Very Rev. Dr. Purey-Cust, Dean of York, and very Worshipful Past Grand Chaplain of England, and Past D.G.M. of Bucks and Birks. At the conclusion of the service, the procession was re-formed, and left by the south porch of the church for the platform at the east end of the chancel, the choir and clergy, headed by the Borough Band, preceding the Masonic body singing the processional hymn, "Forward! be our watchword." At the conclusion of the hymn, the vicar as Chairman of the Building Committee, requested the Acting Provincial Grand Master, J. P. Bell, esq., M.D., J.P., to lay the chief corner stone of the new chancel. The vessels of corn, wine, and oil were then deposited on a pedestal placed for their reception, the upper stone and the lower one adjusted, after which the Acting Provincial Grand Master addressed the assembly. The Past Provincial Grand Chaplain, Brother the Rev. — Kemp, then offered up a prayer. The singing of the Masonic

Anthem; "Hail! masonry divine!" was accompanied by the band, at the conclusion of which the Provincial Grand Secretary, Brother M. C. Peck, read aloud the inscription on the brass plate, as follows:—

> THE CHIEF CORNER STONE OF THIS CHANCEL WAS LAID BY JOHN PEARSON BELL, Esq., D.P.G.M. OF THE NORTH AND EAST RIDINGS OF YORKSHIRE, ON BEHALF OF THE RT. HON. THE EARL OF ZETLAND, PROVINCIAL GRAND MASTER, ON TUESDAY, THE 1st JULY, 1884.
>
> B. C. CAFFIN, VICAR.

The Provincial Grand Treasurer, Brother R. W. Hollon, then deposited the phial containing the current coins of the realm, a scroll of vellum, upon which was inscribed the names of all those connected with the church, and copies of several local newspapers in the crevice prepared for its reception in the lower stone, then covering the whole with the brass plate. Cement was next spread on the upper face of the lower stone, the Acting Provincial Grand Master adjusting the same with a silver trowel, presented to him on behalf of the brethren of the Anchor Lodge by Brother R. H. Sootheran, W.M., for the purpose, after which the upper stone was slowly lowered with three distinct pauses, the band meanwhile playing the National Anthem. The Acting Provincial Grand Master then proved the just position and form of the stone by the plumb, rule, level, and square, and being satisfied in these particulars, gave the stone three knocks with a mallet, made out of the oak of the old chancel. The cornucopia containing the corn, and the ewers with the wine and oil, were next handed to the Acting Prov. Grand Master, who strewed the corn, and poured the wine over the stone with the accustomed ceremonies. He then inspected the plan of the intended building, and delivered the same to the architect, C. H. Fowler, esq., F.S.A., together with the several tools used in proving the position of the stone (all of which were made from oak from the old chancel), and desired him to proceed without loss of time to the completion of the work, in conformity with the plan. Brother J. S. Walton, P.P.G.S.W., Secretary of the Anchor Lodge, then in the name of Brother Sir H. M. de la Poer Beresford Peirse, the lay rector of the parish, thanked the Acting Prov. Grand Master for his presence and services on the occasion, and the ceremony being concluded, the procession returned to the Assembly Rooms, where the Provincial Grand Lodge was closed.

At half-past two o'clock a public luncheon was provided in the Town Hall, over which the vicar presided, supported by the officers of the Provincial Grand Lodge, wearing the collars and jewels of their degrees, and the neighbouring clergy, and at which the usual toasts were given and several warm and interesting speeches were made. In the evening a substantial supper was given to the workmen by the Building Committee, presided over by the rev. J. L. Saywell, curate.

By the Redistribution Bill of this year, the Parliamentary Borough of Northallerton was eliminated from the roll of separate representation, disfranchised as a borough constituency, and absorbed within the parliamentary district or division of Richmond, which now includes the disfranchised borough of Northallerton.

Although the event is one over which the honest and loyal-hearted burgesses of Northallerton may very naturally and mournfully sigh "*Ichabod*," no one can deny that it might have justly and reasonably occurred many years ago, looked at in the light of proportional representation. The grief, therefore, of the electors of Northallerton will be mingled with pride, and their tears with smiles. They need not bend their heads with shame for a lost representation, like the people of Macclesfield and Sandwich, nor blush for a tarnished honour, like the electors of Boston, Canterbury, Gloucester, Knaresborough, Chester, and Oxford; for no stain or blot has ever disfigured or marred the political history and fair fame of the North-Riding capital, chequered though it be. The burgesses of Northallerton have not been unjustly treated, or hardly dealt with; the parliamentary borough of Northallerton, in common with eighty others, has died a perfectly natural and legitimate death, in a good old age, and full of honour; only to rise again in a new garb, as a very important factor in the aggregate constituency of the North-Riding, and powerful enough to turn the scale in a closely contested divisional election. In the future, as in the past, the old town will be true to her principles, and will lose none of her circumspection or vitality on account of her widowed state and altered circumstances. This is what the "Redistribution Bill of 1884" has done for Northallerton, and she will bear her bereavement bravely and resignedly.

A brief *resume* of the political history of Northallerton will here be both interesting and appropriate. The town was first constituted a parliamentary borough in 1298, and returned two stipendiary representatives to parliament. Very soon afterwards, a hiatus of 342 years occurred, but for what

A.D. 1884. reason cannot be exactly ascertained, certainly not for anything disgraceful or dishonourable. In 1640, the privilege of representation was either reclaimed or restored, most probably the former, and a dual representation was continued in unbroken succession until the great Reform Bill of 1832 deprived the borough of one of its members; after which, until the present year, the town regularly and faithfully returned a representative to parliament. During the long political period of 586 years, there has only been one disputed election, and even then, the contention was laid more upon technical than corrupt grounds. But whatever disturbing elements may threaten to ruffle the usually smooth surface of their daily life, the good people of Northallerton will calmly continue on the even tenor of their way, unalarmed by party strife, and uncast down by the adverse turns of fickle fortune's wheel.

1885.
New Clock for the Church.
The very handsome clock recently presented to the church, and put into the tower by Mr. Wm. Emmerson, was dedicated by a short service in the belfry, and formally opened on April 2nd. The vicar and a number of the parishioners were present, and a vote of thanks accorded to the kind donor. The following is a scientific description of the clock, supplied by Messrs. Potts, of Leeds:—It is constructed on the solid horizontal cast-iron bed frame, which is planed, and all the necessary wheels and fittings accurately adjusted upon it. All the bushes or bearings are of gun metal screwed into the frame, so that any wheel can be taken out separately. There are three trains of wheels, namely, going part, striking part for the hours, and striking part for the quarters; three iron barrels, patent wire cords, block pulleys bushed with brass and pivoted in, bevel wheels, universal joints, and other connections. The escapement is the double three-legged gravity by Sir E. Beckett, with compensation pendulum; weight of bob, which is cylindrical in form, about 2 cwt. It has the necessary hammers, cranks, and levels for striking the hours and Cambridge chimes. The clock itself whose melodious chimes are continually sounding the praises of the giver, will, it is hoped, long be a thing of use and beauty to the town and church, and, at the same time, form a fitting memorial to Mr. Emmerson after he is called to rest.

Parliamentary extinction of Northallerton.
On Wednesday afternoon, April 15th, 1885, the House of Commons in Committee resumed the consideration of the Parliamentary Elections (Redistribution) Bill, with Mr. Sclater Booth in the chair. One result of the session was, that the decision of the Boundary Commissioners was reversed, and the name of the Parliamentary division changed to that of Richmond, by a majority of forty in a

division of one hundred and eighty-six. Thus the parliamentary history of Northallerton ends, with the extinction of its name from the roll of parliamentary representation.

It is somewhat singular that the year 1882 should be the starting point of two projects connected with the town of Northallerton, each of them being in its own way both interesting and important, and not dissimilar in its aim. The one was the restoration of the old parish church, and the other the re-compilation of the old " History of Northallerton." Just as a re-beautified and cathedral-like edifice has arisen out of the mouldering ruins of the past, so the old history re-appears in a new and brighter garb, retaining its own peculiar features, but better adapted to the progressive requirements of the times; and just as the work of church restoration and the work of re-compilation began together, so they will end together, the year 1885 marking the period of completion in both instances. The "*Annals*" therefore will briefly notice the doings at Northallerton on Whit-Tuesday, 1885, bid adieu to its old friend the church, and then they will go forth on their respective missions rejoicing; the one to spiritualise, and the other to inform the minds of the people of Northallerton.

The restoration services, which were fully choral, were commenced with an early celebration of the Holy Communion, the vicar being the celebrant, and the curate (the Rev. D. Jacob) the epistoler. The officiating clergy at the second morning service were the Rev. E. S. Carter, of York, who acted as precentor, and the Archdeacon of Cleveland, who read the lesson appointed for the day. His Grace the Archbishop of York (Dr. Thomson) who is a great favourite at Northallerton, again occupied the pulpit, and his local allusions on the occasion are worthy of preservation. He said that Northallerton had long been in possession of a splendid church, but its beauty had been much obscured by the carelessness of the past, which had allowed it to get into a state in which it was less fit for the worship of Almighty God. An attempt had now been made to attempt to restore it, and with due regard to all that was good and beautiful in it, to bring it back to a condition suitable for the worship of the people. It was a great undertaking compared with the town, it was a very large and costly structure, with the restoration of which the community might have found itself unable to cope, but it had been done. And when he told them that £6,000 had been expended, and that a debt of only £300 for unforeseen expenses and for the restoration or the erection of an organ remained, he would give the congregation an account more favourable than he was generally able to do on like occasions. They were asked

A.D. 1885.

Valedictory remarks.

Chancel Restoration Services.

A.D. 1885. to do something towards clearing off this last remaining debt. When that debt had been cleared off the parish would be in the absolute possession of a beautiful parish church inferior to few in the diocese or even in the kingdom. Was it for him to argue with them at this time of day that it was a good work to restore a church? He should do nothing of the kind, because when he came among a number of people who had thus carried out a work of restoration with a splendid liberality it would be a very ungracious thing to argue that liberality was the right thing. Yet he would just remind them that there lay behind the question of beautifying a chancel the whole question of public worship. It was all very well to say that church history showed that people had managed to worship very well when they had only an upper room, a barn, a hillside, or a cave. He knew that when the spirit of the man was right he would worship rightly, but the question was whether spirits did not receive and crave a little help in respect of their worship. Because a cave had been the scene of excellent worship he was not going to ask people to worship in a cave. In times of peace and prosperity, when they could build and restore churches, why should they not show the same interest and liberality in dealing with holy things that they did about the comfort of their own homes and the like. The question was not one of beautifying buildings, but of spiritual work. Their hope was that people would come into that church not to admire a fine building, but to worship Him, who was a Spirit, and to worship Him in spirit and in truth. That was the reason for restoring that church, and why churches were built. We should never forget, while we busied ourselves about beautiful erections, that the church of God was in the hearts of men, and that if there were no spirits to worship Him, God had not found the worship which He sought, and would not delight in it. His Grace's text was, "*I am crucified with Christ; nevertheless I live; yet not I, but Christ liveth in me, and the life I now live in the flesh I live by the Son of God, who loved me and gave Himself for me.*"

At one o'clock there was a public Luncheon in the Town Hall, which was beautifully decorated, when a large and influential company sat down. After the usual loyal toasts, in proposing which it was mentioned that one Prince of Wales (afterwards George the Second), bore among other titles that of Viscount of Northallerton, the Vicar gave the health of the Archbishop, thanking him warmly for his kind sympathy and the interest which he had taken in the work. His Grace replied in a most kind and friendly speech, which cannot but increase the affectionate respect with which he is regarded at Northallerton. The health of the Building

Committee was given by Canon Camidge, and acknowledged by Mr. Jefferson. Mr. Stead proposed the health of the Architect, mentioning also Mr. Carse, the Clerk of the Works, and Mr. Grange, the contractor.   Mr. Fowler, who has taken a deep and loving interest in the old Church, and has attended personally to every detail of the Restoration, replied in kind and courteous words. The Vicar proposed the health of the Churchwardens, thanking them for their services, and acknowledging Mr. Emmerson's liberal gift of the Church Clock. Mr. Emmerson acknowledged the toast in suitable terms. Mr. Jefferson gave the health of the Visitors, which was responded to by the Ven. Archdeacon Yeoman.

A.D. 1885.

At the evening service the Rev. George Body, canon of Durham, (at whose suggestion the work of restoration was commenced) was the preacher. The service was chanted by the Rev. F. Fielding, curate of Helmsley; the lessons were read by the Rev. H. O. Crow, vicar of High Worsall, and the Rev. H. Jones, vicar of Osmotherley. The worthy Canon delivered an eloquent and impassioned sermon from Haggai ii, 9, "*The glory of this latter house shall be greater than of the former; and in this house will I give peace, saith the Lord of Hosts.*" Throughout the day the Union Jack and several banners were floated from the church tower, and the bells ever and anon ringing out merry peals of festivity and gladness. The amounts collected during the day were as follows:—Eight o'clock, £8 5s.; Morning Service, £48 12s. 5d.; Evening Service, £19 4s. 5½d.

The many touching gifts which have been showered upon the church by loving donors, have been crowned by one of singular beauty and costliness in the shape of a burnished brass eagle lectern, of exquisite workmanship and design. It is a splendid offering, and sheds an additional lustre upon the orthodox appearance of Northallerton's miniature cathedral. It is placed beneath the centre of the tower, and stands upon a S. Andrew's Cross of solid oak, carved with medieval faces at the extremities of the arms, which project beyond the lectern itself. The base of the lectern is quadrilateral, the angles resting upon the arms of the cross; each expanding side is in two divisions, the lower consisting of an elaborately pierced circle, with solid centre, and beautifully engraved pelican upon the medallion, the upper division containing a sharply cut Greek Cross with expanding ends, and jewelled in the centre. The shaft is circular, richly engraved with quatre-foils between three equidistant clustered mouldings, the abacus being square, foliated at the angles, and also jewelled between the foliations. Upon the abacus lies a solid globe of brass, at the base of which is a circle of small Greek Crosses, the whole surmounted by a very handsome

Gift of Lectern.

A.D. 1885. and well proportioned eagle. The approach to the lectern consists of two steps, supported by a case of oak with trefoil ornamentations, and balusters of solid brass upon the footpace. This magnificent piece of furniture is the gift of Mr. John Hodgson, of the Lodge, Northallerton.

Conclusion. As a fitting conclusion to the present work, let me remind its readers, and the people of Northallerton in particular, that with them rests the honour, reputation, and well-being of the town. As with the public and private characters of an individual, so with the interests of a community. *Salus urbis est divitiæ populi.* The people only can make or mar. So far no blot has disfigured the historic page of this ancient borough. If its illustrious past is to be crowned with an equally illustrious future, let the words of the poet, who being dead yet speaketh, impregnate every burning thought, every eloquent word, and every heroic action—

"Not enjoyment, and not sorrow,
If our destined end or way;
But to act that each to-morrow
Finds us farther than to-day.

*   *   *

Lives of great men all remind us,
We can make our lives sublime,
And departing, leave behind us,
Footprints on the sands of time."

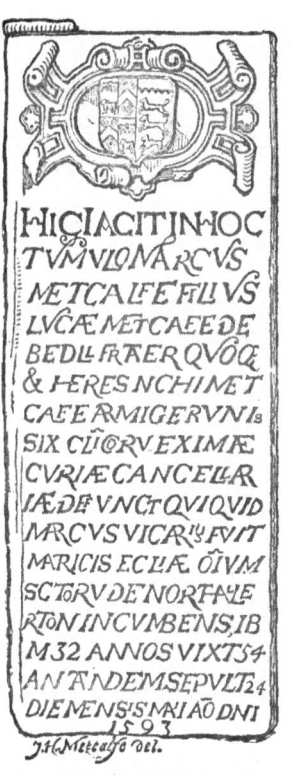

HIC IACIT IN HOC
TVMVLO MARCVS
METCALFE FILIVS
LVCÆ METCAFE DE
BEDLL FRATER QVOQ
& HERES NCHI MET
CAFE ARMIGER VNIs
SIX CTI ORV EXIMÆ
CVRIÆ CANCELLAR
IÆ DEFVNCT QVIQVID
MRCVS VICAR^{IU} FVIT
MARICIS ECLIÆ OIVM
SCTORV DE NORTHALE
RTON INCVMBENS IB
M 32 ANNOS VIXT 54
ANT ANDEM SEPVLT 24
DIE MENSIS MAI AÕ DNI
1593

J. H. Metcalfe del.

The oldest Tombstone in Northallerton Church.

☞ It must be remembered that Northallerton Church has undergone extensive alteration, so that the monuments and brasses are not now in their original places.

NOTE.

RELIGIOUS HOUSES.

In the Cottonian Library some interesting and valuable lists are preserved respecting the dissolution of Monasteries by Henry VIII.

(Cott. Libr. Cleop. E. 4), sec. III.

List of Abbies above the value of two hundred pounds, the Abbots of which were prevailed upon to surrender their houses to the King. These Abbies are not within the Statute for suppressing the lesser Abbies.

(Regni. 30, inter cl alia.)

"Northallerton, Carmel. Yorks., the Prior and 9 Frat." 17 Oct.

List of enrolled Resignations, the originals of which are lost.

(Int. xiii alia).

"Northallerton, Carmel. Yorks., the Prior." 20 Dec.

There is no mention of the Carthusian Monastery of Mount Grace, or of the Augustinian Monastery at Northallerton.

TOWN HALL FROM THE NORTH.

SHAMBLES, CROSS, AND TOLL BOOTH, 1870.

APPENDIX.

I.

ADDITIONAL INFORMATION WHICH HAS COME INTO THE COMPILER'S POSSESSION DURING THE PRINTING OF THE FOREGOING MATTER.

IMMEDIATELY before the battle, Ralph bishop of the Orkneys, deputed by the aged and infirm Thurstan, having assured the army that by fighting bravely, they would purchase the remission of their sins, did, on receiving from them expressions of contrition, actually pronounce their absolution, joining to it his benediction. At the same time the priests in their white vestments, carrying crosses and relics, went among the ranks, encouraging the soldiers by their exhortations and prayers.* Sir Walter Scott's description of the battle is interesting:—" Pledge me in a cup of wine, Sir Templar," said Sir Cedric, " and fill another to the Abbot of Jervaulx, while I look back some thirty years to tell you another tale. As Cedric the Saxon then was, his plain English tale needed no garnish from French trabadours, when it was told in the ear of beauty; for the field of Northallerton, upon the day of the Holy Standard, could tell whether the Saxon war-cry was not heard as far within the ranks of the Scottish host, as the *cri de guerre* of the boldest Norman baron. 'To the memory of those who fought there, pledge me my guests!' He drank deep, and went on with increasing warmth. 'Aye that was a day of cleaving of shields, when a hundred banners were bent forward over the heads of the valiant, and blood flowed round like water, and death was held better than flight. A Saxon bard has called it a feast of the swords, a gathering of the eagles to the prey, the clashing of bills upon shields and helmet, the shouting of battle more joyful than the clamour of a bridal.' "†

A.D. 1138. Battle of the Standard.

* Vide Redpath's Border History.
† Vide Scott's " Ivanhoe," vol. 1, pp. 87, 88.

A.D. 1195.
Election of a
Bishop.

During the vacancy of the see of Durham, which continued nearly two years, the convent, as well as the people of the palatine, appear to have suffered much injury and oppression from the officers of the crown.* The occasion of the delay in electing a bishop does not appear: Geof. of Coldingham says, messengers from the convent were sent to consult the king's (Richard I.) pleasure touching the person they should nominate, when Philip de Poicteu, a native of Aquitaine, one of the king's privy counsellers and chief favourites, was at length pointed out to them as a person most agreeable to the sovereign; on whose election the monks were promised the royal protection, and full confirmation of the liberties they held in former reigns. He was elected at Northallerton, according to Wharton, by the monks assembled there, in the presence of Hubert, archbishop of Canterbury, in the month of November, 1195; but Geof. of Coldingham says, he was elected in the chapter-house on the 11th January. Those various dates are easily reconciled by a supposition that, in full chapter, the act at Northallerton was confirmed at Durham, and then recorded there. He was ordained priest, the 15th June, 1196, and consecrated at Rome by pope Celestine, in the Lateran church, on the 20th April, 1197. Geof. of Coldingham postpones his consecration to the 12th May, 1198.† He died 22nd April, 1208, and the see was vacant for nine years and a half.

1212.
Royal visits.

After a tour in the northern counties, King John and his suite arrived at Northallerton on Friday afternoon, June 20th, 1212, and left the next day for Easingwold. On Saturday, September 1st, in the same year, King John and his Court were again at Northallerton, where they remained over Sunday (most probably attending mass at the parish church), and leaving on Monday morning for Darlington. On the following Thursday the King and suite returned to Northallerton from Durham, and left the next day for Knaresbro'.‡

1213.

On Monday, September 16th, the King and his retainers reached Northallerton where they remained all night, and left for Knaresbro' early the next morning.§

1274.
Dispute settled.

On the death of the rector of Skirpenbeck, Thomas de Chancy, lord of Skirpenbeck, had a violent quarrel with the abbot Robert of Whitby, about the right of presentation to the church. Each party presented a candidate: the matter was examined before the official of the archdeaconry of the East Riding, in a full chapter at Buckrose (a wapentake of the East Riding), held at Scrayingham: who reported to the

---

* Gualter de Ferlington custos Dunelmen castri.—Hen. Ferlington custos castelli de Norham, quæ sumpta in manus regis Hugonem Bardulphum custodem habebant.—Ex lib. Annalium, &c.—Lel. col. v. i. p. 292.
† Ang. Sac. p. 726. ‡ Vide Rot. Lit. Parl. vol. 1, No. xxxiv. § Ibid.

archbishop in favour of the abbot of Whitby, whose claim to A.D. 1274.
the right of patronage was afterwards fully made out before
the king's justiciaries at Northallerton, and was thereupon
confirmed by royal authority, as well as by order of the
archbishop.*

Blind Harry, in his " Actis and Deidis of the Illuster and
Vailyeant Champioun Shyr Wilham Wallace, Knycht of
Elrisle," says that Wallace here fought a bloody battle with
"Shyr Rawff Rymut, captayne of Maltoun," and after lying
some time in expectation of a visit from king Edward I.,
burnt the town.

> "Wallace tranountyt on the secund day,
> Fra York thai passit rycht in gud aray;
> North-west thai past in battaill buskyt boun,
> Thar lugeyng tuk besyd Northallyrtoun."

> " Than Wallace maid full mony byggyng hayt;
> Thai rassyt fyr, brynt up Northallyrtoun,
> Agayne throuch York-schyre bauldly maid them boun,
> Dystroyed the land, as far as evir thai ryde,
> Sewyn myle about thai brynt on athir syde."

This account is evidently unfounded and romantic.

The following is a detailed account of this noted high- 1317.
wayman, a reference to whom has been made in the body of Sir Gosselin
this work under the above date:— Denville.

" Sir Gosselin Denville was descended from very honourable parents at
Northallerton, whose ancestors came to England with William the Conqueror,
and to whom that monarch granted lands in recognition of their services, where
the Denvilles lived in great repute until the days of our hero. He was intended
by his father for the priesthood and for this purpose he was sent to college
where he prosecuted his studies with great assiduity and seeming warmth.
As he was naturally of a vicious disposition, he merely dissembled to please
his father, until he should get possession of his fortune. His natural
habits, however, could not long be restrained, and he soon displayed his
propensity for a luxurious and profligate life; and it appears that so vicious
was his conduct that he broke his father's heart, and his newly acquired
wealth he and his brother Robert soon contrived to dissipate in licentious-
ness and luxury. The first enterprise of note which we find recorded of
Sir Gosselin, is one in which he was joined by Middleton and Selby, two
noted robbers of that time, with a considerable force. Their design was
to rob two Cardinals sent into this Kingdom by the Pope, which they
accomplished with great success — not only travellers, but monasteries,
nunneries, and houses, were the object of their attacks, and they were not
merely content with booty, but barbarously murdered all who made the least
opposition. A Dominican Monk of the name of Andrew Simpson was once
met by our knight and his associates, and obliged to surrender his purse;
wishing, however, to make pastime of him, they compelled him to mount an
adjacent tree, and preach an extempore sermon. The monk selected for his
text these words, "*A certain man went down from Jerusalem to Jericho, and
fell among thieves, who stripped him of his raiment, and wounded him, and
departed, leaving him half dead;*" and he commented thereon in a very
pathetic manner, hoping to move the hearts of his hearers, but without success,
for they were too far plunged in iniquity to reform. They continued their
course and every day became more formidable, and robbed with such boldness

* Young's Whitby, I. p. 317.—R. f. 123. cb. p. 223.

A.D. 1317. that country seats were forsaken and safety sought in fortified cities. They defeated forces sent out to suppress them, and were not deterred from any project, either by the magnitude of the danger, or the greatness of the individuals concerned. The king himself when on a tour through the north of England, was beset by the gang in priest's habits, and he and his nobles had to submit themselves to be rifled. This robbery was highly resented, and several proclamations offering great rewards were issued for the apprehension of any or of every of them. The promise of premium bred traitors among themselves, and in less than a month sixty were delivered up to justice. The last exploit of Sir Gosselin (who was also a partisan of Thomas, the rebel earl of Lancaster) was an attack which he made upon the Bishop of Durham. They rifled his palace at Northallerton (where the bishop then was) of every valuable, and maltreated not only himself, but his servants and family, and also took possession of the manor of Northallerton belonging to the bishop. His amours were many, and among them was one with the wife of a publican whose house he used to frequent, not so much for the goodness of the ale, as the beauty of the hostess. The husband however sought his revenge in due season, and betrayed the knight and his men one evening while they were carousing in his house. The sheriff and five hundred men surrounded the party, who fought desperately, but it was not before two hundred of the beseigers had fallen, and were so completely hemmed in that they were obliged to surrender. They were escorted to York under a strong guard, where, without the privilege of a trial, they were immediately executed to the joy of thousands, the satisfaction of the great, and the delight of the community, who waited upon them to the scaffold, triumphing in their ignominious exit." *

1327.
The Grammar School. The origin of the Northallerton Grammar School is uncertain. There is, however, in the *Liber Præsentationum et Literarum Prioris et Conventus Eccl. Dunelm in Bibl. Cotton.*, the register of the presentation of William de Leeds to the mastership of the Grammar School at Northallerton, in 1385, to which are annexed the following words, "*Consimilem habet Chartam Johannes Podesay v. a. October,* 1327." It seems to be a royal foundation, for in 1818, £5 1s. 8d. per annum was paid by the king's receiver, who deducted five shillings for poundage, two shillings and sixpence for debenture money, and eightpence for acquittance. By whom and when the endowments of a house, garden, and a small close of land (the latter worth about £20 a year), were made is not known. There are no statutes. The school is free only to four boys, for whose education John Eshall left twenty shillings to be paid yearly out of certain lands at Catto.† Soon after 1385, the dean and chapter of Durham became the patrons of it, and have continued so to the present day. During the 17th century, the following eminent men were educated at this school, during the time the Rev. Francis Kaye and Mr. Thos. Smelt were masters: Dr. Grey, eldest son of Sir Ralph Grey, by his second wife, and nephew of Sir Edward Grey, of Howicke; Dr. William Palliser, archbishop of Cashell, in Ireland; Dr. George Hickes, dean of Worcester; Dr. John Ratcliffe, the celebrated physician to king William III; the

---

* Vide "Rymer's Records of Public Executions at York," and "Lives of Notorious Highwaymen."
† Vide pp. 31, 32.

Rev. John Kettlewell, rector of Coleshill, Warwickshire; Thomas Rymer, Historiographer Royal; Admiral Sir Hugh Palliser; Dr. Thomas Burnett, master of the Charter House, London; Dr. Edmund Guest, bishop of Salisbury, and almoner to Queen Elizabeth. The following persons, during the 18th century, were also educated at this school, while the Rev. Wm. Dawson and the Rev. James Wilkinson were masters: Lieut.-colonel Wm. Lambton; George Hammond, the wealthy cheesemonger of London; Sir John Scott Byerley, knight; Thomas Byerley, brother of the above; Dr. Andrew Plaisance, an eminent physician of York, and afterwards of Northallerton; and Thomas Maltby, an extensive lead merchant and banker in London; with many others who filled high and respectable situations in life. A.D. 1327

The following is a list of the masters of the Grammar School since its foundation, but, unfortunately, it is not a complete one:—

 1327. John Podesay
 1385. William de Leeds
     *   *   *
 1593. Rev. Francis Kaye (died 1624)
 16—. Thomas Smelt (died Nov., 1686)
 ? Rev. John Todd
 ? Rev. Abraham Todd
 1734. Rev. William Dawson
 1774. Rev. James Wilkinson
 1821. Rev. J. Bowness
 1844. Jonathan Horner (resigned 1874)
 1874. — Williams (died suddenly)
 1874. W. F. N. Allan
 1877. Rev. W. E. Scott (resigned)
 1880. R. C. D. Nugent

The following inscription, now defaced, appeared upon a tablet in the parish church. It is valuable as an historical record:— 1381. Inscription.

> THIS CHURCH WAS REBUILT AFTER ITS DESTRUCTION BY THE SCOTS IN 1318, BY THOMAS HATFIELD, BISHOP OF DURHAM, ASSISTED BY THE MUNIFICENCE OF HIS ROYAL MASTER KING EDWARD III. OF BLESSED MEMORY. A.D. 1381.

The will of Johanna Smyth de Northalverton, dated April 6th, 1499, contains the following bequests:—A towel to the high altar, a brass pot to the church, to Elizabeth Scrube, my daughter, tway dublers and a dyssh of pewt$^{r.,}$ a mat^{e,} one pair sheets, a gowne, and a ketyll, to Robert Scroby a brass pot. 1499. Curious will.

vi ANNALS OF

A.D. 1534. Cardinal Fisher.

Dr. Fisher, was appointed the twenty-fourth vicar of Northallerton in 1491, but only held the living four years. He was created a cardinal by Pope Paul III., during his imprisonment in the Tower in 1534, in recognition of his opposition to Henry VIII, whereupon the king exclaimed:—"Paul may send him a hat, but I will take care that he have never a head to wear it on." Fisher was executed the following year. After his execution, his head, with that of Sir Thomas More, was fixed upon a pole on London Bridge. Such was the fate of a former vicar of Northallerton. Dr. Nicholas Metcalfe, an ancestor of the Rev. Mark Metcalfe, vicar of Northallerton in 1561, was sometime chaplain to Dr. Fisher, Cardinal-bishop of Rochester.*

1639.

In the ordnance map of Northallerton and neighbourhood (6 inch scale) made for the Government by the Royal Engineers in 1854, the following note appears:—"The Porch House, Charles I. bivouaced here in 1639." †

1646. A disloyal vicar.

The following is an extract from the Journals of the House of Commons, Die Lunæ 30 Novembris, 1646. :—

"A letter from Colonel Sedinham, points of the 27th Septembris, 1646, from York with two copies of letteres not signed and a paper inclosed, concerning an endeavoure to surprise Pontefract Castle, and concerning Malignants and Papists receiving commissions from the King to raise forces against the Parliament, were all this day read. The names of the persons in the copy of the letter written to the committee were Sir James Leisby, &c., and the minister of Allerton.‡

Resolved, &c., that the several persons above-mentioned be forthwith sent as delinquents by the Sergeant-at-Arms attending on this House, his deputy or deputies.

Ordered that Sir Philip Stapilton do prepare a letter to be signed by Mr. Speaker, and sent to the General of the Scots' army, to desire him to be aiding and assisting to the deputy and deputies of the Sergeant-at-arms attending on this House, for the bringing up of the persons of Sir James Leisby, &c., and the minister of Allerton, or of such of them, as are within any of the quarters of the Scots' army."

1660. Parliamentary orders.

June 9th, 1660. Mr. Prynn reported a list of some persons who sat on the pretended trial of the late King's Majesty; that Francis Lascelles, esq., (Member for the borough of Northallerton), sat on the 22nd day of January. Resolved that Francis Lascelles, one of the judges who sat at the trial of the late King's Majesty,§ be discharged from being a member of this house.

12th. Ordered, a new writ be issued for the electing a burgess to serve in this parliament for this borough in the room of Francis Lascelles, discharged from being a member of this house.¶

1661. Will. Maw.

"This noted villain, aged about 50 years when he was hanged, was born at Northallerton in Yorkshire, from whence he came to London, at about 20 years of age, and served his apprenticeship with a cabinet-maker, and for a great while followed that occupation in the parish of St. Giles's, Cripplegate, where he dwelt for above eighteen years together; and for many years before his death having left off working at his trade, he maintained himself by some illegal ways of living, such as the buying of stolen goods, and thereby encouraging thieves and robbers, he had also been addicted to coining, and for some of his irregular actions, had a fine of ten pounds laid upon him, in

---

* Vide "Hist. Cantab. Acad. ed. 1574 ; ed. super, pp. 40, 41.
† Vide page 90. The year 1640 is the more probable date.
‡ Rev. T. Blaikeston.   § Charles I.   ¶ Vide Carew's Boroughs, 1750.

September, 1705, was burnt in the hand in April, 1710, and in September following, was twice ordered to hard labour in Bridewell. Having once committed a robbery, for which he was afraid to be apprehended, when he lived at Golden Lane, he pretended to be very sick at home, and ordered his wife to give out that he was dead. His wife being a cunning baggage, so ordered the matter, that she cleanly executed his command, bought him a coffin, invited about forty or fifty neighbours to the funeral, and followed the corps in such a mournful condition, as if her poor husband had been dead indeed. As they were coming by the Red Cross alehouse, at the end of Red Cross Street, to St. Giles's Church-yard, near Cripplegate, some company being drinking at the door, who were inquisitive to know who was dead, they were told it was old Maw, whom they knew very well.

About five years afterwards, one of those persons that were drinking, as aforesaid, being a prisoner in Wood Street Compter, for debt, and Maw coming in also a little after him, the former person was so surprised at the latter, that at first he had not power to speak to him; but, at length, recovering some courage, as dreading he had seen a ghost, quoth he, Is not your name Maw, sir? Maw replied, Yes, sir; as sure as your name is Watkins. The other said again, Why I thought you had been dead and buried five years ago! Yes, replied Maw, so I was in trespasses and sins: But I mean said Watkins, laid yourself corporally in the grave. No, (replied Maw) I was not dead; but being at that time under some troubles, I was at the charge of a coffin to save my neck, and my wife gave out I was really defunct, as supposing then my adversaries would not look for me in my grave. Shortly after this imprisonment, as he was going up Holborn to be hanged, another person, who, like Mr. Watkins, had thought him dead and buried, seeing him in the cart, he was in a great admiration, calling thus out to him in the cart, Oh, dear, Mr. Maw, I really thought you had been dead and buried five years ago and more. Why so I was, replied Maw, but don't you know that we must all rise again at the day of judgment? Yes, replied his acquaintance, but the day of judgment is not come yet. Ay, but it is, quoth Maw, and passed too, twelve days ago, at the sessions house in the Old Bailey; where I am sure 'twas the judgment of the court to send me to be hanged now. So his friend wishing him a good journey and a safe return, they both parted.

Will Maw having once stolen a trunk from behind a coach, in which were several goods, and among them a clergyman's gown and cassock, great enquiry was made at most of the brokers for the canonical robes, by a friend of the minister who had lost them. Maw had sold them to one Seabrook, in Barbican, with whom they were at length found. Seabrook offered to sell them a pennyworth, and the gentleman bid him bring them to the Sun Tavern, in Aldersgate Street, where the person was that wanted them. The clergyman was there, and having viewed and tried the robes, found them to be the same; whereupon he asked the broker how he came by them; who could neither give much account of the manner he bought them in, nor find the person he bought them of. In a word, but an act of grace having been lately passed, he pleaded the benefit of it, and so escaped the punishment which he must otherwise have suffered, though not the disgrace which attends such practices. After a long course of iniquities, Maw was at last committed to Newgate himself, and at the ensuing sessions convicted of five indictments. 1. For breaking open the house of Mrs. Anne Johnson, and taking thence eight pewter plates, and other goods. 2. For breaking open the house of Mr. John Avery, and taking thence twenty-four pair of leather clogs. 3. For assaulting and robbing Mr. Charles Potts, on the highway, and taking from him a silver watch, five gold rings, money, and other things. 4. For assaulting Mrs. Anne Grover on the highway, and taking from her 3s. 6d. And 5. For assaulting on the Queen's highway, and robbing Mr. Coleman of some money, an handkerchief, and other goods. 'Twas impossible for him now to think of coming off; and if it had been possible for him to have expected any grace, he had been deceived, for on Wednesday, the 29th of October, 1711, this offender met with the punishment he so well deserved, at the usual place of execution."

A.D. 1670.
Henry Jenkins

There is about a mile north-west of Northallerton, adjoining the road leading to Richmond, a low wet piece of ground called "Jenkin," and by some "Jenkins," which is generally covered with water during the winter months, and from report or tradition was once covered with water during the whole year, and abounded with fish. This tract of low land, it is said, derives its name from Henry Jenkins, the centenarian, who was an ardent piscator, and a very frequent visitor there in the pursuit of his favourite pastime.

1679.
Sir Gilbert Gerrard.

Sir Gilbert Gerrard, bart., was Member of Parliament for Northallerton in conjunction with Sir Henry Calverley, knight, from 1678 to 1685. The following incident is related concerning him:—"Whitehall, Jany. 13. This morning Sir Gilbert Gerrard accompanied by Mr. Charleton, Mr. Desborough, Mr. Ireton, Mr. Elias Crisp, Mr. John Smith, Mr, Henry Ashurst, Mr. Johnson of Stepney, Mr. Anthony Selby, and Mr. John Ellis, presented to his Majesty (Charles II) a petition for the sitting of Parliament, saying that it was from the thousands of his subjects in London, Westminster, and places adjacent. His Majesty was pleased to answer, "That he looks upon himself to be the head of the Government, and the only judge of what was fit to be done in such cases, and that he would do what he thought most for the good of himself and his people," adding to Sir Gilbert, "That he did not expect to find one of his name, and particularly him in such a thing, and that he was very sorry for it." Whereupon Sir Gilbert would have said something to the King, but his majesty turned away and would not hear him.*

1735.
The Register Office.

An act of Parliament of the 8 George II., cap. 6, was passed for the public registering of all deeds, conveyances, wills, and other incumbrances, that shall be made of, or that may affect, any honours, manors, lands, tenements, or hereditaments, within the North-Riding of the county of York, after the 29th September, 1736. In pursuance of the second section of the above act, the magistrates assembled at the general quarter sessions for the said Riding, on the 17th July, 1735, adjudged Northallerton to be the market town nearest to the centre of the Riding, for establishing an office for the public registering of all deeds, &c. At the following Easter sessions it was ordered, that a committee then appointed, should have power to lay out any sum not exceeding £200 in the purchase of a convenient piece of ground in Northallerton for building the Register Office; taking care that the ground should be spacious enough, so that it should stand apart from, and not be liable to injury by any other building. It was afterwards ordered, that the committee should draw

* Vide "London Gazette," January 15th, 1679.

upon the treasurer of the Riding for £140; the purchase money for the ground; and for a further sum not exceeding £200, on account of the building and other necessary expenses of the office. The building, which was first used as the office and dwelling-house, and continued as such up to the year 1782, is in Zetland-street, and has a good garden and yard thereto. In or about the year 1782, the present office was erected in the same yard, for the sole purpose of transacting the register business therein : and additional buildings were added to the first office and dwelling-house, so as to render the same a residence for the registrar, and separate from the office. Still further additions have recently been made, so that it is now one of the most complete and commodious offices of the kind in England.* The following is a list of the Registrars and their Deputies.

A.D. 1735.

Date.	Registrar.	Deputy.
1736.	William Turner	Henry Wilkinson
?	,,	John Brown
1757.	Thomas Robinson	William Walker
1771.	Simon Butterwick	William Wailes
1774.	George Crowe	Thomas Walton
1783.	Matthew Butterwick	
1806.	,,	John Sanders Walton
1828.	R. W. C. Peirse	,,
1829.	,,	T. C. Atkinson
,,	,,	John Walker
1832.	,,	Stephen Vasey
1833.	,,	R. W. Peirse
1839.	,,	William Fowle
1844.	Richard W. Peirse	,,
,,	,,	Stephen Vasey
1872.	George A. Cayley	,,

In the year 1740, an issue was tried respecting the parish of Northallerton, and in that case the ancient custom and jurisdiction which was set up by the select vestry was held by the Court to be illegal.†

1740. Select Vestry.

The following is an extract from Todd's MSS. :—

1753. Henry Lascelles.

On opening a small vault in the south transept of Northallerton Church in February, 1814, in order to inter the remains of the late Rev. Benjamin Walker, the leaden coffin containing the body of the late Henry Lascelles, esq., was discovered. The outside wooden coffin was quite decayed, but the leaden one was tight and perfect, upon the lid was a piece of lead bearing the following inscription :—" Henry Lascelles, esq., died October 6th, 1753, in the 63rd year of his age." There was another square brass plate, with the same inscription upon it, laid adjoining the leaden one, which appeared to have been affixed to the lid of the outer wooden coffin. The remains of the Rev. Benjamin Walker were deposited on the north side of the said coffin. Henry Lascelles was the son of Daniel Lascelles, esq., of Stank Hall, near Northallerton, who died October 28th, 1734, aged 78, and who was also interred close to the above. Henry Lascelles was governor of, and receiver of the Crown revenues at Barbadoes for ten years, and afterwards was one of those

* Vide page 137.
† Vide speech of J. C. Hobhouse, M.P., on Select Vestries, April 28th, 1829.

A.D. 1753. unprincipled men who were concerned in the shameful South Sea Bubble business, whereby he amassed great wealth to the ruin of many. In the year 1739 he purchased Harewood, and its extensive manor, and adorned the same with beautiful pleasure grounds. He was Member of Parliament for Northallerton from 1747 to the time of his death in 1753. He had two sons, Daniel and Edwin. He committed suicide on October 6th, 1753, and his remains were brought to Northallerton Church, and there deposited by the side of his ancestors.

1774.
"The Bleeding Vine."

The following account is taken from the *York Courant*, of May 28th, 1835:—

This remarkable and celebrated old vine (long since gone to decay), the largest ever known in this kingdom, was of the kind called Black Hambro', and, though in the open air, generally produced great quantities of fine fruit. Its situation was on the east side of the town, on the front of the large houses formerly the property of Robert Raikes Fulthorpe, esq., on the site of the ancient monastery of the Carmelites or White Friars. The circumference of the trunk, a little above the surface of the ground, was 3 feet 11 inches, the branches of this vine covered the whole fronts of these spacious houses, and also extended along the fronts of the two adjoining houses to the south, turning round the corner of the Masons' Arms inn, a few feet to the east, and to the north it extended along the front of another house to the Pack Horse inn. About the year 1774 or 1775, this vine received, from some impropriety in the pruning of it, a severe injury near the bottom of the trunk, which caused a wound, from which a liquid copiously issued, which ran down to an adjoining brook, and could not be stopped. It happened at that very time that the Duke of Northumberland (formerly Sir Hugh Smithson), grandfather to the present Duke, a native of Northallerton, in passing up the street, seeing the vine (which he well remembered when young) in such a precarious state, he instantly sent an express off to Alnwick castle for his head gardener, who well understood the management of vines, to come immediately to Northallerton; and on his arrival, by his skill the wound was properly healed, and the injured part covered with lead. From this circumstance, it was for many years after called "The Bleeding Vine." This vine in the year 1789 contained 137 square yards, and in 1790, 139 square yards, and had it been permitted, when in its greatest vigour, would have extended over three or four times that area, but from its then great age, and from further injudicious management, it has long since gone to decay. It was supposed to have been upwards of 160 years old, Rymer, the celebrated historiographer royal, who received his education under Mr. Thomas Smelt, at the grammar school at this place, was of opinion that it was planted prior to the year 1600. This vine is noticed in Roebuck's, M'Nevin's, and other Histories of Vines; in the former there is a print of it, but during several periods of its existence, drawings were taken from which prints were published—an engraving by that eminent artist, Sir Robert Strange, knight, was highly esteemed.

1779.
Ancient inscription.

Previous to the rebuilding of the chancel in 1779, there appeared on the north wall of the early English chancel, the following inscription:—

| MARGERI RE GIST ICI A VOUS JHU CRI MERCI. |
| X VOUS KI PASSEZ PAR ICI PRIEZ PUR LALME KE FU MARGERI. |

NORTHALLERTON. xi

The following is a literal translation:— A.D. 1779.

"Here lies Margery Ree (or Ray),
To you, Jesu, she cries mercy;
X All you who go by this way,
Pray for the soul that was
Margery." *

Before the lowering of the roofs of this church in this year, the figures of the twelve apostles were frescoed in full length above the arches and columns on the north side of the nave, and on the south were portrayed the four evangelists.†   1786.

When the churchyard was levelled during the alterations of the church in 1787, a stone coffin was dug up, containing the remains of a human being, nearly all reduced to dust. The coffin was afterwards utilised as a rain-water receptacle.   1787.

In Northallerton church, previous to its being new pewed in 1787, there was an ancient pew belonging to Lazenby Hall, with the coat-of-arms of the Conyers family carved on the upper pannel of the door, which, like the rest of the pew, was of old oak.‡   Conyers family.

While new pewing this church in 1787, an ancient inscription was discovered at the west end of the nave, near the doorway, as follows:—   An inscription

"𝕿𝖍𝖎𝖘 𝕮𝖍𝖚𝖗𝖈𝖍 𝖜𝖆𝖘 𝖇𝖊𝖌𝖚𝖓 𝖙𝖔 𝖇𝖊 𝖗𝖊𝖇𝖚𝖎𝖑𝖙, 𝖆𝖋𝖙𝖊𝖗 𝖎𝖙𝖘 𝖍𝖆𝖛𝖎𝖓𝖌 𝖇𝖊𝖊𝖓 𝖉𝖊𝖘𝖙𝖗𝖔𝖞𝖊𝖉 𝖇𝖞 𝖙𝖍𝖊 𝕾𝖈𝖔𝖙𝖘 𝖎𝖓 𝖙𝖍𝖊 𝖞𝖊𝖆𝖗𝖊 1318, 𝖇𝖞 𝖔𝖗𝖉𝖊𝖗𝖘 𝖔𝖋 𝕶𝖎𝖓𝖌 𝕰𝖉𝖜𝖆𝖗𝖉𝖊 𝖙𝖍𝖊 𝖘𝖊𝖈𝖔𝖓𝖉𝖊, 𝖆𝖓𝖉 𝖋𝖚𝖑𝖑𝖞 𝖋𝖎𝖓𝖎𝖘𝖍𝖊𝖉 𝖆𝖓𝖉 𝖔𝖙𝖍𝖊𝖗𝖜𖎆𝖘𝖊 𝖎𝖒𝖕𝖗𝖔𝖛𝖊𝖉 𝖇𝖞 𝖍𝖎𝖘 𝖘𝖚𝖈𝖈𝖊𝖘𝖘𝖔𝖗 𝕶𝖎𝖓𝖌 𝕰𝖉𝖜𝖆𝖗𝖉𝖊 𝖙𝖍𝖊 𝖙𝖍𝖎𝖗𝖉𝖊, 𝖔𝖋 𝖇𝖑𝖊𝖘𝖘𝖊𝖉 𝖒𝖊𝖒𝖔𝖗𝖎𝖊." §

The Church Sunday school (an institution better calculated to prevent the many evils that spring from ignorance and corruption than anything that has hitherto been devised) was begun in May, 1787, when upwards of sixty poor children were entered upon the books of this laudable establishment. John Ward, schoolmaster, was the first person appointed as teacher of the said Sunday school, and was, after a few years, succeeded by Robert Bray, who was also parish clerk, and who taught many of the scholars to sing in the church.¶   Church Sunday School.

This ancient building was situated at the north end of the town, on the east row, and was built soon after Quakerism sprang into existence. The Society of Friends for a long time were very numerous in Northallerton, but particularly so in the neighbourhood, so that the meeting-house was constantly and numerously attended. The burial-ground, inclosed by a wall, was on the east side of the house, and   1790. The Quaker Meeting House.

* Vide Gale's Hist.   † Todd's MSS.   ‡ Ibid.   § Ibid.
¶ Vide Todd's MSS. vol. 2, page 278, and super page 137.

xii   ANNALS OF

A.D. 1790. many burials took place therein. The last person interred was Elizabeth Burn, of Wearmouth, near Sunderland, who died in 1790, at the house of her brother, the late John Lincoln, surgeon, of Northallerton. A complete list of such burials will be found recorded in the registers of the parish church.

1794. Cock fighting. This inhuman and cruel pastime, which is now happily a thing of the past, was at one time very prevalent in Northallerton and its vicinity. The following is a copy of an advertisement which appeared in one of the local papers towards the close of the last century:—

NORTHALLERTON COCKINGS, 1794.

The gentlemen's (?) subscription meeting will be held at the Cock-pit, Northallerton, on Monday, Tuesday, and Wednesday, the 17th, 18th, and 19th of February, 1794.

Monday, subscription battles for 10 guineas each.
Tuesday, a Welsh main for 100*l.*
Wednesday, a Welsh main for 100*l.*

There will also be three subscription battles on Tuesday, and the same on Wednesday; likewise a long main of five cocks each, for 10 guineas a battle and 20 guineas the main, will be fought on Monday between Mr. Lunn and Mr. Cunliffe.

1800. Curious custom. Towards the early part of this century, a singular custom prevailed in the town and neighbourhood of Northallerton. In the spring of the year nearly all the robust male adults, and occasionally females, repaired to a surgeon to be bled, a process which they considered essentially conduced to vigorous health. For this operation a fee of one shilling was charged, and cheerfully paid. It was doubtless a matter for deep regret to the medical profession when the superstition died out, as this "blood money" periodically amounted to a considerable sum. Indeed there would have been strenuous efforts put forth to keep the custom alive, had not compulsory vaccination come into force, and so averted the pecuniary loss thus sustained.

1804. Wholesale matrimony. During the riot which took place here on the fifth of November in this year, a detachment of the 52nd regiment was marched into the town from Whitby, to keep the inhabitants in awe, and continued quartered on the publicans until the month of June, 1805; during which period no less than thirteen Northallerton women were allowed to be married to soldiers of the said detachment. The following are their names:—Ann Hedley; Ann Dunn, housekeeper to R. Bearpark, Esq.; Margaret Brown; Isabella Gowland, otherwise Goldsbrough; Betty Gowland, otherwise Goldsbrough; Ann Blades; Betty Sedgewick; Mary Prince; Miss M. Hoggart, a milliner's apprentice, and a farmer's daughter; Sarah Wood; Isabella Rigby, and Mary Rigby, granddaughter

NORTHALLERTON. xiii

of Adam Rigby; and Ellen Fearby, cook at Mr. Bulmer's King's Head Inn. Most of these women went abroad with the regiment, and followed their husbands through the campaigns of Calabria, Portugal, and Spain, some of whom were killed in the battle of Corunna, where Sir John Moore lost his life.*   A.D. 1804.

In this year an engagement took place at sea between H.M.S. "Sea Horse" of 38 guns, and two Turkish war frigates. After three hours hard fighting, both the Turkish vessels were disabled and captured by Captain Stewart of the "Sea Horse." The engagement took place at the east end of the islands of Seopulo. The name of the larger of the Turkish vessels was "Badere Taffere," of 52 guns, commanded by Captain Schomderli Kichue Ali; the other frigate was the "Alis Fezzan," of 22 guns. The "Sea Horse" lost five killed and ten wounded, and the Turkish vessels 165 killed and 195 wounded. Dr. William Oastler, of Northallerton, was then head surgeon of the "Sea Horse," and was present during the engagement, in commemoration of which Her Majesty Queen Victoria presented him with a silver medal in 1849.   1808. A sea fight.

After the trial of the much maligned and persecuted Queen Caroline, the people of Northallerton in their joy at her honourable discharge, and the discomfiture of her enemies, forwarded a loyal and sympathetic address to Her Majesty, to which she was pleased to reply as follows:—   1820. Loyal sympathy.

"The gentlemen, clergy, freeholders, and inhabitants of Northallerton and its vicinity will accept my unfeigned thanks for their loyal and affectionate address.

"My enemies have added another testimony to the important truth that "malignity is foolishness." The rancour which has so long (been) fostered in their hearts, made them blind to the consequences of their conduct, and compelled them to measures, which have hitherto been of less misery to me than to themselves. The cruelty and injustice of which they have endeavoured to make me the victim, have so powerfully excited the public sympathy in my favour, that they have occasioned my triumph and their (own) humiliation.

"*January* 10*th*, 1821."†

In excavating the river Wiske, north-west of Northallerton, in 1822, the workmen disclosed several skeletons of men below the bed of the river, supposed to have lain there since the memorable battle of Flodden Field, as the great Conyers, the lord of Lazenby and Hutton Bonville (just adjoining the river where the skeletons were found) had a large army encamped on the neighbouring plains, where he was joined by Stanley from Lancashire, with his retainers, and marched thence to Flodden, in Scotland.   1822. Discoveries.

* Vide Todd's MSS. vol. 2, pages 271, 272, also super page 146.
† Vide super pages 158, 159.

A.D. 1822. An ancient custom.	On June 20th, the boundaries of Osmotherley Common, in the ancient manor of Northallerton, belonging to the see of Durham, were perambulated by the officers and agents of the Hon. and Rev. Shute, Lord Bishop of Durham, attended by a respectable jury, and also by a great number of gentlemen on horseback and others on foot. It was a red letter day for the inhabitants of Osmotherley, work at the spinning mills being suspended and the poor regaled with a plenteous repast. A similar perambulation took place when Nathaniel, Lord Crewe was bishop, in 1704.
Rev. James Wilkinson.	This venerable clergyman died at Northallerton, Nov. 26th, 1822. He had been simultaneously vicar of Hutton Bonville, curate of Northallerton, and head master of Northallerton Grammar School for nearly half a century.
1823.	The postage of a letter from Northallerton to London at this time was 11d., to Thirsk 4d., to York 7d., to Easingwold 5d., to Newcastle 7d., to Gateshead 7d., to Durham 7d., and to Darlington 5d. Letters were conveyed to and from the above towns by coach. There were then four, viz. :—the *Royal Mail*, *Highflyer*, *Wellington*, and the *Cleveland*. Three gold coins, not now current, were then in circulation, viz:—guinea, half-guinea, and seven-shilling-piece. Sixpence was the smallest silver coin at that time.
1826. Rev. George Townsend.	The Rev. George Townsend, M.A., was inducted to the vicarage of Northallerton by the Rev. R. D. Kennicott, curate, on June 14th. He read himself in and preached his first sermon on June 25th.
Legend of Sockburn.	On Thursday afternoon, July 13th, 1826, the Right Rev. William Van Mildert, D.D., Lord Bishop of Durham, arrived at Northallerton, the manor, shire, and halmote of which the Bishop of Durham for the time being is lord. On his arrival he was received by Fletcher Rigg, esq., J. S. Walton, esq. (stewards of the manor), and several other gentlemen. After a short stay in the town his lordship, accompanied by his lady and suite, proceeded to Croft where they stopped all night. Next morning the bishop was met on Croft Bridge by Mr. Rayson, agent of the Sockburn estate, who presented his lordship with the traditional sword used in the destruction of the Sockburn Serpent, at the same time uttering the following formula,—" My Lord Bishop, I here present you with the falchion wherewith the champion Conyers slew the worm, dragon, or fiery flying serpent, which destroyed man, woman, and child; in memory of which the king then reigning gave him the manor of Sockburn, to hold by this tenure, that upon the first entrance of every new bishop into this county, this falchion should be presented." The bishop then returned the falchion with an appropriate reply.

Workmen commenced taking down the old vicarage house on September 15th, 1827, and on October 22nd, the foundation stone of the new vicarage, a little to the south-west of the old one, was laid by the Rev. George Townsend, vicar, attended by the churchwardens of Northallerton, Romanby, Brompton, and Deighton, with the clergy and principal inhabitants of the town and neighbourhood. Previous to laying the stone an appropriate speech was made by the vicar, and after the ceremony the company adjourned to the school room, where they sat down to a very handsome cold collation. The children at the school had a dinner given them, and the workmen also dined and spent the afternoon together. The old vicarage was built about the year 1491, by John Fisher, the then vicar, who became Bishop of Rochester, and was afterwards beheaded on Tower-hill, in 1535. The west end of the old vicarage was of great antiquity, and supposed to be the remains of a former vicarage which was destroyed in 1318, by the Scots, commanded by Sir James Douglas, at which time the town of Northallerton was plundered and burnt. *A.D. 1827. Northallerton Vicarage.*

On Sunday, June 8th, the small theatre at Northallerton, which had been purchased by the Primitive Methodists of the town, was opened for divine service. The Rev. Mr. Towler, of Darlington, preached morning and evening, and the Rev. Mr. Parrott, of Stockton, in the afternoon and following evening. At each of the services the chapel was crowded to excess. The donations added to the sums collected at the chapel amounted to upwards of £84, besides a pair of gold ear-rings deposited in one of the collection boxes by a young lady member of the society. *1834. Primitive Methodist Chapel.*

July 3rd, 1836. In consequence of the lowering of the walls and ceilings, &c. (probably the transepts) of this church, there was no service on this day. C. Spivey, clerk. *1836. Alterations in Church.*

This event was celebrated at Northallerton on Wednesday, May 17th, by a review of the North York Yeomanry Cavalry, by Colonel Clarke, of the 7th Dragoon Guards; a salute of three vollies was fired; and a treat to the school children and seventy old people of the town, workhouse and Maison Dieu. *1837. Majority of Princess Victoria.*

The Rev. George Fyler Townsend, curate, read prayers and preached for the first time on Thursday evening, the 17th of August, 1837, from Corinthians ii, 20. C. Spivey, clerk. *Rev. G. F. Townsend.*

The coronation of Queen Victoria was celebrated at Northallerton on July 28th, by a general holiday. The morning was ushered in by merry peals from the church bells, and all the shops were closed throughout the day. There was a service at the parish church in the forenoon, when the vicar (Mr. Townsend) preached from 2 Kings xi, 12, 17. At one o'clock upwards of 600 poor persons sat down to a substantial *1838. The Coronation.*

A.D. 1838. dinner of roast beef and plum pudding, on tables placed on the spacious land adjoining the vicarage, the castellated turrets of which, as well as the tower of the church, were adorned with numerous flags, &c. In the evening the church Day and Sunday school children, to the number of 700, were regaled with a bountiful tea, as were the children of the schools of the other denominations. The inmates of the Union Workhouse and House of Correction rested from their labours, and enjoyed a good dinner. On this occasion W. B. Wrightson, esq., M.P., and Peter Consett, esq., of Brawith Hall, each sent the sum of £25 to be distributed to the poor of Northallerton, Brompton, and Romanby.

A large confirmation.

On Monday, October 15th, the Lord Bishop of Ripon (Dr. Longley) held a confirmation in Northallerton church for the peculiar of Allertonshire, when upwards of four hundred persons were presented for the holy rite. There had not been a confirmation in Northallerton church for about eighty-three years, in consequence of a dispute whether the duty devolved upon the Archbishop of York or the Bishop of Durham.*

1839. Rev. Dr. Townsend.

On Sunday afternoon, April 14th, the Rev. G. Townsend, D.D., preached his farewell sermon to the parishioners of Northallerton, in the parish church, from 1 Chronicles, xxviii. 2. The church was crowded to excess, and the powerful and impressive discourse of this eminent preacher was listened to with the greatest attention. His telling appeals to the aged, to those in middle life, and to the young, were delivered in such a solemn and impressive manner as will not easily be forgotten by those who heard him, and on the concluding words of his discourse, "Finally, brethren, fare ye well, be perfect; be of good comfort; be of one mind; live in peace, and the God of love and peace shall be with you; farewell." Scarcely a face was dry in the whole congregation. On the following Tuesday afternoon, the whole of the scholars belonging to the Church Sunday schools of Northallerton and Brompton, in number about six hundred, marched in procession, headed by the Northallerton brass band, to the spacious gardens at the vicarage, where they were met and solemnly addressed by the worthy vicar. After tea and other refreshments, the Rev. G. F. Townsend was deputed by the teachers and children to present to his father, in their name, a beautiful silver inkstand, on which was engraved a suitable inscription. This he did in a very feeling manner, the worthy vicar replying with tears. On the next Sunday, Mr. Townsend preached his farewell sermon in the morning to the people of Brompton, and in the afternoon to the people of Deighton,

* Vide Todd's MSS. vol. 1, page 36a.

founding his discourse on both occasions upon Judges iii, 20, **A.D. 1839.**
" I have a message unto thee from God." On Tuesday, the 23rd of the same month, the gentlemen, tradesmen, and respectable inhabitants of the town and its vicinity gave a sumptuous banquet to their late highly esteemed vicar, at the Golden Lion Hotel, William Welbank, esq., presiding, and J. S. Walton, esq., being vice-president. After the repast, the president, in the name of the company, presented to Mr. Townsend an elegant massive silver cup, valued at £40, as a testimonial of their esteem and great regard. The worthy vicar returned thanks in a very feeling and affectionate address.

There was at this time, in the possession of Mr. John **An ancient** Hepton, of Northallerton, watchmaker and silversmith, a **clock.** curious and antique clock, wholly made of iron, with the exception of two brass wheels, which Mr. Hepton (in whose family the clock had been for several generations) said had been put in by the late Mr. Hugh Pannel, of Northallerton, an eminent clockmaker, about eighty years before, in the room of two iron ones which had become defective from long use. The clock was of curious workmanship, and in a good state of preservation. On the back plate of it the date "A.D. 1359" was discernible, so that it was then 480 years old. There is reason to believe, and with some degree of correctness, that the clock originally belonged to the ancient monastery of Carmelites or White Friars at Northallerton, which was built and endowed by Thomas Hatfield, bishop of Durham, in 1354.

Upon a tombstone in the churchyard at Northallerton, **Curious** erected to the memory of three sisters, daughters of Robert **Epitaph.** and Mary Dennison, of Thornbrough House, who died in three successive years, 1837, 1838, and 1839, aged respectively 19, 17, and 26, the following epitaph appears :—

 " Fair marble tell to future days
 That here three virgin sisters lie,
 Whose life employed each tongue to praise,
 Whose death drew tears from every eye.
 In stature, beauty, years, and fame,
 Together as they grew they shone,
 So much alike, so much the same,
 Death quite mistook them all for one."

Northallerton Church first lighted with gas, March 26th, **1840.** 1840. C. Spivey, Clerk.

At the conclusion of the North-Riding Sessions, held at **Archdeacon** Northallerton in April, 1840, the magistrates adjourned to the **Headlam.** inner Court Room for the purpose of witnessing the presentation of a splendid piece of plate to the late venerable Chairman of the Riding, Archdeacon Headlam. The plate was an elegant candelabra of very beautiful workmanship. It has

BB

A.D. 1840. six branches, and is beautifully chased and ornamented. Towards the base are three shields, on the centre one of which is the following inscription:—" To the venerable Archdeacon Headlam, late Chairman of the Quarter Sessions of the North-Riding of Yorkshire, this piece of plate was presented by the Magistrates of the Riding, the Gentlemen of the Bar practising at Northallerton, and the Officers of the Court, as a testimony of respect and esteem for his long and able services in the chair for nearly a quarter of a century, A.D. MDCCCXL." On the left hand shield were engraved the arms of the North-Riding, and on the right hand shield an emblem of justice. The Hon. and Rev. Thomas Monson was deputed to present the plate, which he did in a very neat and appropriate manner, and the venerable Archdeacon, who appeared to be deeply affected, replied at some length in acknowledgment.

1843.
A will case.
Miss Anne Peacock, a venerable old lady of over seventy years of age, was tried at the York Assizes for the alleged forgery of a will, but was honourably acquitted. She was a native of Northallerton, and descended from families of great respectability in the counties of York and Northumberland. She was the grand-daughter of Daniel Mitford, esq., of Northallerton, who was the elder brother of Thomas Mitford, husband to Abigail Mitford, the testator, and whose will Miss Peacock was accused by Thomas Robert Cooper, nephew of the said Abigail Mitford, of having forged. The said Daniel and Thomas Mitford were sons of the late Cuthbert Mitford, an eminent medical professor, resident at Northallerton, and Mary Lascelles his wife, of Stank Castle and Northallerton, who was sister to Henry Lascelles, of Stank Castle and Barbadoes, gentleman, who purchased Harewood House and its estate in the year 1739. The said Cuthbert Mitford was son of Robert Mitford, esq., of Northallerton, and Newby Wiske Hall, who served the office of high sheriff for the county of York in 1702, a descendant of an ancient family of that name, long resident at Mitford Castle in Northumberland.

1844.
The British School.
A British School was established at Northallerton in this year. It was held for some twenty years after its institution in the long row of houses at the east of the town known as Friarage Terrace; but the system of instruction not meeting with public sympathy it was discontinued, and the schoolrooms turned into dwelling-houses.

1848.
Confirmation.
On Monday afternoon, July 3rd, 1848, his grace the archbishop of York (Dr. Musgrave) held a confirmation in Northallerton church, for the parishes situate in the wapentake of Allertonshire, when about three hundred young persons and two adults were admitted to the rite. There had not been a confirmation by an archbishop of York at

Northallerton for more than 120 years, since the time of archbishop Swinburne; nor had the bishops of Durham held a confirmation at Northallerton since the time of Dr. Joseph Butler in 1754, in consequence of the ecclesiastical differences which had prevailed as to the jurisdiction of the peculiar of Allertonshire. In 1836 the revenues of the peculiar were transferred by the Ecclesiastical Commissioners to the see of Ripon, but were subsequently returned to the original possessors, the dean and chapter of Durham.*

A.D. 1848.

II.

MISCELLANEOUS.

NORTHALLERTON FAIRS.

Candlemas and *St. Bartholomew's Fairs* were granted by king John to Philip Pictaviensis (then called Philip of Poictieus) bishop of Durham, according to Leland, A.D. 1200.

St. George's Fair was granted, according to letters patent bearing date at Westminster, the 18th day of February, in the first and second year of the reign of king Philip and queen Mary, 1553—1554, to Cuthbert Tunstall, bishop of Durham, with a fortnight day every other Wednesday until Lammas, for buying and selling all kinds of cattle, on the petition of the following persons, inhabitants of the town of Northallerton and its neighbourhood:

Northallerton Fairs.

Thomas Conyers, Eaglescliffe	John Wilson
Lionel Strangwayes	Alfred Hutton
Edwarde Nornaville	Abel Smithson
Thomas Herbert, Brompton	Lemuel Thwaites
Richard Markenfield	William Danby, Leak Hall
Gyles Fisher	Roger Hawerde
William Metcalfe, N. Allerton	James Gale, Thrintoft
Edwarde Rymer	Charles Waylande
Robert Gouldstone	William Hutton
Hughe Gamble	

* The patronage only of Northallerton and several adjoining parishes remains with the Dean and Chapter of Durham, the Archbishop of York claiming the ecclesiastical jurisdiction.—J. L. S.

St. Matthew's Fair was granted by king James the First, in the eighth year of his reign, A.D. 1610, to William James, bishop of Durham and his successors, lords of Northallerton, with a fortnight day every other Wednesday from Lammas until Christmas, for the buying and selling of all kinds of cattle. Previous to granting the said fair, an inquiry was held at Northallerton, by order of the king, on October 10th, 1609, before sir Francis Hildesley, knight, high sheriff of the county of York, and the following persons, inhabitants of the said town and neighbourhood, on business relating to the propriety of granting the same: *

Gentlemen	Yeomen
William Best	William Britten
Christopher Herbert	William Prest
Thomas Ward	John Hutchinson
George Slinger	Roger Wilson
John Bincke	George Taylor
William Rymer	Peter Coats
Thomas Lumley	John Sigwell
	Thomas Gamble
	Robert Lumley

THE CHURCH BELLS.

The venerable tower of Northallerton church contains a fine ring of eight bells, upon which may be read the following legends and inscriptions :—

1. *Cast by John Warner & Sons, London*, 1871.

2. *Cast by John Warner & Sons, London*, 1871.

Both of the above are quite new, having been added to the original peal of six, in 1871. The key of No. 1 is F sharp, and that of No. 2, F natural.

* Vide Original Grant, 39th part of the Patents, 8 James I.

3. *All glory bee to God on hee.* 1656.
Recast by *J. Warner & Sons,*
1871.
Rev. T. W. Mercer, M.A. Vicar.

The Church Bells.

The above bell was broken, and remained unused for some time, until recast in 1871. It is in the key of B flat.

4. *Jesus bee our speed.* 1656.

This is one of the original bells and is probably as old as the tower. It is much worn, and its key is C sharp, but of course it has been chipped from time to time, in order to maintain its pitch.

5. *God save His Church.,* 1656.

This is supposed to be the oldest bell in the tower, and is also much worn; its key is D. It is called the "Shriving Bell," because it is rung every Shrove Tuesday at mid-day.*

6. *The Mount Grace Bell.*
Re-cast in 1802, and again in 1871, by *J. Warner & Sons,*
London.
Rev. T. W. Mercer, M.A., Vicar.

This bell is supposed to have hung in the bell-turret of Mount Grace Priory for some years after the dissolution of that monastry, until it fell to the ground through the decay of the turret. How long it remained in that abased position, before it was removed to Northallerton, cannot be ascertained; but until the year 1802, when it was broken, its remarkably sweet tones reverberated over hill and dale. It bears the following legend:

In multis annis resonet campana Johannis.

Its key is E, and it is called the "Curfew Bell,"† being rung at eight o'clock every evening.

7. *Thomas Mears, London, fecit.*
1802.

This bell is called the "Fire Bell," but it is never rung in that capacity. Its key is G sharp.

---

* The following distich is recited every Shrove Tuesday by the boys of the Grammar School:—

"The Pancake Bell, the Pancake Bell,
To all you schoolboys now doth tell;
That you may lay your books aside,—
Go home and get your pancakes fried."

J. Horner, 1844.

† Ingledew says that this and other regulations were thrust upon the English people by William the Conqueror as a mark of servitude, and that the signal to curfew (cover fire) at sunset in summer and about eight o'clock in winter was to prevent associations and conspiracies. It is more probable, however, that it was a wise policy on William's part, and not a tyrannical one. Hume says that William had previously established this law in Normandy; indeed, the same law had a place in Scotland and in other European states, being considered necessary on account of the combustible material then employed in the construction of houses, and the numerous fires in towns and villages consequent thereupon. It was continued in England as a police regulation till after the beginning of the sixteenth century.—J. L. S.

xxii   ANNALS OF

The Church Bells.

8. *Thomas Mears, London, fecit.*
          1827.

This is the tenor bell, and it weighs 16 cwt. Its key is F sharp, below. The hour strokes from the clock are struck upon it, and it is always brought into requisition as the "Passing Bell,"* and for funerals. Its tone is peculiarly deep and solemn.

ROMANBY CHAPEL.

Romanby Chapel.

Archbishop Gray (1215-1255) exerted his influence to secure the erection of chapels. In 1233 he took the advice of Pope Gregory IX on this subject. Many of the parishes in the archbishop's diocese were so large that it was impossible for the inhabitants of the widely scattered and distant hamlets to attend the services of the one church of the parish, and more than that the clergyman was often unable to reach the dying person in time to administer to him the last offices of religion. To obviate these difficulties, Pope Gregory advised the archbishop to encourage the erection of chapels which necessitated the residence of a clergyman to serve them, and were to be of no pecuniary loss to the mother churches, which they were designed to assist. Many of these have since become distinct or separate benefices; others have passed away altogether, and nothing remains in many a secluded hamlet save the name of "Chapel Garth, or Field," to show that there was at one time a little House of God set down in that place. Such a chapel was granted to Romanby, June 16th, 1231.

In Canon Raines' Register of Archbishop Gray (p. 45, vol. 56), we find the following Deed of Grant:—

Husthwayth, June 16th, 1231 A.D.

RANDULPH the Prior, and the Brethren of the Church of Durham give saluatation in the Lord to all who shall see or hear these letters. *Let it be known to all.* WE with the assent of Master Robert, our Vicar of Alverton, being urged by godly and pious considerations, have granted to John of Romandby and his heirs and to his men, and the men of that township, a chantry in the Chapel of Romandby in perpetuity on every day of the year except Christmas Day, the Purification of the Blessed Mary, Passion Snnday, Easter Day, All Saints' Day; and on Palm Sunday Divine Service shall be done in the said Chapel as far as the procession and blessing of palms. And the said John shall find a Chaplain at his own proper charges, in return for two oxgangs of land formerly set apart by the Mother Church, for a chantry, in the township of Romandby, which the said Chapel used to hold through the Vicar of Northallerton. The aforesaid Master Robert and his successors shall pay annually half a silver mark to the Chaplain, who for the time being shall minister in the said Chapel, for the maintenance of the service, that is to say, at Pentecost 40 pence, and at the feast of St. Martin in the winter 40 pence. And if perchance it comes to pass that the said Robert or his successors shall

---

* By the sixty-seventh canon of the Church of England it is enjoined that "when any is passing out of this life a bell shall be tolled, and the minister shall not then slack to do his last duty; and after the party's death (if so it fall out) there shall be rung no more but one short peal before the burial, and one other after the burial."—J. L. S.

have withdrawn from the payment of the half mark* for the said purposes, we, by our proper authority, empower them to get satisfaction by withholding the tithe of the hay and corn of the said John and his heirs. But the said John and his heirs, and the men of the village shall swear fealty to the Mother Church, that they will not allow any hurt to the Mother Church by reason of the Chantry granted. And it is provided that in the said Chapel Matrimony shall not be celebrated, nor a font erected for Baptisms, nor shall be done there the Purification of women, nor the Burial of the dead. Likewise the Chaplain ministering in the said Chapel shall swear fealty and canonical obedience to the Mother Church.

And if he shall presume to act contrary to the aforesaid fealty, the Chapel shall cease until suitable satisfaction shall have been made to the Mother Church. In testimony of this matter, our seal on the one part and the seal of the said John on the other part is appended (affixed.)

Randulph Prior of Durham. (SEAL).
John of Romanby. (SEAL).

Romanby Chapel.

ST. JAMES' HOSPITAL, ROMANBY.

There is an interesting record in existence, respecting a hospital at Northallerton, which gives a sort of picture of what were undoubtedly the internal arrangements of many similar houses. It bears date 1244.† From it we gather that the government of the hospital was vested in a warden, who was allowed a serving-man, two foot-boys and three horses. Two chaplains, each with his clerk, had charge of the spiritual welfare of its inmates. A baker and a brewer, with a boy to help, and a cook with his kitchen-boy formed part of the household. Five brethren, who might be either clerics or laymen, had each his allotted work in house and garden; one being specially charged with the care of the sick and bed-ridden. The comfort of the latter was further consulted by their being placed, especially in the night season, under the gentle ministry of female hands. Three who wore the dress and followed the rule of a sisterhood were attached to the hospital. Two of them watched by the sick at night when need required, and all were to take a share in turn of household work. Beds were provided for thirteen sick or infirm poor, who were to be tended *humaniter*, and provided with delicate and tempting food until health returned or death released them from their earthly suffering. Day by day at eventide thirty poor persons were relieved at the gate with half a loaf of bread each and a mess of pottage. If any were too weak or infirm to proceed on their journey or to get back to their home, they had a night's lodging given them in the *hospitium* alongside the gate. The size of the loaves is particularised. A bushel of flour was to be made into twenty-five loaves. If the possessions of the hospital increased in value, a corresponding augmentation was to be made in the

St. James' Hospital, Romanby.

---

* Vide Wolsey's Doings at Romanby, 1523, p. 46.
† Vide Gray's Register, p. 180.

St James' Hospital, Romanby.

alms given to the poor travellers who sought relief at the gate, and to those who were lying on their bed of sickness within.

Leprosy was then a terrible scourge, caused to a great extent, and certainly perpetuated, by overcrowding in the towns, the absolute lack of all sanitary arrangements, and the uncleanly habits and bad food of their inhabitants. Several hospitals for lepers existed in York, and there were many others for the special reception of persons so afflicted in other parts of the diocese. The wills of the period contain constant legacies to the various hospitals. A touching bequest occurs in one for the relief of blind, leprous, or otherwise afflicted priests who could no longer minister at the altar of God.*

RELIGIOUS HOUSES.

Religious Houses.

A more detailed account of the religious houses founded in Northallerton than that given in the body of this work, will doubtless be interesting to those who delight in the mouldy odour of discoloured parchments.

CONVENT OF AUSTIN FRIARS.

Convent of Austin Friars.

The mendicant order commonly called friars first sprang up early in the 13th century, when the monastic orders had, in several instances, begun to degenerate. They travelled where they pleased, instructed youth, heard confessions, and for a long time exercised unbounded influence. "The friars mendicant heretofore would take the opportunity to come into houses when the good women did bake, and would *read a ghospel over the batch*, and the good-women would give them a cake."† They were professedly poor, but obtained large sums from casual charity, which they expended in erecting magnificent refectories and churches. Subsequently it became fashionable for persons of rank to bequeath their bodies to be buried in friary churches. The origin of the Austin friars, or friars eremites of the order of St. Austin is uncertain, but they were first brought into England about the year 1250.‡ The rich who entered this order sold their possessions, and gave the proceeds to be equally appropriated to the use of the brethren. They were not allowed to receive alms unless they delivered the whole up to their superior. When they went abroad they were obliged to go two together, nor were they permitted to eat out of their convent, let the calls of nature be ever so urgent. There were forty-one houses of this order in England and Wales. Unfortunately we possess no record whatever, documentary or otherwise, of any benefaction to

---

* Vide Ornsby's Diocesan History of York, pp. 149, 150.
† Landsdowne MSS. No. 231.   ‡ For the habiliment and rules vide footnote p. 34.

the Convent of Austin Friars at Northallerton, or of any transaction connected therewith, except, of course, the original gift of land in the 14th Edward III; * neither is there any record of its dissolution, or trace of its existence. The curious must therefore be satisfied with the surmise that a house and church of Austin Friars of considerable size and importance did exist in Northallerton from 1340 to 1530. The Fleece Inn which is probably the oldest building in the town, and stands on the site of the Convent, might, if it could speak, give us some valuable information.

<small>Convent of Austin Friars.</small>

Convent of Carmelite or White Friars.

The Carmelites pretended to derive the institution of their order from the prophet Elijah, who, as they asserted was the first Carmelite. The true history of their origin however is given in the foot-note of page 35. After their expulsion from Mount Carmel in 1238, they settled in various parts of Europe. They were brought into England in 1240, by John Vesci and Richard Grey, where they possessed forty houses. They were called white friars from the colour of their habit, and also brethren or friars of the Blessed Virgin. They wore a white cloak and hood, and under it a coat, with a scapulary; but the Saracens, as a mark of contempt, obliged them to adopt parti-coloured garments of white and red, which they continued to wear near fifty years after their arrival in England.† In 1285, the white dress was resumed by order of Pope Honorius III.‡ The prior of the convent was elected unanimously or by the majority. Each monk was to have a separate cell; not to change their places without the prior's leave; and to meditate in their cells day and night. They were permitted to stay in the church, and to walk freely and lawfully *(libere et litite)* at fit hours in the cloisters. They had all things common. They were to carry with them to eat on journeys, dumplings *(pulmenta,* a very equivocal term among the monks) dressed with flesh. Sunday was the only festival during the week from Holyrood-day to Easter; from which the sick and infirm were exempt. Charity and labour were enjoined, and silence after compline till prime, but were permitted to talk moderately at other times.§ The origin of the convent is ascertained from a MS. in the College of Arms, marked L8, from which the following is extracted.—

<small>Convent of Carmelite or White Friars.</small>

"Anno dni Mo. iijc'o., lxvijo. Joh'es Yeu'll mercator Londonen' dedit Regi unam situacionem prope Northalntone ea condicione ut ipse *(sic)* fundaretr. una domus ordi's frum beatie marie de monte Carmelly, ut factum fuit. Et postea dns Radulph' Neville, miles construxit eccl'am integram

---

* Mon Ang. vi., 1603. Tanner's Notitia, 692.   † Tanner.
‡ Dugdale's Warwickshire, 186.
§ Fosbrook's Monachism, 121, and Bullarium Romanum, vol. 1, p. 116.

Convent of Carmelite or White Friars. proprio sumptu. Et in ch[h]oro ead'. eccl'a sepulta est Helena uxor predicti Joh'is Yeu'll. Item ecciam dna Margareta de Percy filia Neville qui obijt anno Mo. iijc'o lxxijo. Et a aud' ordre viij. Religeux."

From the above extract it would appear that John Yole, a London merchant, gave to the king (Edwd. III) a site near Northallerton, on condition that he (the king) built a house thereon for the brethren of the Order of the Blessed Mary of Mount Carmel, which was done. And afterwards Lord Randolph Neville, knight, built a complete church at his own expense. And in the choir of the same church, Helena, the wife of John Yole is buried.

The following benefactions to the Carmelite Convent at Northallerton, may prove interesting to antiquarians, and worthy of preservation as historical records:—

"Grant of a croft called Tentour, and a pasture, together containing 3a. 1r. in Northallerton, from John Yole of the said town, which was confirmed by Edward III." *

William de Neuport, rector of Bishopwearmouth, bequeathed to the brethren of Mount Carmel, at Northallerton, in 1366, one chalice. [unam calicem].

John Percy, of Kildale, by his will in 1382, leaves the following: "Item do et lego conventui Fratrum de Allerton xld.

John, Lord Neville, of Raby, bequeathed in 1836, to the Carmelite brothers of Northallerton, for the repair of their house, "c. marcas."

Sir John Clervaux, of Croft, in 1390, among other bequests gave to the friars [Carmelite] of Allerton 6s. 8d.—to friar John de Yougelby [Austin (?)] to celebrate for Sir John's soul, 6s. 8d.—and to Robert de Rokeby, chaplain, 6s. 8d. [for like purpose].

Sir Bryan Stapelton, in 1394, bequeathed to the "Frers of Richemonde, Yarum, et Allerton, a chescun ordour devaunt nomme xiijs. iiijd."

Richard, Lord Scrope, of Bolton Castle, gave in 1400, to the "Fratribus de Northalverton xxs.

Johanna, wife of *Sir Donald de Hesilrig*, in 1400, bequeathed the following: "Item lego Fratribus in conventu [which convent?] apud Alverton xxs.

Isabella, wife of *Walter Fauconberg*, left to the "Fratribus de Alverton xxs. Here also we are left to conjecture which of the two convents (for they must have been coæval) received the benefit of the legacy.

Sir Thomas de Boynton, of Acklam, in Cleveland, bequeathed in 1402, to "Fratribus de Allerton xjs. viijd." It is to be regretted that Sir Thomas was not more explicit.

Walter Skirlaw, bishop of Durham, bequeathed in 1404, as follows: "Item lego cuilibet domino de ordine Mendicancium infra eandem diocesim xls., inter quos volo illos de Alverton comprehendi, ut ipsi omnes orent pro anima mea, et quod quilibet sacerdos, in dictis locis existens, celebrat pro anima mea xxx missas, infra annum a tempore mortis meæ."

Robert Conyers, of Sockburn, in 1431, gave to "Fratribus de Alverton xjs. viijd.

Johanna Palman, alias *Coke*, in 1436, left the following: "Item lego Fratribus de Alverton j. towell de werk."

Ralph de Neville, earl of Westmoreland, in 1440, left to the Convent at Allerton "pro coquina et aliis domibus ibidem reparandis et ædificandis, xli.

Sir Thomas Fulthorp, of Tunstall, bequeathed in 1456 to "Priori et Conventui Fratrum Mend. de Allerton xiijs. iiijd."

* Dodsworth's MSS., vol. cxxi, f 30, Bod. Lib.

NORTHALLERTON.

Sir Alexander Neville, of Thornton Bridge, in 1457, bequeathed to the Convent of "Convent of the Freris of Allerton for the same to have xiijs. iiijd." {Carmelite or White Friars.}
Ralph Fitz-Randolph, lord of Middleham, in 1457, leaves the following: "Item tribus ordinibus Fratrum, viz., Yarum, Allerton, et Ebor., xv. sol. inter se dividendos per equales porciones,"
Robert Dale, alias *Flesher*, of Great Fencote, in 1470, left "Item lego Fratribus de Allerton viii. sol. Item lego fabrice ecclesie paro. de North Allerton ii. sol."
John Sayer, of Worsall, in 1530, gave to "Ye Frears of Yarme and Aluerton vs."

The Carmelite Friarage at Northallerton was one of the last monasteries dissolved by Henry VIII., as appears from the following copy of the original surrender:— {Dissolution of Carmelite Friarage.}

"Forasmuch as we, the Prior and Friars of the house of brethren, called Carmelites or White Friars at Northallerton, do profoundly consider that the perfection of christian living does not consist in some ceremonies, wearing of a black cloak or coat, disguising of ourselves after strange fashions, docking and becking, wearing of scapulars and hoods, and other like papistical ceremonies, wherein we have been most principally practiced and nose-led in times past; but the very true way to please God, and to live a true christian man, without hypocrisy, and feigned dissimulation, is sincerely declared to us by our Master Christ, his evangelists and apostles; being minded hereafter to follow the same, conforming ourselves to the will and pleasure of our supreme head, under God, on earth, the King's Majesty; and are not to follow henceforth the superstitious traditions of any forensical potentate or power,—with mutual assent and consent, do submit ourselves unto our said sovereign Lord; and with the like assent and consent, do surrender, &c., &c., this 20th day of November, 1539.

(In the absence of the Prior)
Signed by WILLIAM WOMMEFRAYE, Warden,
and nine Friars, his brethren."*

THE PARISH REGISTERS.

The parochial registers, which are generally the sole repository of local history, and from which so much that is interesting respecting prevailing customs and passing events, is usually gleaned, do not in this instance supply either the historian or antiquarian with much that is valuable. The entries therein are much dispersed in consequence of their having been written down consecutively in years as they occurred. The earliest entry in the first volume is that of a burial dated 5th October, 1591. There are, however, a number of old worm-eaten discoloured leaves, the remains of an earlier register, carefully tied up in a bundle, but it would occupy even an expert a very long time to decipher them. The Julian or old style, which made the year to commence on the 25th of March, is used down to the 1st of January, 1752, on which day the new style commenced. The books are in very good condition, and, which is not

---

* Vide super pp. 46-50. This Monastery of Carmelites was dedicated to St. Mary. (Speed). The Augustine Monastery at Northallerton was dissolved January 17th, 1540. Todd's MSS.

The Parish Registers. common, the orthography is particularly correct throughout the earlier volumes. The names Rymer, Danby (Danbi), Metcalf, Peacock (Paycock), Willoughby (Willobie), and Meynell (Mennel) seem to occur most frequently between the years 1590 and 1624, while illegitimacy was certainly more prevalent then than now, if we take the number of illegitimate children baptised as a criterion. Northallerton suffered considerably from that dreadful scourge, the plague, which ravaged England between the years 1602 and 1606. It appears that between 18th January, 1603, and 25th May, 1604, there were buried at Northallerton, that died of the plague, 54 persons. The names of all are recorded, and after each the word "plague" is written within brackets. The following year was still more fatal, for upwards of 90 persons who had died of the plague were buried in Northallerton churchyard between July 16th and Nov. 21st, 1605, which was lamentable, putting down the average annual mortality at 30. The following entries, written in a different hand from those which precede or follow, may supply fuel for those inclined to be jocular:—

1619. Junij 4. —— —— Carbonarius, fulminis ictu.
1620. April 6. Stephanus Lawcock, Curio ibidem per annos 28.
      Maye 10. Alicia Wilkinson, Rogeri filia virgo nubilis.
       ,, 13. Will. Gamble, Samsoni filius, multæ spei juvenis.
       ,, 15. Elisab. Wagget, vidua religiosa, decrepita.
      Nov. 3. Francisca Tru'ble Georgii filia, nata, baptizata, viva, mortua, sepulta.
      Jan. 2. Dorothea Parker, *alias* Daye; excom'unicata extra cœmiteriu' sepulta.
       ,, 16. Ric. Metcalf, eodm. quo mortuus est die, a se'te'tio exco'unic. plene'. absolutus, sepult.
1621. Maij 1. Will. Ashley, generosus, ægrotus ad oppidu' delatus, sepult.
      Junij 18. Jacobus Mead, religiosus, lo'gœvus antiquæ, vir p'bitatis.
      Mart. 19. Jo. Bidsdaill, horrendo sui ipsius suspe'dio vita' finiens, sepult.

The last entry in the first register is dated 11th Sep., 1624. The second register contains a transcript of the first book in the handwriting of Francis Kaye, vicar, but the last entry in the transcript is dated 28th March, 1624. There is an hiatus from the end of the transcript to 29th May, 1625, when the registration re-commences in a different hand, Mr. Kaye having died 15th Sep., 1624. There is no entry of his burial, but in the chancel there was formerly a brass plate, surmounted by a figure in the same material.* A greater part of the year 1627 is lost, and there is also an hiatus between Dec. 13th, 1629, and April 17th, 1631, and another from Dec. 2nd, 1633, to March 1st, 1634-5. On Dec. 26th, 1638, "Elizabeth Best, Cuthb. filia," is denoted first as buried, but

* Vide footnote page 79.

NORTHALLERTON.

afterwards as baptised. She may have been received at this time into the church. The second register ends with the date 1st June, 1640, leaving many blank folios. On one of these next after the general registration is finished, are set down the births of fourteen children in the year 1695. The third register commences in October, 1653, on the 31st of which month Henry Flower was sworn in " Register " before Fr. Lascelles, esq. The last baptism in this third register is dated 30th Dec., 1663, the last marrage 19th June, 1662, and the last burial 8th Sep., 1662. During the interregnum after the year 1653, the marriages at Northallerton were contracted before the following magistrates :—Francis Lascelles, Thomas Lascelles, Leonard Smelt, Ralph Rymere, and George Smithson, esquires, The fourth register does not commence until 25th March, 1670. The following memoranda are on the second page :—

The Parish Registers.

> John Robinson, parish clerk, of Northallerton, entered upon the clerkship August ye 11th, 1678.
> Matthew Bowes was elected clerk of Northallerton, July ye 20th, 1716.

Brompton is wthin ye parish of Northallerton, and so is Deighton, but either of them have registers of their own. Tomas Mann.

> Dr. John Neile was inducted vicar of Northallerton in the year 1669.
> Mr. William Neile was inducted vicar of Northallerton in 1675.
> Mr. John Harper was inducted vicar in July, 1686.
> Mr. Tho. Mann was inducted vicar Sept. 22nd, 1660.
> [The dates are not consecutive.]
> Mr. Charles Neile was inducted vicar of Northallerton July the 28th, 1694.
> Mr. Christoper Hunter was inducted vicar of Northallerton November ye first, A.D. 1718.
> Mr. Thomas Rudd was inducted vicar of Northallerton January ye 22nd, 1725-6.
> [It will be seen that there were three vicars of Northallerton of the name of Neile.]

From 1624 to 1713 the names of Meek, Dunn, Whitton, Dowson, Gale, and Todd most frequently occur, From 1700 to 1706 the date of birth of each child, as well as the date of its baptism, is recorded. The name Flower now becomes very frequent, indeed there is quite a garden of them, between 1670 and 1700. On April 24th, 1701, Ann Campleman was interred at Northallerton; she cut her throat at Osmotherley. The dates of the births of fifteen children are recorded on a separate membrane. The latter entries in this register are written on paper leaves, slightly inserted among the membranes of the book. It is probable that the marriages solemnised between January, 1706-7, and the end of 1713, were also entered upon paper, and that the leaves are lost, but the copies are preserved in the transcript in the following registers. The fifth register commences on the 25th March, 1700. The following entry appears under the head of burials

The Parish Registers. on Jan. 11th, 1726: "Robert Smith, some time servant to Mr. Neile, vicar, whose niece and heiresse he maryed." On Nov. 21st, 1728, "a stranger woman, whose name we could not learn, going to her husband, a soldier." The last entry in the fifth register is dated 22nd March, 1728. The sixth register commences with the year 1729, March 25th. Mem. —"29th Nov., 1754, Edmund Bradeley was chosen by me to be clerk at this church, which choice was signified to the parishioners (according to canon 91) in the time of Divine Service, upon the next Sunday following being 1st Dec., 1754, by me, Robt. Pigot, vicar." On Nov. 28th, 1734, Ann, bastard daughter of Ann Sherrington, bedrid and about 15 years of age, was baptised privately. In this register the number of illegitimate children baptised is something alarming, which is accounted for by the frequent passage of troops through the town at that time. Several adult baptisms took place between the years 1724 and 1781. By the 26th Geo. II., cap. 33, it was provided that a separate book should be kept in every parish for the registration of marriages and banns of marriage; this act came into operation in the year 1754. On Dec. 10th, 1744, a Mr. Peter Deburine, alias Dubern, captain of a French privateer, who was taken prisoner off Scotland, and died of grief on his journey to London, was interred in Northallerton churchyard. The last entry in the sixth register is dated 23rd Dec., 1781. In a separate marriage register commencing 25th March, 1754, the following entry appears:—"1755, Oct. 12th. The banns of marriage between James Grieves and Elizabeth Peacock were published in this church the second time; the publication between James Grieves and Elizabeth Peacock is made void by the dissent of Wm. Peacock, her father." From the year 1778 the name of the officiating minister is appended to all marriages solemnised at Northallerton. The last entry in this register of marriages is dated 29th Dec., 1806. The seventh register commences with the year 1782, and ends with the year 1812, in common with all other registers throughout the kingdom, belonging to the church of England. On the 1st of January, 1813, a new system of registration was introduced under the 52nd Geo. III., cap. 146, commonly called sir George Rose's Act. Among other provisions it was enacted, that the registers of baptisms, marriages, and burials should be kept in separate books, and the entries made according to schedules annexed to the Act, a copy of which is prefixed to every book provided for the registration of baptisms. The last entry in the first register of marriages under this Act, is dated 20th May, 1842, though from 1837 the solemnisations are also entered in the duplicate books provided under the Act of 6 and 7 Guil. IV., cap. 86. There

NORTHALLERTON. xxxi

is nothing worth noticing in any of the later registers. The The Parish
book of excommunications contains two entries of excommu- Registers.
nication for incest, one for fornication, and one absolution,
which have been fully inserted under their respective dates
in the body of this work. The churchwardens' accounts
have also been re-produced, with few exceptions, under their
respective dates.

COURT HALMOT, COURTS LEET AND BARON.

The Court Halmot, and Courts Leet and Baron, are held Court Halmot
after Easter and Michaelmas, when the usual business is and Courts
transacted, such as receiving fines and surrenders, admitting Leet and
copyholders, &c. The following is a list of the stewards of Baron.
the courts from 3rd Sep., 1545, the earliest date in the extant
books. The list of high stewards is incomplete, from the
difficulty, if not impossibility, of obtaining their names, since
they do not appear in the court rolls after 1614.

High Stewards.	Deputies.
1545. Sir George Conyers, knt.*	
1568. Sir George Bowes, knt.†	1568. Thomas Layton.
1580. Thomas Layton, esq.‡	1573. John Conyers.
1585. Sir Thomas Cecil, knt.	1585. Cuthbert Pepper [sits as C. Pepper, knt., from 6th Oct., 1605].
1594. Sir Robert Cecil, knt.	1609. Thomas Lascelles, knt.
1614. William, lord Burghley.	1611. Robert Cooper, [Learned Steward.] ¶
1761. Fletcher Norton, esq.§	
1789. William, lord Grantley.	
1822. Henry, earl of Harewood.	
1841. Henry, earl of Harewood.	

Learned Stewards.
1611. Robert Cooper.
1623. Richard Cradack.
1625. John Waistill
1662. John Blackiston.

                1683. Rowland Norton.
                1694. Christopher Driffield.
                1699. Robert Raikes.
1702. John Cuthbert.   1704. John Rudd.
                1708. Robert Raikes.
                1714. Thomas Crosfield.

* Of Sockburn, co. Durham; born 1510, died 1567. He m. Anne, dau. of sir John Dauncy, of Sessay, in Allertonshire.
† Of Streatlam, co. Durham, and South Cowton, co. York, the knight marshall so distinguished for his loyalty during the rebellion in 1569. He died in 1580. His sister Margery, mar. Knox the Reformer.
‡ Temporal chancellor of Durham, 1562, and attorney-general of the same county palatine in bishop Pilkington's time. Deputy escheator in bishop Barnes's.
§ Created lord Grantley, born at Markenfield, co. York, 9th April, 1782.
¶ This is the first mention of a "Learned Steward" (20th Oct., 1611) and from this period, with the exception of 10th April, 1614, the Learned Stewards have sat, and the High Stewards are not even mentioned; the latter office was abolished upon the death of the earl of Harewood in 1857.

	LEARNED STEWARDS.	DEPUTIES.
Court Halmot and Courts Leet and Baron.	1722. John Fawcett.*	1759. Thomas Crosfield. Roger Gale.
	1761. William Rudd.	Roger Gale.
	1768. George Hartley.	Roger Gale.
		1776. William Wailes.
		1785. John Wailes.
	1780. Thomas Mauleverer.†	John Wailes.
	1785. William Ambler.‡	John Wailes.
	1792. George Pearson.§	John Wailes.
	1798. William Frankland.	1798. John Wailes.
		1812. Peter Rigg.
	1816. Fletcher Rigg.‖	1823. John Sanders Walton
	1829. John Sanders Walton.¶	
	1844. Wm. Thrush Jefferson	
	1845. Thomas Fowle.**	
	1857. James Jell Chalk.	1857. Wm. Thrush Jefferson.
	1871. George Pringle.§§	

EXTRACTS FROM A LECTURE ON "NORTHALLERTON," BY W. T. JEFFERSON, ESQ.

Extracts from a Lecture on Northallerton

Speaking of the Castle Hills, Mr. Jefferson says, "Curiosity led me to examine a singular looking place in Brompton called 'Barrow-pit Holes,' a small artificial hillock, but concave at the top. This was most probably a tumulus in connection with the Castle Hills, from which point the latter could be distinctly seen. * * Many of us must remember the beautiful avenue of trees which stood so majestically on the south side, and all of which were so ruthlessly cut down

* Of Durham, barrister-at-law, and recorder of Durham, second son of Christopher Fawcett, of Lambton, co. Durham; b. in 1676; m. Elizabeth, dau. of Richard Stonhewer, esq., of Durham, by whom he had seven sons and four daughters. Christopher his eldest son was a barrister, and recorder of Newcastle-on-Tyne, whose eldest dau. m. 1780 to Richard Wm. Peirse, esq., of Hutton Bonville; Richard, D.D., vicar of Newcastle-on-Tyne, rector of Gateshead, and prebendary of Durham; John, who assumed the name of Pulteney; Thomas, rector of Green's Norton, co. Northampton; John, William, and Thomas, who died young. Elizabeth m. to Peter Bowlby, LL.D.; Mary, Dorothy, and Elizabeth, died young.

† Of Arncliffe, barrister-at-law, son of Timothy Mauleverer, esq.; m. Sarah Pawson, dau. of John Wilberfoss, esq., of Gainsborough, co. Lincoln, (who died 13th July, 1810) he had issue Thomas, John, and Richard, who died young; Jane, m. to Robert Lindsey, esq., of Lavighry, in the co. of Tyrone; Sarah, m. to Arthur Worsop, esq., Alverley Grange, co. York; Annie m. in 1780 to col. Clotworthy Gowan, Bessingly, co. York, by whom he had issue the late Wm. Mauleverer, esq.; Frances, d. in 1827; Mary, d. in 1833.

‡ Of Durham, barrister-at-law, and steward of the borough of Durham.

§ Of Durham, a barrister, clerk of the peace for Durham 1783.

‖ Of Northallerton, only son of Roger Rigge, esq., of Hawkshead, co. Lancashire, by his wife Mary, dau. of John Fletcher, esq., of Wood Broughton, Lancashire; a deputy-lieutenant of the North-Riding of Yorkshire; clerk of assize of the northern circuit; mar. Susannah, dau. of Joseph Saunders, esq., of Ealing, co. Middlesex.

¶ Of Northallerton, solicitor, b. 17th June, 1781; d. 31st Aug., 1844. He mar. Charlotte C. Diemer, dau. of John Goll, esq., and widow of the rev. J. C. Diemer, D.D., who died 9th Dec., 1850.

** W. D. Walker, held the court for Mr. Fowle, 2nd Oct., 1852, and R. M. Atkinson 18th April, 1857.

§§ Mr. Pringle was afterwards knighted, and sat as Sir George Pringle, knight, at the Court holden on Oct. 6th, 1883.

NORTHALLERTON. xxxiii

to make way for a railway. Would that it had been in my **Extracts from Lecture on Northallerton** power to have stayed that work of destruction." Referring to the castle, he says, "Leland's account certainly bears a traditionary character being descriptive of a place 'where the castle of Alverton some time stood,' and adds that there was no appearance of any walls. At the same time it is highly probable that a castle-like building did once stand upon the summit of the hill, which was afterwards pulled down and merged in the palace or castle within the moat. * * The 'Vine House' and gardens at the rear were undoubtedly part of the lands belonging to the Carmelite establishment." Mr. Jefferson then noticed the following allusions to the town made by eminent writers. In Sir Walter Scott's novel "The Monastery," chapter 16, Sir Piercie Shafton is made to say that he was met at Northallerton, on his way north, by a messenger from the Duke of Northumberland; and Dr. Johnson, in one of his letters, mentions having slept a night at Northallerton, and his impression of the place.* Lady Blessington in her "Confessions of an Elderly Lady," makes the lady state that she happened to be at the "Marquis of Granby" (Inn) at Northallerton at the same time that her old lover and his bride were there.

SIR HUGH SMITHSON, BART.

Hugh, Duke of Northumberland, K.G. (Sir Hugh Smithson,† **Sir Hugh Smithson, bt.** bart.), only son of Langdale Smithson, esq., by his wife Philadelphia, daughter of William Revely, esq., of Newby Wiske; was born at Northallerton,‡ in 1712, baptised at Kirby Wiske, 10th Dec., 1712. Langdale Smithson dying before his father, the third bart., his son inherited the baronetcy in 1729, upon the death of his grandfather, and served the office of high sheriff of Yorkshire in 1738. He married lady Elizabeth,§ only surviving child of Algernon, duke of Somerset (who was created baron Warkworth and earl of Northumberland, 2nd Oct., 1749, with remainder, failing his issue male, to his son-in-law sir Hugh Smithson,

---

* Vide Boswell's "Life of Johnson."
† The family of Smithson have held considerable estates in Yorkshire since the conquest. Robert and Thomas de Smythton, were summoned to appear on a jury, in an inquisition taken on Thursday, the feast of St. Catharine, A.D. 1333; and about this period the family removed from Smithton (Smeaton?) to Yafforth, near Northallerton, which latter estate John Smythson exchanged in 1441 with Robert Danby, for lands in Newsome, &c.
‡ Mrs. Smithson being on a visit to her relative Robert Mitford, esq., then residing at Northallerton, she was unexpectedly taken in labour, and safely delivered of a son, the subject of this account. Elizabeth Mansfield, of Northallerton, was appointed his nurse.
§ Sir Hugh Smithson was considered the most handsome man of his day. A female friend happened to mention to the lady Elizabeth Percy, that sir Hugh had been rejected by a friend of hers; whereupon the heiress observed, that the lady in question was "the only woman in England who would have refused sir Hugh Smithson." The expression soon reached the ears of sir Hugh, who wooed and won lady Elizabeth, and was the only duke created by George III.

Sir Hugh Smithson, bt. bart., and to the heirs male of his body by lady Elizabeth his wife; in default of which the dignities of baroness Warkworth and countess of Northumberland to the said lady Elizabeth, and of baron Warkworth and earl of Northumberland to her heirs male); succeeded to those honours upon the death of the duke in 1750, and obtained in the same year an act of parliament to allow himself and his countess to assume the surname and arms of Percy. His lordship was installed a Knight of the Garter in 1757, and created earl Percy and duke of Northumberland 18th Oct., 1766, with remainder to his issue male by Elizabeth his wife. His grace obtained the barony of Louvaine, of Alnwick, with remainder to his second son lord Algernon Percy, by patent, dated 28th Jan., 1784. His grace died in 1786, and was succeeded by his son Hugh, second duke, K.G., father of Hugh, third duke, and Algernon, fourth duke, K.G., F.R.S., F.S.A., &c.

HAIR POWDER CERTIFICATES.

Hair Powder Certificates. The following list of certificates for using Hair Powder, issued in the year 1795, may be of interest to our readers.

PARISH OF NORTHALLERTON.

Bailey, Mr. B., M.D.	Johnson, Mrs. Amy	Ripley, Mrs. Ann
Bailey, Mrs. Eliz.	Langdale, Mr. James	Reed, Mrs. Eleanor
Bulmer, Mr. Wm.	Lascelles, Mrs. Jane	Sedgwick, Mrs. Mary
Crowe, Mrs. Ann	Leightly, Mr. Wm.	Sedgwick, Mr. Meriton
,, for Sewell, John (footman) *	Metcalfe, Mrs. Ann	Simpson, Mr. Thomas
	Metcalfe, Miss Dorothy	Simpson, Mrs. Cath.
Davison, Rev. Geo.	Mitford, Mrs. Abi	Todd, Mr. Henry
Dent, Mrs. Ann	Parkin, Mr. Jackson	Walton, Mr. Thomas
Dighton, Mr. Richard	Parkin, Mrs. Mary	Walton, Miss Mary
Dixon, Mr. John	Peacock, Rev. Wm.	Walker, Mr. John
Harle, Mrs. Jane	Peacock, Mrs. Eliz.	Walker, Miss Isabella
Hirst, Mrs. Dorothy	Peacock, Miss Annie	Walker, Rev. Benj.
Hirst, Mr. Henry	Peacock, Miss Eliz.	Wind, Mr. Thomas
Jackson, Mr. Richard	Peat, Mr. Samuel	Wind, Mrs. Christiana
Johnson, Mr. Thomas	Peat, Mrs. Henrietta	Wilkinson, Rev. James

TERRIER OF GLEBE LANDS.

Terrier of Glebe Lands. A TRUE AND PERFECT TERRIER OF THE GLEBE LANDS and other Rights and Possessions belonging to the Vicarage of Northallerton, in the county of York, made this First day of September, 1781.†

---

* The custom of wearing Hair Powder came into existence about 1590, but it has now almost fallen into disuse; footmen in noble families only retaining this method of dressing the hair. Duty upon the use of hair powder was first levied in 1795, which yielded at one time to the revenue the sum of £20,000 per annum. The tax was repealed in 1869. John Crowder was the licensed distributor of certificates for using hair powder in Northallerton in 1796.

† The Terrier is so lengthy and its phraseology so dry and uninteresting, that I have only inserted just what the public would care to read, retaining the etymology of the original document.

NORTHALLERTON. XXXV

The Vicarage House* which is chiefly built of brick, but a small part of stone, covered with tiles. It contains eleven rooms, which are all ceiled and have boarded floors. There are beside a large pantry, three cellars, and a good back kitchen or brewhouse. There is a chaise-house built by the late incumbent,† and a corn granary built by the present vicar.‡ The other out-houses are a barn, cart-house, two stables, and a coal-house, * * which with the garden, court, and ground, the buildings stand on, contains in the whole about one acre.

Terrier of Glebe Lands

GLEBE LANDS IN THE TOWNSHIP OF NORTHALLERTON.

	A.	R.
The Rig (divided into four closes)	48	0
Vicar's Croft (meadow land)	7	0
Black Hill (arable land)	17	0
New Black Hill	6	0
Common Close (with lane at east end)	4	0
Chapel Garths (with lane leading to Sigstone)	3	0
Knotta Hill (meadow close)	2	3
Three Arable Lands in Knotta Bottom field; Six Arable Lands in same field; and Eight Arable Lands in same field	5	2
Pinfold Close	2	0
Little Field	2	1

ROMANBY GLEBE.

Mountjoys	28	0

BROMPTON GLEBE.

A Little Garden adjoining Brompton Church-yard	—	
A Little Paddock on the east of Brompton lane	1	3
Sheep Coat Closes	48	0

DEIGHTON GLEBE.

Magdalene Garth	1	2
Webster Closes	15	0
Priest Close	14	0
Priest's Winter Close	4	0
Priest's Summer Close	7	0

TITHES.

	£	s.	d.
From Crosby Coates and Bank Head, in lieu of Tithes	2	10	0
,, Lazenby, in lieu of Tithes	2	10	0
,, Worsall, ,,	1	6	8
,, Spital, ,,	0	10	0
,, Executors of Henry Peirse, Esq., in lieu of Tithes	1	17	0
,, ,, of Tobias Tomes, ,,	0	5	0
,, ,, of Richard Dighton, ,,	0	2	8
,, ,, of Rev. W. Peacock ,,	0	1	4
Salvin's Close in lieu of Tithes	0	5	0
New Closes, sixpence an ox-gang for hay tithe	—		
Stevenson's Close, in lieu of Tithes	0	1	0

---

* Not the present one which was built a little to the west of the old one, above described.
† Rev. Robert Pigot, M.A. ‡ Rev. Benjamin Walker, M.A.

		£	s.	d.

Terrier of Glebe Lands.

Romanby, twopence an ox-gang for hay tithes, and all other tithes .. .. —
Hall Garth, in lieu of Tithes.. .. .. .. 0 0 4
Bridge Mill, ,, ... 0 3 4
Brompton, in lieu of hay tithes 0 8 0
Deighton, in lieu of Tithes 24 0 0

SURPLICE FEES.

The customary fee for a churching is sevenpence, for a burial ninepence, for a wedding by banns two shillings.

EASTER RECKONINGS.

The Easter Reckonings are, for a hen due at Saint Andrew's Day, sixpence; offerings for each communicant, twopence; for each cow, one penny; for each calf, where not a titheable number, an halfpenny; for a foal, one penny; for a plough, one penny; for gelt cattle, each twopence; Bees, each swarm, one penny; monthly tithe for sheep, fourpence a score. Mortuaries are customarily paid.

There are no timber or other trees growing in the Churchyard, and almost none of any considerable value growing upon any part of the glebe.

The vicar pays a yearly sum of sixteen pounds to the Dean and Chapter of Durham.

We have in the church of Northallerton five* bells, a large clock, one silver-plated flaggon, one silver paten (on which the arms of the Metcalfe's are engraved with an inscription underneath *Ex dono E. M.*, 1702), a silver chalice and cover, on the chalice *This cup belongs to Northallerton*, a linen cloth for the Communion table, with a napkin and two surplices, a pulpit cloth and cushion with a valance for the Reading-desk. The books belonging to the church are an handsome folio bible in two volumes, a large common prayer book, another large folio bible† and two folio common prayer books. The parishioners are charged with the repairs of the church and churchyard fence.

The common clerk's wages are, for a burial tenpence, a wedding by banns one shilling, and fourpence yearly from each family at Easter. The sexton's wages are, for a passing bell one shilling, a burial fee one shilling and twopence, for a wedding by banns sixpence.

This is a true and perfect terrier, &c.

B. Walker, Vicar.
Will. Squire ⎫
Edw. Dawson ⎬ Church-   Chr. Welbank ⎫
Ja. Langdale ⎪ wardens. John Walker ⎬ Inhab-
Geo. Ward, Romanby ⎭   John Clapham, jun. ⎪ itants.
                        Will. Wailes ⎭

QUARTER SESSIONS RECORDS RELATING TO NORTHALLERTON.

Extracted from the Published Journals of the North Riding Record Society.

Quarter Sessions Records.

1605. Sessions held at THIRSKE, April 11. [9.] Treasurer named for Lame Souldiours,‡ Francis Lascelles of Northallerton, Gentn.

1605. Sessions held at STOKESLEY, July 9. [11.] [after citing the Statute 18 Eliz. against extortion under pretext of legal process]. Rob. Carver, of

---

* Three others have since been added, bringing up the peal to an octave.
† Now, disused, being quite dilapidated.
‡ A rate of so much, in the pound was assessed upon every parish according to its rateable value for the benefit of disabled soldiers, &c., by the Act.

Northallerton, labr., and Tho. Mathew of the same, butcher, for extorting at the dwelling-house of —— Langley, widow, at Stokesley, 10s., under cover of an information by the said Rob. Carver against Rob. Walker of Marton-in-Cleveland, labr., and also a promise from the said Rob. Walker of the payment of 3s. 4d. more, &c.

1605. Held at RICHMONDE, July 11. [16.] The Churchwardens of Dighton Church, for nonpayment of asssessment in behalf of Lame Soldiours, and the Hospitals.*

Will. Nelson, of Northallerton, indicted for using the art and mystery of a glover,† applies for copy, &c. [bound by Recognizances in £10 to present his Traverse].

1605. Held at RICHMONDE, October 4. Chr. Scarlett, of Romondby, yoman, for shooting two doves in the vill of Romondby "in quodam tormento, Anglice a Foulinge peece, onerato pulvere et glandibus plumbeis, Anglice charged with powder and shott,‡ &c.

Will. Nelson (vid sup) also presents himself, pleads not guilty, and is acquitted by the same jury on the ground that he proves, producing Indenture dated 37th Elizth., his apprenticeship to Anth. Walker of Northallerton, to whom he served as apprentice for seven years, in right of which &c. He is therefore discharged.

1606. Held at RICHMONDE, Jan. 7. [26.] Will. Rainold and John Hutchinson of Brompton in Allertonshire, for tracing and killing hares in snow time.§

[26b.] ORDERS made at the same sessions, or a brief thereof.

ORDERED THAT Roger Robinson of Northallerton be licensed per curiam to kepe an alehouse there and have a License or Tickett for yt. purpose syned by Sir Conyers Darcy, Knt., and Adam Midlam, Esq.

1606. Held at THIRSKE, April 29. The Churchwardens of Dighton, for not paying the sums assessed there for Lame Soldiours and the Hospitals, Gabriell Coates of Northallerton, for keeping an alehouse without license, and also Roger Taylour, Will. Welfoot, Jane Smeaton, John Clarke, and Agnes Hewet, all of the same, for the like. [Per Marm. Rawson et Oswald Taylour, Cap. Const].

[34b.] Anth. Blacklock of Northallerton (and eight others of different places) for killing divers calves under five years old, contra foram &c.‖

1606. Held at HELMESLEY, July 10. [39b.] Henry Buttrye of East Ronckton and Rob. Carver of Northallerton, not considering nor fearing the statute of 18 Eliz. [c. 5] in the case of Will. Lepton of Huton juxta Rudby, blacksmith, taking 4s. from him by the hands of John Mease of Northallerton [Submitted, and fined £10 and to stand in the pillory.]

As Henry Buttry (vid sup) using the office of informer, and is not allowed and by extortion and other deceivable means hath received of diverse persons severall sommes of money &c., therefore he to stand on the pillorie at Northallerton two severall days, with a paper on his head with inscription testifying his cousinage &c., and that he used the office of Informer without the authority or license of His Maties. Attorney in the North, and to pay a fyne of xls. for each offence, in all £4. And, further, as the said Buttry has departed the Court without license, or payment of the said fynes &c., a warrant be made to attach him, and bring him before some Justice, there to be bound with good sureties &c. ; or if he refuse, to carrie him to the Castle of York, there to remeyne &c.

---

* Probably "Hospit'lis Sanct' Jacobi juxta North Alv'ton," and the other religious houses mentioned in the body of this work.
† On suspicion of not having served his apprenticeship.
‡ By a statute 3, Edw. vi, c. 14, no person under the degree of a Lord of Parliament might shoot, under a penalty of £1, within any city or town at any fowl, or at any mark, nor with haile-shot or any more pellets than one at one time ; and by an Act of 33 Henry viii, c. 6, in all plackards (licenses) to shoot, the names of the creatures to be shot at were to be specifically mentioned.
§ The penalty is affixed in 1 James, c. 27.   ‖ 1 James, c. 52.

1606. Held at RICHMOND, July 14.
ORDERS made &c.

[45b.] ORDERED THAT whereas Tho. Mathew of Northallerton, being an Informer, and heretofore indicted for extortion &c, and bound over with suretie to appeare at the then next Sessions to answer &c, and not to depart without license, did nevertheless depart and leave his surety liable, therefore a warrant &c.

1606. Held at MALTON, October 8. The former Order touching Henry Butry (vid sup) shall stand, and that a warrant be made to the bayliffs of the liberties of Langbargh and Allertonshire to see execution done; and the moiety of the fynes imposed upon him to be paid to Rowland Atkinson and Will. Maynard who did prosequute the cause against Butry, and the other moiety to be paid nowe in Court.

1607. Held at RICHMOND, January 16.
RECUSANTS.

Cecilia wife of John Eshall of Northallerton, for not having been to Church for two years and more;* Anne wife of Gabriel Coates, for three years [often presented and still allowed to brewe and keep hostelrie]; Jane Raynold, widow (three years), Chr. Raynold and Anne his wife [married we knowe not where or by whom, have a child christened we knowe not where or by whom, not bene to Church this yeare and more], Tho. Lanchester and Margaret his wife [not at church this yeare and more], Tho. Scott and Jane his wife [married we knowe not &c,] all of Northallerton. [Maxima † peccandi illecebra impunitas. Qui non vetat peccare cum possit jubet. Amicorum vitia ferendo nostra facimus. Milis etiam qui parcit bonis nocet. Illis enim ignoscendo hoc perditum itur]. (Per Fr. Kay,‡ Clericum, et per homagium]. Margaret wife of Rob. Hackforth of Dighton for Recusancy.

1607. Held at THIRSKE, April 14. Geo. Shotton of Synnymyre House, near Northallerton, alehousekeeper, for harbouring men's servants and other suspected persons in his house contrary to the statute, and Tho. Chilton of Northallerton for the like.

[At the Assizes and General Gaol delivery holden at York Castle on July 13, 1607, an Order was made for the provision of a House of Correction at Thirske, "to serve the whole North-Riding;" and for the appointment of a Gaoler "to keepe and sett on worke such prisoners as shall be committed to the same house," a fee of 5/- or 3/4 to be paid by each prisoner according to his ability, either on his delivery or discharge].

1607. Held at RICHMOND, July 7. Chr. Wind, Senr. of Brompton by Northallerton, for an assault committed "uno baculo sive flagello, called a long gadd,"§ on Henry Wilbert less than fourteen years old, and Anne Peycock, less than nine &c.

1607. Held at RICHMOND, October 8. Northallerton towne for not scowring the ditches on either side of the Kinge's highe waie in a lane at a

---

* Recusancy—nonconformity to the established religion of the land. Hitherto the clergy of Northallerton have had no reason to complain of the orthodoxy of their parishioners, but here we have a batch presented from Northallerton, not only as being tainted with papish notions, but for obstinately refusing to submit. The Curate as well as the Churchwardens and other officers of the parish were in all cases under injunction to present Recusants. James 1 in order to protect himself from the odium of secretly favouring popery, found it necessary to press with impartial rigour upon the Roman Catholics. (Mackintosh, England, iv, 184). He therefore issued a proclamation renewing the legal fine of £20 per month upon all Recusants, and even claiming arrears of the same; greater severity in their persecution was shown than of old and as Green states (short History, p. 463) "six thousand Catholics were presented as Recusants in one year. (Vide Qua. Sess. Rec., vol. 1, p. 4.)

† These sentences are inserted in quite a different style of handwriting, and possibly afford a curious illustration of the condition of the writer's mind. (Vide Qua. Sess. Rec., vol. 1, p. 66.)

‡ Mr. Kay was the thirtieth Vicar of Northallerton. (Vide pp. 76, 79.)

§ Halliwell's second sense for the word Gad is "spear; . . . a pole pointed with metal. The last sense is still in use." The gad used in driving oxen, locally ouse-gad, or ox-prod, was a long shaft with a sharp point or prick at one end, and a lash at the other. These were probably the *gaddes* of the text. (Vide Records, p. 78.)

place called Warebranck Lane adjoyning to Vicar's Croft. [fyne xs. assessed upon the original presentment].

Quarter Sessions Records.

John Allason of Northallerton for suffering lewd persons to be in his house, being an alehouse: fined 10s.

1608. Held at MALTON, January 12. Cuthbert Kearton of Northallerton, alehouse-keeper, for useing much drinking with men's servants in the night-tyme.

1608. Held at THIRSKE, April 5. Rog. Robinson of Northallerton, alehouse-keeper, for receyving men's servants and others and suffering them to use drinking and disorder &c.

Rob. Wright of Bedall, for receyving and reteyning Elizabeth Smithe servant to Tho. Danby of Romanby in Allertonshire, without a testimoniall [Per Marm. Rawson et Oswald Tailour: Cap. Const.]

1608. Held at RICHMOND, Oct. 11 and 12. Tho. Best of Dighton for keeping an alehouse and brewing without license.

1609. Held at HELMSLEY, January 10. Fr. Lascelles of Northallerton for buying of greater sommes of barley in Thirske Markett than the markett will beare,* sometimes himself, sometimes his sonne, and other some tymes his man, he keeping three kilnes for drying malt weekly.

1609. Held at NORTHALLERTON, January 12. [136b.] Phillip Deane, Roger Lambe, and Will. Nelson, all of Northallerton, alehouse-keepers, for suffering excessive drinking &c.

Also Rich. Ward, George Staynes, and Will. Nelson, glover, constables of Northallerton, for suffering rogues &c, to wander and beg unpunished &c.

Will. Flower of Northallerton, tailour, Thomas Flower and Rich. Thornton of the same, for taking wages by the daie† contrary to the statute sett downe by the Justices.

Anth. Blacklock, Will. Harrison and Roger Wilkinson, all of Northallerton, for making malt without lycence.

1609. Held at THIRSKE, July 11 and 12. Whereas Chr. Skarlett of Northallerton, on his oath, is in fear his house may be burnt by Chr. Bell of the same, a warrant to be made to attach the said Bell &c.

1609. Held at RICHMONDE, July 14. Chr. Paycock of Romanby, the Constable and Inhabitants of Siggeston, those of Dighton, and those of Birkby, for not keeping the night watch.

1609. Held at RICHMOND, October 6.

ORDERS made &c.

Whereas Chr. Cook of the City of York, inholder, deposeth on oath that John Keath of Danby Wiske, knowing of the warrant graunted from this Court for his apprehension, nevertheless said to Mr. Tyndall and others that he would submit himself to never a Justice of them all, and also that the said Keath being in Northallerton, the Constable of Yafforth and ors. having the same warrant and assaying to take the said Keath, he runn away leaping and shaking his heeles, saying comme take me, comme take me, not yelding himself to the same warrant . . . . a warrant be made directed to the Sheriffs and to all bailiffs and constables to take the said Keath &c.

1610. Held at NORTHALLERTON, July 12. Rob. Duckdale late of Carliell, glover, Geo. Harrison late of Belgrave, co. Lancashire, labr., Rob. Melmerby late of Richmond, butcher, Elizth. Gryme, late of Lincolne, spinster, Anne Gryme late of Nottingham, spinster, Anne Latham of Brunton, spinster, and Andrew Lawson, late of . . . . , labr., as being rogues and vagabonds &c. [Side-note.—Sentence of the Court, the three men to be branded, sedente Curia, with the letter R on the left shoulder, and the women to be whipped at the same time in Northallerton.]

161⁰⁄₁. Held at RICHMOND, Jany. 11. John Clarke of Thirne for playing at cardes for money at Northallerton to the undoeing of his wieff and children.

---

* Under the act for restraining excessive malt-making, 39 Eliz., c. 16.
† Any person retained into service to work for any less time than a whole year in any the arts of a . . . tailor, shoemaker, &c., shall be fined &c.

Quarter Sessions Records.
1611. Held at RICHMOND, Oct. 8. James Kendroe and Will. Nelson of Northallerton for using unlawfull games on the Sabaoth daie, viz. at Nyenholes,* contrarie &c.
1612. Held at THIRSKE, April 21. Rich. Rymer Junr. and Tho. Walker of Allerton, for that they do not exercise shootinge on the long bowe &c.
1612. Held at NORTHALLERTON, July 10th. Rob. Hackforth of Dighton for playing at boules within the Churchyard &c. [Per Joh. Smyth, Ball. de Allertonshire.]

ANCIENT JEWISH DOCUMENTS RELATING TO NORTHALLERTON.

Ancient Jewish Documents
In Part IX of the Journal of the Yorkshire Archæological and Topographical Association, the Rev. J. T. Fowler, M.A., F.S.A., Hebrew Lecturer in the University of Durham, contributes an article entitled: "On certain 'Starrs'† or Jewish Documents partly relating to Northallerton." From this paper the compiler of the "Annals of Northallerton" has made a few extracts which he thinks will be interesting to Northallerton readers:—

"These documents," says Mr. Fowler, "although not historically important, are curious and interesting relics of a remarkable race of men, the Jews in mediæval England." From translations of the original documents given by Mr. Fowler, it will be seen that York, like London, Lincoln, Norwich, and other ancient cities, was a resort of "that cruelly persecuted but much enduring community."‡

In 1286, the Jews of all the principal cities and towns were ordered by Edward I. to raise for him, among their own people, 20,000 marks (£13,333 6s. 8d.,) and the amount not being raised, they were treated with the utmost cruelty. All sorts of absurd accusations were brought against the Jews as pretexts for imprisoning them in order to obtain money for their release; and in transactions between Jew and Jew of that period, which for obvious reasons were recorded in Hebrew, we find together with the promise of payment, the ominous proviso, "unless I am cheated out of my property by any false accusation on the part of the king or the queen." "From Aaron of York§ alone, we learn from Matthew Paris, the king extorted what was equivalent to 32 ounces of gold, and £2,666 13s. 4d. in silver."

A dozen of these "Jewish Starrs" are preserved in the Tower of London, a dozen in the British Museum, and a large collection among the muniments of Westminster abbey. There are also a few in the possession of the Dean

---

* A game played with nine holes cut evenly in the turf, or hollowed out in the soil, in rows of three, so that the nine form a square. Each of the two players has three stones or other small objects of different colours, and he who can get three in a line first wins. The principal is precisely the same as in the game played by school-boys on their slates, and called "Tit-tat-too."

† The word "Starr," is of Jewish origin (Lat. Starrum, Fr. Estar), and was imported into Rabbinical or mediæval Hebrew from the Chaldee (sh'tar) which means a legal contract or obligatory writing. It occurs three times in the Chaldee Targum or paraphrase of Jer. xxxii, 10, 14. It was applied among the later Jews to any legal document whatever, and corresponded in signification to the Latin word "Scriptum," or the English "writing." Among the various explanations which have been given of the term "Star-chamber" (Camera Stellata) one is, that the apartment so called was formerly used for the conservation of these "Starrs" or Jewish documents, but this is mere conjecture.

‡ Vide Ross's History of England, page 127.

§ Aaron of York was a man of considerable importance in the reign of Henry III. He is mentioned by Matthew Paris and later historians, and is believed to be the original Isaac of York in "Ivanhoe." He was the Rothschild of his date in point of wealth.

NORTHALLERTON.   xli

and Chapter of Durham, with the existence of which Mr. Fowler has made us acquainted by the publication of his paper. The first which he quotes has no reference to Northallerton. The next is a quit claim by which Aaron, the Jew of York, delivered to Hugh, Prior of Durham, certain lands at Northallerton, of which he had become possessed, through a transaction between himself and Thomas the Sergeant or Steward of the Prior and Convent at that place. The document is too lengthy for insertion here. No. III Starr is similar to No. II, but No. IV is short enough for insertion verbatim :— *Ancient Jewish Documents*

"Know all men that I, Thomas, the Sergeant of Alverton, owe to Aaron, the Jew of York, six pounds sterling, to be re-paid at the feast of the Apostles Peter and Paul, in the year of grace one thousand two hundred and thirty-seven; and if I do not then re-pay it, I will give to him for every pound for each week twopence for interest, as long as by his favour I shall hold that debt; and therefore I have mortgaged to him all my lands, rents, and chattels until I discharge the said principal and interest, and this I have sworn and confirmed by my seal. Done at York xvii day of June, preceding."

Endorsed. Tomas le Sergunt, of Alverton, 17 June, 1237. (1.)

(L. S.)

The above document shews that Thomas, the Sergeant of Northallerton, had mortgaged lands, &c., to Aaron of York, for £6, and that he covenanted to pay the moderate interest of nearly 44 per cent. if he failed to re-pay the borrowed principal on the appointed day. Thomas failing in this, the land, &c., came into Aaron's possession, and it appears from Starrs 2 and 3, that the land was redeemed by the Prior and Convent of Durham, which accounts for their being found in the possession of the Dean and Chapter. When found they were tied together with a strip of parchment, and Thomas' seal, apparently representing an insect of some sort, but in a very crumbling condition, was attached to No. 4.

BATTLES AT NORTHALLERTON.

A.D. 865. Sharp conflict at Alvertoune between king Elfrid and five Danish kings. Not decided. *Battles at Northallerton*

,, Battle of Alvertoune. The Danes totally defeated.

1138. Battle of the Standard. Defeat of the Scots under David, by the English under Stephen.

1175. Near Northallerton. Defeat of Prince Henry and Sir Roger de Mowbray by Henry II.

1274. Defeat of Sir Ralph Rymount, by Sir William Wallace, knight, of Elrisle. Unfounded.

1644. Fatal skirmish at Northallerton, in which Lieut.-col. Salvin was slain. This was soon followed by the defeat of Charles I. by the Scots at Marston Moor.

MEMBERS OF PARLIAMENT.

List of Members of Parliament returned by Northallerton from its enfranchisement to the passing of the Reform Bill.

1298 John le Clark*
     Stephen Maunsell*

Privilege of political representation in abeyance.

1640 Thomas Heblewaite
     Sir Henry Cholmley, knt.
1658 George Smithson
     James Danby
1660 Sir F. Hollis, bart.
     George Marwood
1678 Sir Gilbert Gerrard, bart.
     Sir Henry Calverley, knt.
1681 Sir Gilbert Gerrard, bart.
     Sir Henry Calverley, knt.
1685 Sir David Foulis, bart.
     Sir Henry Marwood, bart.
1688 William Robinson
     Thomas Lascelles
1690 Sir Willam Robinson, knt.
     Thomas Lascelles
1695 Sir William Hustler, knt.
     Thomas Lascelles
1697 (vice Lascelles, dec.) ———
1698 Sir William Hustler, knt.
     Ralph Milbank
1700 Sir William Hustler, knt.
     Ralph Milbank
  „ (vice Milbank, dec.) ———
1701 Sir William Hustler, knt.
     Robert Dormer
1702 Daniel Lascelles (vice Dormer, elected for co. Bucks.)
1702 Sir William Hustler, knt.
     John Aislabie
  „ Robert Dormer (vice Hustler, elected for Ripon)
     John Aislabie
1705 Sir William Hustler, knt.
     Robert Domer

    Mr. Dormer was subsequently returned to Parliament for the county of Bucks, and in his stead the borough elected
    Roger Gale
    From the Journal of the House of Commons it is ascertained that Thomas Harrison petitioned against the return of Mr. Gale, on the ground of bribery and other corrupt practices, but the petition was unsustained.

1707 Sir William Hustler, knt.
     Roger Gale
1708 Sir William Hustler, knt.
     Roger Gale
1710 Roger Gale
     Robert Raikes
1713 Henry Peirse
     Leonard Smelt
1714 Cholmley Turner
     Leonard Smelt
1722 Henry Peirse
     Leonard Smelt
1727 Henry Peirse
     Leonard Smelt
1733 Leonard Smelt appointed clerk of the ordnance, and re-elected
1734 Henry Peirse
     Leonard Smelt
1740 William Smelt (vice L. Smelt, deceased)
     Henry Peirse
1741 Henry Peirse
     William Smelt
1745 Henry Lascelles (vice Smelt, appointed receiver-general of revenues in the island of Barbadoes
     Henry Peirse
1747 Henry Peirse
     Henry Lascelles
1752 Daniel Lascelles, (vice Henry Lascelles, resigned)
     Henry Peirse
1754 Edward Lascelles
     Daniel Lascelles
1761 Edward Lascelles
     Daniel Lascelles
1768 Edward Lascelles
     Daniel Lascelles
1775 Daniel Lascelles
     Henry Peirse
1780 Henry Peirse
     Edwin Lascelles (vice Daniel Lascelles, resigned)
1784 Henry Peirse
     Edwin Lascelles
1790 Henry Peirse
     Edward Lascelles
1796 Henry Peirse
     Edward Lascelles
1802 Henry Peirse
     Edward Lascelles

* These gentlemen were paid by their constituents.

1806	Henry Peirse Edward Lascelles		1820	Henry Peirse Hon. W. S. S. Lascelles
1807	Henry Peirse Edward Lascelles		1824	Lieut. Marcus Beresford (vice Peirse, deceased)
1812	Henry Peirse Edward Visct. Lascelles			Hon. W. S. S. Lascelles
1814	J. B. S. Morritt (vice Lascelles, deceased) Henry Peirse		1826	Hon. Henry Lascelles Sir John P. Beresford, bart.
			1830	Hon. Henry Lascelles Sir J. P. Beresford, bart.
1818	Henry Peirse Henry Visct. Lascelles		1831	Sir J. P. Beresford, bart. Hon. W. S. S. Lascelles

List of Parliamentary Elections in Northallerton since the passing of the Reform Bill.

Year.	Conservative Candidate.	Votes.	Liberal Candidate.	Votes.
1832	J. G. Boss (Independent)	108	W. B. Wrightson	97
1835	J. G. Boss	Retired	W. B. Wrightson	Returned unopposed
1837	E. Lascelles	Retired	W. B. Wrightson	Returned unopposed
1841	E. Lascelles	114	W. B. Wrightson	129
1847	———	——	W. B. Wrightson	Returned unopposed
1852	———	——	W. B. Wrightson	Returned unopposed
1857	E. W. Lascelles	126	W. B. Wrightson	129
1859	C. H. Mills	136	W. B. Wrightson	138
1865	C. H. Mills *	239	Jasper W. Johns	190
†1866	E. W. Lascelles	224	W. B. Wrightson	201
1868	John Hutton	385	Jasper W. Johns	373
1874	G. W. Elliot	387	W. B. Wrightson	378
1880	G. W. Elliot	484	Albert O. Rutson	384

CENSUS LIST OF NORTHALLERTON
from 1801 to 1881.‡

Year.	Males.	Females.	Total.
1801	1009	1129	2138
1811	1030	1204	2234
1821	1303	1323	2626
1831	1463	1541	3004
1841	1511	1581	3092
1851	1555	1531	3086
1861	1405	1465	2870
1871	1559	1605	3164
1881	1833	1859	3692

* Unseated on Petition. † Bye Election.
‡ These figures do not include the hamlets of Romanby, Lazenby, and Deighton.

VICARS AND CURATES OF NORTHALLERTON
from the most remote period to which they can be traced.

DATE.	VICAR.	CURATE.
12..	Gilbert de Vere	No record
1231	Robert ――	,,
1267	John de Derlington	,,
1302	Peter de Killawe	,,
1311	Peter de Fishburn	,,
1323	Alan de Chiredon, S.T.P.	,,
....	Richard Askeby *	,,
1332	Edmund Cruer	,,
1335	Robert Dighton	,,
13..	John de Haytor	,,
1382	John de Gilling	,,
1393	William Kamell	,,
1396	Robert Redmereshill	,,
1403	John Staynfield	,,
14..	John Corbridge	,,
1421	William Barker	,,
1422	William Middilton	,,
1437	John Thornton	,,
1455	John Treyndon	,,
1465	Robert Walker	,,
1471	Bartholomew Radclyff	,,
1474	Richard Rolleston, A.B.	,,
1475	William Halyman	,,
1491	John Fisher, D.D.†	,,
1494	Robert Clay	,,
1522	Leonard Hutchinson	,,
1533	Robert Askew	,,
1547	Lancelot Thornton	,,
1561	Mark Metcalfe, A.M.	,,
1593	Francis Kaye, A.M.	,,
1624	John Cradock, S.T.P.‡	William Robson ‖
1628	Thomas Blaikeston, A.M.§	No record
1640	Thomas Mann ¶	,,
1669	John Neile, D.D., S.T.P.	,,
1675	William Neile, A.M.	,,
1686	John Harper	,,
1694	Charles Neile, A.M.	,,
1707	,,	Robert Woodifield**
1716	,,	William Robson (?)
1718	Christopher Hunter, A.M.	No record
1725	Thomas Rudd, A.M.	,,
1729	John Balguy, A.M.	,,
1748	Robert Pigot, A.M.	,,
1754	,,	John Robinson
1757	,,	Christopher Place
,,	,,	George Goundril
1758	,,	William Peacock

* Rector of Kirby Sigston, 1332.
† Afterwards Bishop of Rochester, beheaded on Tower Hill, 1535, vide page 40.
‡ Died by poison in 1627, vide page 80.   § Ejected by Mr. Mann, vide page 80.
¶ Vide page 83.
‖ Mr. Robson affixed his signature as a witness to the signing of Rev. Francis Kaye's will
** Died at Northallerton, 5th Feb., 1708, and buried there.

NORTHALLERTON.

DATE.	VICAR.	CURATE.
1761	Robert Pigot, A.M.	David Wray
1764	,,	Nicholas Robinson
1765	,,	Marmaduke Johnson
1766	,,	R. Wilmot
1767	,,	{ John Tickell { John Stoney
1772	,,	{ John Stoney { James Wilkinson †
1774	,,	James Wilkinson
1775	Benjamin Walker, M.A.	,,
1814	Reynold Gideon Bouyer, L.L.B.	,,
1815	,,	Robert Macfarlane
1820	,,	W. S. Temple
1821	,,	R. D. Kennicot, M.A.
1826	George Townsend, D.D.	,,
1830	,,	{ Wilson Beckett { R. Skipsey
1833	,,	{ Wilson Beckett { W. J. Middleton
1837	,,	W. C. Burgess
1838	,,	{ G. F. Townsend, D.C.L.‡ { Henry B. Carr, M.A.
1839	Theodosius Burnett Stuart, M.A.	R. M. Price
1841	,,	S. M. Brasher
1847	,,	John Wood
1849	,,	John Campion, M.A.
1850	Thomas Warren Mercer, M.A.*	John Warner, M.A.
1853	,,	Henry Dawson Moore
1854	,,	C. S. Collingwood, M.A.
1856	,,	Nil.
1857	,,	John Gower Jenkins
1858	,,	Nil.
1860	,,	W. M. Bennett, M.A.
1861	,,	Nil.
1864	,,	T. M. Netherclift, B.A.§
1865	,,	Nil.
1869	,,	Ansell Jones
1871	,,	F. Page Roberts, M.A.
1873	,,	Henry Lateward, B.A.
1874	,,	E. J. B. B. Fellowes, B.A.
1875	,,	A. W. Baldwin
1877	Benjamin Charles Caffin, M.A.	,,
,,	,,	Charles Williams, B.A.
1879	,,	E. S. Rounds
,,	,,	{ J. L. Saywell, F.R.H.S. { W. C. Barwis, M.A.

The above is a correct list of the Vicars and Curates extracted from the Parish Registers. The Chaplains of the Gaol, and Masters of the Grammar School, when in holy orders, frequently assisted the Vicars of the parish from time to time, but were never licensed by the Archbishop.

* Died at Northallerton, after a few days illness, Christmas Eve, 1876.
† Mr. Wilkinson was curate of Northallerton for the long period of forty-two years, during which time he served three vicars in succession.
‡ Son of Dr. Townsend, the vicar.
§ Married Caroline Sarah, youngest daughter of the Rev. T. W. Mercer, vicar.

MINISTERS OF OTHER DENOMINATIONS.

Date	Wesleyan.*	Congregational.†	Primitive Methodist.§
1825	——	J. Benson, M.A.	——
1832	——	Various.	——
1834	——	,,	J. Wilson
1835	R. Tabraham	,,	,,
1836	,,	,,	W. Dent
1838	H. Pedley	,,	M. Lupton
1839	,,	Joseph Walker	,,
1840	J. Whitworth	,,	W. Fowler
1842	M. Banks	J. Elrick, M.A.	W. Lister
1844	,,	,,	J. Borroughs
1845	J. Lewis	William Palmer	,,
1846	J. Whitehead	,,	S. G. Butterwick
1848	J. T. Barr	Samuel Jackson ‡	J. Spoor
1849	F. Barker	J. B. Lister	,,
1850	J. Edgoose	,,	,,
1851	,,	,,	T. Oliver
1853	J. Cadman	Thomas Yeo	J. Wilson
1854	G. E. Young	,,	,,
1856	,,	,,	J. M. Dawson
1857	W. Swindells	,,	,,
1858	J. Dyson	,,	W. Fulton
1861	D. Williams	,,	,,
1862	,,	,,	W. Lister
1864	G. T. Dixon	,,	J. Bendle
1865	,,	R. Crookall	J. Taylor
1866	T. Waterhouse	,,	,,
1869	G. Gregor	,,	,,
1870	,,	,,	M. A. Drummond
1872	J. Anderson	,,	J. Worsnop
1874	,,	,,	E. Rust
1875	Seth Dixon	,,	,,
1876	,,	,,	G. W. Moorse
1878	F. H. Pickworth	,,	,,
1879	J. Johnson	J. W. Parsons	,,
1881	,,	,,	B. Wild
1882	J. J. Sutton	,,	,,
1883	,,	,,	H. Errington

* The Wesleyans may be said to have "had people" in Northallerton from the time of Wesley's visit to the town in 1780 (vide page 135), but Northallerton was regularly visited by the ministers of the Thirsk circuit from 1774 to 1835.

† For some years up to 1825 the connexion was served in Northallerton by students from the Airedale Independent College. The present Chapel is a neat building, erected in 1819 by Mr. George Hammond, (a native of this town, who died in 1839, aged 85 years, leaving £85,000 to charitable purposes), at a cost of £2,000, who also gave £1,000 for the minister's house. It is situated on the west side of the town, opposite Zetland-street, and behind which is a burial ground, closed in 1856.

‡ Died at Northallerton after a pastorate of nine months.

§ The Primitive Methodists first visited Northallerton in 1820, vide Appendix, p. 15.

FREEMASONS.

Past Masters of the "Anchor" Lodge of Freemasons, Northallerton.

Year.	Master.
1871	John Stamford Walton, P.P.G.S.B.
1872	,, ,,
1873	Christopher Palliser, P.P.G.S.W.
1874	Charles Waistell, P.P.G.R.
1875	Joseph Fairburn, P.P.G.A.P.
1876	George Finley Clarkson.
1877	George William Elliot, M.P., P.P.G.S.W.
1878	Henry Rymer.
1879	Moulding Walmsley.
1880	Christopher Palliser, P.P.G.S.W.
1881	Robert S. Palliser.
1882	James Wheldon, jun.
1883	Walker Stead.
1884	R. H. Sootheran.

III.

A BALLAD

ON THE

BATTLE OF THE STANDARD.

The welkin darke o'er Cuton Moore
  With drearye cloudes did lou're—
The woeful carnage of that daye,
  Sall Scotlande aye deplore.

The river Tees full oft dyd sighe,
  As she roll'd her wynding floode,
That ever her sylver tyde soe cleare
  Shoulde bee swell'd with human bloode.

Kyng Davyd hee stode on the rising hille,
  And the verdante prospecte view'd ;
And hee sawe that sweete river that o'er the moore
  Roll'd on her sylver floode.

Oh then bespake that noble kyng,
 And with griefe hys hearte was woo'd :
" And ever I mourne that yon fayre streame
 Shoulde be swell'd with human bloode."

Kynge Davyd hee sawe the verdante moore,
 With wilde flow'res all bestrow'de ;
" And ever I'm griev'd that soe greene a moore
 Shoulde be stayn'd with human bloode."

" But more am I griev'd, alas ! " he cry'd,
 " And more my hearte is woo'd,
That soe manye warriours young and brave
 Muste thys daye shed theyr bloode."

As princely a hoste that kyng dyd leade
 As ever march'd on playne ;
Alas ! that soe manye a warriour brave
 Shoulde be soe soone yslayne !

And firste march'd forthe the Galloway men,
 Of the anciente Picts they sprange ;
Theyr speares all soe brighte and bucklers strong
 For manye myles yrang.

And then cam on the Norman troopes,
 With Englishe them amonge ;
For the empresse Maud they cam to fighte,
 To righte that ladye's wronge.

And then march'd forthe the Scottish foote,
 And then march'd forthe the horse ;
In armoure stronge, all those warriours came,
 A greate and warlike force.

Kynge Davyd look'd athawart the moore,
 And prince Henry hys brave sonne,
And they were aware of the Englishe hoste,
 Cam merrilye marching on.

Oh then call'd forthe kynge Davyd,
 And loudelye call'd hee,
" And whoo is heare in alle mye campe,
 Can descrybe yon hoste to mee ? "

Then came a bearne, besyde the tente,
 An Englisheman was hee ;
'Twas not long since from the Englishe hoste,
 That traiterous wighte dyd flee.

" Now tell mee yon hostes," the king hee cry'd,
 " And thou shalte have golde and fee—
And whoo is yon chiefe that rydes along
 With hys lockes soe aged greye ? "

" Oh that is Walter de Gaunte you see,
 And hee hath beene greye full long,
But manye's the troope that hee dothe leade,
 And they are stoute and stronge."

" And whoo is yon chiefe soe brighte of blee,
 With hys troopes that beate the playne ? "
" Oh that's the young earle of Albermarle,
 Yleading hys gallante trayne.

A more gallante warrioure than that lorde
    Is not yon hostes among;
And the gallante troopes that hee doth leade,
    Like hym, are stoute and young."

" And who yon shynny warriours twoo,
    With theyre troopes yclade the same ? "
" Oh they're the Bruces, that in thys fighte
    Have com t'acquire them fame."

Oh then call'd out kynge Davyd,
    And fulle of woe spake hee ;
" And ever I hold those Bruces false,
    For muche they owe to mee."

" And who's yon chiefe of giante heighte,
    And of bulke so huge to see ? "
" Walter Espec is that chiefe's name,
    And a potente chiefe is hee.

His stature's large as the mountaine oake,
    And eke as strong hys mighte :
There's ne'ere a chiefe in alle the northe
    Can dare with hym to fighte."

" And whoo's yon youthe, yon youthe I see,
    A galloping o'er the moore ?
Hys troopes that followe soe gallantelye,
    Proclayme him a youthe of pow're."

" Young Roger de Mowbray is that youthe,
    And hee's sprang of the royal line ;
Hys wealthe and hys followers, oh, kyng,
    Are allemost as great as thyne."

" And who's yon aged chiefe I see
    All yclad in purple veste ? "
" Oh that's the Bishoppe o' th' Orkney isles,
    And hee alle the hoste hath bleste.

And alle the reste are noblemen,
    Of fortune and fame each one :
From Nottingham and from Derbyeshyre
    Those valiante chiefetaynes com."

" But what's yon glitt'ring tow're I see
    I' the centre o' the hoste ? "
Oh that's the hallow'd *Standard*, of whyche
    The Englishe make suche boaste.

A maste of a shipp it is so hie,
    Alle bedect with golde soe gaye ;
And on the topp is a holye crosse.
    That shynes as brighte as the daye.

Around it hang the holye banners
    Of manye a blessed saynte ;
Saynte Peter, and John of Beverlye,
    And Saynte Wilfred there they paynte.

The aged folke arounde it throng,
    With their old hayres so greye ;
And manye a chiefetayne there bows ydowne,
    And so heart'lye dothe hee praye."

Oh then bespake the kyng of Scotts,
   And so heavylie spake hee ;
"And had I but yon holye *Standarde*,
   Right gladsom sholde I bee.

And had I but yon holye *Standarde*,
   That there so hie doth tow're.
I would not care for yon Englishe hoste,
   Nor alle yon chieftaynes pow're.

Oh had I but yon holie roode,
   That there soe brighte doth showe ;
I wolde not care for yon Englishe hoste,
   Nor the worste that theye colde doe."

Oh then bespake prince Henrye,
   And like a brave prince spake hee :
"Ah let us but fighte like valiante men,
   And wee'l make yon hostes to flee.

Oh let us but fighte like valiante men,
   And to Christe's wyll ybowe,
And yon hallow'd *Standarde* shall bee ours,
   And the victorie alsoe."

Prince Henrye was as brave a youthe
   As ever fought in fielde ;
Full many a warrioure that dreade day
   To hym hys lyfe dyd yeilde.

Prince Henrye was as fayre a youthe
   As the sunne dyd e're espye ;
Full manye a ladye in Scottishe lande
   For that young prince dyd sighe.

Prince Henrye call'd his young foot page,
   And thus to hym spake hee :
"Oh heede my wordes, and serve mee true,
   And thou sall have golde and fee.

Stand thou on yonder rising hylle,
   Fulle safe I weene the syte :
And from thence oh marke thee well my creste
   In all the thickeste fighte.

And if, o'ercome with woundes, I falle,
   Then take thee a swifte swifte steede,
And from thys moore to Dumfries towne.
   Oh ryde thee awaye with speede.

There to the ladye Alice wende ;
   (You'll knowe that lovelye fayre,
For the fayreste mayde in all that towne,
   Cannot with her compare) ;

And tell that ladye of my woe,
   And telle her of my love ;
And give to her thys golden ring,
   My tender faythe to prove.

And stryve to cheare that lovelye mayde
   In alle her griefe and care :
For well I knowe her gentle hearte
   Dyd ever holde mee deare."

NORTHALLERTON.

And nowe the Englishe hoste drewe neare,
    And alle in battle arraye;
Theire shyning swordes and glitt'ring speares
    Shot rounde a brilliante raye.

And nowe both valiante hostes cam neare,
    Eache other for to slaye;
Whyle watchfulle hovered o'er their heades
    Full manye a byrde of preye.

The sun behynde the darke darke cloudes
    Dyd hyde each bermy raye,
As fearfulle to beholde the woe
    That mark'd that doleful daye.

The thund'ring wyndes of heaven arose,
    And rush'd from pole to pole,
As stryving to drowne the groanes and sighes
    Of manye a dyeing soule.

Sterne deathe he hearde tae shoutes of warre,
    That ecchoed arounde soe loude;
And hee rous'd hym to th' embattled fielde,
    To feaste on human bloode.

And fyrste the Pictish race began
    The carnage of that daye;
The cries they made were like the storme
    That rends the rocks awaye.

Those fierce fierce men of Gallowaye
    Began that day of dole;
And their shoutes were like the thunder's roare,
    That's heard from pole to pole.

Nowe bucklers rang 'gainst swordes and speares,
    And arrows dimn'd the playne;
And manye a warrioure laye fulle lowe,
    And manye a chiefe was slayne.

Oh woeful woeful was that daye,
    To chylde and wydow dreare!
For there fierce deathe o'er human race
    Dyd triumphe 'farre and neare.

Dreare was the daye—in darke darke cloudes
    The Welkin alle endrown'd;
But farre more dreare the woeful scene
    Of carnage alle arounde.

Drear was the sounde of warring wyndes
    That foughte along the skyes;
But farre more dreare the woeful sounde
    Of dying warriours sighes.

Laden with deathe's unpitying arme,
    Swordes fell and arrowes flewe;
The wydow'd wyfe and fatherlesse chylde
    That day of dole sall rue.

Ten thousande Scotts, who on that morne
    Were marching alle soe gaye,
By nighte, alas! on that drearye moore
    Poor mangled corps ylaye.

Weepe, dames of Scotlande, weepe and waile
  Let your sighes reecho rounde;
Ten thousande brave Scotts that hail'd the morne,
  At night laye deade on grounde.

And yee fayr dames of merrye Englande,
  As faste youre teares must poure;
For manye's the valiante Englisheman
  That yee sall see noe more.

Sighe, dames of Englande and lamente,
  And manye a salte teare shed;
For manye an Englishman hail'd that morne,
  That ere the nyghte was deade.

The Scotts they fled; but still their kynge,
  With hys brave sonne by hys syde,
Foughte long the foe (brave kynge and prince,
  Of Scotland aye the pryde).

The Scotts they fled; but stille their kyng,
  With hys brave sonne, foughte full welle,
Till o'er the moore an arrowe yflewe—
  And brave prynce Henrye felle.

Alle thys espy'd his young foote page,
  From the hille whereon he stode;
And soone hath hee mounted a swifte swifte steede,
  And soone from the moore hath rode.

And hee hath cross'd the Tees fayre streame,
  Now swell'd with human bloode;
Th' affrighted page he never stay'de,
  Tyll to Dumfries hee hath rode.

Fayre Alice was gone to the holye kirke,
  With a sad hearte dyd shee goe;
And ever soe faste dyd she crye to heav'n,
  "Prynce Henrye save from woe."

Fayre Alice shee hied her to the choire,
  Where the priestes dyd chaunte soe slowe;
And ever shee cry'd, "May the holye sayntes
  Prynce Henrye save from woe!"

Fayre Alice, with manye a teare and sighe,
  To Mary's shrine dyd goe;
And soe faste shee cry'de, "Sweete Mary mylde,
  Prynce Henrye save from woe!"

Fayre Alice she knelte bye the hallow'd roode,
  Whyle faste her teares dyd flowe;
And ever shee cry'd, "Oh sweete sweete Savioure,
  Prynce Henrye save from woe!"

Fayre Alice look'd oute at the kirke doore,
  And heavye her hearte dyd beate;
For shee was aware of the prynce's page,
  Com galloping thro' the streete.

Agayne fayre Alice look'd out to see,
  And well nighe did shee swoone;
For nowe shee was sure it was that page
  Com galloping thro' the towne.

"Nowe Christe thee save, thou sweete young page,
  Nowe Christe thee save and see!
And howe dothe sweete prynce Henrye?
  I pray thee tell to me."

The page he look'd at the fayre Alice,
  And hys hearte was fulle of woe;
The page he look'd at the fayre Alice,
  Tylle hys teares faste 'gan to flowe.

"Ah woe is me!" sad Alice cry'd,
  And tore her golden hayre;
And soe fast shee wrang her lilly handes,
  Alle woo'd with sad despayre.

"The Englishe keepe the bloodye fielde,
  Full manye a Scott is slayne,
'But lyves prynce Henrye?' the ladye cry'd
  Alle else to mee is vayne.—

'Oh lives the prynce? I pray thee tell,'
  Fayre Alice still dyd calle:
These eyes dyd see a keen arrowe flye,
  Dyd see prynce Henrye falle."

Fayre Alice she sat her on the grounde,
  And never a worde shee spake;
But like the pale image dyd shee looke,
  For her hearte was nighe to breake.

The rose that once soe ting'd her cheeke,
  Was now, alas! noe more;
But the whiteness of her lillye skin
  Was fayrer than before.

"Fayre ladye, rise," the page exclaym'de,
  Nor laye thee here thus lowe."—
She answered not, but heav'd a sighe,
  That spoke her hearte felte woe.

Her maydens came and strove to cheare,
  But in vaine was all their care;
The townesfolke wept to see that ladye
  Soe 'whelm'd in dreade despare.

They rais'de her from the danky grounde,
  And sprinkled water fayre;
But the coldest water from the spring
  Was not soe colde as her.

And nowe came horsemen to the towne,
  That the prynce had sente with speede;
With tydings to Alice that he dyd live,
  To ease her of her dreade.

For when that hapless prince dyd falle,
  The arrowe dyd not hym slaye;
But hys followers bravelye rescued hym,
  And convey'd hym safe away.

Bravelye theye rescued that noble prince,
  And to fayre Carlile hym bore;
And there that brave young prynce dyd live,
  Tho' wounded sad and sore.

Fayre Alice the wond'rous tydings hearde,
 And thrice for joye shee sigh'd:
That hapless fayre, when shee hearde the newes,
 She rose—she smiled—and dy'd.

The teares that her fayre maydens shed,
 Ran free from their brighte eyes;
The ecchoing wynde that then dyd blowe,
 Was burden'd with theyre sighes.

The page hee saw the lovelye Alice
 In a deepe deepe grave let downe,
And at her heade a green turfe ylayde,
 And at her feet a stone!

Then with manye a teare and manye a sighe
 Hathe hee hy'd hym on hys waye;
And hee hath come to Carlile towne,
 All yclad in blacke arraye.

And now hath he come to the prince's halle,
 And lowlye bente hys knee;
"And howe is the ladye Alice so fayre,
 My page com telle to mee."

"Oh, the ladye Alice, so lovelye fayre,
 Alas! is deade and gone;
And at her heade is a green grass turfe,
 And at her foote a stone.

The ladye Alice is deade and gone,
 And the wormes feede by her syde;
And alle for the love of thee, oh prynce,
 That beauteous ladye dy'd.

And where shee's layde the greene turfe growes,
 And a colde grave-stone is there;
But the dew-clad turfe, nor the colde colde stone,
 Is not soe colde as her."

Oh then prince Henrye sad dyd sighe,
 Hys hearte alle fulle of woe:
That haplesse prince ybeate hys breaste,
 And faste hys teares 'gan flowe.

"And art thou gon, my sweet Alice?
 And art thou gone?" he cry'd:
"Ah woulde to heav'n that I with thee
 My faythful love, had dy'd!

And have I loste thee, my sweet Alice?
 And art thou dead and gon?
And at thy deare heade a green grass turfe,
 And at thy foote a stone?

The turfe that's o'er thy grave, deare Alice!
 Sall with my teares be wet;
And the stone at thy feete sall melte, love,
 Ere I will thee forget."

And when the newes cam to merrye Englande
 Of the battle in the northe;
Oh then kynge Stephen and hys nobles
 So merrylie marched forthe.

And theye have had justes and tournamentės,
  And have feasted o'er and o'er;
And merrylie merrylie have they rejoic'd,
  For the victorye of Cuton Moore.

But manye a sighe adds to the wynde,
  And manye a teare to the show're,
And many a bleedyng hearte hath broke,
  For the battle of Cuton Moore.

And manye's the wydowe alle forlorne,
  And helplesse orphan poore,
And manye's the mayden that sall rue
  The victorye of Cuton Moore.

The ladye Alice is layde in her grave,
  And a colde stone markes the site;
And many's the mayde like her dothe dye,
  Cause kynges and nobles wyll fighte.

The ladye Alice is layde full lowe,
  And her mayden teares doe poure,
The manye's the wretche with them sall weepe,
  For the victorye of Cuton Moore.

The holye prieste doth weepe as he syngs
  Hys masses o'er and o'er;
And alle for the soules of them that were slayne,
  At the battle of Cuton Moore.

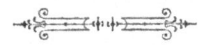

LINES ON VIEWING THE RUINS OF
THE PRIORY OF MOUNT GRACE,
NEAR NORTHALLERTON,
BY SIR JOHN SCOTT BYERLEY, F.R.S.L.

Ye gloomy vaults, ye hoary cells,
  Ye cloister'd domes, in ruins great,
Where sad and mournful silence dwells,
  How well instruct ye by your fate!

Thus every human pride and boast,
  Shall soon or later meet decay;
In dark oblivion sunk and lost,
  The idle pageant of a day.

Ah! what is life! a passing hour!
  A fleeting dream of fancied joy!
No constant blessing in our power,
  But dullest repetitions cloy.

How frail, how weak, is human art,
  By works like these to raise a name!
What empty vapors swell the heart!
  On what strange plans we build for fame!

'Tis virtue only laughs at age,
  And soars beyond the reach of time,
Mocks at the tyrant's fiercest rage,
  For ever awfully sublime.

DESCRIPTIVE POEM ON

THE CASTLE HILLS,

BY MISS A. CROSFIELD,

A.D. 1746.

(Inscribed to Miss Lambton, of Biddick.)

Accept, dear nymph, the tribute of my lays,
Fair patron of my muse, and of the theme ;
The theme, my native shades, the *Castle-hills*,*
From whose aspiring heights amaz'd I view
Thy beauties, Albion ! thy romantic scenes,
Thy future navies, and thy fleecy wealth :
Stretch'd in the amphitheatre below,
Landscape on landscape strikes the dazzled eye,
Floods, villas, golden acres, pastures fair,
And nodding groves, in sweet confusion lie ;
'Till faintly shining from yon distant hills,
Thy silver spires Eboracum arise,
And Studley just presents her magic charms ;
In bolder colours Richmond lifts her head,
And Aske's high tower, aspiring to the sky,
While close behind, the western Alps advance,
Proud that their beacons rous'd their sleepy sons,
And blaz'd security about the isle.
   Eastward I turn, and view thy awful heights,
Stupendous Hambleton : thy dreadful wilds,
Thy gilded cliffs, and blue expanded side,
At once infusing horror and delight :
The hills beneath, comparatively low,
Exalt their flowery tops to grace thy triumph ;
'Till Cotcliff rising conscious of her charms,
Lifts her embowering head, and nobly shews us
Merit can shine, though in the shade of greatness.
Now laughing Ceres re-assumes the plains,
And meadows grow with variegated dyes.
And now *North Allerton*, so fam'd of yore,
Confusedly shews herself the sport of time.
Alas : how fallen, yon *old tower*† proclaims,
Yon ruined tower, by William's bounty great,
Once held the mitred barons of the north :
Still round the town its ancient glories lye,
Still Brompton, once the famous Herbert's‡ seat,
And Romanby, ennobled by its name,
Shine its satellites in fainter brightness :
Still the old *Friarage* shews its bending walls,
Its swelling terras, and encircling trench ;
And northward stretch'd the *Scot-pit-fields* appear,
And *Standard Hill*, sad monuments of war ;
'Twas there the pride of gallant Scotland fell,
And there the warlike Prelate calmly brave,

---

* The history of Allerton Castle will be found in the body of this work.
† The then remains of the Episcopal Palace.
‡ Probably Lord Herbert, of Cherbury, the greatest philosopher of his age.

NORTHALLERTON. lvii

Smil'd on superior strength, and greatly join'd
The golden mitre with the laurel wreath.
  Fain would the muse digress and sing the man,
Who nobly fir'd by this divine example,
Durst, even in times degenerate as these,
Appear the champion of his faith and country;
Oh! wond'rous excellence! unshaken zeal!
Whom power can't bias nor preferment change.
But stop, my muse—stop thy audacious flight!
His virtues soar above the height of praise,
And shall with primitive refulgence shine,
When nature falls, and death itself shall die.*
  Now, lost in thought, I leave the dazzling height,
And seek retirement in the groves below;
Sweet shades! where oft contemplating I rove,
And mourn the gilded follies of the world;
Sweet shades! how shall I sing your peaceful charms!
Come, my Maria, thou shalt be my muse,
Dear patron of the lovely scenes I paint,
And in thy self far lovelier than them all:
Come, my Maria, bless me with thy goodness,
Thy presence can inspire, when all the nine
And bright Apollo tune the lyre in vain:
How oft, my friend, in these alluring shades,
With fair Eliza, sister of thy merit,
We spent sweet hours (too swiftly snatched away!)
In social friendship's ever blooming charms;
O happy hours! when three united hearts,
With gen'rous ardour, planned each others peace,
Sooth'd every care and check'd each rising weakness.
Come, my Maria, let us range the plain,
And trace the winding of yon awful trench,
Which in its circling arms did once contain
The burnish'd conqneror of a yielding world;
Upon this plain the Roman Eagle wav'd,
And here the great Petilius dreadful stood, †
While poor Brigantes, from their utmost bounds,
Trembled beneath the horrors of his sword.
The brave Agricola, whose wisdom beam'd
A double lustre on triumphant Rome,
Perhaps encamp'd his hardy veterans here,
When in the daring march they northward bent,
And conquering all before him, drove thy sons,
Fierce Caledonia! to their inmost mountains.
Nor honour'd less were these auspicious fields,
When proud with great Britannia's sons they shóne,
And gleam'd destruction on the rebel bands;
Here *Wade*, with every gen'rous virtue bless'd,
Inspir'd humanity and courage round him;
Here *Wentworth*, great in cabinet and field,
Assumed the port of Mars; and Huske too here,
With Cholmley, gallantly display'd that fire,
Which sav'd on Falkirk's field their suffering country.
Nor be the foreign chiefs, my muse, forgot;
Britain must always honour a Nassau—
That name alone can strike her foes with terror.

---

* This perhaps too flattering picture is supposed to have been intended for Dr. Herring, Archbishop of York, afterwards of Canterbury.
  † There is no authority for believing that Petilius ever encamped at Northallerton.

Great Swertzenberg must here command a place;
Brave heroes! you convinc'd a doubting world
That, even then, the Dutch rewarded virtue.
   Now smiling peace again illumes the plain,
And gives a humbler, but happier scene:
Now nibbling flocks and lowing heifers stray,
Where late white tents and glittering arms were rang'd;
The thrush succeeds the thunder of the drum,
The flowers rise blooming from their trampled beds,
And lavish nature pours out all her charms.
Hail happy Liberty! Celestial maid!
Thy influence brightens all our smiling scenes,
Adds joy to joy and warms the expanded bosom:
Hail happy Liberty! our noblest pride!
Peace dwells within our walls, and plenteousness
Proclaims around thy ever gentle sway:
Long may'st thou reign the guardian of this Isle!
Long warm her future sons to acts of greatness!
Long may the nations envy Britain's freedom!
Thy gift, great Cumberland! be thine the praise.

A POEM IN
PRAISE OF YORKSHIRE ALE,
BY GILES MORRINGTON,

A.D. 1697.

Bacchus having call'd a Parliament of late,
For to consult about some things of state,
Nearly concerning the honour of his court,
To th' Sun behind th' Exchange they did resort;
Where being met and many things that time
Concerning the adulterating wine,
And other liquors; selling of ale in muggs;
Silver tankards, black pots, and little juggs;
Strong beer in rabits, and cheating penny cans,
Three pipes for twopence and such like trepans:
Vintner's small bottles, silver mouth'd black-jacks,
Papers of sugar, with such like cheating knacks;
Biskets, Luke olives, anchoves, caveare,
Neats tongues, West-phalia-hambs, and such like chear,
Crabs, lobsters, collar-beefe, cold pullets, oysters,
And such like stuffe, which makes young men turn roysters,
And many other things were then debated,
And bills past upon the cases stated;
And all things ready for adjournment, then
Stood up one of the Northern Country men,
A boon good fellow, and a lover of strong ale,
Whose tongue well steep'd in sack, begun his tale:

My bully rocks, I've been experienc'd long
In most of liquors that is counted strong :
Of claret, white-wine, and Canary sack,
Renish and Malago, I've had no lack ;
Sider, perry, metheglin, and sherbet ;
Coffee, and mead, with punch and chocolet :
Rum and tea, Azora wine, Mederry,
Vin-de-Paree, brag, wine with rosemary :
Stepony, vsquebath, besides all these,
Aqua cælestis, cinnamon, hearts-ease :
Brave rosa solis, and other liquors fine,
Rasburry wine, pur-royal, and shampine,
Malmsey and viper wine, all these I pass :
Frontineack, with excellent ipocras :
Lac'd coffee, twist, old Pharoah, and old hoc,
Juniper, brandy, and wine de Langue-dock.
Mum, cherry wine, langoon and lemonad,
Sherry, and Port a Port, both white and red,
Pomgranate, mirtle, and isop-wine I know,
Ipres and Orlearce, Coos, and eke Anjow,
Burgundian-wine, cœcubum, sage and must,
Fennel and worm-wood wine have past my gust,
Hydromel, mulsom, wine boiled with southern-wood,
Opimium, Samirna, and Biæon good ;
Temetum, Lora, and brave Muskadel,
Rumney and nectar too that doth excell :
Silcilian, Naples, and Loraine wine,
Moravia, Malta, and Corsica fine ;
Tent, Muskatine, brandy, and Alicant,
Of all these liquors I've had no scant,
And several others, but none do I find,
Like humming *Northern Ale* to please my mind ;
It's pleasant to the taste, strong and mellow,
He that affects it not is no boon fellow ;
He that in this drink doth let his senses swim,
There's neither wind nor storm will pierce on him.
It warms in winter, in summer opes the pores,
'Twill make a sovereign salve 'gainst cuts and sores ;
It ripens wit, exhilerates the mind,
Makes friends of foes, and foes of friends full kind :
It's physical for old men, warms their blood,
It's spirit makes the cowards courage good :
The tatter'd beggar, being warm'd with ale,
Nor rain, hail, frost, nor snow can him assail :
He's a good man with him can then compare,
It makes a 'prentice great as the Lord Mayor ;
The labouring man that toils all day full sore,
A pot of ale at night does him restore,
And makes him all his toils and pains forget,
And for another day-work he's then fit,
There's more in drinking ale sure than we wot,
For most ingenious artists love a pot :
Nay, amorous ladies it will pleasure too,
Make frozen maids, and nuns, and . . . .
The thing you know : Soldiers and Gownmen,
Rich and poor, old and young, lame and sound men,
May such advantage reap by drinking ale,
As should I tell, you'd think it but a tale.
Mistake me not, custom, I mean not tho',

Of excessive drinking, as great ranters do,
For that would turn a great wit to a sot
I meane the merry quibling o're a pot,
Which makes dull melancholy spirits be,
For criticks and great witts, good company.
Oh the ripe virtues of this barley broth!
To rich and poor, it's meat, and drink, and cloth.
The court here stopt him, and the prince did say,
Where may we find this nectar, I thee pray?
The boon good fellow answer'd I can tell,
*Northallerton, in Yorkshire, does excel
All England, nay all Europe, for strong ale*,
If thither we adjourn, we shall not fail
To taste such humming stuff, as, I dare say,
Your highness never tasted to this day.
They hearing this, the house agreed upon
All for adjournment to *Northallerton*:
Madam Bradley's was the chief house then nam'd,
There they must taste this noble ale so fam'd,
And nois'd abroad in each place far and near
Nay, take it, *Bradley*, for strong ale and beer
Thou hast it loose, there's none can do so well,
In brewing Ale thou dost all else excel.
Adjournment day being come, there did appear
A brave full house, Bacchus himself was there.
This nectar was brought in, each had his cup,
But at the first they did but sipple up
This rare ambrosia, but finding that
'Twas grateful to the taste and made them chat,
And laugh and talk, O then when all was out,
They call'd for more, and drank full cans about.
But in short space, such strange effects it wrought
Amongst the courtiers, as Bacchus never thought
Or dream'd upon: his wise men it made fools,
And made his councellors to look like owles.
The simple sort of fellow it made prate,
And talk of court affairs, and things of state;
And those that were dull fellows, when they came,
Were now turn'd nimble orators of fame.
And such of them was thought to be no wits
Were metamorphis'd into excellent poets;
Those that were lame, and came there with a staff,
Threw't quite away, which made the prince to laugh;
The cripple which did crutches thither bring,
Without them now did hop about and sing;
Some o're the stools and forms did skip and leap,
Some knack'd their fingers, no plain word could speak,
Some shak'd their legs and arms with great delight,
Some curst and swore, and others they did fight;
Some antick tricks did play like a baboon,
Some knit their brows, did shake their heads and frown;
Some maudlin drunken were, and wept full sore,
Others fell fast asleep, begun to snore;
Thousands of lies and stories some did tell,
Their tongues went like the clapper of a bell;
Others were tongue-ti'd, could not speak one word,
And some did cast their reckonings up at board.
Some sung aloud, and did deaf their fellows,
Making a noise worse than Vulcan's bellows;

Some were for bad talk, and some did shout;
Some mist the cup, and pour'd the liquor out,
At every word, some did their neighbours jump,
And some did often give the board a thump.
Some were all kindness—did their fellows kiss,
Some all bedaub'd their clothes, and mouths did miss,
For argument some were, and learn'd discourses,
Some talked of greyhounds, some of running horses;
Some talked of hounds, and some of cocks o'th' game,
Some nought but hawks, and setting-dogs did name.
Some talked of battles, seiges, and great warrs,
And what great wounds and cutts they had, and scarrs;
Some very zealous were, and full of devotion,
But being sober then had no such notion;
Some their were all for drinking healths about,
Some were for bargains, some for wagers laying,
Others for cards and tables cry'd for playing;
Some broke the pipes, and round about them threw,
Some smoak'd tobacco till their nose was blew.
Some in the fire fell, and sing'd their cloths,
And some fell from their seats and broke their nose.
Some could not stir a foot, did sit and glare,
Some called for musick, others were for a dance,
And some lay staring, as if in a trance.
Some call'd for victuals, others for a crust,
Some op'd their buttons, and were like to burst.
Some challeng'd all the people that were there,
And some with strange invented oaths did swear;
Others at such discourse were sore amus'd;
Some shrink'd their drink, did put away the cup,
And some took all that came—left not one sup;
Some whilest they sober were would nothing pay,
But being drunk, would all the shot defray;
Others whilest sober, were as free as any,
But when once drunk, refuse to pay one penny;
Some were for news, and how the state of things
Did stand amongst great potentates and kings;
Some all their friends and neighbours did backbite,
And some in jearing others took delight;
Some of their birth and riches made great boast,
And none but they were fit to rule the roast:
Some filled the room with noise, yet could not speak
One word of English, Latin, French, or Greek,
Or any other language, which one might
Put into sense, and understand aright;
Some laught until their eyes did run on water,
And neither they nor others knew the matter;
Some so mischievous were, they without fear,
Would give their chiefest friend a box on th' ear;
Some were so holy, that they would not hear
Words either that profane or smutty were:
Some in melancholy posture laid,
Others did cry, What is the reckoning paid?
Some burnt their hats, others the windows broke,
Some cry'd, more liquor, we are like to choake;
Lame gouty men, did dance about so spritely,
A boy of fifteen scarce could skip so lightly:
Old crampy chaps, that scarce a sword could draw,
Swore now they'd keep the King of France in awe;

And new commissions get to raise more men,
For now they swore they were grown young again;
Off went their perriwigs, coats, and rapers,
Out went the candles, noses for tapers
Serv'd to give light, whilst they did dance around,
Drinking full healths with cups upon the ground:
And still as they did dance their roundelays,
They all did cry, this drink deserves the bays
Above all liquors we have ever tasted:
It's a pity that a drop of it were wasted;
A stranger coming by, did hear the noise,
He step'd into the house to see the boys;
Such sights he saw, as he ne'er see before,
Which made him laugh until his sides were sore;
His horse did follow, and saw the quaffing,
He neigh'd aloud, and broke his girts with laughing.
These antick sights made Bacchus to admire,
And then he did begin for to enquire
What privileges were bestowed upon
This famous Ale Town of Northallerton; *
The answer was that it was known
To have four fairs i'th' year, a borough town,
One market every week, and that was all:
This mov'd Bacchus presently to call
For a great jug, which held about five quarts,
And filling it to the brim; Come, here, my hearts,
Said he, we'll drink about this merry health,
To the honour of the town, their state and wealth;
For by the essence of this drink I swear,
This town is famous for strong ale and beer;
And for the sake of this good nappy ale,
Of my great favour it shall never fail;
For to promote the quick return of trade,
For all strong ale and beer that here is made.
So to't they went and drank full healths about,
Till they drunk money, wit, and senses out:
For whilst one drop of ale was to be had,
They quaft, and drunk it round about like mad.
When all was off, then out they pull'd the taps,
And stuck the spiddocks finely in their hats;
And so triumphantly away they went,
But they did all agree, with one consent,
To Easingwold they then away would pass,
With Nanny Driffield there to drink a glass;
* * * *

Then they to famous York would haste away,
For thither they'd adjourn the court that day:
The horses were led out, they mounted all,
And each of them did for a flagon call;
Well sirs, said they, we yield, the days your own,
Wee'l try again next time we come to town.
Agree'd, the townsmen said, come when you will,
You'l find us true blue fubling bullies still;
They drank about, the townsmen pledg'd the same,
So took their leaves till they should meet again;
At parting they did kiss, and Bacchus swore
He never met with such boon blades before.

---

* White says, Northallerton was once famous for quoits, cricket, and spell and knurr.

NORTHALLERTON.

Well, noble boys, said he, before 't be long
I hope our lott will be to sing a song :
Great Bacchus, when you come, the townsmen said,
Come well prepar'd, for we are not afraid.
Farewell, good lads, said he, and so away
They took their journey unto York that day.
When they to York were come, they rov'd about
From house to house, to find such nectar out
As they had tasted last, at length they heard
Of Parker's coffee-house i' th' Minster yard ;
The several sorts of strong ale there would find,
Some of which ale would surely please their mind :
Come wench, said they, with strong ale we'll begin :
Sirs, said the girl, we've ale that's strong and old,
Both from *Northallerton* and Easingwold,
From Sutton, Thirsk, likewise Rascal Town,
We've ale also that's call'd Knocker-down,
Well bring a tankard of each in, you maid,
We'll taste them every one, the courtiers said.
The ale came in, each man a tankard had,
They tasted all and swore they were full glad,
Such stingo, nappy, pure ale they had found :
Let's lose no time, said they, but drink around ;
And chear our spirits up with this good creature,
For *miser est qui nummos admiratur.*
About and about it went full merrily,
Till some could neither go, stand, sit, nor see.
Vir sapit qui pauca loquitur ; if true,
The wisest in the company is you,
Said one, to s' opposite beyond the table,
Who was so drunk, to speak he was not able.
They called and drank till they were all high flown,
And could not find their way into the town,
They staggar'd to and fro, had such light heads
That they were guided all into their beds !
And in the morning when they did awake,
They curs'd and swore that all their heads did ach ;
O Yorkshire, Yorkshire ! thy ale it is so strong,
That it will kill us all if we stay long.
So they agreed a journey for to make
Into the south, some respit there to take,
But in short space again, they said, they'd come
And taste some more of the said Yorkshire hum :
Nay Bacchus swore to come he would not fail,
And glut himself with Yorkshire nappy ale ;
It is so pleasant, mellow too, and fine,
That Bacchus swore he'd never more drink wine.

Now I have done, and will hold a piece on't,
That, *nil hic nisi carmina desunt,*
Some men will say, perhaps, here is no wit,
Let such then know, *ex nihilo nihil fit.**

---

* The above rhyme, with a dialogue in the Yorkshire dialect, and a glossary of terms, was printed at York, in 1697, by John White, for Francis Hilyard, at the sign of the Bible, in Stonegate.

OCCASIONAL PROLOGUE:

Spoken at the Opening of the New Theatre, Northallerton,

On Monday Evening, October the 6th, 1800,

By Mr. Meadows.

(Cross and Dibdin, Junior.)

The stoic's plan is futile, which requires,
Our wants supplied, by lopping our desires,
As well by this vague scheme might we propose,
Cut off your feet, 'twill save the price of shoes;
As well might we, thus courting public favour,
To gain your plaudits, lop off all endeavour,
The thought we spurn, be it our constant aim,
By assiduity to gain a name,
Your approbation points the road to fame;
Each effort use, nor e'er a moment pause,
To reap that golden harvest, your applause,
Sweet is the balm, which hope's kind aid bestows,
To lighten grief, or mitigate our woes,
To raise desponding merit, banish fear,
And from the trembler, wipe the falling tear;
To diffidence inspire its dread beguile,
And doubt extinguish, with a cheering smile;
That task be yours, my co-mates with some dread,
Depute me here their willing cause to plead,
Your fiat must our future fates control,
For here our chief has "garner'd up his soul;"
Eager to please, his throbbing heart beats high,
By you depress'd or swell'd to extacy;
Then bid the phantom fear at once depart,
And rapture revel, in his anxious heart,
From you, ye fair, who gaily circling sit,
The galaxy of beauty, and of wit,*

* * *

"The first toast after dinner, which I gave with three cheers,
"Was success to the Town and to its Volunteers;"
I thought that the best way to finish the day,
Was to treat both myself and dear Bet to the Play,
Perhaps you may think that I'm full of my railery,
When I tell you I left her just now in the gallery;
There she is tho' she's lusty I hope she don't throng ye,
You may laugh but by jingo Bet Bouncer's among ye;
Coming down here to buy her some apples and pears,
My old friend Tom Meadows, I met on the stairs,
For all your kind favours I've oft heard him say.
No words can express them no language convey,
On his true hearty thanks you may safely depend,
And with life that his gratitude only will end.†

---

* The portion from the bottom of page 102 to the top of page 107 is unfortunately missing.
† The above Prologue was found in a basket of waste paper at Gisborough, and given by the finder to Mr. R. W. Fairburn, who handed it to his brother, Mr. Joseph Fairburn, of Northallerton, to whom I am indebted for a copy.—J. L. S.

A BALLAD ON

THE HARTLEPOOL TRAGEDY.

———:o:———

Good Lord! I'm undone, thy face I would shun,
I've anger'd my God, and displeased his Son;
I dare not come nigh thy great Majesty,
Oh! where shall I hide my poor soul when I die?

Thy vengeance I dread on my guilty head,
All hopes of thy mercy from me now are fled;
My poor sinful soul is filthy and foul,
And terror and horror in my conscience roll.

The shame of my race, and mankind's disgrace,
My actions all over were wicked and base;
No devil in hell, that from glory fell,
Can now with my blood-guilty soul parallel.

Her affections I drew; how could I embrue
My hands in her blood? Oh! my God I do rue
The curst hellish deed, I made her to bleed,
That never did wrong in thought, word, or deed.

I used my whole art, 'till I stole her heart;
I swore to befriend her, and still take her part;
Thus by my treachery she was beguil'd,
Which made her weep sorely, but I only smil'd.

With sighs and with groans, with tears and with moans,
She uttered such plaints as would soften flint stones;
Oh! where shall I hide my shame, oft she cry'd,
Dear sir, take some pity, and for me provide.

I feared she'd breed strife 'twixt me and my wife,
And that all my friends would lead me a sad life;
Then Satan likewise did join each surmise,
And made me an hellish contrivance devise.

I promised her fair that I would take care
Of her and her infant, and all things prepare
At Hartlepool town, where she should lie down;
Poor soul she believ'd me, as always she'd done.

Thus wickedly bent, with her then I went,
She little expecting my bloody intent;
We then drank some ale, and I did prevail
With her to walk out, which she did without fail.

We then took our way to the brink of the sea,
And there like a fury to her I did say;
You impudent wretch that covets my store,
I'm fully resolved you shall plague me no more.

She dreading her fate, alas! when too late,
Did call out for mercy, whilst I did her beat,
With the whip in my hand; she not able to stand,
Ran backwards and fell from the rock to the strand.

In hopes that the sea would wash her away,
I hastened homewards without more delay,
But was taken soon, to have my sad doom,
And must perish shamefully just in my bloom.

Which makes my heart ache, and ready to break,
I pray, my dear Saviour, some pity now take
On sinners the worst, lewd, bloody, and curst,
Who owns his damnation both righteous and just.

But oh! my God, why should my Saviour die,
If not to save siuners as heinous as I?
Then come cart and rope, both strangle and choke,
For in my Redeemer I still trust and hope.

Let all men beware, when married they are,
Lewd women are surely a dangerous snare;
Then love your own wives; those men only thrive
That are the most pious and chaste in their lives.

THE GARTER:

A BALLAD BY SIR JOHN SCOTT BYERLEY, KNT.*

When Edward England's sceptre sway'd,
Edward the third, I should have said;
At court one jovial holy-day,
The nobles brisk, the ladies gay;
Music and dancing fir'd each part,
Swift mov'd the leg, quick beat the heart.
Just in the middle of a tune
Of *minuet*, or of *rigadoon*;
Which of the two most authors doubt,
Nor have I time to make it out;
A garter dropt, they all agree
From off a Countess' bended knee!
The King with th' odd adventure pleas'd
Stoop'd low, and quick the trophy seiz'd!
"Let this the badge of knighthood be!
This the reward of chivalry!"
He said; her face the Countess veil'd,
And in a blush her pride conceal'd.
But now if when my verse is said,
Ill thoughts should rise in critic's head,
Hear but the Garter's own defence—
"*Honi soit qui mal y pense.*"

* My reason for inserting the above is, its local authorship, and the difficulty of obtaining the works of the gallant knight.—J. L. S.

THE NORTHALLERTON
ST. STEPHEN'S UNION HUNT CLUB.

This Club was formed for social purposes in or about the year 1840, and was set on foot by two or three "comrades in arms"* who met at the Black Bull Hotel, on St. Stephen's Day. It continued to exist until 1850, when its last Anniversary was held, on which occasion the following poetical account of the Club's institution and history, written by MR. EDWARD HARE, of Northallerton, was recited by that gentleman. The poem has been inserted because it alludes to persons and customs well known in Northallerton at that time, and is, on that account, a valuable link in the history of the town.

A Club known far and wide to night will meet;
Yclept, "the Union Hunt," in the broad street
Of old Northallerton, so famed of yore,
Where oftentimes this Club has met before;
At the old hostel with the "Black Bull" sign,
As sure as fate these jovial boys will dine.
Blow high, blow low, naught keepeth them away,
On this the evening of their festal day.

Small its beginning, when ten years ago,
It may be twelve—or more—for aught I know,
On Great St. Stephen's morn, some two or three
Met at the Bull, determined on a spree—
What it should be they scarce could hit upon;
First, this was said—then that—at last one said,
"No sport like hunting†—let us off, and try
How well and fast our gallant hounds can fly.
The first hare caught, we'll have her straight sent home,
And cook'd for dinner, ready when we come
Back to the Bull, where we can take our ease,
Con o'er the day's exploits—or what we please."

A grand idea—sure a better plan
Ne'er emanated from the brain of man—
They all agreed it was the very thing,
And soon our Nimrods bold were on the wing.
They sallied forth on that eventful day
With spirits high, and eager for the fray.
They hunted long—they ranged far and near;
Each bush was beat—each fence and coppice sere;
But all in vain, alas! no game they found,
Although they travelled o'er some miles of ground.
Truth must be told, and truth I now declare,
They nabb'd not one poor solitary hare.
Returning home with appetites as keen
As if they fasting all that day had been;
They call'd to mind what any one may see,
In a most useful work on cookery.
"First catch your hare," you epicurean sinner,
"Then have her dressed as you like for dinner."

* Messrs. J. Horner, T. P. Peckett, and H. Dowson. Mr. Ainsley (Castle Hills), Mr. Wm. Robinson, and Mr. J. Linton joined the Club soon after its formation.
† St. Stephen's Day gave a traditionary license to hunt, provided permission was first obtained from the owners of land over which the huntsmen would pass.

"First catch your hare," I say, "or else the cook
Will not have much occasion for the book."

Something they must have, though, on which to feed,
For they were faint and spiritless indeed ;
Not long they wait,—a glorious dish of tripe
Put all to rights—and then the glass and pipe
Beguil'd the flying hours, and mirth and song
Fill'd up the time, nor seemed the evening long.
But feasts, howe'er prolonged, must have an end,
And so had theirs ;—then friend shook hand with friend,
Each heart elate with friendship and good cheer ;
They vow'd to meet again another year.

And meet they did, with numbers much increased,
To celebrate once more their annual feast ;
But wiser grown than what they were before,
Lest the same scene should be enacted o'er.
No game, no dinner—ah ! a direful sound
To hunters' ears—for all the party round
Beefsteaks were ordered at the hour of Five,
They'd all be there for certain—if alive.

They started forth—a set of " out-and-outs " ;
They made the welkin ring with joyous shouts,
What game they took I do not now remember,
On day the twenty-sixth of that December.
If game was scarce, they'd lots of fun and glee,
Keen was the weather—keen as keen could be ;
Keen too their appetites and sharp, and when
The steaks appeared, they quitted them like men.
Mountains went down before these hunters bold,
What else they did, must all remain untold ;
For here my grey-goose quill her wing must lower,
" Sic' flights as these are far beyond her power."

The steaks, et cetera, vanished—then the mirth
To which are prone all joyous sons of earth ;
A jolly fellow in the chair they placed
(And well that chair he ever since has grac'd—
" Long may he fill it—distant be the day
When he will cease to do so ") all will say.
The Chairman* rises—now the game begun,
The morning's toils enhance the evening's fun.
Well sped the winged hours 'mid joy profound,
Mirth, jest and laughter, and the song went round ;
None thought of home—all were so merry there,
And loud they joined in " Begone dull care,"
Sung by the jovial Vice,† and who but he
Can give it with such tuneful harmony—
My feeble muse unequal is to tell.
The many songs they sung, and sung so well,
The jokes they uttered, and the stories good
I fain would put on record, if I could ;
Yet all the while stern Time kept moving on,
Till grey-eyed morning bid them to be gone.
And, parting with reluctance, all declar'd
They'd meet again next year—should they be spar'd.

* Mr. Henry Dowson was chairman in 1840.
† Probably Mr. Smith, landlord of the " Black Bull."

And now so well establish'd was the feast
Of fam'd St. Stephen, that—next time, at least,
A score was added to the jovial crew,
All honest fellows—of the right sort too.
The tripe and steaks—old friends—had disappear'd,
And in their place, renown'd Sir-loin uprear'd
His noble front, to English hearts so dear,
The savoury haunch, and oceans of good cheer;
And thus they met, where they had met before.

And now, again, behold us here once more,
While mem'ry takes a retrospective view
Of scenes long past, and friends whom once we knew;
And whilst we hold them in remembrance dear,
We pay the passing tribute of a tear,
With grateful hearts to that all-gracious Power,
Whose arm has stay'd us to the present hour.
E'er since our earliest dawn of life began
From feeble, helpless infancy, to man—
No word of discord ever caused a jar,
Nor ill-timed joke burst forth our mirth to mar.
Long may we live to muster at the Bull,
And may our pockets, like our hearts, be full;
And while we meet, still let our motto be,
" Peace and good-fellowship, and harmony." *

A BALLAD ON

THE ROMANBY TRAGEDY.†

Oh! sights are seen, and sounds are heard,
  On Morton bridge at night,
When to the woods the cheerful birds
  Have ta'en their silent flight.

When through the mantle of the sky
  No cheering moonbeams delve,
And the far village clock ‡ hath told
  The midnight hour of twelve.

Then o'er the lonely path is heard
  The sigh of sable trees,
With deadly moan of suff'ring strife
  Borne on the solemn breeze—

For Mary's spirit wanders there,
  In snowy robe array'd,
To tell each trembling villager
  Where sleeps the murder'd maid.

---

* I am indebted for permission to print the foregoing well-written poem to Mr. W. R. Smithson, of Northallerton, in whose Almanac it first appeared.—J. L. S.
† Vide " Ballads and Songs of Yorkshire," pages 164 to 171.
‡ The clock in the tower of Ainderby Church.

It was a Sabbath's eve of love,
  When nature seem'd more holy;
And nought in life was dull, but she,
  Whose look was melancholy.

She lean'd her tear-stain'd cheek of health
  Upon her lily arm;
Poor, hapless girl! she could not tell
  What caus'd her wild alarm.

Around the roses of her face
  Her flaxen ringlets fell;
No lovelier bosom than her own,
  Could guiltless sorrow swell!

The Holy Book before her lay,
  That boon to mortals given,
To teach the way from weeping earth
  To ever-glorious heaven;

And Mary read prohetic words,
  That whisper'd of her doom:—
"Oh! they will search for me, but where
  I am, they cannot come!"

The tears forsook her gentle eyes,
  And wet the sacred lore;
And such a terror shook her frame,
  She ne'er had known before.

She ceas'd to weep, but deeper gloom
  Her tearless musing brought;
And darker wan'd the evening hour,
  And darker Mary's thought.

The sun, he set behind the hills,
  And threw his fading fire
On mountain, rock, and village home,
  And lit the distant spire.

(Sweet fane of truth and mercy! where
  The tombs of other years
Dis-course of virtuous life and hope,
  And tell of by-gone tears!)

It was a night of nature's calm,
  For earth and sky were still;
And childhood's revelry was o'er,
  Upon the daisied hill.

The alehouse, with its gilded sign
  Hung on the beechen bough,
Was mute within and tranquilly
  The hamlet-stream did flow.

The room where sat this grieving girl
  Was one of ancient years;*
Its antique state was well display'd
  To conjure up her fears;

---

* The house has since disappeared, but the village draw-well on the green still occupies its old position directly opposite the site.—J. L. S.

With massy walls of sable oak,
　　And roof of quaint design,
And lattic'd window, darkly hid
　　By rose and eglantine.

The summer moon now sweetly shone
　　All softly and serene;
She clos'd the casement tremblingly
　　Upon the beauteous scene.

Above that carved mantle hung,
　　Clad in the garb of gloom,
A painting of rich feudal state,—
　　An old baronial room.

The Norman windows scarcely cast
　　A light upon the wall,
Where shone the shields of warrior knights
　　Within the lonely hall.

And, pendent from each rusty nail,
　　Helmet and steely dress,
With bright and gilded morison,
　　To grace that dim recess.

Then Mary thought upon each tale
　　Of terrible romance;—
The lady in the lonely tower—
　　The murderer's deadly glance—

And moon-lit groves in pathless woods,
　　Where shadows nightly sped;
Her fancy could not leave the realms
　　Of darkness and the dead.

There stood a messenger without,
　　Beside her master's gate,
Who, till his thirsty horse had drunk,
　　Would hardly deign to wait.

The mansion rung with Mary's name,
　　For dreadful news he bore—
A dying mother wish'd to look
　　Upon her child once more.

The words were, "haste, ere life be gone:"
　　Then was she quickly plac'd
Behind him on the hurrying steed
　　Which soon the woods retrac'd.

Now they have pass'd o'er Morton bridge,
　　While smil'd the moon above
Upon the ruffian and his prey—
　　The hawk and harmless dove.

The towering elms divide their tops;
　　And now a dismal heath
Proclaims her "final doom" is near
　　The awful hour of death!

The villain check'd his weary horse,
　　And spoke of trust betray'd;
And Mary's heart grew sick with fright,
　　As, answering, thus she said—

"Oh! kill me not until I see
  My mother's face again!
Ride on, in mercy, horseman, ride,
  And let us reach the lane!

"There slay me by my mother's door,
  And I will pray for thee;
For she shall find her daughter's corse "—
  "No, girl, it cannot be:

"This heath thou shalt not cross, for soon
  Its earth will hide thy form;
That babbling tongue of thine shall make
  A morsel for the worm!"

She leap'd upon the ling-clad heath,
  And, nerv'd with frensied fear,
Pursued her slippery way across,
  Until the wood was near.

But nearer still two fiends appear'd,
  Like hunters of the fawn,
Who cast their cumb'ring cloaks away,
  Beside that forest lone;

And bounded swifter than the maid,
  Who nearly 'scap'd their wrath,
For well she knew that woody glade,
  And every hoary path.

Obscur'd by oak and hazel bush,
  Where milk-maid's merry song
Had often charm'd her lover's ear,
  Who blest her silv'ry tongue.

But Mary miss'd the woodland stile—
  The hedge-row was not high;
She gain'd its prickly top, and now
  Her murderers were nigh.

A slender tree her fingers caught—
  It bent beneath her weight;
'Twas false as love and Mary's fate!
  Deceiving as the night!

She fell—and villagers relate
  No more of Mary's hour,
But how she rose with deadly might,
  And, with a maniac's power,

Fought with her murd'rers till they broke
  Her slender arms in twain;
But none could e'er discover where
  The maiden's corse was lain.

When wand'ring by that noiseless wood,
  Forsaken by the bee,
Each rev'rend chronicler displays
  The bent and treach'rous tree.

Pointing the barkless spot to view,
  Which Mary's hand embrac'd,
They shake their hoary locks, and say,
  "It ne'er can be effac'd!"

ADDENDA.

Page 46.—Bishop Gheast was not "the principal compiler of the Liturgy of the Church of England now in use," as Ingledew asserts, but he certainly took a very active part in the revision of the Prayer Book in Queen Elizabeth's reign. Strype says, "that Gheast was appointed by Secretary Sir William Cecil, in the room of Archbishop Parker, who was absent some part of the time by reason of sickness. Him the Secretary required diligently to compare both King Edward's (Communion) Prayer Books together, and from them both to frame a book for the use of the Church of England, by correcting and amending, altering and adding, or taking away, according to his judgment and the ancient Liturgies; which when he had done, and a new service book being finished by him and the others appointed thereto, the said Geste conveyed it to the Secretary pursuant to the settlement of the Liturgy; concluding his letter with these remarkable words, which were literally followed, and which have been from that time to the present gradually and progressively fulfilling: 'Thus I think I have showed good cause why the service is set forth in such sort as it is. God for his mercy in Christ, cause the Parliament with one voice to enact it, and the realm with true heart to use it.'"

Page 72.—SCROPE METCALFE.—Named Scrope Metcalfe, after his godfather, Emanuel Scrope, 1st Earl of Sunderland, and 11th Lord Scrope, of Bolton Castle. Mentioned in the will of the Earl of Sunderland, as follows: "To my godchild, Scroope Metcalfe, the sum of one hundred pounds." The Earl's will is dated 26th May, 1630.

Page 112.—The peerage of Viscount Northallerton was created in 1683; merged in the crown in 1727, and became extinct in 1760.

ERRATA.

Page 22.—"Northallerton burnt by Wallace," should be under date 1274.
Page 24, footnote.—For "overshadow" read "shelter."
Page 27, second footnote, line 1.—For "Finchley," read "Finchale."
Page 31, second line from the bottom.—The Master of the Grammar School is appointed by the Dean and Chapter of Durham.
Page 32.—For correct information as to gift of land to Austin Friars, see page 34 under date 1340.
Page 69, line 28.—After 1576, insert—These two tablets were finally removed during the restoration of the Church Nov. 21st, 1882.
Page 72, line 6.—After "September," read—George Metcalfe's kinsmen of the Lincolnshire branch of the family, seated at Louth Park, also suffered much in the royal cause, as appears from the following extract from the petition of Francis, son of Sir Francis Metcalfe, of Louth Park, dated August, 1661:—"Has £2,000 arrears due; was plundered in the wars in which his father, Sir Francis Metcalfe, was murdered, and his four brothers all died."—*Vide State Papers*.
Page 74, last line.—After "Windermere" insert asterisk, referring to footnote.
Page 115.—"Ringing for King Charles's restoration," should be under date 1660.
Page 127, third footnote, 4th line.—For "marriages of cousins" read "cousin-marriage."

NORTHALLERTON:
PRINTED AT THE OFFICE OF J. VASEY.